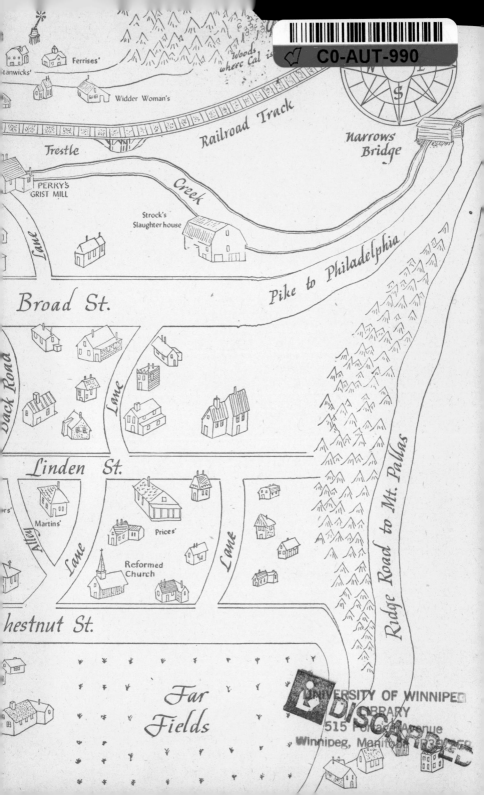

Ferrises'

tanwicks'

Widder Woman's

Woods
where Cal is

$

Railroad Track

narrows
Bridge

Trestle

PERRY'S
GRIST MILL

Creek

Strock's
Slaughter house

Lane

Broad St.

Pike to Philadelphia

Back Road

Lane

Linden St.

Martins'

Prices'

Ridge Road to Mt. Pallas

Allen

Lane

Reformed
Church

Lane

hestnut St.

Far
Fields

BEFORE THE SUN GOES DOWN

Before the Sun
Goes Down

ELIZABETH METZGER HOWARD

Doubleday & Company, Inc.

GARDEN CITY, NEW YORK

Contents

To
THE MISSES METZGER
AND
THE MESSRS. HOWARD

Part 1

SUMMER

Chapter One

AGE FORTY-TWO, six feet three in his socks, weight one hundred and eighty stripped, with thick unruly brown hair, deep-set black eyes, a dead white skin that no amount of weather ever colored, and long thin white twitching hands—this pallor and twitching suggesting narcotics to some—thus stood Dr. Dan Field on an afternoon in the year 1880. He'd been delivering a farmer's wife of child since the previous dawn. Now before entering his Willowspring, Pennsylvania, home he leaned wearily against one of the tall colonial pillars of the big brick house.

It was a late August afternoon and barely breathing, like every other sunny summer afternoon on Maple Street (excepting Saturdays when all of Willowspring hummed with country people and their rigs). Big houses and cottages seemed to be sleeping; trees hardly stirred. Only now and then came slow treads on the walks or soft thuds on the road or the laborious creak of an ox-cart. Occasionally there were voices of children, perhaps the bark of a dog or the moo of a cow or the cackle of a hen. The town clock methodically marked the hours and the half hours; always the mesmeric tapping of hammers sounded somewhere or other. And the gentle buzzing of the bees might be the purr of a contented village heart, Dan Field thought.

His eyes moved across the street to the southeast corner of Maple and Linden. The tapping of the hammers was there today, and had been these many weeks. The new school would soon be finished. Public school, Dan Field meditated, and large enough to include the minute mortal excreta from the frayed fragment of existence called Mudtown, in other words the little Negroes and white scraps who lived across the creek. The old

3

school hadn't been able to accommodate adequately all the children of the town proper.

A small ragged and filthy boy, dragging a huge wash upon a homemade wagon, turned a corner and stopped before the school. Dan Field knew the boy as he knew every man, woman, and child throughout the countryside. He was Ray Stoddard, one of Mudtown's own white scraps. Ray's father, Lem, was a worthless drunk. His mother, Myrtle, expected another child—her ninth in twelve years—come December. Their home was a fetid shanty and their bellies were never full, except during the few summer months when their garden grew. Yet because of the new school Ray Stoddard would have the opportunity of acquiring an education. *Can there any good thing come out of Nazareth?* . . . Ray might someday be mayor of Willowspring. He was smart as a whip.

Pleased with such a heretical possibility, Dan Field's eyes wandered south, between the Norway maples edging the rolling brick walks, by the horsechestnut trees around the vacant corner lot, over Horsechestnut Street, past the Methodist Church and across Maple Street to where two great gray stone houses stood far back under the spreading branches of tall sugar maples. These were the homes of the Albrights and the Sargents, Willowspring's leading families, one might actually say Willowspring's royalty. For although many had tried, never since the town's incorporation had anyone except an Albright or a Sargent held the mayoralty.

Upon the Albright lawn Dan Field saw the two little princesses of the blood, Lillian Albright and Prissy Sargent. He'd brought them both into the world, as he'd brought all the new generation of Albrights and Sargents. Every one of these children was dear to him, but his eyes rested upon Lillian. Miss Muffet, he thought tenderly, using his baby name for her. Jesus! he swore to himself. She grows more like her mother every day, golden skin and all.

"Darling, darling," he whispered, thinking about both mother and child.

His glance shifted from the lovely little girl before the gray stone mansion back to the little scarecrow boy before the new school. Ray Stoddard, he spoke mentally, it'll take more than can be learned in school to give you a Chinaman's chance, smart as

you may be. Suddenly he remembered the mad tramp with whom
Daisy Tatem had eloped, and whose convictions had confounded
Mudtown. Ray couldn't have been more than seven years old at
that time, but he'd listened to the tramp's strange philosophy as
if he understood every word. And there is probably more wisdom
than madness in your theories, tramp, Dan Field thought. Right
now at the new Johns Hopkins University in Baltimore certain
professors were trying to read between the lines of textbooks.

Eventually everyone in Willowspring believed, as sincerely as
the Albrights and Sargents believed, that the first George Albright and the first Rufus Sargent founded the town. Actually
the site had been named, because of a spring which gurgled up
from the roots and out of the trunk of a weeping willow tree,
by a Robert Pierce who'd built a log cabin there in 1750 to
trade with the Indians. In 1829, when the first George Albright
and the first Rufus Sargent arrived, Willowspring already
boasted a dozen homes, a school of sorts, a Lutheran Church
and Jonathan Meigs's store.

George and Rufus, lifelong friends, had been born and reared
among Philadelphia's aristocracy. Left orphans in their early
twenties, with substantial patrimonies, the two young gentlemen decided to leave the city of their birth. Everybody knew,
in 1829, that Philadelphia had reached the limit of population and
all fields open to gentlemen were overcrowded.

One night in a tavern, considering what new region might
be best for their great venture, they happened to overhear a
stranger describe the utter beauty of the country around about
Willowspring. On a fall morning shortly afterward George and
Rufus stuffed saddlebags with Spanish gold dollars, straddled two
fine mares, and rode forth along the Philadelphia–Pittsburgh pike.
Some sunsets later they stopped the mares before Jonathan
Meigs's store.

There stood the weeping willow tree, the spring gurgling up
from the roots and out of the trunk and then into a watering
trough. The mares took their own heads and thrust feverish noses
deep.

Afar George and Rufus saw the mountains with their bur-
nished, dense forests; nearer, the farms on the hills, their houses
and barns, their outlined fields, the fields of buckwheat stubble

vermilion under the setting sun. Below the hills the thin line which was the blue Juniata was winding its way through the valley. Before them they saw, down the lane, a row of neat sturdy houses of frame or fieldstone and the log Lutheran Church. The lane was edged by Norway maples, crimson and gold then in October. In their ears was the cool tingle of the willow spring falling into the trough. And in their nostrils was the smell—*that* smell. Years later the grandchildren of George and Rufus, returning from the far corners of the earth, would say they could tell when they reached Willowspring with their eyes shut, by that smell—a mingling of clean air and rich sod and damp moss and sweet fern, with always something else floating through, lilacs or apple blossoms or locust trees in bloom, new-mown hay or buckwheat or clover, then in October spruce and burning leaves.

George spoke at last: "Here we might build us a kingdom." Rufus nodded. "I was thinking the same thing myself."

George the First died in 1866 and Rufus the First less than a year later. Side by side they lie on the green hill, which is across the Juniata and a mile beyond Willowspring's last street, Limestone Avenue. But upon a huge tomb is inscribed:

GEORGE ALBRIGHT AND RUFUS SARGENT
FOUNDERS OF WILLOWSPRING, PA.

For they had built them a kingdom. Because of their gold a small settlement became a thriving town. They had the village incorporated and later made the county seat. They established the Willowspring Savings Bank, paying for the original capital stock themselves. They loaned money at fair interest to merchants and farmers and for new homes and churches. They even loaned the Catholics money to build their church, overlooking personal opinions concerning papacy.

George and Rufus prided themselves upon their tolerance, although the tolerance was never extended socially. They and later their wives and children (excepting Tim Albright) didn't even dream of mingling personally with a soul beneath their own status. However, the valley possessed many families of ancient lineage and there were any number of sizable estates and fortunes. And as time went on not a few of these "best families" moved into Willowspring, so that when, in 1839, George and Rufus brought brides back from Philadelphia, a local aristocracy was already established.

George married a Miss Lillian Sammal and Rufus married a Miss Priscilla Lane. And if the brides found some opposition, as George and Rufus surely did, the passing years established their social supremacy and they came to be regarded as queens of a sort, as George and Rufus were thought to be kings.

George the Second (addressed as Captain George after the Civil War) was born in 1840. A handsome, stalwart boy, he grew into a handsome, stalwart man, with yellow curls, round blue eyes, and fine white teeth, and he followed in his father's footsteps. But Tim Albright, born in 1848, became the family black sheep. A thin dark sensitive wisp of a child, at eleven he began writing poetry and at fifteen left home.

Rufus's first child was Priscilla (called Pris), born in 1843. From childhood she was a picture, slim, with straw-colored curls, a complexion the color of pale honey actually darker than her hair, and shadow-filled gray eyes. She had music in her finger tips, too, and had studied a year at the Boston Conservatory. Pris and Captain George were married the time he came home on furlough during '63.

After Pris, the Sargents had a stillborn son and then in 1845 came Rufus the Second. His nose was always too big and his mouth too small, but he had brilliant black eyes under sweeping lashes. These eyes, however, were weak from his birth, and because of this affliction Rufus the Second could not join the army and spent the war years studying to follow in his father's footsteps. During 1867 he married a Miss Lou Walton of Germantown, Pennsylvania, a pretty, tiny, strong-minded girl of Quaker descent.

But George the First and Rufus the First not only built a kingdom; they established a dynasty. After their deaths Captain George and Rufus the Second ruled the town from the bank on Broad Street. In the Albright home lived Gramma Lillian Albright, Captain George and Pris, and their three children, Rufe, Sammy, and Lillian. In the Sargent home lived Gramma Priscilla Sargent, Rufus the Second, and Lou, with their two children, Prissy and Bert.

By 1880 the spring had dried up and the weeping willow tree was dead, but the town of Willowspring had more than three thousand souls. Beside numerous lanes and alleys there were five long wide streets—Broad, Linden, Horsechestnut, Oak, and Maple—lined by brick walks and with lampposts on every corner. A good town to see, everybody thought, with great tree branches spreading over the staid, lovely mansions of the best families and the tidy, pretty cottages of the townspeople. A progressive town, with the steeples of the four Protestant churches, the cross upon the Catholic Church, the dome of the courthouse, and the flag topping the post office, all breaking through the leaves. And now the new public school. A clean town if one could forget that across the blue Juniata, across the "crick" in the section called Mudtown, lay Limestone Avenue. Cramped and cluttered, its days were brightened only by the sun and its nights were lightened only by the moon and stars or the headlight of an engine brushing by on the adjacent trestle.

And this August afternoon, contemplating Mudtown, Dan Field thought, One rotten apple . . .

Captain George and Rufus the Second strolled along. Dan Field smiled. He'd reached Willowspring in time to know George the First and Rufus the First and it amused him to see their sons strolling along together, immaculately attired and holding their haughty heads high, so like their fathers before them.

"Hello, Dan," George called.

He and Rufus stopped beside the gate and Rufus said, "Haven't you anything better to do than let a pillar support you, Dan?"

Dan Field yawned. "Letting a bed support me might be a better idea. I've not closed my eyes since night before last."

"Who's your lady?" George joked.

"Farmer's wife near Mount Pallas, nine-pound boy," Dan Field said.

But he wondered what would happen if he'd up and tell George who his lady really was. He chuckled to himself: *Thou hast ravaged my heart with one of thine eyes, with one chain of thy neck.*

George the Second and Rufus the Second began their education under tutors and finished it at the University of Pennsylvania, where Dan Field was studying during part of George's time. They met, however, through a Philadelphia girl named Viola Larsen. No one could tell what George really thought, he being a taciturn fellow. Yet obviously he'd fallen head over heels for Vi and seemed appreciative when Dan Field withdrew his attentions. And the very month the war ended George wrote Dan Field:

"Our one medico, Dr. Berkley, has just dropped dead. Here is a splendid opportunity."

He met Dan Field at the depot and said, "I'm married."

"Vi?"

George flushed to the roots of his yellow curls and his answer was the only time he made Dan Field a confidant until years later.

"Not Vi, Dan. It's Pris Sargent, Rufus' sister. Or didn't you meet Rufus? Anyhow, Dan, the Albrights and Sargents are practically royalty. Both lines go away back, are indisputable, and my father and Uncle Rufus (he isn't my real uncle—I simply call him that the way Pris and Rufus call my father Uncle George) they built a little kingdom here. Since we were born it's been understood that Pris and I would marry. And she's—well, wonderful, Dan. You couldn't help seeing what I thought of Vi. . . . Pris is the right wife for me though, Dan."

Before the war Dan Field had spent several summers traveling abroad. He meant to stay in Willowspring merely long enough to earn sufficient money so that he might return to Vienna and begin research work. The Field family lineage was also indisputable and the Field mansion had stood a hundred years on Rittenhouse Square. But the elder Field, who'd been a lawyer, was forced to retire because of a heart condition and the income left barely maintained his establishment. Yet after fifteen years Dan Field still lived in Willowspring.

He had never married and, what was more, he'd never seemed interested in any local girl or woman. Every spring he spent a week in Philadelphia and a week in New York. He went to Philadelphia to visit his parents, people knew, so the rumor was he had a girl in New York. The truth happened to be that Dan Field had been in love with George's wife, Priscilla Sargent Albright, since the first moment he saw her. But this truth Dan Field had carefully concealed, not only from the world but from Pris herself.

There was a girl in New York, however, many girls, always a different one.

Once a year in New York Dan Field found a woman whose body was slim and whose hair was fair and whose eyes were gray and he took her to bed, and for an instant out of all time he let himself believe that her flesh was the color of ripe wheat.

Dan Field's eyes followed Captain George and Rufus the Second along the street. On the vacant lot under the horsechestnut trees children played, Rufe and Sammy Albright among them.

As if it had all happened yesterday Dan Field remembered again the look in Pris's eyes when he'd put the first baby, Rufe, in her arms. He remembered, too, when Baby George and Sammy and Lillian were born, and when Baby George died. How he'd fought to save the little fellow for Pris, and to save Lillian. She'd been a blue baby.

Rufe and Sammy and Lillian . . . George Albright's children. He was just Uncle Doc. Uncle Doc . . .

Dan Field shrugged and brought his eyes back to the school. Ray Stoddard didn't seem to have moved a muscle. The eight Stoddard children had survived and the ninth would probably live likewise. Maybe we're supposed to exist like swine. . . . Then he recalled the vast strides the medicos had made during the last few years. The next generation, he concluded, will know definitely why babies of the Stoddard ilk can be born sound while Baby George Albright comes into the world with his lungs defective. Why Lillian Albright arrives looking like a little purple monkey, and Dolly Tatem . . .

Dolly Tatem, whose mother had run off with the mad tramp, was another of the Mudtown scum. But Dolly happened to be the first Willowspring baby Dan Field had delivered. After he'd washed her he'd held her up in one hand. She had reminded him of a little plump white rosebud, a whiff of perfume in a dung heap. And Cal was another Mudtown scrap who looked like a tiny angel but whose mother was a whore. It wouldn't be long, though, before Cal began spewing forth bloody bits of his lungs the way Baby George Albright had done. Dan Field shuddered.

He looked back toward the Albrights'. Prissy had disappeared and with Lillian now was Alexander Jennings—poor scared little Alexander whose mother kept telling him that if he trusted in God there was nothing to fear, when all the time her own poor scared heart stuck in her throat. Captain George entered the gate, said a few words to the children, and Alexander fled.

Rufus the Second moved toward his own gate. Another boy,

Gregory Beamer, walked a few feet behind. Gregory never dreamed of catching up and walking beside him. When he reached the Sargents' place, Gregory would go around back because he'd come to see their hired girl, Maggie. Maggie was supposedly Gregory's sister; still, he always visited Maggie and not Nellie, the Albrights' hired girl, who was also supposedly his sister.

Watching Gregory, Dan Field remembered Prissy Sargent: a little princess and a little bastard under the same roof. And Bert Sargent flashed through his mind—Bert, age nine, the small heir apparent who during the past year had spent most of his waking hours hobnobbing around Mudtown.

From the vacant lot came the voices of Rufe and Sammy Albright mingling with those of several town children—Mollie Reynard, a carpenter's daughter; Helen Boyd, the little Jewish girl; Bertha Richards, a Catholic; Buzz Standing, son of the village seamstress; Walt Butler, the butcher's son; Perse Hershberger, the blacksmith's son. Again Dan Field smiled. Times certainly had changed. Captain George and Rufus the Second boasted that they'd never associated with any of the town children during their boyhoods.

Gabe (short for Gabriel) Williams, the Albrights' colored hired man, stopped before Dan Field's gate. "Mr. Doc, hear 'bout Old Man Mr. Meeker?"

Dan Field shook his head. "No."

"Well, sir," Gabe explained, "a little while back Old Man Mr. Meeker gits loosen his wife and daughter and gits right uptown and into the Grand Central Bar, blind as he is."

"Did Old Man Meeker find what he sought?" Dan Field inquired.

Gabe shook his black head. "No, Mr. Doc, he didn't. Mr. Leonard say it pretty nigh bust his heart not to of give Old Man Mr. Meeker a drink. But it'd been worth his license to of give him a drop. Mrs. Meeker and Mrs. Diggers couldn't budge him out'n the bar, though. They had to git Mr. Williams. Sure caused a heap of excitement 'long Broad Street, Mr. Doc."

Broad Street was the business mart. Along the north side ran Strock's Market complete with meat counter, a rarity in 1880; Miss Gunther's Ladies' Emporium, carrying all the latest women's accouterments; the Elite (usually pronounced "Elight") Tonsorial Parlor; the Grand Central Hotel and Bar, with a wooden Indian at the steps and a watering trough on the curb; Carl's Novelty Shop; and Heckshire's Drugstore. Among changing medicinal jars, the drugstore window had for many years displayed another jar which contained the seemingly immortal carcass of a two-headed squirrel preserved in wood alcohol.

Along the south side of Broad Street ran the Willowspring Savings Bank; the Western Union Telegraph Company, and Smith's Livery Stable, with the blacksmith shop, the iron pile, and the wheelwright shop behind. Across Oak was Hardy's Office Building, the Willowspring Printing Office, where the Willowspring *News* was issued weekly; then Frazer's Family Clothing Palace, and Morgan & Sons Hardware & Tool Company.

Other, no less important, places straggled here and there between vacant lots for more than a mile at both ends of Broad Street. The last one west was Fulton's Flour, Seed, and Feed Warehouse, and the last two east were Perry's Grist Mill and Strock's Slaughterhouse.

Yes, Dan Field could readily imagine the excitement caused by Old Man Meeker's escapade. This August afternoon Broad Street, even as Maple, would have been basking in lush lethargy. Maybe from the blacksmith shop an anvil rang; maybe footsteps sounded or the rattle of a wagon or the creak of an oxcart. An occasional shopper entered a store. Before his livery stable Jake Smith probably leaned back in his chair, half asleep, while Floyd Shires, his hack driver, dozed in the hack on the curb, as the horse, with its head almost touching ground, swished a trenchant tail over a fly-ravished rump. Perhaps Ralph Pettigrew stood before Hardy's Office Building, wherein was his office, staring up and down the street, wondering what the hell else could be said or done to push those bastards George Albright and Rufus Sargent off the throne and make himself king of Willowspring. George and Rufus would be balancing the books, oblivious of Ralph Pettigrew. Likely against the bank's front loitered the colored policeman, Mr. Williams, Gabe's father, his red helmet pushed far back on his white wool and beads of sweat rolling down the deep dark furrows of his face. No doubt Tracy Whitlock, owner and editor of the Willowspring *News*, darted here and there, hoping to discover a spicy bit. Certainly Mr. Leonard (Nard to his friends), owner and proprietor of the Grand Central Hotel, lounged in the saloon, empty during the afternoon lull, talking to Shorty Clapp, the bartender.

And that would be all until Old Man Meeker groped his blind way along, or so Dan Field thought.

That was not all, however. Ralph Pettigrew had been standing before Hardy's Office Building prior to Old Man Meeker's appearance but his thoughts for the time being did not include George Albright nor Rufus Sargent.

Ralph Pettigrew had been a poor farm boy who'd worked his way through law school and come to Willowspring eight years ago, politically ambitious. And others beside himself believed that if George Albright's henchmen had not bought votes last election Ralph Pettigrew instead of George Albright would have been elected mayor.

Next to George Albright and Rufus Sargent, Pettigrew's detestation focused upon Judge Hart Martin, William Price, and Channing Taylor, heads of three other families who considered themselves equals of the Albrights and Sargents. The judge (known as Judge Hart because his father, who'd been a judge before him, still lived and was addressed as Judge Martin) had one son studying art in Paris, another attending Princeton, and a third at Lawrenceville. What Pettigrew particularly detested about Judge Hart was that, although he had three sons, he extended no clemency to boys brought before the bench. And William (Billy) Price! Thinking of him, Pettigrew usually sniffed. Old Man Price had made a fortune out of lumber and consequently the bank gave Billy a berth as cashier. He had one daughter about seven who looked like a frog and a pink-haired wife who looked like a tart. And Channing Taylor (who'd married Madge Kimbell and become president of the Kimbell Coal, Coke, and Iron Company) had two daughters, aged seventeen and sixteen, who knew no more about life than babies. And this afternoon these three men left the bank building in the order named and each one passed Pettigrew without recognition, as usual, which never failed to gripe his guts.

No sooner had Channing Taylor turned the corner of Oak Street than Pettigrew saw Margaret and Dorothy Taylor coming the other way. They were handsome girls, chestnut-haired, brown-eyed, and red-cheeked, with big breasts and thighs—the type Pettigrew admired. "Give me a woman you don't have to shake the sheets to find," he expressed it. He liked particularly the looks of the older one, Margaret, and every time he chanced to meet her he wished he was seventeen again and could get her in a haymow and show her what it was all about. He'd have to show her, of course. What could girls who'd been raised as in a convent, attending Old Maid Fisher's school, ever know about boys or men?

Pettigrew always eyed these girls openly and today he eyed Margaret boldly, his gaze lingering over her thighs, then her breasts, lastly her face. She seemed oblivious of the attention until directly before him. Then she glanced up through her lashes and smiled.

Pettigrew watched Margaret Taylor until she turned the corner. If I could get that girl on her back . . . He smacked his lips. Besides, it would be sweet revenge. A hurt to one of the best families would mean a hurt to all of them.

Suddenly Pettigrew forgot Margaret Taylor. He saw Old Man Meeker groping his blind way toward the Grand Central Bar.

"Yes," Dan Field told Gabe Williams, "I can imagine the excitement on Broad Street."

Gabe nodded. "Never did see a street fill up like that 'cept'n the night 'fore 'lection when Mr. Pettigrew says his speech. One minute, Mr. Doc, hardly nobody's 'bout and next minute seems like the hull town, 'cepting the best families, buzzed 'round. Even Miss Fisher and her mama and Miss Aunt Tillie Whitlock."

Gabe moved toward the Albrights'. Dan Field looked the other way, past the Catholic Church (on the northeast corner opposite the new school), up Maple Street to where Miss Fisher and her blind mother lived. Miss Fisher conducted the private school where the best-family children had gone since Pris and Tim Albright's childhood. The phenomenal Miss Fisher, Dan Field thought. Since girlhood she'd been practically perfect physically and now, nearing fifty, she'd lost little of her animal allure. But Miss Fisher had never had a beau. She and her blind mother and Aunt Tillie Whitlock (maiden aunt of Tracy Whitlock of the Willowspring *News* and called Aunt Tillie by almost everyone) along with Mrs. Meeker and Mrs. Mame Diggers (wife and widowed daughter of Old Man Meeker) were the leaders of the town's Women's Christian Temperance Union.

Dan Field often thanked God that the town's one other doctor, Brown Walsh, and not he, happened to be the Meekers' physician.

In 1880 Mr. Meeker was well past seventy and had long been known as Old Man Meeker. He'd been a fixing fool. He could fix anything—watches, locks, guns, furniture, and what not. For almost fifty years Mr. Meeker had spent his days going around town from place to place fixing this and that, and always carrying a bottle out of which ever so often he'd take a nip. Yet truly no one ever remembered seeing Mr. Meeker really drunk, as truly no one ever remembered seeing Mr. Meeker really sober. During almost fifty years he had merely existed in a state of mellowness.

Strangely, this mellowness interfered not a whit with Mr. Meeker's business progress. He was not only a clever fixer but an astute businessman. Besides earning enough to buy his drink he gave Mrs. Meeker a weekly amount sufficient to support the family, buy a house, and deposit tidy sums in the bank.

However, Mrs. Meeker and Mrs. Diggers considered themselves eternally disgraced by his drinking. Ably assisted by other members of the W.C.T.U., they had done everything possible to reform the culprit, from threatening Mr. Leonard with arrest if he ever sold Mr. Meeker another drop to continually entreating Mr. Meeker to sign the pledge.

All of which Mr. Meeker took good-naturedly. In fact he never took anything other than amiably. His round pink face, framed by snow-white hair, beamed upon whatever confronted him. Until one day during May 1879 a gun he was fixing exploded and blinded him and since that day his wife and daughter had seen that he'd not even smelled a cork. In fact two months later blind Mr. Meeker, Mrs. Meeker guiding his hand, signed the pledge. This was all well enough except that Dr. Walsh would sometimes be called to treat what Mrs. Meeker and Mrs. Diggers called "one of papa's indigestion attacks." And today Old Man Meeker, blind though he was, had been able to grope his way uptown and into the Grand Central Bar.

"Poor old desiccated devil," Dan Field thought, out loud.

His eyes came back to the Catholic Church and he hoped fervently that no case of his would interrupt Father Callahan's Sunday night call.

Ray Stoddard moved, pulling the wash-laden wagon along. I'd give a pretty penny to know what the little beggar's been thinking, Dan Field meditated.

He called, "Think you'll like going to the new school, Ray?"

Ray called back, "Yes sir, Mr. Doc."

Dan Field turned at last and one of his hands lingered on the colonial pillar.

Practically every unmarried girl and woman around Willowspring had set her cap for Dan Field. When he built the big brick house, gossip had him married to ladies all the way from Willowspring via New York to Virginia. Why would a bachelor build a mansion? Why would he go to Virginia and buy pillars and furniture? There were plenty right on hand. Sometimes Dan Field, himself, wondered why he'd built such a big place. Maybe because he'd been born and raised in a large house. But he knew definitely why he'd gone back to Virginia and bought the pillars and furniture.

Dan Field had seen the destruction of the South but he had also perceived what he termed its "dead truth." The Confederacy had admitted an aristocracy and acknowledged slavery, while, if the North admitted an aristocracy, it never had and probably never would acknowledge shackled labor.

Not that there was anything of the iconoclast about Dan Field. Only one night, marching through Virginia, his regiment came to a plantation where fire had left nothing of the mansion but two tall pillars standing straight and strong in the moonlight. They had seemed a monument to the South's dead truth. And he liked having them before his house as he liked having the furniture and Ackley in it—Ackley, who'd been the slave of the Ackleys of Virginia from whom Dan Field had bought the furniture.

Dan Field's hand left the pillar. And now for the golden bourbon, he was thinking, and food and a dream of you, my Pris. I'll dream that all I have to do is open a door to see your golden body stretched upon the bed, the bride's bed, the bed I've sworn to myself no one but you shall ever occupy again.

He stepped into the wide hall. On the right was his office with its outside door opening upon the drive.

Dan Field turned left into the parlor, calling, "Ackley."

Almost immediately Ackley appeared. "Yes suh."

"Anybody here this afternoon?"

Ackley wrinkled his black nose. "Mudtown scum."

"Who?"

"Lem Stodda'd's wife."

"What did she want?"

Ackley shrugged. "She says next time you goes by huh place to bring moh' tonic. Huh back's bad liftin' washtubs all day long, she says."

Dan Field nodded. "All right."

He reached a decanter and glass. Thank God for the golden bourbon, he was thinking. He chuckled once again to himself. *O Jerusalem, Jerusalem, . . . how often would I have gathered thy children together, even as a hen gathereth her chickens under her wings, and ye would not!*

Chapter Two

THIS late August afternoon Lillian Albright was ten years and eleven months old and Prissy Sargent was ten years and seven months old. Lillian was a tall, slim little girl who, like her mother, had shadowy gray eyes, straw-colored curls, and a complexion, Dan Field called golden, which was darker than her hair. Prissy Sargent was short and plump, with brilliant black eyes under sweeping lashes like her father's, dimpled rosy cheeks, and a thick brown pigtail.

From the Albright lawn the two little girls could hear the hammering on the new school, and they were both thinking the same thing. Excepting themselves and Ginny Price, who was only seven years old, and Margaret and Dorothy Taylor, who were seventeen and sixteen, soon all the children would be going to the new school. Even Rufe, Sammy, Bert, and Alexander would be going, because best-family boys could do lots of things best-family girls couldn't do. Why, at the moment Rufe and Sammy were playing on the vacant lot with some town children, though Rufe was fifteen and too old to be playing children's games.

Lillian and Prissy enjoyed carrying their little noses high. Still, they were lonely at times; there was not a single other best-family little girl their own age. Today they'd rolled their hoops around and around the yard and they'd dressed and undressed their big wax dolls.

"Sometimes I wish I was a boy," Lillian sighed.

"Why?" Prissy demanded.

There she goes, Lillian thought, acting like she doesn't know what I mean when she always knows what I mean, like I always know what she means. Like now she knows I want to be a boy 'cause boys can play with town children and have fun.

"What do you want to be a boy for?" Prissy went on. "Boys are grubby."

"Rufe's not grubby," Lillian defended.

"Bert's not grubby either." Prissy giggled. "But look at Sammy."

Lillian flushed: that mean Prissy, saying Sammy was grubby. But how could she answer Prissy? Even Mama said Sammy was never clean.

And Prissy announced loftily, "You ought to be thankful you're born who you are and not common, Lillian Albright."

Lillian sighed once more. "I suppose so." Then her heart missed a beat. "Oh, here's Alexander."

"I see him," Prissy said. Her heart also missed a beat.

Alexander was a frail, brown-haired boy of twelve, who had a rose-leaf complexion and timid brown eyes. Before entering the Albright gate he could see the children playing on the vacant lot. And the sight of the children and the pounding of the hammers on the new school made him quake inwardly.

Alexander's mother continually told him that if he trusted in God he'd nothing to fear. On the very day his father died, she told him over and over, his father had said, "I have trusted in God and I've nothing to fear." Alexander kept telling himself that he really did trust in God so he'd nothing to fear. But the town boys and Sammy Albright, too, made his life a misery. And now he'd not be going back to Miss Fisher's school with Lillian and Prissy but to the public school.

However, coming up to the little girls, he tried to speak lightly. "Guess the new school's pretty near done."

"Do you think you'll like going, Alexander?" Prissy asked.

"Of course," Alexander lied.

And there goes Alexander, Lillian thought, making believe we don't know he'll hate the new school, like he lets on he don't know we hear when the other boys call him "sissy."

A voice from next door called, "Prissy."

"Oh dear," Prissy fussed, "Mama's calling. I'll have to go home. You'd better go, too, Alexander. Auntie Pris will be calling Lillian, soon."

"You don't have to go, Alexander," Lillian announced. "Mama's out."

Next to his mother Alexander loved Lillian and Prissy more than anyone. However, until today he never could decide which one was his favorite. But sitting propped against the trunk of a big maple tree, Prissy gone and his eyes on Lillian, he suddenly knew. It was Lillian he loved best, Lillian with her gray eyes and fair curls. Maybe after he grew up he'd find words to tell her how much he loved her.

This day the best he could muster was, "Well, Lillian, I'll miss not being at Miss Fisher's with you."

Captain George entered the yard.

"Hello, Papa," Lillian called.

"Hello, dear." He came along. "How are you, Alexander?"

"Well, thanks," Alexander gulped. He always felt fearful of the great handsome figure who was Lillian's father.

"Better run along home," George instructed. "Time Lillian came indoors."

Alexander ran as fast as his legs would take him.

"Where's Mama?" George asked Lillian.

"She's out," Lillian answered, hoping Papa wouldn't mind. He always wanted Mama home to greet him.

Today he didn't seem to mind. His blue eyes crinkled and his white teeth flashed the way they did when he was quite pleased. Wondering, Lillian picked up her wax doll and followed him into the house.

At the time the brides were brought to Willowspring, George the First and Rufus the First already had built the identical great gray stone houses standing far back under the spreading branches of tall sugar maples. And until the grandchildren were well grown the outsides of each place remained the same—the pump on the back porch; the gray stone icehouse covered by rambler roses; the outhouse with one room for the family's use and one for the hired help; the tall trellis between the yard and garden where the Concord grapevines grew; the lilac-lined path along the flower garden to the chicken coop, barn, and vegetable fields; the apple trees and the plum and cherry and peach trees around the far fields, where the cows were pastured and the hog sties stood and where violets and daisies grew in springtime.

Within each house was a wide entrance hall and a wide winding stairway. Double doors on both sides of the hall led left to the thirty-foot parlor and right to the sitting room, dining room, and kitchen. The second floor had five bedrooms and in 1880 a bathroom. And the third floor had three rooms: the playroom, the hired girl's room, and a storage room. The walls of the first and second stories were fifteen feet high and the walls of the third story were twelve feet high. While, if the furnishings of the two houses were not uniform, there was such a similarity about them that any piece in one house might be taken to be a counterpart of one in the other—massive oak chairs and tables and huge walnut beds and bureaus and washstands and marble-topped pedestals to hold the big lamps. Even the great square pianos were alike.

Entering the Albright house Lillian went upstairs. Captain George hung his hat on the hall rack, stepped through the portieres into the sitting room, and settled himself in an easy chair. At forty George had gained some weight and his yellow curls were a bit gray, but his eyes were as blue and his teeth as fine and white as they'd ever been.

He took a copy of the Philadelphia *Public Ledger* out of a pocket and his eyes rested upon a certain item. All right, he thought, for perhaps the third time since the paper had been delivered. "PROGRESSIVE MAYOR OF WILLOWSPRING, PA.," the column began, and it went on to say that although Willowspring was a small town it was one of the most progressive places in the state because of a mayor like Captain George Albright, through whose influence a modern temple for the education of its youth was being erected.

As he had done many times before, George wished his father might have lived to see how he was carrying on. Although Pa, George speculated, would be aghast at his grandsons playing with town children, not to mention their going to the new public school. How he'd worried because Tim couldn't be kept away from the rabble! But George himself felt his boys would be the better off for having played with and gone to school with men they must later meet in the business world. And he also felt it wasn't a bad idea if Rufe and Sammy associated a bit with the town girls. Until he'd attended college he'd never had a girl . . . and then he'd met Viola Larsen. Vi . . .

Still, his father would be proud of him, George knew. And Uncle Rufus would be proud of Rufus, no doubt. Rufus's only trouble was never being satisfied to let well enough alone. Now his arc-light scheme . . . Rufus didn't seem to understand tradition was what counted. George shrugged, remembering that upstart Ralph Pettigrew who'd run against him last election. Why, since the days of their fathers no one had ever held the mayoralty except an Albright or a Sargent. What was more, no one ever would hold that office while there was an Albright or Sargent of proper age upon the horizon.

Lillian entered the room. What a lovely little girl she is, George thought fondly. And fine boys, Rufe and Sammy. And Pris . . . George's eyes grew tender. There was a wife, lovely and dutiful. The only time he could ever remember Pris being obstinate was when she would name their first baby Rufus, after her father. Yet Pa had been living then and the first Albright baby should by all rights have been George the Third. But Pris had absolutely defied him. And the second baby, named George, lived a short four months.

But where was Pris?

"Lillian, where is your mother?"

Lillian, who had seated herself, bent over some embroidery, began wiggling. "I—I—said Mama's out, Papa."

Finally the front door opened and Pris came breathlessly into the room. Lillian sighed, relieved. Pris, at thirty-seven, was quite as lovely as she'd ever been—her gray eyes shadowy, her straw-colored curls fairer than the skin Dan Field called golden but which was more the color of pale honey, and her figure slimmer than the day George had married her, excepting the roundness of her breasts. Today she'd been hurrying and her cheeks were a bit flushed, making her look all the lovelier.

"George, I'm sorry I'm late," she panted. "I was over helping Mrs. Lanning pack the missionary box, the one we're sending our missionary in Africa. There was quite a stack of things and we started packing and the time fairly flew."

He smiled. "Perfectly all right, my dear. Have a look at this."

He handed her the *Ledger*. Her eyes ran down the column.

"Splendid, George. It really is. . . . Where can Rufe be?" she wondered out loud.

Rufe Albright was fifteen. Much too old to be playing with the children on the vacant lot, but he couldn't keep away when Mollie Reynard was there. Strange the effect Mollie Reynard had on him, common, noisy little thing that she was, and only twelve years old, Sammy's age. Rufe knew Mollie liked Sammy more than she did him. Well, why shouldn't she? Sammy was her kind, noisy, rough, even if he was an Albright. But there was something about Sammy made you like to look at him. Maybe it was his yellow curls which Gramma Albright said shone like Grampa Albright's used to shine.

There was nothing worth looking at about himself, Rufe felt. Too tall for his years, he walked with a slouch, his chest caved in. His nose was too big, and his lashes were too long for a man's. Lately, though, he'd tried to straighten up, to act like a man. And he'd been shaving the fuzz off with his father's razor and putting grease on his hair to keep the cowlick back.

And here he was playing silly games he hated—I spy and kick-the-stick—to be near Mollie. But his mind wouldn't stay on the games. His thoughts were driven by the hard young body of Mollie as loose leaves by a wind: Mollie's black curls bobbing . . . Mollie's blue eyes dancing . . . Mollie's slim legs flying. Girls shouldn't be allowed to play games, Rufe speculated bitterly, with their legs flying so everybody could see—Buzz Standing and Walt Butler and Perse Hershberger and Sammy, too. Suddenly Rufe wanted to kill them all, Sammy included. And he wanted to kill Mollie's parents; they ought to know better than to let Mollie run with boys, no matter if Mr. Reynard was only a common carpenter and his wife did her own work.

"First chooser for prisoner's base," Sammy cried. "I choose Rufe."

No loyalty about Sammy, Rufe knew. Sammy chose him because his legs were long and he could run. He wished he could run now, so he'd never see any of them again, Sammy included.

"Second chooser," Mollie cried. "I choose Helen."

Soon they were lined up, the teams across the lot from one another. At a given signal each team would try running past the other to the opposite side of the lot without being tagged. Across from him Rufe saw Mollie. You little devil, he thought, I'll show you.

"Go," Sammy yelled.

Mollie was coming. Rufe lunged. He had her. You weren't supposed to hold a person, just tag, but Rufe held Mollie in his arms, against his breast. You little devil, I'll show you. . . . His arms crushed her closer and closer against him.

She was struggling. "Let me go. It ain't in the rules to hold."

"Rules," Rufe choked. "Who cares about rules?"

She broke loose. She was the stronger and he knew it now. He hadn't been able to hold her. His face flamed and, facing him, her face flamed.

"I hate you," she screamed.

"I despise you," he snarled.

This was the end. He'd had all he could stand. He wanted never to see her again. He threw back his shoulders and tried to walk the way a man should walk.

Moving away, he heard Sammy's voice, loud, furious. "You, Mollie, now you've went and made Rufe mad."

Mollie yelled, "He cheated. He held me. It ain't in the rules to hold. But I'm stronger'n him. I got away."

"You're a liar," Sammy bawled. "I'm stronger'n you and Rufe's stronger'n me. Then Rufe's stronger'n you."

Loyal Sammy, lying to save him. Sammy knew he was stronger than Rufe, and three years younger. But what boy wants to admit he's stronger than his big brother? Rufe choked.

He went on up Maple Street. There was the new school house being built. In another month school would begin and he'd be going. No more lessons at poky old Miss Fisher's beside a bunch of babies and Dorothy and Margaret Taylor who thought they were so much because they were sixteen and seventeen. There'd be boys of his own age in his class—Tom Leonard, whose father ran the hotel, Ben Smith, whose father owned the livery stable, Jack Sturdevant, whose father was a plumber. Until a few months ago these three boys had been his friends. Then all of a sudden they had stopped coming around and if he looked them up they acted as though they didn't want him. Rufe didn't know what had happened to make the boys act like this. Still, they'd been his friends and maybe they'd be again, once they were going to school together. And it would be a long, long time before he'd not be able to recognize them socially.

Papa had told him that himself. "Of course, I was never allowed to associate with the rabble," he'd said. "But you go ahead and make friends among the village boys and girls. It will be time enough, after you've finished college, to let them see you can't recognize them socially."

Papa had outlined Rufe's future quite clearly too. After he had graduated from the new school here he would go to the University of Pennsylvania and eventually take Papa's place in the bank, the way Papa had taken Grampa Albright's and Uncle Rufus had taken Grampa Sargent's.

Rufe sat down on a pile of boards beside the new schoolhouse, supposedly to watch the carpenters at their work, but his mind was hardly upon them. Although once he had wanted to be a carpenter. . . . But that was before he was old enough to know that gentlemen didn't build things with their hands. What he was really thinking about right now was that one of the men pounding away was Mollie's father, the one with the black curls and the long mustache. . . . Mollie's father, a common carpenter. Rufe thought of Mollie's mother, a nice, neat-looking little woman, but she did her own work. And Mollie's family ate in the kitchen. One night at suppertime Rufe had walked by their place. The front door was open and Rufe could see clear through the house to the kitchen, were Mollie and her father and mother were sitting around the table.

What would his own father and mother think if they knew the way he felt about a girl who had a family like Mollie's? Of course Papa'd said to make friends among the village boys and girls but what if Papa and Mama, too, knew the way he felt about Mollie? That nothing else mattered, nothing else in the whole wide world.

Suddenly Rufe realized the carpenters had gone. Bert Sargent moved along the pavement toward home, so it must be nearly dinnertime. Bert was only nine years old, yet he walked as if he'd never be afraid of anything, his head high and his shoulders square. Funny how different cousins can be. . . . Rufe could think of just one thing to be thankful about: at least his voice didn't crack any more.

Back on the vacant lot the other children had regarded Sammy aghast. No one could remember seeing Sammy mad before.

"You, Mollie," he yelled, "if you wasn't a girl I'd beat you."

"Beat her anyhow," Buzz Standing sneered. "I'd just as lief beat a girl if she made me mad."

Terror filled Helen Boyd's lovely, gentle Jewish eyes. "No, Sammy, you mustn't hurt a girl."

Sammy fled toward home and the three girls started down the street: Helen, like a little brown dove; Mollie with her black curls and blue eyes; and fat, jolly Bertha Richards, who was a Catholic. These three were the same age, twelve years old, and since babyhood had been inseparable.

"That Rufe!" Mollie spluttered, ignoring Sammy's wrath.

Bertha trembled. "I never knew Sammy could be like that. He might of killed you, Mollie."

Mollie shrugged. "I wouldn't care."

Helen said, "I'd care."

Prissy had picked up her dolly and made her way home sullen-faced. Lillian was mean, letting Alexander stay if Prissy couldn't, trying to make Alexander like her best, that's what Lillian was doing. And if he did, Prissy knew she'd die. For she loved Alexander more'n anybody 'cept Mama and Papa and Bert. And she felt so sorry for Alexander—no father (Mr. Jennings, who'd been the Methodist minister, had died a long time ago) and his mother delicate and poor as a church mouse, but a best family anyhow. They lived in a tiny little cottage way at the end of Maple. The church gave Mrs. Jennings thirty dollars a month and Papa and Uncle George had paid Alexander's tuition at Miss Fisher's, and Mama and Auntie Pris called on her and invited her to their big parties. But the town children and that Sammy treated Alexander terrible, called him sissy and everything.

Prissy went into the sitting room where her mother sat knitting. "What did you want, Mama?"

"It's after five o'clock. Time you came in."

Lou Sargent was only a few inches over five feet tall. Approaching thirty-five, she had become a bit plump but there was a certain beauty about her. Straight, glossy chestnut hair rolled in a shining coil at the nape of her neck. Her eyebrows were arched and black. Her nose was fine and her lips bowed, if her chin was square. But Lou's eyes were her most dominant feature, deep hazel; she could turn them on a person and keep them fixed minutes without batting a lash. Now they were fixed upon Prissy.

Lou wasn't thinking about Prissy; she was wondering where Bert could be. Prissy, however, sank uneasily into a chair—Mama's eyes upon her always gave her a guilty feeling. Still, Prissy thought Mama was a wonderful person, maybe because she'd been born near Philadelphia. She could settle almost any question simply by saying how in Philadelphia they do it this way.

Even Papa listened to Mama, although Mama pretended Papa decided matters. When Prissy asked Mama might she do something, Mama'd say, "Ask Papa," but Papa never answered until he'd consulted Mama.

Only once a long time ago Prissy had asked Mama if she could go in her bare feet and Mama said to ask Papa and he said it was all right.

Later Mama found her running around the lawn in her bare feet and fairly shrieked, "Prissy, what do you mean by being outside in your bare feet?"

"You told me to ask Papa," Prissy choked, "and he told me I could."

Mama had taken her by the hand and led her to Papa.

"Rufus," she said, "Prissy said you told her she could go in her bare feet."

"I suppose I did," Papa answered.

Mama groaned, "Rufus, if you can't take enough interest in your own daughter to see that she acts like a lady, please remember such conduct reflects on me."

Then Mama explained how if in Philadelphia a little girl went in her bare feet no other nice little girl would ever speak to her again. Prissy had cried and Mama had told her to forget all about it now, it was all over.

But it wasn't all over. Ever afterward Mama's eyes upon her gave Prissy a guilty feeling, because she'd loved running bare footed, and what was more, she had dreamed she and Alexander were running in their bare feet together on a lawn which was so big there wasn't any end.

"Prissy, don't sit idle, dear. Get your embroidery."

Prissy jumped guiltily. Still, she knew she was silly. Mama'd never find out the truth. Why couldn't she look at Mama the way Bert did, his eyes unflinching too? Suddenly it occurred to Prissy, Why, Bert treats Mama like Mama treats Papa. Mama asks Papa might she do something, knowing all the time he'd never tell her no and that's the way Bert asks Mama, knowing she never says no to him.

Bert Sargent was nine but he was a big fellow for his years, almost as tall as Prissy, and far wiser. Sturdy, straight-backed, with a sleek black head, deep hazel eyes, and a large mouth, Bert went his way. A determined way it was, Lou knew.

Lou had never known happiness until Bert was born. Not that she had ever been unhappy, merely indifferent. She did not realize the fact herself that, despite her small stature, she should have been a man—free to shape a personal destiny. Only a sense of discipline, generated by her Quaker upbringing, had made her a dutiful daughter and a conscientious wife. Her father had died before she was eighteen, a few months after Rufus Sargent had requested his daughter's hand in marriage. But the wedding did not take place until 1867, the year following her mother's death. Whether she loved Rufus or not Lou did not consider, and the marital relation was another duty she schooled herself to accept.

But when the baby Bert was in her arms Lou's life took on a different aspect. For, although she did not realize this fact either, he was the little boy she might have been. He was not only her son, he was herself. And truly he was herself. As a baby his hazel eyes could look longer at an object without batting a lash than Lou's own hazel eyes could look. Lou had a great affection for an only brother, Bert, after whom she named her son. He had been studying medicine at the time of her marriage and had later joined the navy. But Bert Walton, who was two years her junior, had been under her thumb, so to speak, and she had never respected him a great deal.

Bert Sargent was another story. He is just like me, Lou told herself. From early babyhood he defied her authority. Not aggressively, however; if she tried to force him to eat a dish he disliked, Bert simply clamped his small jaws and kept them clamped until Lou surrendered. Or if he didn't want to sleep, he'd not fuss, merely lie wide-eyed until all hours. Bert was never really naughty, but if he made up his mind, nothing could change him. Fearless, was the way Lou thought of him. For more than a year now he'd been starting out early every morning (excepting Sundays and school days), often not returning home until evening.

"Bert dear, where have you been all day?" Lou would question.

His unflinching eyes always met hers. "All over, Mama."

"Can't you tell Mama one place?"

"No one place. Lots of places."

"You didn't come home to lunch. Weren't you hungry?"

"If I was hungry, Mama, I'd of come home to lunch."

Where he spent his time Lou couldn't imagine, although she knew it was some place or places perfectly all right. Blood would tell and Bert could do no wrong. But the truth was that for more than a year Bert had been hobnobbing around Mudtown.

At the corner of Broad the dwellings on Maple Street ended. Along the east side, from there on to the creek, was a woods where lovers often met. On the west side, directly before coming to the covered bridge, stood an old house whose door opened upon the walk, and over the door hung a sign:

M. A. WOODWARD—CABINETMAKER

However, M. A. (known as Ma) Woodward's specialty did not happen to be cabinets. During the past thirty years he'd been making coffins (and better coffins never were, fashioned of sound seasoned pine boards held together by hand-turned wooden pegs) and Ma's coffins had incarcerated most of Willowspring's dead. In 1880 Ma was a plump, white-haired, white-bearded old fellow who would have looked exactly like Santa Claus if he'd worn a red suit and boots, instead of blue jeans and boots. His workshop, right off the house, was set back from the walk and before it a number of tombstones of various sizes and shapes always stood on sale.

Across the covered bridge a left turn led to the depot. If no turn were made, a mile due north, past the colored graveyard, was the Greenhill Cemetery where George the First, Rufus the First, and Baby George Albright (as well as the rest of Willowspring's white dead) rested. But the right turn, a couple of hundred yards off the covered bridge, past the lime kiln and beyond the railroad trestle, led to Willowspring's last street—Limestone Avenue.

The turn leading to the depot chanced to be uphill, while the turn into Limestone Avenue was a sharp descent. When the spring freshets came the creek seeped and sometimes rushed over Limestone Avenue. Often the water reached higher than a man's knees. Of course it went down eventually but it took a long arid spell to dry up the mud. Hence the section was called Mudtown.

Twenty shanties cluttered Limestone Avenue. seventeen of them inhabited by Negroes, the other three by whites—the Stoddard family; Red Tatem, who'd fought Indians and killed buffalo out West, and his two daughters, Dolly and Belle; and Lottie Lawler, Willowspring's one professional whore, called the "Widder Woman," and her three children, Ella, Wilbur, and Calvary.

Bert knew Lem and he knew Red and he knew Lottie. He played with Lem's and Lottie's children and with the little Negroes, who, thick and busy as traveler ants, swarmed around among hogs, chickens, dogs, cats, a couple of mules, and an occasional cow. Shaddock Stanwick, called Shad, a round-eyed, rangy black boy of thirteen, was Bert's shadow. During a single day Shad taught Bert more about *life* than he could have found out in years among his own class.

After the birth of the last Stoddard, Lem had gone staggering along Limestone Avenue.

"How come Mr. Stoddard he gets drunk, Shad?" Bert had inquired.

"Mr. Stoddard he git drunk fer plenty of fers, Bert. Most any fer's good nuff fer Mr. Stoddard ter git drunk. But Mr. Stoddard's gittin' drunk now 'cause they git nother young'un."

"If they don't want young'uns, how come they get 'em, Shad?"

Shad rolled his round eyes. "Mr. Stoddard he jest probably can't help goin' after the missus."

"What you mean, Shad, going after the missus?"

Shad told him.

"Shad"—Bert's eyes widened—"do best families get babies that way too?"

"Mighty likely, Bert. I never did hear tell of gittin' young'uns no other way."

Shad told Bert about Lottie Lawler, the Widder Woman, too, about men sneaking into her shanty.

"If the men do that, Shad, how come she lets them in?"

"They gives her money."

And Shad told about the colored gentleman over at Pleasantburg whom the mob got. "See, Bert, them men kivered theirselves with long white sheets and kivered their horses and in the middle of the night they catches that thar colored gen'leman and they lynches him." Shad chuckled appreciatively. "Yes sir, Bert, they puts a rope round his ol' neck and string him up on a tree and then they shoots him chock-full of holes."

"What did the colored gentleman do, Shad?" Bert demanded.

"The colored gentleman he done aplenty all right, Bert; he rapes a white lady."

"What's rapes, Shad?"

Shad gave a graphic delineation of this act of violence. Bert accepted all the information according to his own philosophy. He couldn't understand, he didn't try to understand; all these things just were. But this knowledge made Mudtown's people all the more fascinating. If Lem happened to be sober enough to talk, Bert would sit hours on the shanty steps listening, Shad lurking somewhere near, and the three oldest Stoddard children—Harry, Rita, and Ray, aged twelve, eleven, and ten respectively—perched around ready to burst into peals of laughter at any witticism on their father's part. Usually a baby or two or three toddled about the porch. Always from within the shanty came the sounds of fretting or screaming babies, Myrtle's ceaseless harangue, and a stench, which was a mixture of dirty diapers and unwashed flesh and scorched turnips. If the weather were cold Bert would join Lem and family in their kitchen where the turmoil and stench were far worse.

Lem, usually shirtless, his hairy chest and arms displayed, his eyes bloodshot, a black stubble on his chin, his mouth tobacco-juice-smeared, was willing enough to talk to Bert. He found few listeners.

His stock stories concerned the fine family he had come from and the inferior family his wife had come from. Between long spirals of brown juice—which from the porch were directed at and missed any objective, and in the kitchen were directed at and missed the coal pail—Lem would begin:

"Jesus Christ! Was my folks refined. My mam she wouldn't think-a lettin' us young'uns call a pee pot a pee pot. A chamber's what she called it." Here were always peals of laughter from Harry, Rita, and Ray. "And by God! Us young'uns had ter call the pee pot a chamber or git our God damn necks wrang. I recollects oncet when I was a-goin' on ten or, now, maybe I was a-goin' on twelve—now let me think . . ."

Where concerning Myrtle's lineage Lem would begin: "Her!

Why, God damn me soul, if'n her folks didn't use the same can fer a chamber and cook pot." Again peals of laughter from Harry, Rita, and Ray, and Myrtle would interrupt the subject she'd been haranguing upon long enough to snort, "Black liar" or "Bastard."

Often Lem would orate about how the country, not to mention the town, should be run. "Now, Bert, I ain't a-claiming yer pa and yer uncle ain't smart. But fellers like 'em ain't had a chance ter know what's what, like a feller what's had fer ter make his own way. Fer instant, who's President of the United States? Rutherford B. Hayes, a man of the people. But what kin he do? He ain't got a chancet with all them rich bastards a-fightin' over gold and silver and greenbacks, and what with industries. Let me tell yer what I'd do. . . ." Lem's solution was equal distribution of wealth.

The Widder Woman didn't nonplus Bert either. Another day he took Shad to play with Lottie's three children, Ella, Wilbur, and Calvary. Ella, aged eight, and Wilbur, aged six, were filthy, lousy-headed children. But Calvary (whom Lottie, some thought, had named Calvary because the euphony pleased her ears rather than from any bitter symbolism, Lottie being incapable of such) was a silver-headed, blue-eyed baby of three, whose pallid skin miraculously appeared almost clean.

"Know sumpin, Shad?" Bert said. "Cal he's a pretty baby."

Shad nodded. "They says Cal's papa he's a preacher."

"Here?" Bert asked.

Shad shook his head. "Nope. Four or five years back the Widder Woman she git run out'n town."

"Run out of town?"

Shad rolled his round eyes. "See, Bert, they's some figgers whores is downright bad, and they was some church folks tells the Widder Woman if'n she don't git out'n town they was a'gonna tar and feather her, so she had ter git."

Bert nodded. "I see." But he didn't see at all. "They let her come back afterward, though, didn't they, Shad?"

"Nope. She jest come back and brang Cal 'long. And, Bert, he never did cry a-tall. My mama she says Cal he never did cry a-tall."

The Widder Woman's place was the last one on Limestone Avenue before you came to the woods leading to the mountains.

It was a stone's throw beyond the next place, and verily a little meaner-looking than any of the other shanties; perhaps because its once vivid orange paint had become faded and streaked, giving it beyond the meanness and dilapidation a jaded tawdriness. Ella, Wilbur, and Cal ran to meet Bert and Shad. They were glad to see the boys. Even the little Negroes shunned them generally.

"We us playin' so'jers," Cal lisped.

"All right," Bert said.

They began marching up and down before the shanty, along the road ankle-deep with powdered dust during the dry season, sticks over their shoulders for guns, Shad leading because he was the tallest, little silver-headed Cal bringing up the rear. Lottie came out of the shanty. She was no cleaner than Ella and Wilbur, her infested, greasy hair hanging over her shoulders, a dirty stained wrapper around her.

"Hey, yer nigger," she called to Shad, "git going. Who yer guess yer air playing with my young'uns?"

"Listen what that old whore's saying," Shad whispered to Bert. "Telling me not ter be playing with her bastards."

Bert fixed his unflinching eyes upon Lottie. "Know sumpin, Mrs. Lawler? I brought Shad here."

"Who the hell air yer?"

"Bert Sargent."

Lottie sneered. "Bert Sargent, air yer? So yer brang Shad, did yer? Wall, I ain't having my young'uns playing with the likes of yer nohow neither. Yer git going and stay on yer own side the crick now and after yer growed too."

Laughing uproariously at her implication, she grabbed the stick Ella had been playing was a gun and whacked her sharply over the head. Wilbur dodged but Cal received a clip across his tiny shoulders. The three of them ran back of the shanty, Ella and Cal sobbing from pain.

Lottie shrieked after them, "God damn yer! I'll larn yer ter play with niggers."

Shad had ducked behind a tree, legs ready to fly if Lottie came near him. Bert had not moved. Lottie struck him across the face. Still Bert did not move and still his unflinching eyes were fixed upon the Widder Woman.

"Hit me again if you want to," he said. "But know sumpin?

The more you hit me the longer I'll stay. And Shad he's going to stay too."

Suddenly Lottie threw the stick away and began laughing. The God damn little brat ain't skeered, she was thinking.

Bert seldom laughed aloud and seldom even smiled. But hearing Lottie's laughter, one of the occasional smiles crossed his serious little face.

"Please go on back in the house, Mrs. Lawler," Bert said, "and don't mind if Cal and Wilbur and Ella plays with Shad and me."

The Widder Woman went back into the house.

The sun was going behind the mountains on the late August afternoon in 1880 when Bert made his way across the covered bridge from Mudtown. His sturdy legs dragged wearily but he wasn't aware of the fact. This afternoon he and Shad had been hunting rabbits with Red Tatem.

Next to Shad, Bert had a higher opinion of Mr. Tatem than of any other inhabitant of Mudtown, Mr. Stoddard included—Mr. Tatem, who'd fought the Indians and shot buffaloes out West. Mr. Tatem could line bottles along a fence and fifty yards away show how he'd made redskins bite the dust; and every rabbit he potted seemed a buffalo to Bert.

"Come on, m' lads," Red had said, tossing a gunny sack to the boys and whistling to Duke, his liver-spotted hound dog.

He shouldered his musket (the very one he'd used to shoot Indians and buffaloes) and started toward the woods leading to the mountains, Duke at heel and Bert and Shad a safe distance behind, swinging the gunny sack between them.

In the woods Red said, "M' lads, watch me every move and walk likes I walk, the way I larnt ter walk a-scouting Injuns— nary a sound."

Soon Duke trotted ahead, nosing the underbrush, his long ears flapping forward and his long tail flapping sideways, but with nary a sound. Wonderful the way Red moved, too, Bert thought, with nary a sound over stiff stubble and dry branches and twigs. Stealthily Bert's square feet crept, imitating Red.

Duke yelped. A buffalo (Bert had been hoping an Indian would be uncovered) scuttled from the brush. Red raised the musket. Bang! He had him.

"Fat as a bugger," said Red, sticking the rabbit in the sack.

He reloaded and they were off again.

By the time they returned to the Tatem shanty there were eight rabbits in the sack. Red took it from the boys and dumped the rabbits on the ground. Bert looked at them, at their soft brown hair, blood-streaked. One moved.

Bert leaned over and picked it up. He could feel the little heart beating. "Know sumpin, Mr. Tatem? This one's still breathing."

Red was already skinning another. But he reached out a bloody hand. Bert knew he would crush the live rabbit's skull between his fingers, easy as most people could crush an egg. Bert had seen him do it before.

Bert stood back. "Know sumpin, Mr. Tatem? I'm going to keep this here little rabbit. You got seven others and me and Shad we toted the sack."

"All right," Red agreed.

Shad smacked his lips. "It'll taste mighty good in stew, Bert."

"We ain't going to kill it, Shad. Come on."

Reaching the Stanwick shanty, Bert went on, "Shad, I'm going to keep this here little rabbit alive."

Shad wrinkled his nose. "How come, Bert?"

"To see if I can. You fetch me some hot water and the littlest knife your mama's got."

Shad entered the shanty and came back carrying a kettle full of simmering water and a paring knife.

Shad's mother stuck her head out of the door. She was a fat Negress with round rolling eyes like Shad's.

"What you boys doing, taking my kittle and paring knife fer?" she demanded.

"We'll give 'em back," Bert told her. "Know sumpin, Mrs. Stanwick? I'm going to save this little rabbit's life."

"What'd anybody want ter save a rabbit's life fer? Rabbit makes mighty good stew."

Shad nodded vigorously. "That's what I tells Bert, Mama."

Bert didn't hear the conversation. He was examining the rabbit more closely. The shot had only cut through the flesh of the breast. Bert washed the wound and probed as gently as possible with the paring knife.

"There it is, Shad," Bert said finally, rolling the bloody ball between his fingers.

Mrs. Stanwick picked up her kettle and paring knife, rolling her round eyes and shaking her head. Mrs. Stanwick's private opinion was that Bert Sargent might be addlepated.

Bert took the rabbit into the woodshed behind the shanty and fixed a nest of straw between some blocks of wood.

Going home, Bert forgot how tired he felt because he was thinking about the rabbit. He had saved its life. Bert had never seen his uncle Bert, who was a doctor on a boat, but Bert resolved to be a doctor like him when he grew up and he wished now there'd be a wounded rabbit every day to make well. It occurred to Bert that Red's dog, Duke, had sores. Tomorrow he'd find some salve and find out what could be done about Duke.

By this time Bert was passing the school. Rufe was sitting on a pile of boards. Rufe didn't speak to him, mighty likely didn't see him. But Sammy always saw Bert.

Chapter Three

Rufe arrived home and found the family assembled on the big front porch, where they gathered every summer evening before dinner. Papa was reading the *Ledger*, Mama knitted, and Gramma Albright was crocheting. Lillian was doing her embroidery, while Sammy sat on the steps fooling with a slingshot.

"Well, Rufe," Captain George said.

"Evening, Papa."

Rufe couldn't tell exactly what his feelings toward his father were. Of course he loved him. It would have been a sin not to love your father. And he admired him, the money he had and the way people looked up to him. Only once Rufe had seen Tom Leonard and his father going hunting together, laughing and talking like two boys, their guns over their shoulders, the sleek lean pointers, Rex and Queen, following. . . .

"Rufe dear," Pris was saying, "I wish you'd not stay out so late."

"Yes, Mama."

Late! She thought six o'clock late for a boy fifteen years old to be out! Rufe loved his mother. He knew he loved his mother. Sometimes he loved her so much he ached. But the things she would worry about—uneasy now because a boy fifteen years old wasn't home before six! Rufe sank upon a chair. What if she knew the way he felt about Mollie Reynard?

"Rufe, you didn't speak to your grandmother or sister," George corrected.

"Evening, Gramma; evening, Lillian."

They answered something Rufe didn't hear. His eyes shifted to Sammy, wondering if he suspected anything. Sammy ignored him.

Rufe heard Lillian's voice. "Mama, I've only three more roses and a daisy and I'll be through."

Three more roses and a daisy, Rufe thought. That was all a girl had to worry about, at least a girl from a best family. But Mollie—what about a girl from a family like Mollie's?

Sammy couldn't look at Rufe. He knew how bad Rufe must feel, letting a girl get the best of him. And it wasn't Rufe's fault—Mollie was stronger. Sammy liked Rufe more than anybody in the world except Mama, and he didn't care if it was a sin to like a brother more'n your father. Papa was all right, only he was always telling you what to do or what not to do. Rufe never did, and Rufe could draw and make things. Rufe could make bows and arrows and reed whistles and he'd made a little boat whose sail really caught the wind. Last spring they'd taken it down to the crick when the water was high after the thaw. Rufe had a string tied to the boat. But it bobbed and pulled and Sammy suggested Rufe cut the string.

"We'll lose it if we do," Rufe said.

Sammy nodded. "Mighty likely. But we could follow it down the crick a long ways."

Rufe cut the string. All afternoon they followed the little boat, past the shoals beyond the depot on to Elm Bank, where the water was deep enough for the ice cutters in winter to take out chunks of ice thicker than Sammy was tall. And the little boat never turned over once; its sail bulging in a stiff breeze, it bobbed along and along. Near dusk, though, it struck the eddies at the pine ford and smashed against a rock. Then a current pulled the wreck into a pool and they saw what was left of the little boat go under and come up and then go down again forever.

"She's gone," Rufe said.

But Sammy knew Rufe was glad he'd cut the string. Wonder what a real boat looks like? Sammy asked himself. Bert and Prissy had an uncle who was a doctor on a boat. Sammy decided he wouldn't want to be a doctor, but maybe he'd be a sailor some-day—that is, if he could get away from Mama and Papa. Maybe he could run away from home the way Uncle Tim had done.

Nobody remembered that Sammy knew about Uncle Tim. But a long time ago Papa had brought Gramma Albright a letter.

"Here's a letter from Tim," Papa had said.

"From Tim?"

Gramma Albright didn't cry if she got upset the way Gramma Sargent did, but this day she looked like she was going to cry.

Papa nodded. "His name's on the envelope and it's postmarked London, England."

"London, England?"

Reading the letter, Gramma Albright's hands trembled and Sammy had felt sorry for her.

"Sammal," Gramma Albright said now (she always called him Sammal because it had been her family name), "your hair shines just like your grampa's used to."

"What do you suppose his grampa would say if he got a look at his hands?" There went Papa.

"Sammy dear, you should try and keep yourself cleaner!" There went Mama.

"Sammy's grubby." There went Lillian, agreeing with Papa and Mama.

After dinner, Pris was thinking, I'll ask George to take me over home.

Pris always referred to the Sargent place where she had been born and raised as "over home" and to the Albright place where she'd spent her married life as "back home." Whenever she was in the Sargent place she'd think about going back home and when she was in the Albright place she'd think about going over home. And similar as the two places were, back home never meant to Pris what over home meant. Often, entering the Sargent house, she would have the sensation of having returned from a long journey. There was a familiarity about the big oak and walnut pieces, the marble-topped pedestals under the lamps, and the rest, which their counterparts in the Albrights' never possessed. Sometimes she would linger in the icehouse and around the flower garden. Again the cold, musty, sweet smell of the icehouse, where a ton of ice was buried every winter, mingled with the cool, rich, smooth breath of new milk in gallon crocks and the delicate acrid aroma of the butter churns filled Pris's soul full of a dear nostalgia never experienced in the icehouse back home. And the Sargent garden—with the crocuses and lilies of the valley and lilacs and snowballs in the springtime, and in the summertime

the roses and hollyhocks and mignonette and babies'-breath and larkspur and dahlias and sweet William—made Pris's nostrils quiver from a perfume which the same flowers in the Albright garden never seemed to exude.

Because Pris had been worrying a bit about her own children she particularly wanted to go over home this evening. Perhaps she could catch a fleeting sense of the little girl she'd been who had known no worry. Pris knew how foolish she was to worry about her children. Indeed, they were everything children should be: dutiful, healthy, and good-looking. Of course Rufe had been growing too fast, but truly he'd been the most beautiful as well as the best little boy who had ever lived. And after his face grew up to his nose and he filled out he'd make a handsome man. Sammy was still adorable-looking, with his yellow curls and his round blue eyes. And Lillian was perfect. Yet lately a feeling had come over Pris that she didn't really know her children, especially Rufe.

She remembered again the dawn when Dan Field had put the baby Rufe on her shoulder. George had been upset from the time her pains began, and about midnight Dan had given him a powder and George was still sleeping and did not hear Rufe's first wail. Dan had sent the nurse downstairs (to where the grandparents had been waiting on and off all night) to say it was a boy. Then Dan put the soft little mouth against her breast. She looked up and saw him bending over her, his white face whiter than ever and tired and drawn, as if he were the one who'd been suffering. It had seemed that there was nobody else in the whole world but the baby and Dan and herself. And during this moment it had seemed Dan was Rufe's father.

How often she remembered how, during the time Rufe was beginning to talk, he insisted upon calling Dan "Da-da" and George "Ga-ga."

Dan would say to the baby, pointing to himself, "Not Da-da. Uncle Doc." He'd point to George. "There's Da-da."

"No, Ga-ga." Rufe would shake his small head toward George and gurgle at Dan, "Da-da, Da-da, Da-da."

George thought the situation very funny.

" 'It's a wise child,' " he'd laugh.

But George had been terribly upset because she insisted upon naming the baby Rufus instead of George. It wasn't, though, that

Pris particularly wanted to name the baby after her father; it was simply that she couldn't call him George, remembering the moment Dan had put the little mouth against her breast. She had really wanted to name him Dan—Dan Field. When Baby George died, Pris had felt that perhaps God was punishing her. And she never crossed her husband again, openly.

George was in the room the times Dan put Baby George and Sammy and Lillian on her shoulder and she had looked at George instead of at Dan. But she'd always felt Dan there bending over her, nearer, much nearer than George. No husband could ever be as close to a woman as a doctor whose merciful hands had lifted her from the valley of the shadow of death to lay against her breast a soft little mouth.

Not that she didn't love George, Pris would tell herself. She had always loved George, and after Rufe's birth came a new side to their relations. Then what she had accepted passively became an ecstasy. Only—and Pris could never understand this—George's body over her in the darkness wasn't a body. It was a spirit, or an essence, which seemed to release her from a bondage as the sweet kind whiffs of chloroform Dan Field would give her toward the last of childbirth lifted her from a bed of agony onto a cloud of rapture. Ga-ga, Da-da, Rufe, Rufe darling . . .

He slouched in his chair, his long thin legs stretched before him. His eyes were a thousand miles away. Where are his thoughts? Pris asked herself. Rufe had never been like Sammy and Lillian, who kept their thoughts to themselves. Until lately he'd always brought her his joys and little worries. Rufe, my son, what is it? Now when I look at you your eyes don't see me. If I try to talk to you there is nothing you want to tell me. . . .

Perhaps Rufe needed the companionship of boys his own age, of his own kind. She'd been thankful enough when he dropped that Tom and Ben and Jack. It might amuse Rufe if she invited a few young people to the reception for the principal of the new public school—the Taylor girls and Laird Culver.

"Rufe," Pris said, "why don't you go and see Laird Culver?"

Rufe started. Why under the sun would she want him to go and see Laird Culver? Laird was the Presbyterian minister's son and he had white eyelashes and buck teeth and a voice that sounded like a frog with a fishbone caught in its throat, and he was stuck on that big tub Margaret Taylor.

"I don't want to go see Laird, Mama."

"Well, if you don't want to go see Laird why don't you invite him around to see you, dear?"

"I don't want to invite him around to see me, Mama."

All right, Rufe, Pris thought. Her eyes turned toward Sammy. Pris could remember George at his age looking the same. And Sammy was exactly like George. He'd never admit any secrets and yet no one could ever find out what he really thought. Sammy should have been called George. Baby George had been a dark wisp of a baby who would have looked like Tim if he'd lived. How cold it was that winter he died, and how Dan Field fought to save the tiny life! Dan had made George take her from the room and it was Dan Field's arms which held the tiny racked body choking to death. She had gone with George but she'd wanted to stay beside Dan while he held her dying baby.

Lillian heaved a great sigh. Oh dear, Pris thought, she sounds and looks as if all the troubles of the world were upon her shoulders.

"Darling, whatever is the matter?" Pris asked, knowing Lillian wouldn't tell.

"Nothing, Mama."

The truth was that Lillian sighed because she'd told the family Sammy was grubby. The idea of saying such a mean thing about Sammy! I'm always saying and doing things I don't mean to please Papa and Mama, and that Prissy, Lillian fumed inwardly. But I'm glad I stayed out and talked to Alexander, Lillian decided, no matter how mad Prissy is. The idea of her saying Sammy's grubby. . . .

Bert Sargent found his family assembled on their front porch: Papa reading the *Ledger*, Mama knitting, Gramma Sargent crocheting, and Prissy embroidering.

If I'd a knife as little as Prissy's needle I could of done it better, not hurt the rabbit at all maybe, Bert was thinking.

"Good evening, Bert," Papa said.

"Evening, Papa. Evening, Mama. Evening, Gramma. Evening, Prissy." Bert was thorough or nothing.

Suddenly Mama screamed. "Bert, you're covered with blood. Rufus, look, Bert's covered with blood."

Rufus sprang to his feet. "What? What?"

Prissy moaned.

Gramma Sargent groaned.

Bert looked down. "Rabbit blood. Nothing but rabbit blood. I ain't hurt."

Lou sighed with relief. "However would you get rabbit blood on you, dear?"

"Off a rabbit what's got blood on it." Bert knew how to change the subject. "Mama, I'm so tired. Please come upstairs and help me change."

"Of course, dear."

Rufus sank back upon his chair and forgot his son's bloody shirt. He gave his children little thought. After Prissy came, Rufus had wanted to mind the baby a bit, cuddle her, spoil her mildly. But he hadn't a chance. Lou monopolized the management of the child as she monopolized the management of the household. If Rufus began by protesting he soon saw that an argument with Lou was never finished until she won—or thought she won. By the time Bert arrived Rufus had become so used to ignoring Prissy that he was hardly aware of the boy.

At thirty-five Rufus Sargent was a distinguished-looking man. He had gained weight and the added fullness of his face made his nose appear a normal size. He wore a mustache which widened his small mouth and even the thick-lensed glasses didn't detract from the brilliant black eyes under their sweeping lashes.

Well, whatever the condition in his home, Rufus continued thinking, he ran the bank and the town. If he fed George's vanity, George ate out of his hands. George certainly was set up over the *Ledger* squib, never suspecting that he, Rufus, inserted the column to put George in such an amiable mood that he'd agree to incorporating an arc-light company. George believed the position he held in the town was his because he was George Albright. But George the First and Rufus the First had found dissenters among the townspeople, and Ralph Pettigrew might have been elected mayor of Willowspring if Rufus hadn't managed George's campaign shrewdly. Now perhaps the town didn't need arc lights but again an arc-light company might mean a new fortune. That fellow Edison at Menlo Park was trying to make an electric lamp suitable for use in homes and offices. Of course such an idea might be merely a flash in a pan. On the other hand, electric-lighted houses weren't improbable, and if the idea did prove practical the arc-lighting company could be easily converted. The only way to make money was to take gambles, Rufus speculated. Certainly Pa and Uncle George took chances and hadn't always won. During the panic of '57 they'd made another gold strike by buying and holding supposedly worthless railroad bonds. But on the other hand, a corner of the bank safe still held Confederate bonds that had been bought—just in case . . .

However, despite shortsightedness, George was all right, Rufus decided. He had really worked like a dog making the legislature appropriate a sum sufficient to build a modern school large enough to take care of all the Willowspring children. And Pris thought George about perfect. Rufus held the greatest affection for his sister, and he was sincerely glad she was happily married. Too, George seemed contented. Rufus wondered whatever had happened to Vi Larsen. George had certainly gone wild over her. He would have married her if his father hadn't gone to Philadelphia and raised hell, telling the Larsen family he'd disinherit George. Pris had never known a thing about the affair.

Rufus began wondering, and not for the first time, if perhaps a man weren't more content married to a woman he wasn't mad about. The hell he'd been through and still went through. And what a fool he was, knowing—and knowing the way he did— nothing could make Lou respond.

Rufus's eyes rested upon his daughter. For the first time in years a tenderness toward her flooded him. Poor little devil, he thought, she means no more to her mother than I do. It's all Bert, Bert, Bert with Lou. He wished he could call Prissy to him, take her on his lap, cuddle her a bit. But they'd grown so far, far apart.

"Prissy."

"Yes, Papa."

He saw the brilliant black eyes under their sweeping lashes, so like his own, the dimpled rosy cheeks and the thick brown plait, hanging over a shoulder now. Why, she's beautiful. . . . He wanted to tell her she was beautiful, tell her she was beautiful and she was his little girl and he loved her.

Instead he said, "Did you have a nice time today, Prissy?"

"Yes, thank you, Papa."

Prissy had been thinking, Bert didn't tell Mama how he got the blood on him and he won't. But she was hoping fervently no one had seen Bert coming along the street all over blood. It would be terrible if anyone had seen him, after telling Lillian Bert wasn't grubby.

Lou and Bert came back on the porch. Bert wore a clean suit and his face was soap-shiny.

Maggie, the hired girl, a gaunt, rawboned woman, wearing a starched calico dress and apron, stuck her head through the door and said, "Supper's ready."

Prissy knew that across the lawn at the Albrights' Nellie, who was Maggie's sister and looked and dressed like Maggie, was saying the same thing. The next minute both families would be settling around like tables to eat the same bounty—tonight a huge roast, mashed potatoes, gravy, peas, lima beans, corn on the cob, hot biscuits, butter, cream, strawberry preserves, and custard pies and doughnuts.

The grandmothers, if unable to ignore the fare, were wont to wince inwardly as Maggie and Nellie announced, "Supper's ready." When they had charge, they often remarked, it was: "Dinner is served." Nor could the grandmothers accustom themselves to having only one hired girl in a house. Before Lou and Pris took over, there were never less than three or four girls in each house.

"But you didn't have Maggie and Nellie," Lou and Pris would tell them, to no avail.

Where in those days the young people took their lot for granted, in after years they all loved to dwell upon the bounty of the households when they were young. They told of the great roasts, dripping with their own abundance, sent away from the table only half finished but never to be seen again, no one caring what happened to the leftovers. Their tongues would linger upon stories of quart pitchers full of yellow cream, huge slabs of golden butter, how both families kept two cows, and the hogs got the milk. Their lips would roll over tales of giant tureens brimming with fresh vegetables in summer and put-ups in winter. They'd tell about peas big as marbles, beans thin as needles, limas rich as butter, corn sweet as sugar, and juicy, red, round beefsteak tomatoes. And then about the piles of potatoes and onions stored all year round in the icehouses, and the jellies and preserves, pies and cakes, and on Sundays the gallon freezers full of ice cream.

And Maggie and Nellie—such girls couldn't be found in days to come. Why, they did all the work—the cleaning, cooking, baking, churning, preserving, for a dollar and a half a week. Of course on Mondays and Tuesdays Mrs. Race came to the Sargents' and Mrs. Schiller to the Albrights' to do the washing and ironing. And they came a week every fall and a week every spring to help with the house cleaning.

In 1880 Maggie and Nellie had lived with the Albrights and Sargents ten years. They were well past thirty but neither had married. Maggie and Nellie were Catholics and on Sundays their parents, Mr. and Mrs. Beamer, brought the little boy Gregory Beamer in to mass from the farm at Four Mile Run. But Maggie and Nellie never visited the farm. And although Gregory was supposedly their brother, it was Maggie he went to see every month when he came to confession. And it was Maggie who bought his clothes, as well as her own, out of her dollar and a half a week. Sometimes Maggie would be sitting beside the kitchen lamp until midnight, making shirts and pants or mending the little boy's things. And now Maggie wanted to keep Gregory all night Saturdays. Prissy had heard Mama telling Papa.

"It seems," Mama had said, "Father Callahan is taking an interest in that boy, Gregory Beamer. He wants to give him Latin lessons Saturday afternoons and Maggie asked if she might keep the boy here Saturday nights. What do you think, Rufus?"

"Whatever you think, my dear," Papa had answered, the way he always did.

"He's to walk in from the farm Saturday afternoons and his grandparents" (Prissy wondered why Mama called Mrs. and Mr. Beamer Gregory's grandparents; they were his mother and father) "will take him back Sunday mornings after mass. Of course Maggie knows he mustn't have a thing to do with Bert or Prissy."

"Of course, my dear."

"For this food we are about to receive make us grateful, O Lord," Prissy heard Papa saying.

She knew Uncle George was saying the same thing.

Chapter Four

THE CATHOLIC CHURCH was across from the new public school; the Methodist Church on Maple was across from the Albrights'; the Reformed Church was on Horsechestnut; the Presbyterian on Linden; and the Lutheran on the northeast corner of Linden and Oak streets directly opposite the post office and diagonally opposite the courthouse. The jail and fire house were just behind the courthouse. Every day and every night, year in and year out, the town clock on top of the courthouse struck the hours and half hours, until people became so used to these booming sounds that they were no more apt to hear them than they were the early morning crowing of cocks or the chirping of birds. But the church bells were a different thing.

Come nine o'clock Sunday mornings they began sending forth such a pealing that none save the very deaf could miss the clangor. Nine o'clock was the first Sunday-school bell, nine-thirty the second Sunday-school bell, ten o'clock was the first church bell, ten-thirty the second church bell.

Shortly after nine o'clock every Willowspring street would fairly swarm with boys and girls, teachers and parents, all dressed in their best, and on the way to Sunday school. Shortly after ten o'clock the streets would again be swarming with some of these boys and girls going home, and more men and women, all dressed up and on their way to church.

The Albright and Sargent children didn't attend Sunday school, yet every Sunday, health permitting, all members of the Albright and Sargent family went to church.

Lillian and Prissy loved church. They loved swishing up the aisle dressed in their best, beside their mamas and papas and

47

grammas and brothers, also wearing finery. Even Sammy and
Bert looked spick in their Sunday suits, faces soap-shiny and
heads sopping wet and smooth. All the townspeople and Alexander, beside his mother in their pew, looked at the Albrights and
the Sargents. Prissy would give Lillian a sidelong glance, as much
as to say, "Aren't you glad you're who you are?"

Once the Albrights and the Sargents were settled—the Albrights in the Albright pew and the Sargents in the Sargent pew
—the Rev. Mr. Lanning, a tall, gray-faced man, came into the
pulpit. Mr. Lanning always entered the pulpit directly after the
Albrights and the Sargents were settled no matter if they were
a bit early, no matter were they a bit late.

Then the music began: "Jesus, Lover of My Soul," "Rock of
Ages," "Just as I Am without One Plea," or "Nearer, My God,
to Thee." Miss Fisher played the organ, her feet pumping very
fast, and the choir sang the first hymn. The choir members were
town girls whom Miss Fisher had trained, and Mollie Reynard
was one of them.

The music filled Prissy's soul full of a tremendous longing. She
wished she might do something to make the world a better place,
the way Mr. Lanning said everybody should strive to do. Prissy
wished she could save all the unsaved souls in the world. She
wasn't sure she'd ever seen an unsaved soul because 'most the
whole town went to church (excepting Uncle Doc, who was
excused to look after the sick). Mr. Lanning said townspeople,
and perhaps Catholics, who went to church would be saved the
same as best families. But Prissy had heard Mr. Lanning describe
lost souls so often she knew exactly how they looked: tottering,
red-eyed, garments rent, screaming to God for mercy after it was
too late. Prissy could see herself, an angel of mercy, wearing
flowing robes of white and wings and maybe a crown, floating
over the heads of the lost, telling them that she, Prissy, would
save them yet. And Alexander would be looking at her, worship-
ing, and Lillian would be perfectly furious.

The music made Lillian feel the way the smell of roses made
her feel, or the stars shining, or a little baby . . . warm, tender,
giving. She saw herself at the organ, her fingers running up and
down the keys, the notes of music falling like raindrops or perfume or the petals of roses onto everybody in the world, including Prissy, but most of all upon Alexander.

When the sermon began Lillian and Prissy sat erect in the stiff pews, even though they didn't hear all Mr. Lanning said. By and by, however, they'd gradually settle down and almost sleep, although their eyes never quite closed. The way Sammy did must certainly be a sin, they felt.

Sammy, brazenly and unashamed, dozed off the minute the sermon began and slept through its length despite the fact that his father ever so often leaned over his mother to give him a shake.

Bert's mind was occupied by various subjects during Mr. Lanning's exhortations—Shad, Red, Lem, Lottie, Duke. He operated upon rabbits, fixed Duke's sores, trailed Indians and buffalo, joined Uncle Bert on his boat, burned Mr. Lanning at the stake, or cold-bloodedly cut open the front of the reverend gentleman and removed his heart, lungs, stomach, bowels, and such other organs as he was aware of at the time.

Rufe accepted the service casually. He had been attending church so long—twelve years, since the age of three. There was nothing Mr. Lanning could possibly say that he had not heard before. Now he couldn't keep his mind upon anything anyhow except Mollie up there in the choir.

Rufe during the years had seen many ministers come and many of them go. Only one who had gone had died—Alexander's father. Others who had disagreed with Papa or Uncle Rufus were dismissed. Rufe remembered the last one—Mr. Yates. Mr. Yates had claimed the part in the Bible about fire and brimstone wasn't to be taken literally. It was symbolism (whatever that might be). And he went on to explain that a merciful God would not torment His children with actual fire no matter how wicked they'd been.

Papa and Uncle Rufus got rid of Mr. Yates in a hurry. "Heresy," they called what he'd said. Rufe heard afterward Mr. Yates couldn't get another church because of his views. Mr. Yates had been an old man and Rufe had pitied him, not only about not getting another church but because what he had said wasn't true. Rufe thought it would be terrible to believe such a —well, such a beautiful thing when it wasn't true. Rufe himself wished he could believe that a merciful God would not torment His children with actual fire no matter how wicked they'd been.

"A fine sermon. No nonsense about Mr. Lanning," Captain George said to Rufus one morning around the middle of September.

Rufus nodded. "None of this modern rubbish in his sermons. Splendid text: 'God will surely gather the ungodly and the unbelievers together in hell!' "

"Give me the good old-fashioned gospel translated literally every time," George went on. "Boys"—this to Sammy and Bert—"walk like gentlemen. No pushing. See how nicely Lillian and Prissy are walking. Here, Ma, let me help you."

"Help me? What for?" Gramma Albright chirped. "I don't need your help. I could walk long before you could and I may be walking long after you're bedridden."

Captain George and Rufus laughed indulgently. Gramma Sargent was already holding Rufus's arm, as they followed Rufe. A little ahead were Pris and Lou and the little girls, who were trying to step exactly as their mothers stepped.

Before the corner was reached Rufe and Bert had disappeared, and at the corner Sammy turned north toward Broad Street.

Walking along Broad Street, Sammy thought how funny the town looked on a Sunday, the stores closed, their steps and pavements swept clean, and hardly any people about. It looked uncomfortable on a Sunday, the town, rather like Sammy felt in his Sunday clothes. Wonder if a boat looks different on a Sunday? Sammy mused.

But no matter how uncomfortable he felt in his Sunday suit he must wear it all day, and if he got it dirty he got scolded, because on Sunday you weren't supposed to do anything to get a suit dirty—not play or run or anything.

Still, things might be worse than they were. If he was a girl, like Lillian and Prissy, he'd have to go straight home after church and stay all day. Papa wouldn't even take them out driving; he believed horses, like people, should have a day of rest. Only sometimes if Uncle Doc drove out in the country he'd take Lillian and Prissy along.

But a boy could get off by himself, Sunday or no Sunday, and do what he wanted, so long as he kept his suit clean and got home by dinnertime. (On Sundays the Albrights and the Sargents had the big meal at two o'clock.) Bert, now, was on the way to

Mudtown and Rufe was probably walking up and down Linden Street past where Mollie Reynard lived. Lately Sammy had seen Rufe walking down Linden on one side and up on the other. Though what was the sense Sammy couldn't make out. Rufe never looked toward the Reynard house and if Mollie was in the yard he'd never act like he saw her. They didn't speak when they met on the street either. It was all beyond Sammy.

Sammy, at this point, stopped to survey the wonders displayed in the window of Carl's Novelty Shop. This was Sammy's favorite window. Of course he must disregard trifles like dolls and baby toys and watches and jewelry, but he found a wealth of wonders besides—guns and knives and drums and bugles and fishhooks and balls and what not. The prices were plainly displayed and after figuring some twenty minutes he decided all he needed to make life perfect was four dollars and three cents, and sauntered along.

Mr. Smith sat on one of the chairs before the livery stable. He looked funny, too, Sammy thought, wearing his Sunday suit without a collar. And the livery stable sounded funny—or rather, seemed funny—without the sounds of the hammers and anvils ringing behind in the blacksmith shop.

"Hullo, Sammy," Mr. Smith said.

"Hullo, Mr. Smith," Sammy said.

"Been to church?" Mr. Smith inquired, he being a Methodist like unto Sammy.

"Yes sir."

"Good sermon?"

"Fine sermon."

"What was the text?"

Sammy wrinkled his brows. "I can't seem to remember the text, Mr. Smith. But it was a fine sermon. Ain't none of this modern rubbish 'bout Mr. Lanning."

"You're right thar, Sammy."

"Yes sir." Sammy nodded. "And give me the good old-fashioned gospel translated lit—let—lit—well, anyhow, it was a fine sermon."

"Glad to hear it. Couldn't go myself this morning." Mr. Smith got to his feet and remarked with forethought, "Likely I better be having a look at my pups."

"Pups," Sammy echoed. "You ain't got pups, honest, have you, Mr. Smith?"

"Bet your life," Mr. Smith said. "Six of the cutest little houn's you ever set eyes on."

"Mr. Smith"—Sammy's voice had acquired an almost reverent tone—"do you suppose I could look at 'em?"

"Sure." Mr. Smith thought he might get rid of the bitch.

Mr. Smith went on into the barn. He was so fat and round he appeared to roll instead of walk but now, following him, Sammy wondered how he could have ever thought Mr. Smith funny-looking. Mr. Smith was a mighty kind-looking man.

They passed the stalls, where the five horses comprising the stable stock stood, and moved along through the harness room, which was also the office, to a box stall. Mr. Smith swung the door open, entered, and Sammy stepped behind him. Rolling in the straw were a mother hound and six black and white puppies.

Recalling the scene later, Sammy always grinned gleefully. Why, the very first thing, out of all those pups, Spotty ran to meet him, wagging a little tail. And when Sammy held out a hand Spotty licked it, just like she knew him, not scared a bit.

"Glory Ned!" Sammy exclaimed, a lump in his throat. "Ain't he a beauty?"

"Spotty's a bitch," Mr. Smith informed. "I'd leave her go cheap."

"Leave her go . . . Glory Ned! Mr. Smith, you ain't selling the pups, are you?"

Mr. Smith nodded his round fat head. "I gotta get rid of 'em. They's over four months old now. I was astin' five for the dogs and three for the bitch but I come down to three for the dogs and I'd leave you have Spotty for two dollars, Sammy."

Two dollars. Sammy's heart sank. He had no more chance of getting two dollars to buy Spotty than he had of getting the four dollars and three cents to buy what he wanted in Carl's window. But he'd sooner have Spotty than anything.

Sammy shook his round yellow head. "I never could get that much money, Mr. Smith. Two dollars is a mighty lot of money, Mr. Smith."

"Not for a dog like Spotty."

"I know that, Mr. Smith. A dog like Spotty mighty likely's worth a lot more'n two dollars. A dog like Spotty mighty likely's worth a hundred dollars. 'Cept I ain't got two dollars, Mr. Smith."

"Your papa's rich, Sammy," Mr. Smith informed.

Sammy shook his head sorrowfully. "The most he ever did give me was a quarter, and that only special times."

"Too bad, Sammy, too bad," Mr. Smith sympathized. "I'd like to see you own Spotty. You could see yourself how she took to you aplenty."

"I could see all right, Mr. Smith." Sammy rubbed Spotty's soft little ears between his fingers. "Spotty she run to me like she knows me, like she's my dog, licked my hand and everything. Mr. Smith, ain't there some way I could get Spotty 'out paying money? Ain't there any favor I could do, like currying the horses, or cleaning stalls, or something?"

"Mighty likely, Sammy," Mr. Smith speculated. "My nigger, Harry, he went off for a couple months. That lazy Ben he won't do a thing to help his papa out. Boys ain't what they was in my day. I tell you what, Sammy, if'n you'll come here around four-thirty mornings and scrape stalls—you can get home 'fore seven —after Harry gets back I'll give you Spotty."

Sammy could hardly believe his ears. "You mean—do you honest mean, Mr. Smith, if I'd do a little thing like scraping stalls you'd give me Spotty?"

Mr. Smith nodded. "Sure, Sammy. Sure."

"Glory Ned! Mr. Smith . . ."

A lump filled Sammy's throat. He threw himself flat on the straw, his face rubbing against Spotty's little cold nose. Spotty wiggled and wagged and bounced and barked joyously. Spotty, his dog, his dog. His Spotty. Something must have got in his eyes, Sammy thought, wiping away the tears with a sleeve.

Mr. Smith's corpulent body was fairly bursting from suppressed laughter. Of course Sammy wouldn't keep the job. He'd not come more than a morning or two. But what a story to tell —Ralph Pettigrew would split his sides—one of George Albright's boys shoveling hoss shit. Such a story would be better than a sale.

Even as Captain George, most of Willowspring's people believed horses, like people, needed a day of rest, and on Sundays hardly a rig was to be seen on the streets except around the Catholic Church. But Catholics drove dozens of miles to mass and

from six o'clock in the morning until past noon all along Maple
and Linden streets buggies and wagons stretched before hitching posts, with oxcarts to boot.

Maggie and Nellie attended six o'clock mass because the Sargents and Albrights had their big meal at two o'clock on Sundays, and Mr. and Mrs. Beamer (whom Gregory called "Papa"
and "Mama") also attended early mass. But times the Beamers and
Gregory would stay on for late mass. They had stayed this certain Sunday around the middle of September, and, coming out
of the church door after service, Gregory had seen Bert Sargent
trudging toward the bridge.

Gregory Beamer was eleven years old in 1880. Two years later
a visionary artist was to have him pose for what was to be the
beginning of a long succession, by many artists, of paintings portraying a revolutionary-looking Christ child. Gregory's soft hair,
almost colorless above the high forehead, fell back to rise in a
golden crest. His brows, a bit darker than his hair, were slightly
arched, and his fawn-colored eyes were actually luminous under
lashes that, like his hair, were seemingly colorless at the base but
curled into a chestnut fuzz. His nose was straight, his lips curved,
and his chin piquant. His face and neck were sun-browned, as
were his forearms and hands, but where the tan ended the skin
was milk-white and his shoulders sloped as smoothly as a lovely
girl's.

However, there was nothing feminine-looking about Gregory
Beamer. His chest was deep and his arms and legs were strong.
Nor was he considered beautiful by his family and their friends
(excepting perhaps by Maggie, who never expressed herself upon
the subject). His appearance was too great a departure from the
accepted standards of what a farm boy should look like to be
admired.

Gregory climbed into the buggy between the Beamers, and
Mr. Beamer turned the horse's head toward Four Mile Run. But
Gregory continued thinking of Bert, and of Prissy too. When
Maggie said she could keep him Saturday nights Gregory's first
thought had been how he'd be able to play with Bert and Prissy.
Maggie had talked about them many times and of course he'd
often seen Bert and Prissy. Now he would know them.

The first night after supper he'd asked Maggie if he mightn't go into the rest of the house, or ask Bert and Prissy out in the kitchen to play.

Maggie fairly snapped at him. "No, you mightn't ever go into the rest of the house. And you can't ever ask them out in the kitchen. And you mustn't ever play with them. Do you understand?"

He shook his head. "No, I don't understand. Why mustn't I ever play with them?"

Maggie hadn't answered. She'd taken his face between her hands and looked and looked, until he squirmed away.

Going home this Sunday, Gregory still didn't understand. But there were plenty of things Gregory Beamer had not been able to understand during his short life. He had never been able to understand why his mama and papa seemed so much older than the parents of other children his age; nor why they never spoke to each other and seldom to him; nor why Maggie made his clothes and was nicer to him than Nellie. And lately Gregory couldn't understand why Father Callahan made him walk to town every Saturday afternoon to take Latin lessons.

Sammy hadn't come home for dinner and Mama was worried and Papa was mad and Lillian was glad enough to get out of the house and see Prissy coming across the lawn. They sat down under the trees and Lillian wondered where Sammy could be and Prissy wondered why Mama never scolded Bert if he wasn't home for meals, while if she was a minute late it was a sin.

Pretty soon the little girls saw Uncle Doc's buggy coming up the street drawn by Nervy. They both loved Nervy (short for Minerva, the Goddess of Wisdom, Uncle Doc said) and enjoyed nothing better than a trip behind her shafts. Nervy was the smartest horse in the world. She never had to be tied and Uncle Doc didn't have to tell her to go—the minute she should, Nervy would start on her own.

"There's Uncle Doc," Lillian said.

"I see him," Prissy answered.

They sprang up, ran across the lawn, and stood on the front walk waiting hopefully. And Uncle Doc didn't have to tell Nervy to stop; she drew up along the curb herself.

Dan Field saw the two eager little faces. "I don't suppose any amount of coaxing could persuade you young ladies to take a ride."

"Please, could we, Uncle Doc?" Lillian gurgled.

"Could we, please, Uncle Doc?" Prissy gurgled.

"Run tell your mothers."

They scampered off. When Lillian reached the porch Pris and Gramma Albright were coming down the steps. Dan Field knew where they were bound. Every Sunday afternoon, following the hearty two o'clock meal, George slept an hour or so, and Pris and Gramma Albright took themselves over to visit Gramma Sargent and Lou.

Dan Field crossed the yard to meet Pris and Gramma Albright. "Mrs. Albright, you're radiant today." He smiled. "And you, my dear Pris, look like a hag."

Both women laughed. Dan Field chuckled to himself, imagining what they might do if they knew what his eyes upon Pris really saw—naked lovely golden breasts, round slim golden loins. Darling, darling, he thought.

Lillian and Prissy skipped back, wearing absurd little bonnets, or so Dan Field regarded them.

"Uncle Doc, please may I drive first?" they both chirped.

Pris and Gramma Albright started across the lawns.

"I never could understand why Dan never married," Gramma Albright said.

"Some men don't," Pris answered.

She had often contemplated the possibility of Dan's marrying. She always told herself she wanted him to marry: he would make such a wonderful husband and father. Still, she knew if Dan did marry she would feel that she had lost something very precious. What she couldn't imagine. If Dan married it wouldn't interfere with his being her doctor and George's and her friend.

She glanced along the road to where Dan's buggy had become a speck. I wish, Pris thought, I could be Lillian's age once again and Dan would take me driving out in the country.

Entering the coolness of the Sargent house from the summer outdoors, Pris drew a deep breath. Home. Lou and Gramma Sargent were waiting in the sitting room. Pris kissed her mother. She wished she were small enough to crawl into her lap. . . . Why, Pris wondered, must I worry over the children? Now, Sammy not coming home to dinner . . . She often felt she'd like to discuss her worries with Ma (or Ma Albright) but their ideas and opinions were so old-fashioned.

"Good afternoon, Mrs. Albright," Gramma Sargent said.

"Good afternoon, Mrs. Sargent," Gramma Albright said.

Those two, during forty some years, had lived side by side, their lives and destinies as intertwined as the roots of the sugar maples under the sod. There had been days they had loved each other, minutes they had hated each other. They had clung together in happiness and in sorrow, in sickness and in health. They had loved each other's children in the way they loved their own, and if Gramma Sargent were grandmother to them all, Rufus's two also considered Gramma Albright their own. Yet the grandmothers always had and always would address each other as Mrs. Albright and Mrs. Sargent, and they always referred to their husbands as Mr. Albright and Mr. Sargent.

Gramma Albright and Pris seated themselves.

"Hot, isn't it?" Lou said. "Doesn't seem possible it's the middle of September."

Gramma Albright nodded. "That's right, it is the middle of September. I'd like to go to Philadelphia earlier this fall. About the middle of October."

"It would be a good idea," Gramma Sargent agreed.

Ever since the grandmothers had been brought as brides to Willowspring they had returned to Philadelphia twice a year, a week in the fall and a week in the spring. At first, of course, their husbands had accompanied them, and now George, Pris, Rufus, and Lou went along. At first there had been many relatives and friends to visit, but one by one these had died or become lost and now they all stayed at a hotel, "doing the town," Captain George put it, and shopping. Not one member of the Albright or Sargent family had ever worn a stitch bought or made in Willowspring, so the shopping took considerable time.

And almost to the days of their deaths the grandmothers walked as pridefully as when brides and took the same interest in wearing "the right clothes." They were inclined to be disdainful of any new family which came to Willowspring and was accepted. But there were a number of their old friends left in 1880—Mr. and Mrs. Harley (whose father had entertained President Washington), Mr. and Mrs. Kimbell (who had inherited the iron and ore lands over half the county), Mrs. Dr. Berkley (the death of whose husband had been the reason George had urged Dan Field to come to Willowspring), and so on. All of this "older crowd" enjoyed a hand of whist and the younger folks joked, saying the grandmothers attended far more parties than they.

Now Gramma Sargent said, "Seems to me Prissy and Lillian are pretty near big enough to take along to Philadelphia. You couldn't have been more than twelve when we first started taking you, Pris."

"She was fourteen, Mrs. Sargent."

"Was she really, Mrs. Albright?"

Dan Field sat between the two little girls, letting them take turns flapping the reins over Nervy's dapple shanks, although Nervy turned her head every so often to make certain he was still there.

Lillian giggled. "She'd not go a step if she didn't know you were here. Would she, Uncle Doc?"

Prissy giggled. "Of course Nervy'd not go a step if Uncle Doc wasn't here. Would you, Nervy? Wouldn't you think, smart as Nervy is, that she could talk, Uncle Doc?"

"Maybe that's the reason she doesn't talk, because she is smart."

"What do you mean?" Lillian asked.

Prissy cocked her head. "You're teasing, Uncle Doc."

"I am not teasing. If you know how to talk you have to talk and there are some people it's much better not to have to talk to."

Both the little girls thought this remark excruciatingly funny and burst into peals of laughter.

Dan Field loved having them with him. They chatted all the time but he could answer them mechanically and have his own thoughts. Strange he never grew weary of his own thoughts when they were always with him and they were about all he could call his own, except Nervy and the house and Ackley. How different his life was from the one his youth had anticipated—research and travel, money and fame, a wife and children. Then George had got him here and he had seen Pris. She was pregnant with Rufe, although he'd not suspected the fact until she'd come to him that day . . . that day . . . when his hands first touched the golden flesh and his eyes first saw . . . She had come to him because he was the doctor, of course, but she had come to him, and she didn't tell George about her condition, but let him find out himself.

Yet Dan Field's hands had never touched her in any other than a professional way. Not that he held scruples; in his thoughts and dreams he was forever possessing her. Though he felt certain he could make her love him, that sort of romance would bring only unhappiness to Pris. Still, ever his heart held a hope, if a faint hope, and a damn fool hope, Dan Field told himself over and again. The only solution possible would be George's death, and he certainly didn't want George to die. George's death would be an irreparable loss to the town, not to mention the family, and Dan Field himself was genuinely fond of George. Besides, Pris was happy enough with him (she'd never heard a word concerning the Vi Larsen episode) and Pris adored her children.

Prissy was driving and Lillian sat on Dan Field's left, patiently awaiting her turn. He looked down and her eyes, shadow-filled like her mother's, met his.

"Uncle Doc," she chirped, "I can understand how you could bring one baby in your little black bag. But, Uncle Doc, you brought Mrs. Beemiller two babies at the same time and I can't see how you could bring two babies in such a little bag."

Dan Field smiled. "When I took you out of that little black bag you were all folded up like a rosebud and hardly a whit bigger than one, either."

But he thought tenderly that she had looked more like a little purple monkey than anything he'd seen before or since.

Prissy flapped the reins. "Lillian, you know Mama and Auntie Pris said we weren't to talk about how Uncle Doc brought us in the little black bag."

Lillian shrugged. There went Prissy again.

Aloud she asked, "Uncle Doc, isn't it my turn to drive now?"

"I think it must be."

Prissy released the reins reluctantly. Dan Field noticed the intensity of the little face. God, how she's going to suffer! he thought with a twinge. This child was also dear to him as were so many of Willowspring's people.

It wasn't only Pris who had held him. There was something about the valleys and hills which had seeped into him like a drug. Here today was the country road winding through the fields, with their goldenrod and haystacks and buckwheat stubble and corn shocks, and the farms and the barns and the cattle grazing, and the mountains forever. And the smell of it all—you forgot the smell when you were here all the time, except at intervals—clean air and rich sod and damp moss and sweet fern, with always something else floating through—dust now in September. Dan Field smiled. Dust, even the dust, seemed sweet in his nostrils. *And the Lord God formed man of the dust of the ground.* . . .

"Where are we going, Uncle Doc?" Prissy asked.

"Don't you know?"

Both little girls piped, "To Mrs. Miller's."

"That's right."

He couldn't help Mrs. Miller's rheumatism much. But the old soul lived alone and every so often Dan Field paid a friendly visit and left a new paper of pills. Mrs. Miller always inquired how much she owed him and Dan Field always said he'd let her know later. Perhaps his practice continued outstripping Brown Walsh's because he never pressed a bill and often didn't send one. But sometimes Dan Field felt he received far more than his services were worth.

Today, reaching Mrs. Miller's place, Nervy would stick her nose into the mountain brook flowing across the road and thereafter nibble sweet clover along the fence. Mrs. Miller would be glad to see him and glad he'd brought Lillian and Prissy along —the two little princesses, she called them—and they'd all sit on the front porch and chat, and pretty soon Mrs. Miller would hobble on her rheumatic legs to the kitchen and come hobbling back again, bringing cool milk and gingerbread or cookies.

"Sammy, where have you been?"

"Why—why—why, Papa?"

"It's almost six o'clock. Why weren't you home for dinner?"

"I must have forgot dinner, Papa."

Pris came upon the scene. "Sammy, look at your best suit, all over hay. And the smell. You haven't been playing in a stable on Sunday, have you?"

"No, Mama, I wasn't playing in a stable. I wasn't playing at all."

"Well, you get along upstairs, young man," George instructed, "and take off those clothes and go to bed. And perhaps next Sunday you'll remember your dinner."

Climbing the stairs, Sammy sniffed. They *would* spoil it, the very best time he'd ever had in all his life. Playing, huh; Sammy sniffed again. Anybody what had any sense'd know training a dog wasn't playing. And he wouldn't tell them a word about Spotty until she was his and then they couldn't not let him keep her. But he'd have to get overalls or something or the stable smell on his clothes would give him away; Papa and Mama would never let him work in a livery stable.

He went into his room. Sammy's room opened off the back porch. He went through the room now, onto the porch, for no particular reason. But he saw Bert coming along the street from Mudtown and it occurred to Sammy that Shad wore overalls and maybe Bert could borrow a pair.

He slid down the porch post and dropped on the grass. "Bert," he called softly.

Bert turned and Sammy motioned him to make no noise, by putting one hand over his mouth and pointing toward the house with the other one.

Bert came close and Sammy whispered, "Could you get me the loan of a pair of Shad's overalls?"

"Yes," Bert said.

"I got to have 'em 'fore five o'clock tomorrow morning."

"I'll get 'em," Bert promised.

Sammy knew Bert would bring the overalls if he said he would. He climbed up the post and, back in the bedroom, started undressing. Suddenly his stomach began turning around. He wished he hadn't forgotten his dinner. Then the door opened softly and Pris entered, carrying a tray. There was chicken and bread and butter and milk and ice cream. Sammy smiled gratefully.

Pris put the tray on a table. "Here, dear, give me that filthy suit. And go wash before you eat."

She took the suit onto the porch and gave it a thorough brushing. When she returned to the room Sammy had about finished his supper. She saw his face and hands.

"Sammy, did you wash before you started to eat?"

"Oh, Mama, I forgot."

"Oh, Sammy! Won't you tell Mama why you didn't come home to dinner?"

"I wasn't doing anything bad, Mama. Honest."

"Of course you weren't, darling."

She ran her fingers through his yellow curls and bent to kiss him but he wiggled away. All right, she thought, all right, Sammy. She picked up the tray.

As she went out the door he smiled. "Good night, Mama."

Pris returned the smile. "Good night, darling. My darling. And please go wash right away before you forget again."

He trotted toward the bathroom.

Why do I love them so utterly? Pris pondered, taking the tray down the back steps, the way she had come up. George had an idea it wasn't punishment to send the boys to bed unless they were hungry. But in the kitchen Pris saw, through the window, that George already had begun his Sunday evening stroll around the grounds. During many years she had accompanied him on the strolls. She began wondering at what point and for what reason she had stopped and if walking about the Albright place now made George remember a long ago, dear like the nostalgia she experienced over home. Then suddenly it dawned upon Pris; the times she kept longing for of late were not her childhood years but the months when she was merely biding time until she and George would be married.

George had been in her dreams forever, of course, but he had hardly noticed her until she grew up. It was Tim who loved having her play with him (little thin dark Tim, so unlike the handsome yellow-haired, blue-eyed George), little Tim who had wanted to be a poet. Wherever could Tim be now? Ma Albright had answered his letter but she had never heard another word. Pris wondered how she would feel if Rufe or Sammy ran away. Here Pris gasped, amazed—certainly she had always known it but never before had the fact struck her that Tim was only fifteen when he ran away, Rufe's age.

Well, thank goodness! Rufe had stayed home all afternoon. Directly after dinner she had heard him going up to the third-floor playroom and he was still there, probably drawing; he was really clever at drawing. But Rufe wasn't drawing. He had found a book hidden in Papa's closet, and in the playroom, where he'd not be disturbed, he'd been reading. The book was *The Scarlet Letter*, by Nathaniel Hawthorne.

Pris put the tray down. Nellie would wash the dishes later. Nellie and Maggie had Sunday evenings off. Pris often wondered what the girls did during their time off. They didn't seem to have any friends. But every Sunday afternoon they dressed themselves all up and out they'd go. And good girls as they were, they couldn't have beaus because they were so homely. Still, there was that boy Gregory. People said he was Maggie's son. Poor soul, Pris thought about Maggie, I suppose she worries about Gregory too.

Pris remembered Rufe again. She fixed a snack if anyone wanted a bite Sunday evening.

She went into the hall and called, "Rufe, don't you want some supper, dear?"

"No, thanks, Mama," he answered.

"Hadn't you better light the lamp, dear, if you're going to stay up there?"

"It's not dark, Mama."

No, it wasn't dark, only shadowy. Twilight, and twilight of a Sunday.

"Pris." Gramma Albright spoke from the sitting room.

"Yes, Ma?"

"Would you mind lighting the lamp?"

Pris entered the sitting room and lighted one of the big lamps. Gramma Albright was reading her Bible. "My eyes aren't what they once were," she said.

"Would you like a bite to eat?" Pris asked.

"After that dinner I should say not." She rested the Bible on her knees. "Oh deary me, I often wonder if Tim has enough to eat."

"He said he was doing just fine in the letter, you know."

Gramma Albright nodded and returned to her reading. Pris wondered again what George could be thinking, out there walking around the place. She began reminiscences—about the beautiful year she had spent at the Boston Conservatory of Music and how handsome George had looked, and how envious the other girls had been, the time he came on to see her. She thought of how splendid he had appeared wearing his captain's uniform and of that night he had said, "Pris, I might not come back again and I'm going to marry you before I leave this time."

Then it came to Pris, why, George had never said, "I love you." Not when he was asking her to marry him nor in all the years they had been married. Of course he loved her, truly and deeply, the way she loved him, but never once had he said so. And come to think of it, Pris realized, she had never once told George she loved him either. She wondered what Dan Field would say to a girl whom he wanted to marry. What the girl might say to him. . . .

Entering the parlor, Pris sat down before the big square piano. She began playing Chopin's Opus 48 in C minor, Dan's favorite. He called it *the* nocturne because he said there was never another by comparison worth considering. Perhaps if Dan heard her playing when he brought Lillian home he'd stop a few minutes.

There was just one season of the year wherein Lem Stoddard really worked and that was springtime. As soon as the air began growing mild and the earth softened, something entered Lem's soul and he became sober and industrious. For Lem truly had green fingers and he loved making not merely his own garden but those of a number of townspeople as well; everybody said, "Lem Stoddard can make anything grow." The rest of the year, however, the family sustenance depended upon Myrtle, who took in washing, and he deviled the life out of Myrtle for money to buy liquor. Although once in a blue moon she liked a swig herself and would send Ray over town to buy a jugful. At such times Lem's attitude toward his wife was affable and gracious, after his own fashion, of course.

On the certain Sunday afternoon around the middle of September Bert, Shad at heel, arrived and found Lem and Myrt in one of these unusual friendly moods. Sprawled upon the porch, tin cups in hand, the jug between them, they chatted pleasantly. The children gathered around were almost quiet, too, because if Myrt bought herself a swig she had Ray purchase enough licorice sticks to keep their big mouths shut a spell, as she put it.

"Here you, Ray, give Bert a licruse stick," Myrt instructed.

"Please give Shad one, too, Mrs. Stoddard," Bert said.

"Sure." Myrt nodded agreeably. "Give Shad one, Ray. Give Shad two, Ray. Give Bert three, Ray."

Ray followed the biddings.

Lem shot a spiral of brown juice at the porch's one step, missed, filled his cup again, and beamed benignly toward his wife.

"Give the God damn shirt off'n yer God damn back, wouldn't

yer?" He took a drink, which he adroitly let slip over the quid down his throat. "Bighearted Myrt. Some likes 'em fat and some likes 'em thin, but me, I likes 'em jest like Myrt."

Bert fixed his eyes upon Myrt. She'd got fat, all right. He wished he could see a baby getting born. He would, someday.

Beaming toward Lem, Myrt filled her cup again. "Yer ol' bastard yer. Yer God damn ol' bastard. Ray, give everybody another licruse stick. Give everybody two licruse sticks."

The current baby, who was eleven months old, stretched beside her and she pulled the licorice stick out of his mouth and flung it across the porch. "Ray, give Teeny 'nother licruse stick. He's been a-chawin' that un plenty long. Why don't yer think 'bout yer lil brother oncet in a blue moon?"

Ray, whose life this day might be likened to Gunga Din's, dashed here and there, obeying instructions. Harry and Rita, their stomachs already chock-full of licorice, were trying to emulate their father's proclivity by emitting long spirals of licorice juice across the porch.

The next three—Maggie, seven, Lista, six, and Bud, four—were drawing licorice pictures on the floor. While Sonny, three, and Tiny seemed content enough merely to suck and drool licorice.

Myrt continued instructing, "Ray, give yer pap a licruse stick. Why don't yer think 'bout yer pap oncet in a blue moon?"

"I don't want no licruse stick," Lem said, taking another swig and still beaming toward Myrtle. "Give the God damn shirt off'n yer God damn back, wouldn't yer?" He turned to Bert. "Jesus Christ! Was my family refined." Here, Harry, Rita, and Ray set themselves to burst into laughter but today their father's story took a new twist. "Yer know, Bert, family ain't everythin'. Now thar's Myrt. I wouldn't trade Myrt fer the Queen of England."

"God damn black liar," Myrt responded affectionately.

"Th's right, Bert." Lem nodded. "It ain't all refinement. It's w'a's here." He tapped his heart. "An' here." He tapped his forehead. "An' they sumpin else, Bert. Gold! Gold! Whar'd yer folks 'a' got 'out'n money, Bert?"

Bert shook his head. "I don't know, Mr. Stoddard, where my folks would have got 'out money."

"Listen, Bert! I gonna tell yer sumpin. That gang hangs round Jake Smith's Livery Stable—Jake an' Floyd Shires an' Fat Hubbard an' all of 'em. See, Bert, last 'lection they thinks as how they gonna 'lect Ralph Pettigrew mayor o' Willerspring. And Ralph he makes some pretty God damn fine speeches. Yer hears them speeches, Myrt. What was it Ralph Pettigrew says?"

Myrt nodded amiably, pouring another drink. "Tha's right. Tha's 'zactly right. Tha's 'zactly wha' the God damn ol' bastard says."

Lem refilled his cup. "God damn fine speeches."

Ray spoke. Ray Stoddard at nine years and ten months of age had never known a day's schooling and could not read or write his own name. His straight, black, unkempt hair hung to his shoulders. His face was so thin it appeared cadaverous despite the dirt. But his black eyes were alert and his bony shoulders square.

"I kin tell yer what Mr. Pettigrew said, Pap." Ray spoke. "But we jest hears Mr. Pettigrew make one speech, Pap, last May, the night 'fore 'lection. And Mr. Pettigrew he says, says he, this here givern—givern—givernment of the United States was found—found—foundered by the people fer the people. But here in Willerspring——"

Ray stopped and looked at Bert.

"What else did Mr. Pettigrew say, Ray?" Bert asked.

"I wouldn't go fer ter hurt yer feelin's, Bert," Ray said.

"I ain't got feelings, Ray," Bert informed.

"Wall," Ray continued, "Mr. Pettigrew he says, says he, the reason Captain George Albright and Mr. Sargent is al'ays 'lected mayor is 'cause they got gold fer ter buy votes. And he said it is a sin fer ter buy votes."

Lem bellowed, "If'n tha' ain't the God damnedest talk I ever hear. If'n I kin git five dollars fer ter vote fer George Albright it's a sin fer ter take it."

Now came wafting across Limestone Avenue a medley of voices singing, "Wash Me and I Will Be Whiter Than Snow."

It was four o'clock. During the past fifteen minutes, from every Negro shanty men, women, children, and babies, dressed in their Sunday best, had been pouring and strolling past the Stoddards' toward Mr. Williams's shanty. (At the approach of Mr. and Mrs. Stanwick and the five other young Stanwicks, Shad had momentarily disappeared under the Stoddard porch.) Willowspring as yet boasted no colored church but at four o'clock every Sunday afternoon service was held in Mr. Williams's shanty.

Thomas Williams, addressed as Mr. Williams by practically everyone both black and white, including his wife and eleven children, was a patriarchal-looking old Negro somewhere around sixty. He was not only the colored preacher but Willowspring's one policeman. In his "pulpit"—a small platform he'd erected at one end of his "parlor"—Mr. Williams wore a stiff collar, a long-tailed coat, tight pants, and a high silk hat. Some believed this raiment had been acquired at a point in Mr. Williams's career when he was coachman for rich Pittsburgh people. On the beat Mr. Williams wore no collar and a simple coat and pants, while upon his white wool perched a red helment with "Police Chief" across its front. No one had any idea where this feature had originated and there was no subsidy provided by Willowspring to uniform the law.

The singing, which drifted across Limestone Avenue, was surely loud and sweet, but because Mr. Williams's congregation lacked hymnals the words seldom conformed to text. Also the congregation overflowed the parlor and was scattered through the kitchen and bedroom. And now came the words, if loud and sweet on different keys, from different rooms:

> *"Wash me and I will be whiter than snow,*
> *Whiter than snow, whiter than snow,*
> *Wash in the blood, yes, wash in the blood,*
> *Wash me and I will be whiter than snow,*
> *Whiter than snow, yes, whiter than snow.*
> *Wash me and I will be whiter than snow."*

The singing in Mr. Williams's shanty ceased but Myrtle took up the refrain:

> *"Whiter shan sho, yesh, whiter shan sho,*
> *Wash me and I will be whiter shan sho."*

Lem nodded approvingly. "Purty, Myrt, purty. God damn if'n I ain't gonna take yer dancin' sometime. 'Member how we uster dance, Myrt? Look. . . ." Lem pointed toward the Tatems' shanty.

Red was sitting on the porch smoking his corncob pipe, and Dolly, his younger daughter, was walking along Limestone

Avenue toward the woods. Once Red had possessed a wife and thirteen children. But when the youngest child was a year old Red's wife ran off with another man. The other man was a tramp who'd ambled along the track and stopped a few days in Mudtown. Of course everybody on Limestone Avenue who ever heard the tramp talk knew he was crazy as a loon, yet what he'd wanted with Daisy Tatem couldn't be imagined. Still more, he let her take the five youngest children along. They were never heard of again and they had last been seen walking along the railroad track, Red's wife carrying the baby, the tramp holding the next smallest on a shoulder, and the other three children trudging behind. After their mother left, one by one other children wandered away, until now at home were only Dolly, fifteen, and Belle, sixteen.

Where Red's hair was brick-colored, Dolly's and Belle's was like living flames and both had deep, deep blue eyes shaded like purple pansies (or so Ralph Pettigrew thought) and skins whiter than milk, if their mouths were wide. Red had raised a terrible row over his wife's elopement, got himself drunk, and sworn to use his musket upon both miscreants if they ever showed up again.

When he finally calmed down, however, Red felt more than pleased at being relieved of the six who had fled. Not that responsibility had ever rested on him heavily, but his wife's constant nagging had kept one shoulder, anyhow, under the wheel. And the last year Red had been more satisfactorily situated than he'd been since his marriage. Dolly and Belle were waitresses at the Grand Central Hotel, earning three dollars a week, half of which Red made them give to him. All he had to do was put a bead on bottles, or pot rabbits, or sit on the porch smoking and dreaming of the days when a mighty hunter of Indians and buffalo was he.

"Look," Lem guffawed, pointing to where Dolly was disappearing into the woods. "Know whar 'at slut ish a-goin', Bert?"

"Seems like Dolly she's going to the crick, Mr. Stoddard."

"Tha's right, Bert. Tha's 'zactly right. Tha's 'zactly whar she's a-goin'. Know wha' fer, Bert? Dolly she's a-goin' down in them bushes by the crick fer ter meet tha' big black buck nigger Gabe Williams, and his own pap over thar preachin' the gospel. Yer knows Gabe, Bert, yer uncle George Albright's hired man?"

"Yes, Mr. Stoddard, I know Gabe."

"Bert, wash yer s'pose yer uncle'd say if'n he knowed tha' God damn big black buck nigger wash a-layin' down in the bushes by the crick wif a white slut?"

Again Bert shook his head. "I couldn't hardly tell what Uncle George would say, Mr. Stoddard."

Now from the shanty of Mr. Williams the voice of Mr. Williams could be heard shouting, ". . . eternal hell," and then was lost again. But across Limestone Avenue once more Myrtle's voice wafted.

> *Whiter shan sho, yesh, whiter shan sho,*
> *Wash me and I will be whiter shan sho. . . .*

"And thar gosh Floyd Shires, reg'lar ash clockwork," Lem guffawed.

Floyd Shires was the one customer who did not sneak into the Widder Woman's shanty. Floyd, Jake Smith's hack driver, had a wife, three married daughters, and seven grandchildren. But every Sunday afternoon, rain or shine, Floyd ambled across Limestone Avenue at exactly half past four.

"Mr. Shires' clock must keep mighty good time," Shad said, rolling his round eyes.

"Bert," Ray Stoddard went on as if there had been no intervening conversation since his last remark, "even if'n Captain George and Mr. Sargent do buy votes Mr. Ralph Pettigrew gittin' 'lected mayor wouldn't have did no good. It'd take a mighty sight more'n Mr. Ralph Pettigrew gittin' 'lected mayor of Willerspring fer ter make him the likes of Captain George and Mr. Sargent."

Chapter Five

RUFE FINISHED the last word and closed *The Scarlet Letter*. His face burned. Of course, what the minister and the lady had done was terrible. But maybe they couldn't help themselves, and why must people who did things they couldn't help have to suffer? Rufe remembered again what Mr. Yates had said, that no merciful God would torment His children with actual fire, however wicked they had been. Even if that wasn't true it would be fine if people wouldn't torment each other, no matter who was right.

Rufe tiptoed down the third-floor stairs, put the book back in Papa's closet, and tiptoed on down the back steps and outside. Mama was playing the piano—the piece she was always playing lately—but Rufe was making sure she didn't hear him. She never liked having him go out this time of evening and he simply had to get away, go somewhere, anywhere. He saw his father wandering around the garden, the way he did every Sunday evening, and Gabe Williams, their hired man, and Charlie Raub, the Sargents' hired man, were coming along the walk on their way to feed the livestock and milk the cows. Before the Sargents', Uncle Doc was talking to Bert, and Lillian and Prissy were sitting in his buggy.

When he was a little fellow Uncle Doc had taken him on rides all the time. Rufe guessed it must be his own fault Uncle Doc had stopped taking him along, as it might be his own fault that Tom Leonard and Ben Smith and Jack Sturdevant had stopped playing with him. Until not very long ago these boys had stopped by for him often and there'd been plenty of fun swimming and skating and fooling around the livery stable and hotel. And Rufe'd never forget the time Tom asked him to stay for supper.

It was the only time Rufe had ever eaten in a hotel dining room. The Leonard family—including, besides Tom, Mr. and Mrs. Leonard and Tom's older sister, Jean—lived at the hotel, had several rooms on the third floor. After supper they'd all gone up to what they called their private parlor and played card games. Mr. and Mrs. Leonard had seemed to enjoy the games as much as the young people. And there was the time Rufe could never forget either when he'd seen Tom and his father starting out hunting together, laughing and talking like two boys, their guns over their shoulders and the two sleek lean pointers, Rex and Queen, at their heels. . . . Then suddenly the boys had stopped coming around and Rufe never did know the reason. But it must have been his own fault again, Rufe thought.

He passed Linden Street, his shoulders up. He didn't intend walking past Mollie Reynard's house this evening, nor maybe any other evening either. Rufe guessed, though, he might walk up to the hotel and see if Tom and Jack and Ben were around. Approaching the livery stable, Rufe saw the crowd assembled there. (Winters they gathered in the harness room and summers on chairs along the walk.) There was Ralph Pettigrew himself, and Jake Smith, Floyd Shires (just back from Limestone Avenue), and Fat Hubbard, not to mention a number of lesser personages.

Ralph Pettigrew made Rufe quake inwardly. Not, however, because of the Pettigrew antagonism toward the Albrights and Sargents. Ralph Pettigrew reminded Rufe of a bull who'd all but got him once.

In 1880 Ralph Pettigrew was thirty-three years old. He was six feet tall and weighed over two hundred pounds but, as he put it, he was "all beef and not an ounce of fat." He had black curly hair, a high forehead, beady black eyes, a flat nose, red cheeks, a letter-box mouth, and a square jaw. There was that about his "beef," though, which made lesser men regard him as a wall of strength. He had an indisputable charm whenever he pleased, and words often rolled from his tongue that made his hearers wonder and doubt and believe. Approaching the livery stable, Rufe heard the Sunday evening calm broken by one of Pettigrew's bull roars. As Mr. Smith had anticipated, he did split his sides over the story about Sammy Albright.

Rufe crossed the street and walked along to the hotel. The

Grand Central was built directly upon the walk, the bar and ladies' entrance on the right, the office door on the left. Across the front of the office was a huge window behind which the guests, mostly traveling men, sat during the winter. Now in September they lined the benches along the pavement. Inside the office to the left was the stairway, to the right the desk, and a door beyond the desk led to the dining room. Looking through the big window, Rufe saw Jerman Stanwick (who was Shad's father and the hotel porter) opening the dining-room door, which indicated that supper was ready. As if they had received a telepathic message, the men on the benches arose almost simultaneously, filing through the office into the dining room. Mr. Leonard, who was behind the desk, nodded amiably to each man who passed. Pretty soon Tom and Ben and Jack came out of the dining room (Rufe thought they must have been having early supper for some reason) and went on upstairs. They pretended not to see Rufe standing there looking through the window.

Rufe started down Broad toward Maple. Before the telegraph office Mr. Williams passed him and nodded pleasantly.

"Evening, Mr. Rufe."

"Evening, Mr. Williams."

Floyd Shires went by in the hack on the way to the depot. Before he was halfway home Rufe heard the whistle of the evening train at the narrows, and then the rumble of the train coming nearer and nearer, and again the whistle before going into the station.

Rufe thought, I wonder if even Mama would care if I got on that train some night and never came back?

Tom Leonard and Ben Smith were sixteen years old and Jack Sturdevant was fifteen, three months older than Rufe. Tom was a tall, sandy-haired boy who'd honest blue eyes, a freckled nose, and a wide smile. Everybody liked Tom Leonard. Ben Smith was short, plump, with nondescript features, but he kept all the other boys in stitches—he was so funny. Jack Sturdevant was medium height; he'd long lean dark features and a hollow chest, but he was far shrewder than either one of the other boys.

Tom had invited Ben and Jack to supper and they had eaten

early because they wanted to be in the dining room before anybody else got there to "have some fun pulling Dolly's leg." Belle was all right; any fellow could do anything he wanted to Belle. But Dolly got mad if you even touched her.

Tom had a room of his own on the second floor and, once the boys were there, they began discussing the situation.

"I can't figure Dolly out," Jack said. "She'd liked to scratched my eyes out if she could of."

"She was pretty near crying," Tom said. "Maybe we better lay off her."

"Can't see we've laid on her yet," Ben remarked, and the other two boys went into stitches.

"Did you see Rufe looking through the window?" Tom asked. "Wonder what he wanted."

"Probably wanted us to play tag." This, again from Ben, caused considerable laughter.

"The only trouble with Rufe is he ain't grew up," Jack explained.

Tom nodded. "That's right. We used to have a lot of fun playing."

"Christ sakes!" Ben ejaculated. "We can't keep on playing all our lives. It's pretty near time he found out a thing or two. Let's go hide back the stable door and hear what Ralph Pettigrew's saying."

After Bert left the Stoddards' he strolled over to Red Tatem's to inspect Duke's sores and then home. Passing Uncle George's, Sammy stopped him and asked him to get the loan of a pair of Shad's overalls. Bert's room, like Sammy's, opened onto the back porch, but Bert seldom felt compelled to take advantage of a pole as a means of exit. He guessed, however, he'd better shinny down the pole tomorrow morning because if Mama did happen to catch him going out around four o'clock she'd be sure to ask plenty of questions.

Bert saw Uncle Doc's rig stopping before their place to let Prissy out. He realized he'd not seen Uncle Doc to have a talk for a long time. In fact he had not seen Uncle Doc since he'd saved the rabbit's life.

"Hello, Bert," Uncle Doc was calling.

"Hello, Uncle Doc," Bert called back, going beside the buggy.

Prissy and Lillian were still on the seat and he gave them a significant glance. "Uncle Doc, would you mind letting me tell you something?"

"Of course not, Bert."

Dan Field crawled from the buggy and took Bert to a spot along the walk where they'd be out of the little girls' earshot.

"What's on your mind, Bert?"

"Know sumpin, Uncle Doc? I saved a little rabbit's life."

"Good boy. How?"

"See, it was like this. A couple weeks ago Mr. Tatem took me and Shad along potting rabbits. He potted eight. When we got back one was still alive. I could feel its little heart beating. Mr. Tatem said I could keep it and I took the little fellow over to Shad's house and washed the sore and dug the ball out."

"And the rabbit lived?" Dan Field asked.

"It lived," Bert informed. " 'Cept, it didn't live for keeps," he added quickly. "It died the next morning. But I saved its life all right. Don't you think, Uncle Doc?"

"Of course you saved its life," Dan Field agreed. "Nothing lives for keeps."

Bert nodded. "Know sumpin, Uncle Doc? All I had was a nicked paring knife. If I'd had a little real sharp knife mighty likely I'd not hurt the little rabbit at all and maybe it'd lived— wall, it might have lived to be an old, old rabbit."

Dan Field smiled. "You're right about the knife. To do a job well one must have the proper instrument."

Again Bert nodded. "There's sumpin else I want to tell you, Uncle Doc. I fixed Duke's sores."

"How?"

"I washed 'em and put sa've on 'em."

"What kind of salve?"

"Some of the blue sa've you give Mama last month."

The "blue sa've" given Lou last month was for a vaginal inflammation. Dan Field chuckled inwardly, imagining Lou's reaction were she to realize her vaginal jelly was being applied to the scabrous hide of Red Tatem's hound—and by her Bert.

But Dan Field asked seriously, "How did the salve work, Bert?"

"Not so good," Bert admitted.

"I tell you what, Bert," Dan Field said, "drop in the office tomorrow morning and I'll let you have some salve a dog's hide might find better to its liking. And another thing, you'll no doubt be called upon to save a rabbit's life again one of these days. I wouldn't be surprised if somewhere around the office is a little real sharp knife to spare."

Across Bert's face one of the occasional smiles flashed. "Thanks, Uncle Doc."

He made his way along the walk to the gate. Down the street Rufe was going toward town, and Gabe Williams and Charlie Raub were coming from Mudtown to feed the livestock and milk the cows. Even as Nellie and Maggie, Gabe and Charlie were a part of the Albright and Sargent life. At this time Gabe had been employed by the Albrights and Charlie by the Sargents four and five years respectively. Besides looking after the livestock and milking the cows, Gabe and Charlie kept the lawns, made gardens, and during the winter tended the furnaces and shoveled snow. Bert liked Charlie all right—a short wiry Negro who was about thirty years old—but Bert's admiration for Gabe was tremendous.

Gabe Williams was twenty-five years old. He was coal-black but his features were more Arab than Negroid. His hair was almost straight, his eyes long and narrow, his nose aquiline, and his lips thin. He was six feet tall and he had the shoulders, arms, and chest of a glorified galley slave. The far fields, where the cows were pastured and the hog sties stood, were remote from the Albright and Sargent houses, and, working there sometimes, Gabe and Charlie would take their shirts off. Charlie was nothing to see; but stripped to the waist, Gabe's flesh, from the shoulders and arms down the chest to his flat belly looked as smooth and lustrous as black satin, while underneath his mammoth muscles rolled and rippled. In the fall Gabe and Charlie took the Albright and Sargent hogs up the creek to Strock's Slaughterhouse. Mr. Strock and Lykes Butler, his butcher, were supposed to do the killing but Gabe would pitch in. Once Bert had seen him, stripped to the waist, holding alone a mad, fighting sow with one arm and hand while he slashed her throat with the other hand.

Going toward the house, Bert could hear hog squeals from the far fields and he knew Gabe and Charlie were moving the garbage barrels from their places behind the barns; the hogs evidently were able to smell the swill clear across the fields and gardens because the squealing began the minute the barrels were touched. Charlie always rolled the Sargents' barrel on a barrow but Gabe lifted the Albrights' onto a shoulder and carried it along. Remembering, Bert could see Gabe's great muscles moving under his shining black skin.

When Bert reached the steps Gramma Sargent, like Gramma Albright, was reading her Bible by lamplight in the sitting room, but Rufus and Lou were on the porch.

Seeing Bert, Rufus thought: Lou surely knows exactly where the boy spends every minute of his time. But it's beyond me. He's never home.

Lou thought: Of course Rufus wants Bert to be a banker. But he should be a minister. This moment the expression upon his face is positively spiritual.

Bert was thinking: I wonder why Gabe'd want to go laying down in the bushes by the crick with a white slut.

Once Bert had left Mudtown, Ray Stoddard slipped off their porch, around the shanty, across the bridge, and up Broad Street. He was still thinking about the speech Mr. Ralph Pettigrew had made on the May night before the election. Now Ray had gone over town because he knew Pettigrew and his crowd would be gathered before the livery stable, as on every Sunday night, and he wanted to have another close look at him to confirm the opinion made after the speech.

That May night before the election had been the greatest event ever to happen in Ray Stoddard's young life. Lem and Myrt had had a jugful (Ray guessed it was purchased with part of the five dollars Lem received to vote for Captain George Albright) but neither Pap or Mam—so Ray expressed it—was clean soused and about nine o'clock they'd locked the younger children in the shanty and taken Ray and Harry and Rita over town.

Broad Street was a blaze of torches, the band was playing, and crowds were pushing over walks and streets. A platform had been built in the middle of the road before the hotel, and pretty soon Mr. Ralph Pettigrew leaped upon it. Above the blare of bugles and the rat-a-tat-tat of drums arose a thunder of cheers and applause. Ray Stoddard had quivered, thrilled. Then from the

Pettigrew tongue rolled words to make many men wonder and doubt and believe.

"Your forefathers died, your forefathers and mine," Ralph Pettigrew had begun, "they died to free themselves from the oppression of tyrants. 'We, the people of the United States, in order to form a more perfect Union, establish justice, insure domestic tranquillity, provide for the common defence, promote the general welfare, and secure the blessings of liberty to ourselves and our posterity, do ordain and establish this Constitution for the United States of America,' our forefathers wrote. The government of these United States was founded by the people for the people. But . . .

"Captains of industry promised the people 'golden harvest fields, whirling spindles, turning wheels, open furnace doors, flaming forges, and chimneys filled with eager fire.' Prosperity, they meant. Prosperity *for themselves.*

"Enterprises which should have been a blessing to the people have become a yoke around our necks. The railroads, for instance. The total debt of the Revolutionary War was reckoned well under seventy-five million dollars. By 1872 the federal government had given—*given*, do you understand?—railroad promoters one hundred and fifty-five million acres of land, an area almost equal to Pennsylvania, Massachusetts, Connecticut, Rhode Island, Vermont, Maine, New York, and New Hampshire. The Union Pacific Railroad alone secured a loan of fifty million dollars. In other words, the railroads were *given* land whose area almost equaled the area of the thirteen original states and a single one of them received a goverment loan amounting to three quarters of what it cost to free ourselves from England, while it is we, the people, who must pay this debt even as the railroad magnates become millionaires.

"But the railroads are not the only menace to our freedom. Last year oil companies in Pittsburgh, Philadelphia and Cleveland, Ohio, united in a price-fixing agreement. What this will lead to unless the people take steps to stamp out the evil is evident. There will be price-fixing companies not only for oil but for steel, lumber, clothing, food, and labor. And . . .

"In this beautiful little town of Willowspring," Ralph Pettigrew concluded, "the yoke of the tyrant has ever been upon the necks of the people. George Albright and Rufus Sargent, and their fathers before them, have seen to that. Why should the Albrights and the Sargents, and the twenty other families, more or less, around here who also consider themselves royalty, loll in riches when the great majority of the rest of us must sweat to make a bare living? Why? I'll tell you why. Because you have let them buy your votes. It is as much a sin to buy votes as to steal. But votes will be bought this election, as they have always been, either directly or indirectly, for there will be many, as there have always been, who would be above taking a gold piece but who will be afraid not to vote for George Albright because they owe his bank money. But give yourselves a chance, men. Vote for me and you will have an opportunity of becoming richer and more important than George Albright or Rufus Sargent. I pledge my word that no matter what the conditions in the rest of the country may be, if I, Ralph Pettigrew, am elected mayor of Willowspring, in this town there will be a government of the people for the people."

If at nine years of age Ray Stoddard had never had a day's schooling and could not read or write his own name, he could and did form his own opinions. None of the Stoddard children had ever known a minute's coddling; before each one was old enough to understand a need for affection a new mouth was at Myrtle's breast. And from the time he could walk the whole family had imposed upon Ray. Not alone from his mother was it, "Ray, do this and, Ray, do that." Since he was seven, it was Ray who had gone to the woods and found fallen logs, cut the kindling and made the fires in the kitchen stove and under the pot behind the shanty where Myrt boiled her washes; Ray carried the water from the creek—there being no pipe line throughout Mudtown—for the family's use and to fill the pot; and it was Ray who collected and delivered the washes over town on the little wagon he'd made from a box top and four barrel staves. The only task Ray didn't do was to make the garden in the springtime when Lem's green fingers sought the soil. All this was not from lack of spirit upon Ray's part, however; he just didn't mind doing the chores and concluded, therefore, that it was senseless trying to dodge them the way Harry and Rita did.

Ray Stoddard had never possessed a store toy and all he knew about picture books was the sight of their covers in Carl's window. But collecting and delivering the washes, he passed the homes of the rich, and the Albright and Sargent places particularly appealed to him. He'd look at the lovely big graystone houses and their yards and the gardens behind, and at times he'd see at a distance the beautiful ladies and the little girls and Captain George and Mr. Sargent upon the street, and Ray would look at all this as another little boy would turn the pages of a picture book. He'd never darst, so he put it, enter the gates or speak to one of these people unless spoken to first, yet he couldn't help wondering how it would seem to live in one of the houses, the way Bert Sargent did, and belong to people the likes of them.

The night before the election Ray Stoddard had stood among the crowd, his straight, black, unkempt hair hanging to his shoulders, his face so thin it appeared cadaverous despite the filth, his skinny body covered by rags, his bare toes black and stubbed, his belly so empty it would have ached had it been accustomed to the feel of a square meal. But with his black eyes alert and his bony shoulders square, he missed not a word nor a move on Ralph Pettigrew's part. Nor was Ray swayed by the eloquence and the glory of such a night as the boy had never known before, what with the torches and the band and the cheering crowd. For after the speech, when the crowd was cheering and the band playing once more, Ray Stoddard was thinking: Maybe this here givern—givern—givernment of the United States was found—foundered by the people fer the people. And maybe if'n the Albrights and Sargents didn't have no gold fer ter buy votes som'un else'd been mayor of Willerspring long ago. And maybe it is a sin fer ter buy votes. But it'd take a mighty sight more'n Mr. Ralph Pettigrew gittin' 'lected mayor fer ter make me the likes of Bert Sargent and it'd take a mighty sight more'n Mr. Ralph Pettigrew gittin' 'lected mayor fer ter make him the likes of Captain George or Mr. Sargent.

Ray's approach to the livery stable, even as Rufe's, was preceded by one of the Pettigrew roars and the loud if lesser laughter of the other men, as out of sight behind the stable door Ben Smith and Tom Leonard and Jack Sturdevant were stifling their mirth. Ralph Pettigrew had told a new one about a traveling man and the farmer's daughter.

Of course Ray knew all the crowd by sight. Besides Pettigrew,

Jake Smith, Fat Hubbard, and Floyd Shires, this evening the other followers of Ralph Pettigrew chanced to be Frank Hershberger, the blacksmith, Alex Richard, the harness maker, Lykes Butler, Walt Strock's butcher, and Pen Sturdevant, the plumber. Fat Hubbard was the only man without an occupation; his tiny, emaciated, nervous, fluttering wife supported him, herself, and their three children by clerking in Miss Gunther's Ladies' Emporium. Standing on the edge of the crowd, Ray's eyes didn't miss a detail, from the blue stubble on the Pettigrew chin via Jake Smith's collarless fat neck to the buttons missing on Fat Hubbard's fly.

Ray was thinking how right he'd been about it taking more than electing Mr. Pettigrew mayor to make him the likes of Captain George or Mr. Sargent. What was more, he furthered his conclusion: Why, the likes of the whole bunch put tail ter tail ain't as good as the likes of Captain George or Mr. Sargent nohow.

Ralph Pettigrew saw the boy, the filth, the cadaverous face, but he also saw the alert eyes fixed upon him, and the Pettigrew intuition discerned no admiration in those eyes. In spite of his muscle and might, Ralph Pettigrew possessed a sensitive streak and a certain generosity. He never admitted, except to himself, how easily his feelings could be hurt, but he often said his heart was too big for his own good.

"What's your name, boy?" he asked, not unkindly.

"Ray."

"Ray what?"

"Ray Stoddard."

"Him's one of Lem Stoddard's up-and-comin' citizens," Fat Hubbard informed, confusing his pronoun per habit.

Pettigrew ignored Fat's remark and spoke to Ray again. "Why don't you like me, Ray?"

"Who says I don't like yer?" Ray demanded.

"Looks speak louder than words. And you better like me, Ray. I'm the best friend a boy like you could have in this town. Come here and hold out your hand."

Ray followed instructions. Pettigrew pulled something from his vest pocket and put it in Ray's outstretched palm. It was a quarter. Ray looked at the money.

"Now what do you think, Ray?" Pettigrew asked.

"I tell yer what I think," Ray said. "I think if'n it's a sin fer ter buy votes it's a sin fer ter try and buy som'un ter like yer. Thar's yer money."

He tossed the quarter at Ralph Pettigrew and shot down the block. Reaching the corner, he slowed his pace, looked over a shoulder to ascertain that no one was pursuing him, and then turned south on Maple Street. He was feeling particularly valiant, although unaware of the word or the emotion. All Ray knew now was he had stuck up for Captain George and Mr. Sargent and right to Mr. Pettigrew's face, and it made him want to see the big houses, perhaps catch a glimpse of the lovely ladies or little girls or Captain George or Mr. Sargent, again this evening.

Before the new schoolhouse Ray stopped a few minutes, however, wondering, as he always did, what going to school would be like, how it would feel to hold a book in his hands, to move a pencil over a slate. Once someone had given Shad Stanwick a pencil and slate and Shad had let Ray make marks on it. But what Ray wanted was to be able to write words on the slate and read the words. And there was something else Ray wanted to learn, learn more'n anything else in the world—how to do numbers.

Ray knew simple addition and subtraction. But adding and taking away were only the beginning of doing numbers, someone had told him. The someone who had told him was the tramp gentleman Mrs. Tatem run off with. The tramp gentleman had tarried about Mudtown a week before the elopement and he had talked a great deal. Ray was just seven then but he had never forgotten what the tramp gentleman had said about numbers. He had said people who knew about numbers could find out anything they wanted to know in the world—like how far it is around the world, how many miles to a star, where the North Pole is at, or where a ship still in the middle of the ocean would land. And there was something else the tramp gentleman had said anybody who knew enough about numbers could find out, something else Ray wasn't able to understand at the time, even though he never forgot the words: "If you know enough about numbers it is as easy to measure the depths of a soul as it is to weigh the pounds of a body."

Ray had never been inside of a church but long before he was

seven he knew what a soul is: something which flies out of you
when you die and goes to heaven or hell.

Seeing the new schoolhouse, Ray remembered all this and
speculated, It'll mighty likely take me more'n a year fer ter larn
everything 'bout numbers.

Moving along, he saw Mr. Doc's house over the way and Mr.
Ackley out front, probably waiting for Mr. Doc. Ray considered
Mr. Doc's house quite equal to the Albright and Sargent places.
And Mr. Doc was a fine gentleman like Captain George and Mr.
Sargent. Ray also admired Mr. Ackley, now all dressed up in a
white coat and pants, although Mr. Ackley never noticed any of
Mudtown's whites. For Mr. Ackley was a Southerner and put
on airs plenty among Mudtown's whites as well as colored. Folks
knew Mrs. Gordon's Bessie and Mrs. Wilbur's Tom and Mrs.
Stanwick's Willie were Mr. Ackley's young'uns but Mr. Ackley
never did let on. Mr. Stanwick had stopped speaking to Mr.
Ackley because he was too uppity to let on Willie was hisn.
Still, Ray considered, there was sumpin about Mr. Ackley made
him seem different from the likes of the Mudtown niggers, like
there was sumpin about Mr. Doc and Captain George and Mr.
Sargent made them seem different from the likes of Mr. Ralph
Pettigrew and his gang.

Ray stopped and drew his breath. There was the Albright house
and there was music coming from it and way back in the yard
he could see Captain George walking around the garden. Course,
Captain George'd never know how he'd stuck up for him right
to Mr. Ralph Pettigrew's face, but the knowledge of what he
had done gave Ray a mighty proud feeling. Then he saw Mr.
Doc's rig stopping at the gate and Lillian Albright hop out of the
buggy. Miss Lillian, Ray thought of her. Of course he had seen
her often before but never close enough to know how she really
looked. But today she passed him so near that if he had put out a
hand he could have touched her.

Ray had never seen the inside of a picture book and he didn't
know what a princess is, nor a knight, let alone a dragon. Yet,
looking after Lillian Albright, Ray Stoddard was thinking: She's
beautifuler'n a flower. I wisht—I wisht—oh, I wisht the biggest
ol' fightin' hog'd come after her and I'd throw myself right 'twixt
the two of 'em.

Ray had meant to speak to Mr. Doc, now he forgot all about him. And *the* nocturne was in Dan Field's ears and he did not notice Ray Stoddard on the edge of the walk.

Nervy started down the street on her own and Dan Field laughed. "Got more sense than I have, haven't you, Nervy?"

Going the block home, Dan Field remembered how Rufe had not so much as waved on his way toward town. Come to think of it, he'd not seen the boy except at a distance these many days. Used to be the youngster spent half his time playing around the office or going along on calls. What a funny little chap he'd been, insisting on calling him Da-da. But Rufe was growing up, Dan Field speculated. Why, he must have been fifteen on August fifteenth. August fifteenth! That date was never to be forgotten! The look in Pris's eyes when he had put the baby on her shoulder. Now Rufe was fifteen. And probably going through hell, a worse hell than most boys his age had to endure. He'd always been too sensitive. Rufe, Dan Field thought, Rufe, my son . . .

Nervy drew up at the gate. Ackley was waiting. Funny, Dan Field thought, the satisfaction I get out of Ackley in his white coat and his bows and smiles, and my colonial pillars and furniture and the candelabra with their lights flickering across the age-old wood. Life had compensations. Tonight Father Callahan would come and they'd sit upon chairs where long ago crinoline skirts had rustled and they'd drink golden bourbon until they loved each other even as Damon and Pythias, and they'd talk of everything the world had ever known from Aesculapius to the new laboratory at Johns Hopkins, from Faraday to what this odd fellow Edison was up to, from the Ten Commandments chiseled upon a stone to the latest novel Father Callahan had received from its publisher. And just as they were becoming a bit too mellow Ackley would usher them into the dining room and they'd eat fried chicken and spoon bread and apple pie while the lights from the candelabra flowed across linen and plate and silver until Ackley came bearing the pie—which he designated as Yankee shortbread, because no Ackley of Richmond "evah 'bided pie" —and then the candle flames would flicker and dim an instant. Of course Ackley was responsible for the phenomenon but Dan Field had never been able to discover how the feat was accomplished, nor did he question Ackley. It amused him to pretend the spirits of the South's dead truth blew breath across the lights at the sight of the Yankee shortbread.

When the door opened and Lillian called, Pris kept on playing. But in an instant Lillian was standing by her side alone and Pris lifted her hands from the keys.

"Is that your favorite piece, Mama?" Lillian asked.

"Why, dear?"

"You're playing it all the time lately."

Pris nodded. "I suppose it is my favorite piece."

She turned on the stool and peered at the little girl. How lovely she looked, the twilight gray of the room outlining her fair curls and making her eyes two deep dark pools. Oh, my dear, Pris thought, what will the years hold for you? Whom will you love? Who will love you?

Even as outside on the edge of the walk Ray Stoddard still stood lost in a dream.

Chapter Six

 R ALPH PETTIGREW caught the coin Ray
Stoddard tossed to him and stuck it back in his vest pocket.

"Ought to have him bottom tanned," Fat Hubbard snorted.

"All them Stoddards too big for their stinking britches," Jake
Smith sniffed.

Pettigrew didn't make a reply. He was wondering if the boy's
words might not be true. There probably wasn't any difference
between buying votes and trying to buy a person's liking. And
what Ralph Pettigrew wanted to do above all else was to discover
the truth of things, and not only why people acted certain ways
but why they thought so and so. He had an idea maybe Ray
Stoddard had been actuated by a liking for George Albright and
Rufus Sargent rather than by a dislike for him. There was no reason why the boy should dislike him, he felt. Filthy little beggar,
Pettigrew thought, but without prejudice. He admired Ray's
spunk despite his sass.

Glancing across the street, Pettigrew saw the Taylor girls
sauntering along. From the ridiculous to the sublime, he mused,
a Stoddard and now the Taylor girls. He pulled himself out of
his chair, said he guessed he'd better be getting over to supper
or the dining room would be closed, and started toward the
Grand Central. He lived at the hotel. Carefully he timed his steps
to meet the girls at the corner and again Margaret looked up at
him through her lashes and smiled.

He returned the smile openly and thought, I'm going to get
hold of you someday, young lady, come hell or high water. Today, however, Pettigrew was not mindful of the sweet revenge
the seduction of one of their members would bring upon all the

best families. He thought only of the pleasure of possessing the girl.

On the way to the dining room Pettigrew stopped in the bar. Shorty Clapp shoved a bottle of rye and a water tumbler across the counter. Pettigrew poured the tumbler half full and emptied it. When he entered the dining room no one was left except Dolly Tatem.

He sat down at the table and stuffed a napkin into his collar. "Guess I'm late."

"We got fried ham, ham and eggs, beef stew and . . ." Dolly began.

Then he saw she was crying.

"What's the matter?" he asked.

"I guess I gotta quit my job," she choked.

"Why?" Pettigrew demanded.

"It's them boys," she continued choking, "Tom and Ben and Jack. They won't let up on me."

"There, there," Pettigrew said. "They don't mean any harm. All they want's a little fun."

"Fun!" she cried. "Sure, fun's what they's after. Not one of 'em thinks I'm fit'n to have nothin' 'cept fun with. I tell you, we got fried ham, ham and eggs, beef stew, and sausage. Coffee, milk, and buttermilk."

"Sausage and buttermilk," Pettigrew said.

But he'd lost interest in food. Mudtown, he was thinking, Limestone Avenue . . . Ray Stoddard . . . Dolly Tatem . . . scum of creation. Ray Stoddard's eyes fixed upon him accusingly, and Dolly Tatem crying because Tom and Ben and Jack had acted fresh. It don't make sense, Pettigrew thought. He remembered Margaret Taylor, her round thighs and big breasts. A dull red suffused Pettigrew's face. Like Dolly, Margaret Taylor was just a kid. Maybe she'd cry, too, if he'd act fresh.

Dolly returned carrying a big tray. She put the sausage and buttermilk, bread, butter, and a half-dozen little vegetable dishes before him. Pettigrew ate but the food afforded no relish.

"We got custard pie, peach pie, and vanilla ice cream for dessert. The chocolate cake's all," Dolly said pretty soon.

Pettigrew pulled his napkin from his collar, wiped his mouth, reached a toothpick, and began prodding his gums.

"I don't want any dessert. And look here, Dolly, don't quit

your job. Just don't pay any attention to those boys. Boys are all ornery and men're just as ornery till they fall in love. After a man loves a woman it's different. One of these days a nice girl like you will find a fellow who wants to marry you."

Her white face turned whiter and her hair was like a living flame and her blue eyes were shaded like purple pansies and, looking at her, Ralph Pettigrew thought that this moment she was beautiful. He wondered if her body could be as white as her face.

She said, "I found a fellow wants to marry me."

Pettigrew smiled. "I'm glad, Dolly. I really am glad."

She didn't return the smile. She began piling the dishes on a tray.

Ralph Pettigrew shoved his chair back. Going out the door he was thinking, Wonder what Margaret Taylor would feel like if I wanted to marry her.

In 1880 Father Callahan was fifty years old—a tall, lean, blond Irishman whose salty sense of humor was only outwitted by a sensual love of beauty, even as both of these characteristics were overshadowed by his "spirituality." Since coming to Willowspring five years before, he and Dan Field had found each in the other a congenial outlet for opinions and sentiments, which God knew—Dan Field put it—would have caused Willowspring's Parsifals, papists, and paynims to rise up in holy horror. Actually the only unorthodoxy concerning the deity Father Callahan ever uttered was, as he himself put it, "Sure, it may be God the Father placed a bit too much faith in human nature when He sent so many unholy lovelies roaming over the earth."

During the last year Father Callahan had taken to spending every Sunday evening with Dan Field, the doctor's practice permitting. They did discuss everything under the sun, usually in dialogue, one beginning a subject and the other carrying on, a fact which amused them both no end. Too, Father Callahan experienced a pleasurable sensation in the atmosphere—the colonial pillars, Ackley, and the candelabra's gentle glow across the age-old wood, not forgetting the golden bourbon.

This Sunday evening Father Callahan and Dan Field sat upon the chairs where long ago crinoline had rustled and Father Callahan's eyes wandered appreciatively around the room again.

"You have never told me," he said, "and if you consider me presumptuous ignore my interest. But sure, I've been curious, too, concerning the colonial pillars and the furniture and Ackley."

Dan Field smiled. "The rest of the town wouldn't understand if I explained. It all goes back to Praxiteles."

" 'Greece had to submit to Rome,' " Father Callahan quoted, " 'and Rome to conquer part of the ancient world, before Italy and the west of Europe at last participated in the radiance of this manifestation.' Sure, I am beginning to understand."

"Only beginning to understand, Padre." Dan Field sipped the gold. "Kentucky bourbon. A gentleman's drink. Let me go on. In this enlightened year of 1880 practically everyone in these United States believes the original Pilgrims, Puritans, yeomen, Huguenots, and the poor but proud Virginia gentlemen comprised the majority of our original settlers, even as practically everyone believes also that the original Constitution gave equal rights to all men."

Dan Field stopped and Father Callahan continued the strain. "As a matter of fact many of the immigrants were rich men and with few exceptions all had property. And the number of bondmen, not to mention Negro slaves, outnumbered them all. In Pennsylvania alone, between the opening of the eighteenth century and the Revolution, two thirds of the immigrants were bondmen. At the time the Constitution was adopted slavery was lawful in all the Northern states except Massachusetts. Even in 1850 there were more than five million bondmen in this land of the free." Father Callahan stopped, sipped his bourbon, and smiled. "The platform is now yours, Dr. Field."

Dan Field bowed, sipped his bourbon, and smiled. "Then when bondmen and black men were freed from one master, another arose to draw blood with a far more insistent lash than any that Simon Legree ever flourished. By some strange coincidence during the hundred years following the birth of this nation greater strides have been made than in all previous ages." Dan Field sipped his bourbon and smiled. "The platform is now yours, Father Callahan."

Father Callahan bowed, sipped his bourbon, and smiled. "At the beginning of the century there wasn't so much as a sewing machine nor a railroad on the globe. But the blessings machinery should have brought to the people have been overshadowed by greed. Now in factories men, women, and little children work from dawn until night for less than living wages. Which I should think about explains why your colonial pillars and furniture and Ackley all go back to Praxiteles."

Dan Field nodded. "Exactly. Greece had to submit to Rome, Rome conquered part of the Western world before the radiance of Praxiteles' manifestation could be appreciated. Commerce will have to conquer the whole world before the glory of the Old South is reverenced. I fought to defend the Union and not to destroy the South. But the fact the slaves were taken from one master did not deliver them from another. Only today both black and white have the same hypocritical master who chortles of freedom to the rhythm of a quirt. *Totidem verbis*, Padre, I revel in the luxury of an aristocracy which was honest enough to call a slave a slave. It may be someday the world will appreciate the radiance of the South's dead truth—even as Praxiteles finally found an audience capable of recognition, *ad valorem*."

Father Callahan smiled. "Sure, what the pity such reverence cannot be directed toward heaven. Still, contemplating Harmes reminds me, have you seen the boy Gregory Beamer of late?"

"Only in passing."

"He is the most beautiful boy I ever did set eyes on."

Dan Field chuckled. "We seem to be in Greece, so why not do what the Greeks did?"

Father Callahan chuckled. "Sure, don't you lose any sleep over that, Dr. Field. I mean to save his soul."

"He'll probably not thank you."

"Perhaps not. But he's too beautiful to let any save the Virgin have him. The first time I saw him I thought, sure, and that's how the little Saviour should have looked, if perhaps he didn't. By the way, would you happen to know who the boy's father might be? Gossip says Maggie is the mother."

"All I know is rumor. From what I've gathered, Mrs. Beamer officiated at the birth and let no outsider enter the house until several weeks later. Then she tried to make out the child was hers. Later the report started that Beamer is the father."

"What would you think?" Father Callahan asked.

"I believe he is. And that conclusion is arrived at by observation. Neither Maggie nor Nellie ever goes home. What is more

significant, they never have anything to do with men. It's a standing joke among the street-corner element."

"That doesn't necessarily follow——"

"Not necessarily," Dan Field put in, "yet if one, or maybe both
of them, had been badly treated by their father, a distaste, or
possibly a fear of sex, might have developed. Look here"—Dan
Field shook a finger—"you wouldn't be thinking, would you,
about an immaculate conception?"

"You good-for-nothing rapscallion!" Father Callahan chortled.
"I'd be thinking somebody ought to try and save your soul."

"For what?" Dan Field reached the decanter and refilled the
glasses.

"Because you're too lean to sizzle nicely on a spit."

Outside the evening church bells began to ring, first the
Lutheran, then the Methodist, then the Presbyterian and the
Reformed.

"There's your answer," Father Callahan said. "Civilizations
come and civilizations go but the need of God was from the
beginning and will be until the end."

Dan Field nodded. "You're right. Still, I believe the time will
come, and before long, when no one will worship a God who
runs a race with a Devil, with said Devil always ahead. These
children who are growing up today—Lillian Albright and Rufe
and Sammy, Bert and Prissy Sargent, your Gregory Beamer, the
Stoddard young ones in Mudtown—are beginning to think their
own thoughts and not what their fathers have believed. Charles
Darwin may not have been the first to comprehend evolution but
his book has sent thoughts whirling through the universe, and
these thoughts, if not believed by all, will revolutionize doctrines
as dynamically as the theory of the conservation of energy has
revolutionized science. Think what electricity will do to both
dogma and physics during the next few years."

"Sure," Father Callahan's tone became dry, "it all goes back
to Praxiteles. Darwin will have to submit to electricity, or we
might say Darwin will have to submit to Tom Edison and Edison
conquer the rest of the world before the radiance of God's manifestation can be appreciated."

"Good, good," Dan Field laughed. "You grow better by the
thimbleful." He filled the glasses again. "Truly, we're both unusually eloquent and witty tonight. What the pity we have no

more ambition. You with your souls and I with my bodies—
easing each for but an instant out of all time."

Starting on his Sunday evening stroll, Captain George had
walked to the front gate and looked at the great lovely house
under the sugar maples. Going around back, his eyes had rested
upon the pump on the porch, the gray stone icehouse covered
by rambler roses, the outhouse with one room for the family's
use and one for the hired help (the family room now being for
Nellie and the hired help's for Gabe). He wandered by the huge
trellis where the Concord grapevines grew, along the lilac-lined
flower garden, past the chicken coop and stable to the vegetable
fields, edged by the apple trees—now in September gay as Christmas trees bedecked with the red, red late fruit—and the plum and
cherry and peach trees. Beyond he could see the far fields where
the cows were pastured and the hog sties stood, and beyond the
far fields the mountains rising like the mountains about Jerusalem.

Permanent, is what he was thinking, nothing changed since the
days of George the First and Rufus the First. And the reason was
obvious, because he and Rufus the Second, after a fashion, had
carried on the traditions of their fathers. Certainly this country
was a democracy, but there had to be leaders not of the people.
The veritable fathers of the nation, all aristocrats who had inherited wealth, had protested against indiscriminate powers. They
had limited office-holding to men of property, and Jefferson himself wrote against granting suffrage to "the urban masses and
mobs of great cities," where when the people had finally been
granted the vote and Andrew Jackson elected President panic
overtook the land. Only in Willowspring, and a few other places
where aristocracy still held sway, was disaster averted.

Certainly since the days of Jackson to the present, matters in
Washington had gone from bad to worse. Sometime, perhaps,
Abraham Lincoln would become a hero of sorts. But during his
presidency not merely the South approved Wendell Phillips's
opinion: "a more unlimited despot than the world knows this side
of China." While if Rutherford B. Hayes was no worse, he was
certainly no better than other "sons of the soil." And concerning
the conditions of the country today, James Russell Lowell had
recently written (George had memorized the opinion): "What

fills me with doubt and dismay is the degradation of the moral tone. Is it or is it not a result of democracy? Is ours a 'government of the people, by the people, for the people,' or a Kakistocracy, rather for the benefit of knaves at the cost of fools?"

George shook his head sadly as he always did when bent upon this subject. And matters were going from bad to worse because things had come to such a pass that the average man could not distinguish between the real aristocracy and the pseudo articles —quick fortunes made with railroads, steel, oil, and so forth. What could such upstarts do except promise the people wealth and give them nothing?

The train whistled at the narrows and rumbled nearer and nearer. . . . George frowned. The railroad—the Juggernaut under which man had cast his most cherished possessions: individuality and free will. Once everyone who had a mind could own his own business, come and go the way he chose. Now, since the North and the South and the East and the West were united, the little fellows had been wiped out and were herded like cattle into sweatshops, factories, and mills.

Looking toward the street, George saw the lamplighter, Eddie Perkins, moving from corner to corner, the little ladder and torch a part of him. George smiled. For twenty years, since the street lights had been installed, Eddie had gone the rounds. He was truly one with the landscape, like the mountains or the church steeples or the town clock or the blacksmith shop or the trees or the houses or the livery stable or the blue Juniata. Suddenly George frowned, remembering Rufus's arc-light scheme. It simply wasn't thinkable not to have Eddie going the rounds. This idea of lighting whole towns by means of what was called a "dynamo" was nothing more or less than a wild-goose scheme, George decided.

There was Rufus's trouble! Never satisfied to let well enough alone. Money invested in mortgages, especially farm mortgages, couldn't be lost. Still, there was money enough to let Rufus speculate a bit, and until this arc-light scheme he'd been mighty lucky. The California cable-car bonds paid handsomely despite the prejudice toward this type of street railway and the fact that Eastern cities weren't apt to adopt such a mode of transportation. Horsecars met every practical purpose. The whole world would be better off if it knew enough to let well enough alone.

George saw Dan Field's rig stopping before the gate and Lillian hopping out of the buggy. He shook his head. Dan seemed actually to enjoy the children's society. Queer, Dan never had a real girl. Of course he had his fling during college days, probably was still having a time on his New York trips, but there seemed to be a lack in his character which made him incapable of loving a woman. From a fine old family like the Fields there should be some ambition, if nòt to carry on the line at least to replenish their estate. But Dan spent half his time looking after paupers and it was like pulling teeth to get a bill out of him. Why, George remembered, it had taken Dan ten years to repay the money the bank loaned him to build his house, not to mention the three thousand-odd dollars advanced to further that idiotic idea of bringing pillars and furniture all the way from Virginia. Queer world . . . George strolled along.

Rufe turned in at the gate. George noted how tall the boy had grown. Wondering where Rufe had been this time of day, George smiled indulgently. Probably up to a bit of mischief and do him good to play around the town girls a bit. Nothing wrong of course. Rufe could be depended upon to do the right thing. Fine boy, Rufe.

The church bells began their tolling and George went around front again. Pretty soon people began swarming along the pavements to evening service. Among others George noted Reynard, the carpenter, and his wife and little girl. He had noticed the little girl in the choir. "Vivid" was the word to describe her. George remembered the first time he had seen Vi Larsen he had thought the same thing—vivid. Vi . . . Vivid . . .

But how wise his father had been. Pris was the wife for him. Although, George had often thought, sometime in Philadelphia it might be interesting to find out whatever had become of Vi. Merely out of curiosity of course. He had Pris. . . . And he most certainly would see that Rufe and Sammy and Lillian had no opportunity to fall in love with, or rather, become infatuated with—"love" was hardly the word—anyone outside of their own social class. However, George's eyes chanced to fall upon a small figure standing outside on the edge of the walk, and he wondered what such a filthy little upstart meant by hanging around the place.

Turning toward the house, George forgot Mollie Reynard and

Ray Stoddard. He was thinking of his own family again—Pris, Rufe, Sammy, Lillian, and the walls of the big house surrounding them, the town and the mountains surrounding the town. House of rock . . . town built upon a rock . . . mountains like giant sentinels. Permanency.

If the Rebs had beaten us at Gettysburg, Captain George concluded, they could never have gotten across the mountains. And if there's ever another war Willowspring will be the safest spot on earth.

Captain George mounted the front porch steps and Mrs. Schiller went down the Albrights' cellar steps, even as at the same moment Mrs. Race was going down the Sargents' cellar steps. Every Sunday evening Mrs. Schiller and Mrs. Race arrived right before dark to put the washes to soak. They would drag the big round wooden tubs up the cellar steps to the back porch, carry water in pails from the kitchen to fill them, pull the clothes out of bags hanging on the walls, douse each article separately, soap them collectively, and be off, returning next morning before dawn to do the washes.

Chapter Seven

𝒰NLIKE A MOTH emerging cautiously from a cocoon, on Saturdays Willowspring fairly soared from its shell and spread wings; the quiet village became a busy metropolis, a Mecca where all roads ended. In those days when there were no country stores, every Saturday, long before dawn, in farmhouse kitchens all over the valley, candles or lamps would be gleaming, stoves crackling, coffee boiling, frying pans sizzling, while outside livestock was being tended, horses and oxen hitched. Soon through the darkness, in either summer dew or spring rain or perhaps autumn fog or winter snow, wheels would begin turning or runners sliding—on toward town. By daylight not an available hitching post could be found on any of Willowspring's main streets. Come nine o'clock, vehicles lined alleys and lanes unto the town's boundaries and Broad Street buzzed—a teeming, thriving, endeavoring center.

Saturday in town was as much a part of farm life as sowing or copulating, harvest or travail. On this day provision must be made for the coming week—supplies bartered or bought; materials and wearing apparel purchased; horses and buggies taken to the blacksmith and wheelwright shop; bank loans negotiated, interest paid; and in the fall grain had to be hauled to the gristmill.

First, every farmer and his family took themselves to Strock's Market, there to linger in the redolence of coffee beans and ginger cookies, molasses and pickle barrels, cinnamon sticks and sweet cider, plug tobacco, cigars, coal oil, dried cod, mackerel, and raw red meat.

Behind the butcher's counter Lykes Butler presided, his huge raw red hands, themselves like chunks of raw red meat, deftly sawing or chopping stiff carcasses upon a block or scooping snow-

95

white lard from deep brown crocks while he took another order or did a neat bit of bartering.

"Five pounds to the very ounce, Simon. A dollar even. Howdy, Eben. What can I do for you?"

"Two pound spareribs'll see me over. Gonna butcher myself Tuesday. Hogs done good this year."

"Good hog year. Fourteen cents, Eben. What's yours, Art?"

"What you askin' for beef, Lykes?"

"Six cents up."

"Swap you two dozen right fresh eggs for two pounds twelve-cent beef."

"Can't do that, Art. Give you two pounds eight-cent beef."

"All right, Lykes. Now don't you go makin' it all bone."

"See this here piece. Hardly no bone, Art. What'll you have, Don?"

"What'd ten pounds good draw'd lard be worth, Lykes?"

"Let me see . . ."

Behind the grocery counter Mr. Strock waited upon the women. Brown sugar, coffee, butter (if cows were dry), eggs (if chickens were moulting or setting), risings, cinnamon, salt, pepper, lye to make soap.

"Two pound coffee," Mr. Strock would say, words filtering through his bushy black mustache, "five pound sugar, one pound salt. Let me see. Eighty-seven cents. There you are, Mrs. Fodder. How about a pound of ginger cookies? Eleven cents. Cheaper'n you can bake."

"Don't hold to store cookies."

"Couldn't tell'm from homemade. Save you baking."

"If I get too lazy to do my own baking I'll say so."

"All right, Mrs. Fodder, but they's mighty good. Wouldn't you like to try 'em, Mrs. Clark?"

"I might try a nickel's worth. Let me think what I'm needin'. Two pounds of sugar, one of coffee . . ."

All the children large enough to be out of their mothers' arms hovered around the candy counter—peppermint lozenges, lemon drops, cinnamon balls, licorice sticks, popcorn balls.

"I wanna penny, Mama."

"Ma, give me a penny."

"Penny, penny, please, Mam."

Often a penny dropped into an eager little palm. Again a screaming child would be dragged away. Sometimes a bottom was smacked soundly because a mite refused to move without a sweet.

The shopping at Strock's over, the men, the bigger boys in tow, were off to the bank or repair shops, as the women, accompanied by the bigger girls and children, hurried along to Miss Gunther's Ladies' Emporium.

For if Willowspring on Saturdays was Mecca to the country people, it was Babylon besides. To the great majority it was the only innovation life had to offer. Many a soul had lived and many a soul was still to live on many an isolated farm from birth till death without experiencing any other dissipation than Saturdays in town. And to them whose eyes were used only to barnyards and cow pastures, the streets of Willowspring were midways, what happened upon them revelry.

Business having been attended, the farmers dropped into the Grand Central Bar. They'd drink and talk weather and crops and tell stories and laugh. Shorty Clapp never failed to have a new story, and pretty soon the farmers would forget drought and debt and that the mare had lost her foal or the bull couldn't hold on. There sure had to be a break next year by the law of averages.

Necessities purchased, the women still lingered hungrily about Miss Gunther's, their eyes feasting upon luxuries—perfume from Arabia, silk from the Orient, lace and colored muslin, ruching and ribbons. And the pair of silk stockings Miss Gunther kept in a drawer. Of course she couldn't display them on a counter because a gentleman might come in to make a purchase but she was proud to let any woman look or touch the wonder of their sheen.

The older girls also lingered about Miss Gunther's. But before long they'd be gone. The older boys were off the moment a father's back was turned. Boys and girls would be looking for one another, each with a certain person in mind. When any two found each other they'd link arms and go to Heckshire's Drugstore and drink root beer. There were, however, girls who had no regular fellows, and they'd wander around the streets, hope high in their hearts. They wanted any kind of fellow. If a town fellow could be had, all the better. And the country fellows who had no steady sweethearts wandered around looking the country girls over, their eyes out for any of the town girls who might be abroad.

On corners, or before the livery stable and drugstore, certain Willowspring males loafed. Often an acquaintance would be scraped between a town boy and a country girl. Yet most of the town element enjoyed merely baiting the country girls, whistling and winking and making suggestive remarks. Some of the country girls might answer back hotly, others pretend not to see or hear the miscreants. But even in such proceedings ran a strain of high tension.

The last Saturday of September during the year 1880 an unusual exhilaration vibrated throughout Broad Street. A rumor had started early that morning. By nine o'clock the rumor had been verified. By ten o'clock every country man and boy big enough to be out of knee breeches, not to mention the town element, knew the tale. The farmers in the stores whispered it, in the bar they roared over it. The corner loafers, their eyes hot and their voices hilarious, kept calling to the country girls:

"Been to Miss Gunther's yet?"

"What did you buy at Miss Gunther's?"

"Let's see what you got at Miss Gunther's."

Miss Gunther was forty years old. She was a tall, thin, dark, fine-looking woman, who'd these last twenty years been style director for most of Willowspring's female population, as well as for the farmers' wives. Every spring and every fall Miss Gunther went to Philadelphia and did her buying. She kept her stock right up to the minute and always returned home bringing a late novelty, like the pair of silk stockings she'd brought back last spring. Just last Thursday, she'd returned from Philadelphia and her latest novelty was the cause of all the flurry.

The first thing this Saturday morning Miss Gunther had said to the early shoppers, "Wait till I show you the latest novelty."

She had pulled open a drawer, the one where the silk stockings were kept out of sight, and put something on the counter. Mrs. Fat Hubbard giggled nervously and the country women gasped.

Miss Gunther's latest novelty was a pair of ready-made women's drawers.

"Several of the Philadelphia stores are carrying them," Miss Gunther informed. "But I don't believe they'll last. Think of all the different sizes it would be necessary to keep on hand if ready-made drawers became popular."

Ralph Pettigrew's law office, on the second floor of Hardy's Office Building, was a corner one looking out upon both Broad and Oak. About three o'clock in the afternoon of this last September Saturday Pettigrew stood looking out of the window at the still teeming street. He was thinking about the days when as a boy he had come to town Saturdays, his eyes full of wonder and his head full of dreams. Those were the days George the First and Rufus the First were kings. Pettigrew remembered well the elegant figures walking along the streets holding their haughty heads high, as he remembered Captain George and Rufus the Second, as boys. He remembered Tim, the one who had run away from home, who was about his own age. Tim hadn't been like the others. He was friendly. Several times Tim and Ralph Pettigrew talked together. Pettigrew had long since forgotten what the conversations were about but he never forgot a decision, made during those days, that no matter how rich and important he might become there wouldn't be anybody too lowly to treat decently, white or black.

Now across the street Pettigrew saw Sammy Albright standing, holding the hound pup in his arms, a wide grin across his face. Jake Smith had been wrong about Sammy; he had stuck on the job, pretty near two weeks now. What was more, Pettigrew was sure Sammy would see the thing through. One morning he had stopped by the stable around six o'clock and there was Sammy, wearing a pair of ragged overalls, working like a Trojan, his young muscles straining to lift the heavy shovelfuls and the sweat pouring down his cheeks. Pettigrew ceased thinking it was funny to see one of George Albright's boys working at such a job, because the boy was doing the job right and all for a God damn hound bitch not worth a cent over two dollars.

Mollie Reynard and Bertha Richards stopped beside Sammy. The wide grin still across his face, Sammy put the pup down. The pup wiggled and wagged and bounced, and, laughing, Mollie picked it up and kissed the sleek little head. Pettigrew smiled. What that Mollie wasn't going to do to the boys before long! The Richards young one wasn't bad either—fat but cuter than a button. Pettigrew wondered where Helen Boyd could be.

Since they were babies Mollie and Bertha and Helen had been inseparable. Then he remembered the talk about the Boyds being Jews. Probably Reynard and Richards had put a stop to the friendship. Pettigrew thought Helen was the sweetest one of the three, like a gentle little brown dove.

His mouth straightened grimly. Probably the next thing would be Reynard not letting Mollie play with Bertha because the Richardses were Catholics. Pettigrew attended the Lutheran Church, yet he could see no reason why Protestants considered themselves on a higher social plane than Catholics, nor why gentiles believed themselves better than Jews, all things being equal. Sure, some Jews were low as niggers, but plenty of gentiles weren't a whit better, and no decenter fellow ever lived than Eli Boyd. And Vera Boyd was a lady from the top of her black curls to the tips of her small feet. Eli earned a living by clerking in Fulton's Feed & Seed Warehouse, but he could fiddle like nobody's business, and Vera had a voice sweet as a nightingale's. They had come to town when Helen was a baby, attended the Presbyterian Church, and were popular until their heritage was discovered. Now Eli and Vera didn't go to church and lived by themselves in a cottage at the end of Horsechestnut Street.

Oh well, Pettigrew shrugged, and his eyes moved along the street to where Tom Leonard, Ben Smith, and Jack Sturdevant were standing, talking to three country girls. The sight of the boys set Pettigrew thinking again about Dolly Tatem and then Ray Stoddard. Why was it the boy disliked him? Why?

Rufe Albright came along. He passed Sammy, Mollie, and Bertha, as well as Tom, Jack, and Ben and the three country girls, without giving any one of them a glance. A true Albright if ever one lived, Pettigrew sniffed. But God damn them; he'd show them, the vote-buying bastards. Yet Pettigrew knew he'd give all he possessed to be invited to the reception tonight. On Monday the new school was opening, and tonight the Albrights and the Sargents were introducing Professor and Mrs. Phelps, the principal and his wife, to Willowspring society.

The Taylor girls were going, Pettigrew had heard. He wondered how Margaret would look wearing a party dress and if she'd dance. For an instant Margaret Taylor was in his arms and they were waltzing. . . .

Suddenly a commotion on the street attracted Pettigrew's attention. Probably more flurry over the ready-made drawers. Then he saw there was more than a flurry. Red Tatem stood in the middle of the street yelling and waving his hands as a crowd gathered around. Pettigrew guessed he'd better go down and find out what was going on.

By the time it reached Strock's Slaughterhouse, Broad Street had dipped north until it was hardly a stone's throw from the creek. Thereafter it wound by the bank of the river for more than a mile eastward to the covered bridge which crossed the creek at the narrows. This stretch of road was part of the turn-pike—"the pike"—between Philadelphia and Pittsburgh.

About three o'clock this September Saturday Dan Field's rig moved toward town along the pike beyond the bridge. He had been on a baby case since yesterday noon. The baby was born perfect, a fourteen-pound boy. The mother, a great strapping nineteen-year-old farm girl, had bled to death. The father, a great strapping twenty-year-old farm boy, had screamed and cursed and refused to look at his son. But the girl's mother, a wraithlike old woman, gnarled and bent, her old eyes dry, had rocked the baby in her withered arms. Probably no tears left to shed, Dan Field thought.

Someday we'll know how to prevent such tragedies, he told himself, going home. He began remembering another girl he had lost—or rather, murdered—years ago. The husband was to inherit a sum of money if he had a child. When Dan Field found out it had to be the mother or the child he asked the husband which one should be saved. That is the law; if only one of them can be saved the husband has the right to choose. This husband chose. Dan Field saved the baby. Only the day before the girl, her eyes shining, told him how kind her husband had been since he knew she was going to have a baby. She said she was sure she wasn't going to die, of course she didn't want to die, but she felt as if she'd gladly give her life to make her husband happy. She loved him like that, the girl had said.

Nervy's hoofs clumped across the covered bridge and softened to clops again. Dan Field noticed a mist on the far horizon. Near by, quail began calling. Along the river bank the trees were splashed with the gentle yellow and rose coloring which always precedes the resplendent autumnal gold and crimson. But the blue

Juniata, seemingly oblivious of time or reason if obviously aware of tide and rhyme, trickled and gurgled and broke here over stones, there around diminutive isles, again falling into pools where bass and suckers basked, sunnies flashed, minnies and catfish and pike darted, and occasionally naked boys splashed, as if it were a June or July or August day rather than September's last Saturday.

Near the slaughterhouse was a swimming hole practically beside the road. Approaching, Dan Field saw a young naked figure standing upright, back turned, ready to dive. Dan Field saw sunlight upon a crest of golden hair, milk-white shoulders and arms smooth as a lovely girl's, straight slim thighs, but straight sturdy legs. *His legs are as pillars of marble.* . . . Jesus! Dan Field swore, It is the most beautiful creature I ever saw, but is it a boy or a girl? He put his fingers between his teeth and whistled. The figure turned and Dan Field saw who it was. "Jesus" is right, Dan Field chuckled, it's the immaculate conception. What the pity if the padre does save his soul; the delight he might bring to both sexes!

Dan Field waved. "Hello, Gregory."

Gregory Beamer waved back and dived into the pool.

At the corner of Maple and Broad Street Nervy turned toward home but from the other direction Dan Field heard someone calling him. He pulled Nervy's head around and saw Belle Tatem running along the street.

She began shrieking, "Pap tried to kill Dolly. Pap tried to kill Dolly. . . ." She caught up to the buggy and jumped in. "God sake, Mr. Doc, hurry! Maybe Dolly's dead a'ready."

Dan Field flapped the reins and Nervy trotted toward Mudtown. "What's the trouble, Belle?"

Belle sniffed. "Pap found out about Dolly and Gabe Williams."

"What about them?"

"They been laying together. 'Cept Pap's trying to make out Gabe raped Dolly. He's gone over town to get a mob to tar and feather Gabe. But it ain't all Gabe's fault, Mr. Doc. Dolly's crazy mad about him. He's the only fellow she ever let put a hand on her."

Nervy's hoofs clattered across the bridge and thudded onto Limestone Avenue, among the sunlight and the shadows and the swarming little Negroes, though there was no more stir this afternoon than on any other afternoon. What matter if Red had beaten Dolly? Hardly a week passed without some Mudtown father or husband or lover taking fists to a girl or woman.

Before the Tatem shanty Dan Field drew Nervy to a stop. Belle jumped out of the buggy and he followed her. In the shanty Dolly was stretched unconscious upon the dirty floor, her face pounded to a bloody pulp, her flaming hair streaming out behind her, a ragged quilt covering her body. At her head Bert and Shad were kneeling and at her feet Mr. Williams crouched.

Mr. Williams, the red helmet with "Police Chief" across its front pushed back on his white wool and tears streaming down the deep dark furrows of his face, raised his eyes to Dan Field. "Thank the good Lord you come, Mr. Doc."

Bert and Shad shuffled to their feet.

Bert said, "Know sumpin, Uncle Doc? I covered Dolly up. But I didn't do nothing else 'cause the time old Mr. Prosser died I heard you say he'd mighty likely of got well if his folks hadn't doctored him 'fore he come to."

Dan Field nodded. "You're right, Bert. Thank you."

He pulled his big gold watch out of his vest pocket, dropped on his knees beside Dolly, and, reaching under the quilt, took one of her small white wrists between his long fingers. The feeble pulse made him remember what a strong and lovely baby she had been, a little plump white rosebud. And Lillian Albright had looked like a little purple monkey.

Mr. Williams began to talk. "Mr. Doc, I'm skeered fer Gabe. I's mighty skeered fer Gabe. Red he's went clean crazy. But he ain't a big enough man hisself ter go after Gabe so he's making out a lie ter git folks on his side. Mr. Doc, he's making out Gabe raped Dolly. He's went over town ter git a crowd ter tar and feather Gabe. Mr. Doc, they might likely lynch Gabe. If'n Red makes them believe it was rape they sure will lynch Gabe. Mr. Doc, it wasn't rape. Dolly she's crazy mad about Gabe. My Gabe's a good boy. All my children's steady but Gabe he's the steadiest. Nothing was his fault. Dolly she jest wouldn't let him be. Dolly she——"

"Shh!" Dan Field cautioned. "She's coming out of it."

He was thinking, *Look not upon me, because I am black, because the sun has looked upon me: my mother's children were angry with me.* . . .

By the time Red Tatem had appeared on Broad Street, Rufe was on the way home and Sammy was walking toward Linden Street, between Mollie and Bertha, the pup under his arm.

Rufe was going home because he didn't know what else to do. Entering the house, he found the place a dither, Mama and Auntie Lou buzzing around arranging flowers and Nellie and Maggie rushing about straightening things. And in the kitchen, Rufe knew, great bowls of chicken were ready to be mixed into salad, pans and pans of biscuits waiting to be shoved into the oven, while the table was covered with huge frosted layer cakes, and out on the back porch the gallon freezers of ice cream stood already packed. This was how things always were the afternoon before one of Mama's parties. Stuff and nonsense, Rufe thought, all this fuss about an old party.

He said, "Hello, Mama and Auntie Lou."

"Hello, dear." Pris smiled across the top of a great bowl of asters.

Lou said, "Never in my life did I see anyone grow the way you do, Rufe Albright. Bert's going to be tall. . . ." She turned toward Pris. "Pris, those asters should be arranged with the darker ones clustered center. In Philadelphia they always arrange asters with the darker ones clustered center."

Rufe went on upstairs. "In Philadelphia they always arrange asters with the darker ones clustered center"; he sniffed. Stuff and nonsense again. What did Auntie Lou know about what "they" did in Philadelphia any more than Mama knew? If Auntie Lou had been born near Philadelphia, since Uncle Rufus married her she'd not been to Philadelphia any oftener than Mama had. But all she had to do to make Mama let her have her own way was say, "In Philadelphia they do so and so."

Passing Gramma Albright's room on the second floor, Rufe could hear her and Gramma Sargent talking. My God! he ejaculated silently. The grammas were upon the same subject he had heard them discussing directly after lunch. They didn't believe the Albrights and the Sargents should be introducing the principal of a public school and his wife to Willowspring society, no matter if their lineage appeared all right.

"I can't help feeling, Mrs. Sargent," Rufe heard Gramma Albright saying, "too many social barriers are being let down these days."

"I agree, Mrs. Albright," Gramma Sargent answered, "the young people of today are entirely too democratic."

"Of course," Gramma Albright continued, "George says both Professor and Mrs. Phelps are from really fine stock. But it's hard to understand how a man of any refinement would want to be principal of a public school."

"Still I suppose somebody must be principal."

Stuff and nonsense, Rufe thought once more; next they'll be fussing about Mama and Auntie Lou keeping only one hired girl. "But when we had charge of things there were always three and four girls," he mimicked the grandmothers, climbing the third-floor steps. In the playroom he could have some peace, he hoped. And damn the party! Why did Mama make him go? What was worse, she'd make him be nice to those big tubs, Margaret and Dorothy Taylor. And there'd be no relief because Laird Culver was so stuck on Margaret he'd be scared to open his mouth. Laird Culver! Rufe wrinkled his nose as if smelling something none too pleasant.

His nose still wrinkled, Rufe entered the playroom, sank into a chair, and stretched his long legs before him. All sorts of toys lay around, but Rufe's eyes rested darkly upon Lillian's dollhouse. The sight of it always offended him. It didn't look any more like a real house than a coop. He had once wanted to build Lillian a better one. But that was long ago, Rufe meditated. He didn't want to do anything any more—nothing. Mollie had been laughing when he passed the livery stable. . . . Tom and Ben and Jack had been laughing, talking to the country girls. One of the girls was holding her skirts up and you could see her leg.

Suddenly Rufe buried his face in his hands and began sobbing silently. Maybe, he choked to himself, if I prayed, God would help me. But why would God help me any more than He'd help all those people who went to hell? And some of them must have prayed. Oh, if Mama wouldn't make me go to that damn party.

Downstairs Pris was feeling happier than she had felt these many days. Of course, she was letting Lou have her own way about the decorations (it was so much easier to let Lou have her own way than to argue) but tonight would be another story. The new waltz she had discovered—everyone was sure to be mad about it. And she'd wear the blue crushed satin and after Dan arrived she'd play the new waltz. Then Miss Fisher would take charge of the music and she and Dan would dance. No one could dance like Dan, and this new waltz—well, its purpose was to interpret the rhythm of lilting lovely blue water. She and Dan would float on lilting lovely blue water.

And Rufe—Pris smiled—Rufe would have a good time even if he dreaded the evening. A party might be the very thing to bring the boy back to normal. Anyhow, Rufe would eventually come around all right, like Sammy. Why, Pris reflected, the change that had come over Sammy lately seemed almost a miracle. To pull him out of bed mornings once was a siege and to get Sammy in a bathtub a major operation. Now Sammy was up and into the tub before anyone else had stirred, emerging scrubbed until he fairly shone. To think I ever worried about Sammy, Pris concluded.

Sammy, however, walking between Mollie and Bertha, began wondering where Helen could be. "Where's Helen?"

"Helen's a Jew," Bertha informed.

Sammy nodded. "Everybody knows the Boyds are Jews. What if Helen is a Jew?"

"We're getting too big to play with Jews," Mollie explained. "It was all right when we were little but now we're growing up our folks won't let us play with a Jew."

"Balls!" Sammy ejaculated.

It was a livery-stable expression recently acquired which Sammy considered particularly forceful. And Mollie winced under the rebuke. She really loved Helen. Nobody could help loving Helen, she had told her parents. Yet this situation gave Mollie a certain amount of satisfaction. It made her feel important, this not being allowed to play with *someone*, like Lillian Albright and Priscilla Sargent weren't allowed to play with *anyone*.

Mollie hoped Sammy'd tell Rufe, let him know there were some people she was better than. If Rufe heard this maybe he wouldn't think he was so important—the way he'd dared maul her in that game, and the way he walked up and down before the house, too stuck up to look at her, let alone speak. Only lately Rufe hadn't been walking by the house. Mollie frowned; she did hate him, like she had told him she hated him.

Still it was funny, Mollie speculated, before the game she had wanted Rufe to grab her and hug her. Rufe was so tall and his shock of brown hair fell over his forehead in a peak and his light gray eyes made his long black lashes look longer and blacker than they really were. And before the game, looking at Rufe across the lot, she had thought, What if he grabs me and hugs me hard? Only once Rufe had her in his arms she had become frightened and struggled to be loose, and after she got away she'd told him she hated him. And she did hate him. Oh, Mollie did hope Sammy would tell Rufe she wasn't allowed to play with someone.

They'd reached the Reynard place, which was on Linden Street a half block beyond the new school. Sammy didn't stop. He was on his way to show Ginny Price the pup, the Price place being farther along on Linden. Ginny Price was seven years old and skinny and homely, with red hair and green eyes and freckles, and she cried if most people looked at her cross-eyed. The first day she'd been at Miss Fisher's school Ginny had hollered till Sammy gave her the sourball he'd been saving to suck during recess. But Sammy liked Ginny, because he couldn't help feeling sorry for her, he guessed.

Next to the Reynards' cottage stood the great brick Taylor mansion. Passing, Sammy caught a glimpse of Dorothy and Margaret through an upstairs window. Mama had invited them to the party tonight, and Laird Culver. Mama said she was having these young people to amuse Rufe. Sammy knew Rufe hated the whole idea. Rufe thought Margaret and Dorothy were big tubs and he didn't like Laird. Sammy wondered if Margaret and Dorothy and Laird hated the idea of the party like Rufe did.

Within the Taylor house Margaret and Dorothy were more excited than they'd ever been. The reception tonight was the first grown-up party at which their presence had been requested. All afternoon they'd been making up and changing their minds concerning what dresses to wear. Finally, after Dorothy had selected a pink ruffled mull, Margaret decided upon a red embroidered nainsook.

"It may not be as becoming as my blue mull," Margaret said, "but it makes me look much older than anything else I own. With my hair up, I really believe I'd pass for twenty in it. Don't you think, Dot?"

Dot nodded. "It does make you look terribly old, Meg, especially with your hair up. But what difference will it make tonight? Laird's only sixteen and Rufe's a mere child."

"Those striplings!" Meg sniffed. "You may have them both. It's not how I'm going to look at the reception that concerns me. After we're dressed you and I are going uptown before dark."

Dot gasped. "Meg, you don't mean you'd dare walk uptown if you've no errand, just to see him?"

Meg shrugged. "Why not? If a cat can look at a queen I can look at him. How often need I tell you, darling sister, dearest of sisters"—Meg now assumed the lingo employed by the characters in her favorite series of books—"that I know our paths lie far apart, our lips will never meet, perhaps we shall never even clasp each other's hand? But none other shall ever call me wife. And do not be distressed, darling precious little sister, my suffering is not unendurable."

The tears started in Dot's eyes, as they were wont to start each time Meg talked like this. And Dot knew what was expected of her.

"Darling sister, dearest of sisters," Dot said, also following the fictional pattern, "if I might bear it for you."

"No, no!" Meg cried. "That were far worse, far worse."

"Perhaps were I to read *that* part of the chapter to you once more it would bring comfort," Dot suggested.

Meg bowed pathetically. "Please, darling precious little sister, do read *that* part of the chapter to me once more. Hearing of another's strength always gives me a bit of succor."

From a nearby table Dot took the last volume of their favorite series—*Elsie's Widowhood*, by Martha Finley. And after fingering through the pages an instant she read:

"His features were convulsed with pain but his eyes wandered restlessly around the room as if in search of something. As Elsie drew near they fixed themselves upon her face, and his was lighted up with a faint smile.

" 'Darling precious little wife,' he murmured, drawing her down to him till their lips met in a long loving kiss, 'don't leave me for a moment. Nothing helps me to bear this agony like the sight of your sweet face.'

" 'Ah, beloved, if I might bear it for you!' She sighed, her eyes filling with tears, while her soft white hand was laid tenderly upon his brow.

" 'No, no!' he said, 'that were far worse, far worse!'

"Her tears began falling fast.

" 'Ah, do not be so distressed; it is not unendurable,' he hastened to say with a loving tender look and an effort to smile in the midst of his agony. 'And He, He is with me; the Lord my Saviour! I know that My Redeemer liveth and the sense of His love is very sweet, never so sweet before.'

" 'Thank God that it is so! Ah! He is——' "

"Dot," Meg interrupted suddenly, "we'd better start getting dressed. He usually goes over to the hotel from the office about six. If we slipped uptown just before dinner we'd be pretty sure to see him."

Uptown Ralph Pettigrew had forgotten the existence of Margaret Taylor. When he reached the street to find out what was going on, Red Tatem, followed by a group of muttering men, was entering the Grand Central Bar. Floyd Shires stood on the curb beside the hack.

Floyd Shires reminded others besides Ralph Pettigrew of a turtle. From his thick shoulders, rounded like a shell, his long thin neck protruded chinlessly to his jowls and his little round eyes were black, bright, and beady. Floyd had no teeth, either, and a piece of straw always stuck out of his mouth, upon which his gums would clamp at intervals. Whenever Floyd's gums clamped upon the piece of straw Pettigrew was reminded of a turtle snapping over a fly, and Pettigrew sometimes wondered if Floyd took the straw out of his mouth even when he visited the Widder Woman.

Approaching him, Pettigrew asked, "What's all the excitement, Floyd?"

Floyd batted his little round black beady turtle eyes and answered, his voice drawling, "Gabe Williams he raped Dolly Tatem."

"What!" Pettigrew ejaculated.

Floyd drawled on, "Red he's trying to get a mob to tar and feather the nigger. They'll mighty likely end by lynching him."

Rape, Pettigrew thought. Across his mind's eye flashed the picture of Dolly's white face turning whiter than ever and her hair like a living flame and her blue eyes shaded like purple pansies. He remembered how for a moment he had thought she was beautiful and had wondered if her body could be as white as her face.

Again Floyd began to talk, and at this instant his eyes reminded Pettigrew of a turtle's bent upon a fly, the instant before the catch.

"Yah, they'll sure end by lynching him," Floyd drawled. "After dark they'll get him. They'll string him up, but 'fore his ornery neck cracks they'll shoot his stinkin' hide full of holes. No nigger around this here town's gonna rape a white gal and not get what's a-comin'."

Was it rape? Ralph Pettigrew asked himself. Dolly had cried because Tom and Ben and Jack had fooled with her. Dolly had cried and said, "I know a fellow wants to marry me." No, it wasn't rape.

Poor little devil, Pettigrew thought, what chance did she ever have? Brought up as she was, living in niggertown, with an old bastard for a father and her mother running off with a tramp, and no white fellow ever thinking she was fit for anything except to handle. Poor little devil, Pettigrew thought again, and that poor big black dumb nigger. What chance did he ever have to hold out against that red hair and that white skin and those blue eyes? But they'll get him all right. They'll string him up all right, and before his black neck cracks they'll fill his poor big black dumb body full of lead. And Ralph Pettigrew remembered the day Old Man Meeker had escaped from his keepers and groped his blind way uptown and how the streets filled like magic and people laughed and pointed as Mr. Williams dragged him out of the bar.

Floyd's jaws clamped upon the straw. "And nobody'll ever know who done it, Ralph. Remember that nigger they lynched over to Pleasantburg? And nobody ever did find out who done it."

Ralph Pettigrew turned and went back upstairs to his office. Lynching or no lynching, court week was not far off and his desk was piled high with records still to be gone over. But all afternoon, every once in a while, Pettigrew couldn't help thinking about Gabe Williams. The nigger didn't have one chance in a million. Even if someone warned him and he took to the mountains, the mob'd run him down. And Floyd Shires was right: nobody would ever find out who was in the gang. The very members of the gang wouldn't be sure of each other. Only by rumor would it become known that at such and such a place at such and such a time a meeting might be held and after dark men would ride forth, their faces and bodies and horses covered by sheets of white cloth. Funny! Pettigrew couldn't help thinking every once in a while, all afternoon, how the smell of nigger blood makes killers of men, of men who are supposed to be civilized, men who love their wives and children and who go to church Sundays.

Around six o'clock Pettigrew went downstairs again and crossed to the livery stable, where Jake and Floyd and Fat were gathered.

"Anything new?" Pettigrew asked.

Jake shrugged and Floyd's jaws clamped on the straw.

Fat hawked and spat before he spoke. "Nothin' exciting. Red him went off stinkin' drunk. Dolly and Belle ain't come over town yet. Bet them ain't."

Dan Field, Bert Sargent on the seat beside him, drove up and stopped.

Chapter Eight

Having done everything possible to ease Dolly's suffering, Dan Field told Bert to come along, and the two of them left the shanty and got into the buggy.

When Nervy's feet were thudding again among the sunlight and the shadows and the swarming little Negroes Bert said, "Know sumpin, Uncle Doc? Shad says they really did lynch a colored gentleman over at Pleasantburg 'cause he raped a white lady. Know sumpin, Uncle Doc? Shad says they'll mighty likely lynch Gabe if Mr. Tatem makes them believe it was rape."

Dan Field nodded. "They mighty likely will lynch Gabe, Bert. That is, if they can catch him. But you and I are going to see to it that they don't catch him, I hope."

"How, Uncle Doc?"

"At the corner of Horsechestnut I want you to jump out and run to your uncle George's, fast as your legs will take you. Find Gabe and tell him I must see him right away across the far fields. And don't tell him anything else, Bert, except to hurry."

"What you going to do then, Uncle Doc?" Bert asked.

"Drive Gabe across the old mountain road to the Mount Pallas depot, where he can catch the evening train. By the time they discover he's gone Gabe will be miles away, I hope."

"Uncle Doc, who's 'they'?" Bert demanded.

Dan Field smiled. "Who 'they' are, my good fellow, is a matter of speculation."

"Is it the same 'they' Mama's always talking 'bout when she says in Philadelphia 'they' do sumpin?"

Dan Field chuckled. "Practically the same, Bert. Except one 'they' inhabits Philadelphia and the other 'they' resides in Willowspring. But all 'theys' are the same 'they,' one in spirit and——"

Bert interrupted, "Like the Father, Son, and Holy Ghost, Uncle Doc?"

Dan Field became serious. "Hardly, Bert. 'They' merely means certain people whose names we don't know, as we don't know who would lynch Gabe if he could be caught, so we say 'they.' "

When they reached the corner of Horsechestnut Street Bert jumped over a wheel and tore toward the Albrights'. Dan Field turned Nervy's head east, drove along Horsechestnut and through a lane which ended beyond the far fields. He felt reasonably sure no one would be around this spot to see Gabe meeting him and there was hardly a chance of an encounter on the old mountain road.

The old mountain road began a half mile beyond the far fields and ran east over a steep grade known as "the ridge." But the pike going east crossed the creek at the narrows bridge and finally passed right by the Mount Pallas depot where the old mountain road kept on through the woods and didn't reach the creek until it dipped to the ford which led to the depot. This pass over the ridge hadn't been a thoroughfare since the pioneer age. These days it was used only by lumber cutters and hunters, no mills had been operating for over a year, and no hunter was likely to be abroad at this season.

Pretty soon Dan Field saw Bert and Gabe hurrying across the far fields, Bert jogging to keep pace with Gabe's long strides.

Coming near, Gabe called, "What's all this 'bout, Mr. Doc? Bert says you wants to see me quick. It's got to be quick, Mr. Doc. My chores got to be done. I was jest fixing to do my milking."

Gabe and Bert came beside the buggy and Dan Field said, "Your chores must wait this evening, Gabe. Get in."

"Mr. Doc, I can't go nowheres. My chores——"

"Get in," Dan Field commanded.

Gabe hesitated and then climbed in beside Dan Field.

"See you later, Bert," Dan Field said.

Bert's face fell. "Can't I go 'long, Uncle Doc?"

"Not this time, I'm afraid, Bert."

Bert stood back. Dan Field clucked and turned Nervy's head toward another lane leading to the old mountain road.

Gabe frowned. "Mr. Doc, this here must be mighty important. Captain George he's going to work hisself to a lather if'n he gits home and my chores ain't done. Where you taking me to anyhows?"

"I'm taking you to Mount Pallas, Gabe."

"To Mount Pallas? What you taking me to Mount Pallas for?"

"Gabe," Dan Field went on, "this afternoon Red beat Dolly to a pulp and afterward went over town to get a mob to tar and feather you—or so he said. What he meant was to lynch you."

Dan Field heard Gabe suck in his breath.

"Lynch me!" Gabe's breath oozed out. "What'd anybody'd want to lynch me for?"

"Red's claiming you raped Dolly."

Gabe gasped, "Red's claiming I raped Dolly—I raped Dolly! As Jesus is my Saviour, Mr. Doc, it wasn't rape. Dolly she likes me. As Jesus is my Saviour, Dolly she——"

Suddenly Gabe grabbed the reins and yanked Nervy to a standstill. Dan Field turned toward him and saw Gabe's huge muscles writhing under his cotton shirt, the great tendons of his thick neck bulging out, and through the blue of Gabe's eyeballs fine rivers of blood ran.

"You ain't taking me to no Mount Pallas," he snarled. "You ain't taking me nowheres. I'm going back. Hear me? I'm going back. I don't care if'n they do lynch me. I'd be better off dead anyhows. But 'fore they ketch me to lynch I'll git Red. I'll pound him to a pulp like he done Dolly. 'Cept when I gits finished of Red he'll be dead."

Dan Field shrugged. "If you want to go back it's all right. If you want to kill Red that's all right too. No one would miss him much, least of all Dolly. But, Gabe, if you died suddenly Dolly would miss you. And if you go back nothing can save you. They'll get you as sure as God made sour apples. Don't you think Dolly has suffered enough without having to live, knowing you were lynched because of her?"

Gabe dropped the reins. Dan Field felt the big body slump. "I'll go 'long, Mr. Doc."

Presently they reached the old mountain road. It was narrow and hemmed by dark woods; the treetops often met over the pass, making the way gray. Loose stones rolled under Nervy's hoofs and the buggy creaked, bouncing up and down over ruts.

It was three miles across the ridge to Mount Pallas and for two of these three miles the silence was broken only by the rolling stones and creaking buggy and birds calling from the thickets.

Finally Gabe spoke. "Taking the hard road, ain't you, Mr. Doc?"

Dan Field nodded. "The pike wouldn't be safe. Someone might spot you."

"Why you doing this for me for, Mr. Doc?"

"Why wouldn't I do it for you, Gabe?"

Gabe sniffed. "I ain't nothing but a nigger. What's the good doing sumpin for a nigger?"

Dan Field shrugged. "You're black all right. But you know, Gabe, it wasn't God who imagined that men who have dark skins are to be looked down upon by those of fair complexion. That idea, you know, is merely one of the presumptuous conceptions of the white race. Know what I'm talking about, Gabe?"

Gabe nodded. "Mighty likely you's trying to tell me a black man's good as a white man. 'Cept it ain't true. Look at me, Mr. Doc. I always was steady. From the time I was a little bitta teeny boy I always was steady. Mr. Williams he always say all his children's steady but Gabe's the steadiest. I always worked hard. I don't drink or cuss, hardly ever. And I reads the Bible (Mr. Williams he made every last one his eleven children larn to read the Good Book). And I never whored, much. After I begin liking Dolly I never whored none. But what's I good for, Mr. Doc? Lynching, that's all I's good for."

Gabe stopped talking and Dan Field didn't say anything, and again the silence was broken only by the stones rolling under Nervy's hoofs and the buggy creaking as it bounced up and down over the ruts and birds calling from the thickets.

Again it was Gabe who began talking. "I knowed all along, Mr. Doc, no good could come to Dolly and me. She'd say, 'Don't you want to marry me, Gabe?' I'd tell her I'd jest lief be skinned alive if'n I could marry her. But it didn't seem right." He blew his nose. "And as Jesus is my Saviour, Mr. Doc, if'n I could of knowed Dolly'd ever start thinking 'bout the likes of me I'd never have went over that first night. But how could I have knowed, Mr. Doc?"

"You couldn't have known, Gabe."

Gabe nodded. "No, I couldn't have knowed. Belle she was

always off with a feller nights and after Red goes to bed Dolly'd set on the porch alone. I'd see her setting thar and I'd think how lonesome she looked and so . . ."

"And so, Gabe?" Dan Field said.

"And so one night I walks over. But you knows, Mr. Doc, 'fore that first night I always thought 'bout Dolly being jest a little bitta girl. I recollects good when she was jest a little bitta teeny baby. Her hair was that red and she had the cutest little round freckles on her nose. Mr. Doc, do you recollect them cute little round freckles Dolly had oncet on her nose?"

"Yes," Dan Field told Gabe, "I remember very well those cute little round freckles Dolly once had on her nose. And I remember the day she was born. After she was clean I picked her up and held her in one hand and she made me think of a little plump white rosebud."

From somewhere deep within Gabe a great sob arose.

"You knows how I feels, Mr. Doc. You knows all right. But thar ain't another white man on earth, least none I ever hears of, what could know. Maybe you're right, Mr. Doc, 'bout God thinking us colored folks is good as white. Mr. Williams he's pretty sure 'bout God feeling that way too. And Mr. Williams is mighty sure what God thinks is right. But sometimes I feels what God thinks ain't worth shucks, Mr. Doc. What difference kin it make what God thinks if white men's running things to suit theirselves?"

"Maybe things will be different someday, Gabe."

"Maybe someday, Mr. Doc, but not now."

You're right, Gabe, Dan Field thought, maybe someday but not now. Now ahead between the trees beyond the gray road Dan Field could see sunlight on the ford across the blue Juniata and over the creek the railroad track gleaming, and the depot beyond.

"I guess this is as far as I go, Gabe."

They both got out of the buggy. Dan Field took off his coat and pulled a roll of bills from a trousers pocket.

"Gabe," he said, "to be on the safe side you'd better wait here until the train comes. And don't get off until you reach Altoona." He handed Gabe his coat and the roll of bills. "You'll need these until you find work."

Dan Field followed the pike home to Willowspring. But crossing the ford, he heard Gabe calling.

"Mr. Doc," Gabe was calling, "I'll pay you back."

Jesus! I'm tired, Dan Field swore to himself. Jesus! I am tired.

Over the ford and the railroad track Nervy jogged along the pike. Every so often a buggy or wagon passed on the way to a farm. Across the covered bridge the shadows were lengthening in the evening's prelude. By the slaughterhouse Bert waited and Nervy stopped automatically, starting automatically once Bert was on the buggy seat.

"I guessed you'd come home by the pike, Uncle Doc," Bert said. "Is Gabe all right?"

Dan Field nodded. "I believe so, Bert. He's going to wait in the woods until train time."

"He'll be all right, Uncle Doc," Bert assured. "Know sumpin, Uncle Doc? Mr. Williams he sent Matt over to Uncle George's to tell Gabe to run off and to do Gabe's chores. I told Matt Gabe run off over to Kinton's Knob."

"To Kinton's Knob?" Dan Field inquired.

Bert nodded. "See, Uncle Doc, 'they' might get Matt and make him tell where Gabe's at. And if Matt tells 'they' Kinton's Knob it'll be all right. 'Cause Kinton's Knob's just where Gabe ain't, Uncle Doc."

Dan Field laughed. "You're right, Bert, Kinton's Knob's just where Gabe ain't. That was a smart idea, boy."

At the corner of Maple Street, Dan Field looked ahead along Broad. It seemed the same as on any other Saturday afternoon near suppertime, sunlight fading and shadows long, a few rigs and country people still lingering about, townspeople here and there, walking or loitering. But Dan Field drove on up Broad and, seeing Jake Smith, Floyd Shires, Ralph Pettigrew, and Fat Hubbard before the livery stable, he drew the rig along the curb.

"Anything new today?" he asked.

"Where you been at?" Fat demanded.

"Went over to Lutz yesterday noon, delivery," Dan Field answered. "Just got back."

Fat guffawed. "Ain't heard about Miss Gunther's latest novelty then?"

Dan Field shook his head. "No."

Fat bellowed, "When Miss Gunther come back from Philadelphia Thursday her brung a pair of women's ready-made drawers."

He roared and Jake Smith cackled but Floyd Shires's little round black beady turtle eyes darkened.

"I don't call it decent to be having women's ready-made drawers in a store," Floyd snapped. "If I catched any of my womenfolks looking at ready-made drawers there'd be trouble aplenty. Ready-made drawers and rape—what'll be going on next in this here town?"

"Rape?" Dan Field acted surprised.

Floyd nodded. "Rape. Gabe Williams raped Dolly Tatem."

Fat put in, "They's talk of lynching he tonight after dark, Doc."

"Think they'll catch him?" Dan Field asked. "He might take to the woods. Gabe knows the land around Kinton's Knob pretty well."

"Kinton's Knob?" Fat's tone seemed whetted.

Dan Field shrugged. "I'm not saying Gabe would make for Kinton's Knob. But he was mighty interested in Davy Jones's cave. I heard Gabe say once, no wonder that outlaw was never caught if he hid in that cave."

"Do tell!" Fat ejaculated.

Floyd's turtle eyes blinked. "What do you think, Doc? Think the nigger he ought to be lynched?"

Dan Field shrugged again. "You know what the Bible says, don't you? *Look not upon me, because I am black, because the sun has looked upon me: my mother's children were angry with me.* Good afternoon, gentlemen."

Dan Field smiled and chirped at Nervy.

"What's Doc quoting the Good Book for?" Jake inquired. "Doc he never goes inside a church and him and that Father Callahan's thick as thieves."

"A man don't have to go to church to know his Bible," Pettigrew spoke at last.

Fat nodded. "That's right, Ralph. A reverend I knowed oncet tells I a infidel named Ingersoll—Robert Ingersoll—knows the whole Good Book by heart. What's more, this reverend tells I all doctors is atheists or Catholics and if'n you see a doctor inside a Protestant church him's just there to get patients."

"I hears Doc quote out'n the Good Book before," Floyd drawled. "The time I be round to take Ed Lester's ma to the poorhouse. The old woman she says she ain't a-going to no poorhouse. Ed he drug her fur as the front porch, squealing like a stuck sow. But Ed he didn't like dragging her out'n the yard for fear the neighbors'd see. So the old woman she stands on the porch hollering and I be standing round wasting time."

Floyd hesitated and Ralph Pettigrew asked, "What about Doc, Floyd?"

"Wall," Floyd continued, "then Doc he come 'long the road and draws 'side the curb. He gets out'n the buggy and goes up on the porch and takes holt the old woman's hands. She stops squealing just like that"—Floyd snapped his fingers—"and Doc quotes out'n the Good Book. The part 'bout mansions in your Father's house. Recollect?"

Pettigrew quoted, " 'Let not your heart be troubled: . . . In my Father's house are many mansions: if it were not so, I would have told you. I go to prepare a place for you.' "

Floyd's jaws clamped upon the straw. "That's right. That be the one, Ralph. And after Doc quotes out'n the Good Book he says, 'Mrs. Lester, it don't matter where you live in this here world,' or sumpin like that. And by God! The old woman she goes right off and gets in the hack."

"I'll be damned!" Jake ejaculated.

Fat spat. "Doc's mighty queer in the head times. It might be him takes drugs. Did you ever take note of that white skin Doc's got and how him's hands shake? Yah, it might be Doc takes drugs."

"If he does take drugs," Ralph Pettigrew said evenly, "it might not be a bad idea if some other people followed suit."

"What you mean?" Fat demanded testily.

Pettigrew didn't answer. He was thinking, Kinton's Knob, hell! I bet Doc's got Gabe someplace safe. And oh, my God! I do hope he's got that poor big black dumb nigger someplace safe.

Pettigrew started toward the hotel when he heard Fat snicker, "Here comes the Taylor girls. Me's going to ask if'n them's seen Miss Gunther's latest novelty."

Pettigrew's right hand shot out and his iron fingers pressed upon Fat's butter neck.

"If you say one word to those girls," Pettigrew snarled, "I'll push my fingers through your God damn dirty windbag."

He let loose of Fat and when the girls passed Pettigrew stood between Fat and them. And he did not so much as cast a glance at Margaret Taylor.

Around the corner Bert asked, "Don't all women wear drawers, Uncle Doc?"

Dan Field smiled to himself but answered soberly, "I believe they do, Bert."

"Then what were Mr. Hubbard and Mr. Smith laughing at, Uncle Doc?"

"They were laughing because the drawers to which they referred were ready-made instead of homemade," Dan Field explained.

Bert shook his head. "How come ready-made drawers're funnier'n homemade drawers?"

"I honestly don't know," Dan Field told Bert.

"And, Uncle Doc," Bert went on, "Mr. Shires didn't laugh and he said ready-made drawers wasn't decent. Why did Mr. Shires say that, Uncle Doc?"

Dan Field smiled. "The reason Mr. Shires said that, Bert, is because Mr. Shires happens to be a gentleman of very little wit."

Bert pondered an instant. "Mr. Pettigrew didn't laugh either. How come Mr. Pettigrew didn't laugh, Uncle Doc?"

Dan Field smiled again. "The reason Mr. Pettigrew didn't laugh, Bert, is because Mr. Pettigrew happens to be a gentleman of quite some wit."

Bert nodded. "Yes, Mr. Pettigrew's smart all right. Know sumpin, Uncle Doc? Mr. Stoddard says Mr. Pettigrew'd been 'lected mayor of Willowspring long ago if Uncle George and Papa didn't have gold to buy votes."

"Did it ever occur to you, Bert," Dan Field asked, "that everything Lem Stoddard says might not be true?"

"It's true about Uncle George and Papa buying votes, all right," Bert informed. " 'Cause Ray Stoddard says so and Ray wouldn't lie. But know sumpin, Uncle Doc? Ray says it wouldn't of done no good if Mr. Pettigrew did get 'lected mayor. Ray says it'd take a mighty sight more'n Mr. Pettigrew getting 'lected mayor to make him the likes of Uncle George and Papa."

Dan Field laughed. "Are those Ray's own conclusions?"

"Sure they are. Ray's smart. He's smarter'n any the fellows round town 'cept me."

Dan Field patted Bert's sleek black head and looked down into the straightforward hazel eyes. "You are a smart boy, Bert. I don't know a smarter."

Bert's serious young brows came together. "Uncle Doc, maybe Ray Stoddard's smarter."

"I must have a talk with Ray one of these days."

Nervy stopped before Dan Field's place. Bert jumped from the buggy. After having wound the reins around the whip, Dan Field followed suit and Nervy moved toward the barn.

"Uncle Doc," Bert said, "is it true about Gabe being mighty interested in Davy Jones's cave? Or did you make that up so they'd think he really went to Kinton's Knob, like I told Matt?"

"I made that up, of course, Bert."

Bert's eyes widened. "Uncle Doc, you don't think Mr. Smith and Mr. Shires and Mr. Hubbard and Mr. Pettigrew is that 'they,' do you?"

Dan Field shrugged. "Hardly, Bert. It's just the way I explained. No one knows who 'they' are. I simply felt sure if the gentlemen gathered around the livery stable got the idea Gabe might be headed toward Kinton's Knob the news would spread."

"Mighty likely. But know sumpin, Uncle Doc? I don't think Mr. Pettigrew believed you."

Dan Field smiled. "You know sumpin, Bert? I am quite certain he didn't believe me. But unless I am greatly mistaken Mr. Pettigrew will keep his own counsel."

"You mean he won't tell, Uncle Doc?"

"Exactly."

Bert looked up at Dan Field. "When's Dolly going to have her baby?"

Dan Field looked down at Bert. "Is Dolly going to have a baby?"

"Sure she is," Bert informed. "You know how people get babies, Uncle Doc. You know even best-family people get babies the same way."

Dan Field concealed a smile. "I believe I do know, Bert. And now, boy, if I were you I'd run along home and stay home tonight. There may be trouble in Mudtown and you won't help matters by being among those present. You've done a good job today; let it go at that."

"All right, Uncle Doc. 'By."

" 'By."

Dan Field's eyes followed Bert's square little figure along the street and farther. Ray Stoddard, dragging his rickety wash-laden wagon, was passing the Albrights', while on the lawn Lillian and Alexander rolled their hoops. Wondering where Prissy could be, Dan Field glanced toward the Sargents'. Prissy was nowhere in sight but Gregory Beamer was entering the gate.

Suddenly, like a flash out of the blue, the Norway maples filled Dan Field's eyes. As if in a minute, he noted, the trees had become splashed with the resplendent autumnal crimson and gold —the Norway maples always turned first in the fall—which was no less glorious under the evening's gentle light.

Thank God for trees, Dan Field thought, and the end of day. Now for the golden bourbon and food and sleep and a dream of Pris. But, turning toward the gate, Dan Field saw George and Rufus nearing the corner and waited.

Chapter Nine

$\mathcal{B}$ERT REACHED HOME, opened the front door, and called but no one answered, and he remembered about the party tonight and guessed Mama and Maggie were over helping Auntie Pris and Nellie. He went upstairs and through his room to the back porch. On the porch stood a large chest where Lou stored old newspapers and in this chest under the newspapers, safe and sound from sight and smell, Bert kept his prize possessions. They were the "little real sharp knife" Dan Field had given him and currently the *corpus delicti* of a once blooming bullfrog, now pungently putrefied, practically skinned, and partially dissected.

Bert's purpose now was to complete the frog's disintegration. But, about to open the chest, his glance fell over the porch railing and on the ground below Bert saw Gregory Beamer kissing Prissy. Bert cautiously focused his ears, as well as his eyes.

Not long before, Prissy had come home from the Albrights', her little heart nearly breaking. All the whole afternoon Alexander had hardly said a word to her. It was Lillian this and Lillian that, until Prissy couldn't stand it any longer. At home she had run around back and fallen down upon the soft grass beside the kitchen porch. The tears rolled down her cheeks. Why, she had choked to herself, can't anybody like me best? Everybody likes Lillian best, Auntie Pris and Uncle George and Rufe and Sammy and now Alexander, and Mama likes Bert best and Bert and Papa doesn't like anybody best.

Presently Prissy became aware of footsteps approaching and, looking up through her tears, she saw Gregory Beamer stopping before her. For the first time Prissy noticed how beautiful Gregory was. He looks 'zactly like a picture of a angel, Prissy thought.

And suddenly Prissy's troubles rolled away, her thoughts as well as her eyes full of Gregory.

Gregory knelt beside her. "You're crying, Prissy."

Prissy rubbed her eyes. "No. No, I'm not crying, Gregory."

"You are, Prissy."

He leaned forward and Prissy felt his lips touch hers in a gentle fluttering kiss, like the brush of a butterfly wing. Then he leaned back and looked at her.

"Why—why—did you kiss me, Gregory?" Prissy stammered.

Gregory smiled. "Didn't you like it?"

Like it? Prissy meditated. Yes, she had liked it maybe more'n she'd ever liked anything else before. Her heart beat like a little hammer.

"Yes, I liked it. Yes, I did like it, Gregory," Prissy admitted. "How did you know I'd like it?"

Gregory cocked his golden head to one side. "There's plenty things you can tell 'out you knowing."

"Plenty things," Prissy repeated. "You mean other things 'side kissing?"

Gregory nodded. "Other things, Prissy."

"What?" Prissy demanded.

"Well"—Gregory cocked his golden head to the other side—"well, like you can tell before you've went how good water's going to feel if you go swimming bare. Ever go swimming bare, Prissy?"

Prissy gasped. "Course not. Boys go swimming—go swimming—well, go swimming like you said. But girls, even town girls, wouldn't dare."

"They do, Prissy," Gregory informed. "Lots of girls go swimming bare together. And I know a girl at Four Mile Run—her name's Marjorie, Marjorie Bowers—and she goes swimming bare with fellows."

"Oh, Gregory!" Prissy could hardly believe her ears.

"And Marjorie's older'n you are, Prissy," Gregory went on. "She's fourteen."

"But, but," Prissy was still gasping, "she didn't go swimming like you said with you, did she, Gregory?"

"No," Gregory had to admit, "she goes with big fellows, Ed Raub and Hank Burke and all them. But I seen her bare oncet." Gregory hesitated an instant but as Prissy seemed stricken speechless Gregory continued. "Me and Russ Armitage hid 'hind some trees when they was swimming and Marjorie clum out and stood on the bank bare."

Dan Field smiled, watching George and Rufus approach. The sight of the two of them walking along a street together, holding their haughty heads high, so like their fathers before them, amused him once more. Still, like their fathers, there was something fine about George and Rufus. George was nonchalant, inscrutable; Rufus was shrewd, calculating; both were pompous, unbending, yet either one would give his life or last cent to further a cause which he believed would benefit the village. Monarchs of all they surveyed perhaps, as some of the dissenters facetiously claimed, yet fashioned of the same sovereign substance as the Continental fathers—those astute aristocrats who, creating a government they believed to be "founded on the consent of the governed," vested the rule and the vote in the wealthy, working nevertheless for the good of the masses so far as their light carried.

George and Rufus had come beside him and Dan Field asked, "Hear the excitement uptown this afternoon?"

Rufus smiled faintly. "Do you mean Miss Gunther's latest novelty?"

George smiled faintly. "Lady Godiva probably wouldn't have caused such a flurry." George laughed. "And, Dan, you should have heard Chan Taylor. He was convulsed."

Dan Field smiled faintly. "Chan's always been a bit of a boy. But I'd forgotten the ready-made drawers. I was referring to the talk about Gabe Williams raping Dolly Tatem."

"Nothing to it," George expostulated. "Talk, that's all. The Tatem girl's scum of creation."

"Whether she's scum or not, George," Dan Field said, "a mob might be incited to lynch Gabe."

Rufus's black eyes under the sweeping lashes blazed behind the thick-lensed glasses. "They'd never dare do such a thing in Willowspring."

"Certainly they'd not dare even attempt such a thing here," George proclaimed.

Dan Field lifted an eyebrow. "'They' covers all the different kinds it takes to make a world. And Gabe has skipped town. I understand Mr. Williams sent Matt over to take his place, George."

George frowned and then shrugged. "Gabe has probably heard the report and is scared to death. It doesn't take much to scare a nigger, Dan. By tomorrow everything will have blown over."

"I hope you're right, George."

Rufus nodded. "Certainly he's right, Dan. Tomorrow all the excitement will be with last winter's snow."

They went along. Watching them go, Dan Field was thinking, Perhaps someday men will be able to penetrate the darkness beyond where their light carries now.

Hoping to God no one was waiting in the office, he started toward his front entrance.

Ackley threw the door open. "Mr. Doc, suh, when I goes uptown to do my ma'keting I heah Gabe Williams raped Dolly Tatem and they's going to lynch him. Am that correct, suh?"

Dan Field entered the hall. "So I hear, Ackley."

He went on into his parlor and, pouring himself a drink, sank into a chair.

Ackley had followed. "Mr. Doc, suh, when you all think they's going to lynch Gabe?"

Dan Field downed the drink and poured another. "After dark, I suppose."

"Aftah da'k!" Ackley grunted. "Humph! Down in Vi'ginny they nevah waits till aftah da'k, suh. And down Vi'ginny no poo' white trash'd be involved. The quality'd officiate. Yan-keys do have some triflin' ways shu' nuff."

Dan Field downed the second drink and poured a third. "Ackley, don't you worry about a thing. When your time comes to be lynched I'll see to it personally that the quality officiates and during broad daylight."

Ackley beamed. "Thank you, suh. By all means, suh." Suddenly an ashen mask spread across Ackley's black face. "Whawhat—wha' you mean? I ain't nevah going to be lynched."

Dan Field laughed.

An instant later Ackley's face had resumed its natural shade. "You all shu' nuff had me skeered foh a little old minute, suh."

In 1880 Ackley was somewhere around forty years old, a short, stocky, pompous Negro. But he had been no less short, stocky, and pompous at the age of twenty-seven when Dan Field brought him to Willowspring. Ackley's forebears through generations had served the house of Ackley. Not one of his "shu' nuff kin," he boasted, had ever been a field or barn hand. And during the first weeks in Willowspring Ackley had rebelled sullenly over having to look after the yard and stable besides the house. Yet it wasn't the extra work Ackley resented. Ackley hadn't a lazy hair in his head, but the pride of his house-servant forebears fell before these tasks. Dan Field had tried to explain the situation, saying times had changed and these days even white Virginians were laboring in fields and barns. Then one day Dan Field happened to remember Colonel Ackley's parting words to Thomas Jefferson Ackley.

"You black buzzard"—Dan Field loomed above Thomas Jefferson Ackley, employing the colonel's words—"if I catch you shirking any of your work I'll break every bone in your body. Understand?"

Ackley had understood all right. From that time on he found the same interest in yard and barn as in the house. Ackley's pomposity gave Dan Field no end of amusement—the airs he put on among Mudtown's white as well as colored population, and the way he seduced the wives of the other Negroes and refused to acknowledge any of his offspring.

The night Mrs. Stanwick brought forth the boy later christened Willie, Mr. Stanwick, his tone somewhat proud, had told Dan Field, "This young'un's Mr. Ackley's."

When he reached home Dan Field said, "Ackley, Martha Stanwick has an eleven-pound boy. Stanwick says the child's yours. What do you intend doing about it?"

Ackley had drawn himself up to his full five feet four. "What do I 'tend doing 'bout it, suh? What do a Vi'ginny gentleman evah do, suh, if a house wench produces? What do a Vi'ginny house niggah evah do, suh, if a field wench multiplies?"

There was also a nostalgia about many of Ackley's reminiscences, stories which had fallen like gentle cascades over generation after generation. Stories first told by gentlemen wearing white wigs and satin breeches and gleaned by slaves whose nostrils still remembered African air, stories about before and after the war.

"My fi'st gran'pappy away back, suh," Ackley would tell Dan

Field, "couldn't talk rightly. The fi'st Massa Ackley buy him off a ship in No'folk ha'boh." Or, "Foh the damn Yan-keys come, suh, we'd a hundah sixty slaves on the plantation but Old Massa'd not let none but my pappy tend him. Old Massa say, 'Jeff's wo'th moh'n all the othah niggahs rolled togethah.' " Or, "My pappy go off to the wah with Young Massa. Old Massa say to my pappy, 'Jeff, I's gonna have to make out with Little Jeff tending me 'cause if you's with youh Young Massa I'll know no God damn Yan-key'll cotch him.' " Or, "The damn Yan-keys didn't bu'n the house but they stomped the crops and took the stock. And aftah the wah we all neah sta'ved. Most the niggahs run off but I stayed, 'cause foh my pappy go he say, 'If you all don't look aftah Old Massa like I done, Little Jeff, when I git home from the wah I'll break every bone in youh body.' But Pappy and Young Massa nevah did come home." Or, "Old Massa fall off his ho'se away back and couldn't go to the wah. Reckon if Old Massa could have got to the wah we all'd licked the God damn Yan-keys shu' nuff."

The day he went to the Ackley plantation was one of Dan Field's poignant memories. After he'd bought the pillars the idea of the furniture occurred and he made inquiries.

"Try Colonel Ackley," an agent suggested. "There are no finer pieces in all Virginia and a little money would be a godsend. Young Ackley, their only child, was killed at Gettysburg. They're broken and the colonel's lame. . . ."

If the colonel (the title by courtesy, Dan Field suspected) were broken and lame, no evidence was apparent the afternoon he met Dan Field. He stood on his mansion's broad veranda tall and straight, his hair and beard and suit immaculately white.

"I have been given to unde'stand, suh"—the colonel's eyes, cold as blue steel, were on a level with Dan Field's—"that you are interested in the pu'chase of a few of my hei'looms. Any preliminary conve'sation is unnecessary. Step inside, suh."

"A minute if you please, sir," Dan Field said; "before we step inside I want you to know the reason I am interested in your heirlooms."

Then Dan Field had told the colonel about the night his regiment was marching through a plantation and he had seen the pillars, all that was left of the great house, standing straight and strong in the moonlight, and how they had seemed a monument to the South's dead truth.

"I returned to Virginia to find those pillars," Dan Field had concluded. "I wanted them before my house. And I hope to have the privilege of owning furniture capable of upholding their significance."

The blue of the colonel's eyes grew warm. "Suh, may I offah you my hand. You are the first Yankee gentleman I have evah had the honah to meet."

After Dan Field had selected enough pieces to fill his house Colonel Ackley said, "Unfortunately, suh, I am not in a position to offah hospitality. But with youh kind pe'mission, suh, I shall make you a gift."

He clapped his hands together and a short, stocky, pompous Negro appeared upon the scene.

"This, suh," Colonel Ackley continued, "is Thomas Jeffe'son Ackley. Befoh the wah gold couldn't have bought him. Today he is moh precious than gems. But he dese'ves a fah finah fate than I can provide. Take him No'th with you, suh. He, too, will uphold the pillahs' significance." He turned to the Negro. "Little Jeff, from this day fo'th you shall be called Ackley. This is youh new mastah." The colonel's tall figure loomed over the little Negro. "And, you black buzza'd, if I catch you shi'kin' any of youh wo'k I'll break every bone in youh body. Unde'stand?"

Ackley had understood all right. And he understood all right when Dan Field finally employed the colonel's words. Thence Ackley not only admired but respected his new master; at last Ackley felt at home.

"You shu' nuff had me skeered," Ackley was repeating. He snapped his fingers. "I fo'get. Mrs. Boyd and her little girl's in the office."

The foxes have holes, and the birds of the air have nests; but the Son of man hath not where to lay his head. Dan Field yawned, crawling to his feet.

Taking leave of Dan Field, George and Rufus immediately forgot Gabe Williams.

Rufus, his tongue in his cheek, said, "I've concluded, George, a telephone company is a venture worth considering."

"A telephone company!" George ejaculated testily.

But he saw Eddie Perkins, his little torch and ladder a part of him, lighting the lamp on the corner—Eddie, who was truly one with the landscape, like the mountains or the church steeples or the town clock or the blacksmith shop or the trees or the houses or the blue Juniata. It wasn't conceivable not to have Eddie going the rounds at twilight, George thought, and laughed.

"A telephone company," he repeated, laughing. "What about your arc lights?"

Rufus shrugged. "You know what about my arc lights. I had another letter from Charles Brush yesterday. There's a big demand for his dynamos since the Wabash street lighting. But it won't be long before my order's filled."

"No doubt," George agreed, "your toy will arrive eventually. But I'd have to see to believe the electric lighting of a whole city could prove practical. As I've mentioned on several occasions, employing arc lights in store windows, the way Wanamaker does, attracts considerable attention and might be worth the cost. But this idea of lighting whole towns by means of dynamos is merely a flash in a pan."

" 'There are more things in heaven and earth . . . than . . .' " Rufus began to quote.

George wasn't listening. They had reached the corner. The street lamp was burning, if hardly discernible in the afternoon light. And Eddie was starting off, the torch in one hand, the ladder under the opposite arm.

"Eddie," George called; he and Rufus stopped.

Eddie waited, raising the hand holding the torch to his cap respectfully. He was a grizzly little old man whose legs were stumpy like whittled lead pencils.

"Eddie," George continued, "what is your opinion concerning the modern idea of lighting towns by electricity?"

Eddie pursed his grizzly lips. "I'd hardly like to say, sir, about electricity—don't overly understand. They say it's like lightnin'. I'd hardly like to say, sir, but it seems to me monkeyin' with what's like lightnin' might be temptin' Providence. Seems to me, sir, might be best to let well enough alone."

George's blue eyes twinkled and his white teeth flashed. "I agree with you, Eddie. It's always best to let well enough alone."

Eddie raised the hand holding the torch to his cap once more before moving on.

Passing the corner, tongue in cheek again, Rufus said, "You and Eddie put one over on me, didn't you, Captain? Consider the telephone idea, nevertheless."

"I'll do nothing of the kind," George insisted. "Great heavens! Rufus, don't you remember the gadget at the Centennial Exposition? Buzz—buzz—buzz . . ."

Rufus didn't answer; from long experience he knew just how far to go with George when introducing a new project.

They'd reached the Albright gate. Lillian and Alexander Jennings played on the lawn (Rufus wondered where Prissy could be) and Pris, Lou, and Gramma Sargent stood outside the front door. Pris waved and Lou and Gramma Sargent came down the porch steps, along the walk.

Rufus's eyes followed Lou, Lou with her tiny rounding figure, her tiny filling bosom. Tonight, Rufus was thinking, she will wear a gown cut low and the crease between her breasts will show. Other men will see and hold her in their arms and dance but they will mean no more to her than I.

He said, "Good evening, Lou and Ma."

They spoke to him and George.

George nodded. "All goes well, I hope, ladies." He turned to Rufus. "I'm expecting you tonight in time to assist entertaining the reverends and their fraus. Don't leave all the hospitable duties to me. This is also your affair, don't forget."

Whenever the Albrights or the Sargents gave one of their big parties the custom was to entertain the clergy and their wives from eight until ten and the socialites from ten thereon. But no matter how Pris and Lou strained, it was an effort to amuse without cards or dancing, so George and Rufus were expected to pull an oar—a duty which they both despised.

"All right," Rufus told George, "I'll be over about eight."

"*At* eight," George emphasized.

Rufus nodded, moving along between Lou and Gramma Sargent.

"Where's Prissy?" he asked.

"Probably at home," Lou answered abstractedly. "Truly, Rufus, I've never seen lovelier flower arrangements in the Albright house."

"I'm glad you're pleased, my dear."

Gramma Sargent shook her head. "Of course, Rufus, if you

say it's all right, it must be all right. But Mrs. Albright and I don't feel that we should condone such an occasion."

"Ma," Rufus said, "I've told you, and George has tried to make Ma Albright understand, that both Professor and Mrs. Phelps are of splendid stock."

"Perhaps, perhaps."

"Ma, Professor Phelps's ancestors came over on the *Mayflower* and Mrs. Phelps is a descendant of John and Priscilla Alden."

Gramma Sargent sniffed. "Mr. Sargent used to say, 'There is only one group which outnumbers the *Mayflower* clan and that is the Alden tribe.'"

Rufus smiled. "Pa was a bit of a wit, Ma."

"Wit or not, who were John and Priscilla Alden? If a poem hadn't been written who'd care to claim them as ancestors?"

Rufus smiled again. "But the poem was written, Ma, so stop your worrying."

"I'm not worrying," Gramma Sargent insisted. "And I know the affair will be lovely. Pris and Lou always entertain beautifully, even if Mrs. Albright and *I* can't imagine how it's done with one servant in the house. You remember, Rufus, when Mrs. Albright and I managed the houses we never kept less than three or four girls."

"Of course, Ma," Lou put in, "and Pris and I have often kept three and four girls. But Maggie and Nellie can do more work than any three or four we ever had. You know, Ma, how often I've explained the situation. You remember the time I had that second maid and Maggie said she just got under her feet."

Gramma Sargent nodded. "I suppose you're right, Lou. I can't help thinking, though, that if we'd several girls one might be trained to say, 'Dinner is served,' and not 'Supper's ready.'"

Bert heard the front door open and the voices in the lower hall.

He leaned over the porch railing, calling softly, "Prissy, Mama and Papa's home."

Prissy heard Bert's warning but she got to her feet slowly, as if recalled from a trance. Then in an instant the situation's enormity struck her and she flew around front.

Gregory Beamer raised his eyes. "Are you going to tell, Bert?"

Bert shook his head. "No."

"Why not?"

"Why would I tell?"

"I ain't s'posed to play with Prissy and you."

"Don't pay no 'tention," Bert instructed. "Just don't let Mama or Maggie or Papa catch you."

"I won't," Gregory promised. "Do you know why I ain't s'posed to play with Prissy and you?"

"I know all right."

"Why?"

Bert waved a hand. "Don't pay no 'tention, I told you."

Bert saw Maggie coming around the house and dived under the railing.

"I heard you talking, Gregory," Maggie said. "Who was you talking to?"

"To myself," Gregory lied.

George mounted his porch steps and kissed Pris upon the cheek. It was good to have her waiting there, he felt. No matter how harrying a day might be, when Pris greeted him George felt beatified. The sight and touch of Pris had never bedizened George's senses, he had never felt a lust—only a need—a need, like the need a man has for air or water or sleep. My Pris, he thought now, and he kissed her upon the lips gently, his own lips lingering but an instant, according to their habit.

Pris was saying, "George, Gabe was ill and left this afternoon without telling me. About five-thirty his brother Matt came and said Gabe was 'took sick' and he'd come to do the chores."

George nodded. "I know. Nothing really serious wrong, though. Gabe will be back shortly." His glance fell back to where Lillian and Alexander were playing. "It seems to me the Jennings boy is spending entirely too much time around here lately."

Pris smiled. "George, they're just babies. Besides, Alexander's like a little girl himself. And don't forget his father was our pastor." Her eyes rested on Lillian. "Isn't she lovely, George?"

George smiled. "She looks exactly like you did."

Pris saw Sammy coming through the gate. "And Sammy is exactly like you were, George."

"Where's Rufe?" George asked.

Pris shook her head. "Probably upstairs. He came home early. George, you know I think Rufe's growing too fast. He hasn't been a bit like himself lately."

George shrugged. "Nonsense. Rufe's all right." He went on into the house, calling over a shoulder, "Hope there's plenty of hot water."

As if there isn't always enough hot water for him anyhow, Pris thought, and looked at Sammy crossing the yard. Pris didn't see, but Sammy, passing Alexander and Lillian, fixed his round blue eyes on Alexander and clinched a fist. Alexander winced and Lillian flushed miserably. Smiling over Alexander's discomfiture, Sammy hurdled the steps. Pris thought, How beautiful he is. Sammy, she thought, with his yellow curls and his round blue eyes and smiles; Sammy who looks just like George.

"Why are you smiling, darling?" Pris asked.

Sammy blinked his round blue eyes. "Smiling? Was I smiling, Mama? Oh, I smile lots, Mama."

He darted past her.

Sammy not only looks exactly like George, Pris speculated, he is exactly like George. Neither one would ever admit any secrets but no one could ever find out what they really thought. And Lillian was like George in one way, too, keeping her thoughts to herself. Yet Lillian was affectionate where Sammy from babyhood had actually seemed to resent attention. Pris sighed, and now Rufe—Rufe who used to bring her all his little joys and sorrows—had drawn in unto himself. Sometimes I feel, Pris told herself, that I know no more about my own family than I do about strangers. Then suddenly it seemed to Pris that this life she was leading, this man who was her husband, these children she had borne, were all dreams, not realities. And out of the whole wide world Dan alone seemed real, Dan whose long thin white twitching strong merciful hands had lifted her from the valley of the shadow of death.

Why am I thinking about Dan so much lately? she questioned herself. Of course I have always thought about Dan, only lately he is in my mind constantly. Dan, Pris smiled, Dan—tonight we will float on lilting lovely blue water. The smile faded; a fear had seized her. What if Dan should forget the reception? He had forgotten about Peggy Martin's birthday party last year.

Her heart in her throat, Pris went into the house, entered the sitting room, and sat down at the desk.

In the office Dan Field found Vera and Helen Boyd waiting, sitting stiffly upon two chairs.

He smiled, seating himself. "You're two of the rosiest-looking prospects I ever beheld. Which one is the patient?"

Neither Vera nor Helen answered his smile.

Helen spoke soberly. "I'm supposed to be the patient, Dr. Field, but there's nothing the matter with me. I told my mother so."

Vera, her voice also sober, said, "Perhaps I am unduly alarmed, Dr. Field. Helen isn't a bit like herself, though. She's always been one to be off playing with the other girls and these last few days she won't go near any of her friends."

"Honestly, I'm not sick," Helen insisted. "I—I just don't want to go near any of my—my fr-friends."

Dan Field heard Helen's voice break and he saw the blood mount in her little thin brown cheeks. He knew where the trouble lay all right. No, my child, you're not sick, he thought, at least your body is sound. And you know it, Vera. But you are afraid to face the truth so you are hoping without hope, trying to make yourself believe it is Helen's flesh which is ill. *And they spit upon him, and took the reed, and smote him on the head.*

He smiled again, however. "We'll see, Helen. Stick out your tongue."

He looked down her throat, took her temperature, counted her pulse. Presently he leaned back in his chair. Vera was certainly a fine-looking woman, with her black curls and big brown eyes and dainty figure. And what a lovely child Helen is, he thought, with her soft brown hair and her brown eyes wide and gentle as a little fawn's.

"Vera," he lied, "all Helen's trouble—if you can call it a trouble—is boredom. Helen's an unusually thoughtful girl and the time has come when she no longer finds children of her own age congenial. Isn't that right, Helen?"

Helen's face flamed. "What's the use of all this pretending? You know the truth, Dr. Field. Everybody knows the truth.

I didn't want to tell my mother because I knew how she'd feel. But she must know someday so it might as well be now." Helen's eyes looked straight into Vera's. "Mother, it's not that I don't want to go near my friends. It's—it's my—my friends don't want me any more."

Vera's face didn't move a muscle and her voice was even. "Thank you, Dr. Field. I'm sorry we've taken your time about nothing. Come, Helen."

They started to their feet but Dan Field waved his hand. "Just a minute. I'm the doctor, you know. And the case hasn't been dismissed. Helen, I'd like to tell you a story. May I?"

Vera and Helen settled back and Helen said, "Of course, Dr. Field, if you want to."

"Once upon a time," Dan Field began, "there was a young man we shall call John, who happened to fall off a high mountain peak and by chance landed unharmed in a valley far below. This valley was entirely surrounded by unsurmountable cliffs and had no access whatsoever to the outside world. However, there were beautiful villages and cities and the inhabitants seemed to John quite like the people in the outside world. But John soon discovered that every man, woman, and child throughout the entire valley had been born without ears."

"Without ears, Dr. Field?" Helen put in.

Dan Field nodded. "Without ears, Helen. Birds sang and trees rustled and brooks gurgled and children laughed (because the deaf do laugh and cry, you know), but not a single soul had ever heard a solitary sound until John arrived. Of course, immediately everyone noticed the queer little flaps on John's head but they were friendly folks and overlooked these peculiarities. And before very long John had learned their sign language and was accepted as one of them. Then John fell in love with a beautiful young girl and the beautiful young girl fell in love with John."

Dan Field hesitated an instant and Helen asked, "Did John and the beautiful young girl get married, Dr. Field?"

"They became engaged," Dan Field continued, "and they were very, very happy until one day John told his girl, by means of the sign language, how he wished she might hear. 'Hear!' she exclaimed. 'What do you mean by "hear"?' So John explained how birds sing and trees rustle and brooks gurgle. And he told his girl about pianos and violins and cellos and flutes and tunes, and about the sweetest music, the laughter of children. And how do you think John's girl felt, Helen?"

Helen sighed. "Sad, I suppose, because she wasn't able to hear the beautiful sounds."

Dan Field shook his head. "No, Helen, she wasn't sad. She was afraid."

"Afraid!" Helen echoed. "What was she afraid of, Dr. Field?"

"She was afraid because she believed John was cursed rather than blessed. It has been said, evil is what we cannot understand. Because the girl couldn't comprehend sound she was convinced that to hear was to sin. So she told John unless he destroyed his hearing she would never marry him."

"What did John do, Dr. Field?" Helen demanded.

Dan Field lifted a finger. "Wait! John had two courses. First, he could deafen himself, marry the girl, and become one with the earless people. Or, secondly, he could retain his hearing, lose the girl, and become an outcast. Which course do you think John chose, Helen?"

Helen shook her head thoughtfully. "I don't know, Dr. Field. John would feel awfully bad about losing his girl and becoming an outcast but he'd feel awfully bad about losing his hearing. What did he do?"

"John kept his hearing. He felt to destroy this gift God gave him would be a denial of truth, for no one could believe a man willing to destroy a blessing. Of course at first John was terribly lonely but presently he found happiness. His soul found peace in the knowledge that he had done the right thing. Every time John heard a bird sing or a tree rustle or a brook gurgle or a child laugh he thought, This gift God has seen fit to bestow upon me is more blessed than any benefit which earless mortals could possibly bestow."

Dan Field finished and Helen asked, "Why did you want to tell me the story, Dr. Field? I—I don't think I've ever betrayed any trust and I've certainly no blessing other girls don't have."

"You certainly haven't ever betrayed any trust, Helen," Dan Field said, "and what's more, you never will. But your heritage— the people of God, Israel, Bethlehem—is a blessing you possess no other girl here can claim. Why, Helen, no matter what the fate of the Jewish race may be, their history is written not only across the face of earth but over heaven, and not to be proud of these records would be a denial of truth more witless than the destruction of John's hearing. What's more, Helen, not another little girl in town has the advantage of parents with such exceptional musical ability. You must have talent too. Don't you, Helen?"

Vera spoke at last. "Yes, she does, Dr. Field. Truly, before Helen was five years old she could play the piano. And if I do say so myself, I believe Helen has real talent."

Dan Field clapped his hands together. "There you are, Miss Helen. What other little girl in town could play the piano before she was five years old? Not one. You may become a great musician. Mozart could play pieces before he was five years old. How'd you like to be a lady Mozart?"

Helen nodded. "I'd be willing to work my fingers off if I might become a great musician. And if I had something like that to work for I might not mind about the other girls. But, Dr. Field, you know it's a—a shock when you've had friends all your life and then all of a sudden they—they——"

"I know, my child. But, Helen, don't think your race and you alone are martyred. Long before Christ was born the Greek philosopher Socrates was forced to drink poison. In fact, Helen, the majority of those whose efforts have benefited humanity have been persecuted. Schubert breathed his last in a wretched garret. Milton, the poet, was blind. Through twenty years Bizet struggled to have *Carmen* recognized and died before the opera was ever produced." Dan Field shrugged. "One could go on indefinitely citing such instances. Helen, the point is, no matter what genius suffers there is joy in creation, accomplishment. It may be some divine power directing the other girls, making them not play with you, so that you will have more time to contemplate music."

Helen smiled faintly. "If I believed that I might not mind. If I really knew I had a gift, like John knew, being lonely wouldn't matter. I'd not care how the other girls acted."

"Good!" Dan Field ejaculated and turned toward Vera. "Vera, other mothers have endured worse. During my student days a woman brought the corpse of a tiny girl to the morgue. She offered to sell it for two dollars. The tears were streaming down her face. We asked if she had to sell the little body. She said she did. Her husband was dead, she'd no money to bury the child, and she'd four other children starving, she said. 'After all, this little one can suffer no longer and the others are starving,' she finished. Medical students are not sentimental but this night we got together and found enough money to bury the child and give the woman fifty dollars besides."

"Did the mother and the four other children get along all right afterward, Dr. Field?" Helen asked.

"We never heard from them again, Helen." He chuckled. "The story was simply to cheer up your mother. Often the best way to shake a person's blues is to let them know others are worse off. Vera, you've plenty to make you happy—a devoted and talented husband, a lovely and talented little girl. All the years of your life aren't too many to devote to the development of Helen's talent."

Vera smiled faintly. "You're right, Dr. Field, such a story does make one appreciate blessings. I know I've plenty to make me happy. And thank you for all the time you've given us when— well, when Helen's really all right."

Dan Field smiled broadly. "I enjoy talking to you two. I wish you'd invite me down some evening and let me hear Eli and Helen play and you sing."

"We'd love to have you any time, Dr. Field," Vera said, she and Helen both smiling broadly, too, at last.

Dan Field asked, "Helen, do you know Chopin's Opus 48 in C minor?"

"Yes, yes, Dr. Field," Helen cried. "Do you like it?"

"Like it! I call it *the* nocturne because by comparison another was never worth considering."

Vera laughed. "*The* nocturne. Oh, Dr. Field, that is rare. I must remember to tell Eli."

They left. Dan Field returned to the parlor and poured himself another drink. The evening train whistled at the narrows.

He raised his glass and whispered, "Good luck, Gabe, good luck, you poor big kind honest blackamoor. Good luck, Vera and Eli, and good luck, Helen, you lovely little Jewish girl with wide and gentle eyes."

He thought, I'm dead upon my feet, and sank into a chair. And Dolly, he meditated, Dolly whose mother had run off with a tramp. Her belly flabby and her breasts sagging from carrying and suckling thirteen children, her face lined from constant worry and her shoulders stooped from ceaseless labor, with the smell of age creeping over her, Daisy Tatem had eloped with a tramp.

Dan Field had encountered the tramp a few days before he and Daisy started along the railroad tracks, the five youngest children along, Daisy carrying the baby, the tramp holding the next smallest on a shoulder, and the other three trudging behind, none of them ever to be seen or heard from again.

One afternoon, driving over Limestone Avenue, Dan Field had noticed the tramp sitting on Mr. Williams's steps, orating to an audience consisting of Mr. Williams and Ray Stoddard. Dan Field had heard about the tramp and his queer talk and he drove beside the steps and stopped Nervy. Mr. Williams nodded and spoke politely but the tramp seemed oblivious of Dan Field's arrival and kept right on talking.

The tramp was a man of indeterminate age, tall and thin and dark. Everything about him was thin and dark; clothes, face, hair, beard, hands—all were thin and dark. And his thin dark eyes held the burning, shifting gleam which sometimes marks a genius and more often brands a madman, but again bespeaks a combination of both genius and madman.

"There is nothing mysterious about eternity to me," the tramp was saying, his voice also thin and dark. "And after I've explained there should be nothing mysterious about it to you. See, in the universe there are two kinds of time, earth time and space time. Now on earth, time flows only one way; it goes and as it only goes it must end. But in space, time flows two ways; it ebbs but it rises again, like the ebb and rise of the sea; hence even as it goes it returns, so there can never be an end to it. Understand?"

Mr. Williams scratched his white wool thoughtfully. "Can't hardly say as how I do understand."

"It's perfectly simple," the tramp continued. "Like in this world life must end because it is regulated by earth time, which ends, but in infinity life can't end because it is regulated by space time, which never ends. But someday men will be able to reckon earth's time by space's tide of time and eternity will be made clear as the nose on your face."

"And jest how's men going ter do all that?" Mr. Williams asked.

"By numbers."

"By numbers?"

The tramp nodded. "Certainly, by numbers. See, today any-one who knows enough about numbers can measure the tide of the sea and someday enough will be known about numbers to measure the tide of time."

Mr. Williams scratched his white wool again thoughtfully. "I can't hardly think as how God'd expect us ter larn nuff 'bout numbers ter measure—what is it now?"

"The tide of time."

"Yeh, the tide of time. Wall, as I was saying, I can't hardly think as how God'd expect us ter larn nuff 'bout numbers ter measure the tide of time jest so eternity'd be clear as the nose on yer face. Seems ter me like it's a mighty sight easier ter read 'bout eternity in the Good Book and take God's word fer it."

The shifting gleam in the tramp's eyes dilated. "That is where you are mistaken. Only by numbers can anything be proven. Why, anybody who knows a half about numbers can find out anything he wants to know in the world, like how far it is around the world, where the North Pole is at, how many miles to the stars, or where a ship still in the middle of the ocean will land. And if you could know enough about numbers it would be as easy to measure the depths of a soul as to weigh the pounds of a body."

"How yer come ter know all this?" Mr. Williams demanded.

The tramp smiled, a thin dark smile. "My father was a hunch-back and my mother was a midget, just three feet eight inches tall. But I am not the Wandering Jew."

Mr. Williams nodded. "I see, I see, yer father was a hunch-back and yer mother was a midget, jest three feet eight inches tall. But yer ain't the Wandering Jew. Who is this here Wan-dering Jew yer ain't?"

The tramp ignored Mr. Williams's question and for the first time looked directly at Dan Field. "And who might you be?"

Dan Field smiled. "I might be but I'm not the Wandering Jew either."

"Ah, so you have heard of him too," the tramp went on. "By any chance have you ever happened to meet him?"

"I'm afraid I haven't had that privilege," Dan Field had to admit. "By any chance have you ever happened to meet him?"

The tramp's thin dark eyes narrowed reflectively. "I am not certain. I met a Jew on the island of Madagascar——"

"Madagascar," Dan Field interrupted. "Why, Madagascar's off the eastern coast of Africa."

The tramp lifted an eyebrow. "Certainly it's off the eastern coast of Africa. Where else would Madagascar be? And what a spot! The harbor's full of giant man-eating turtles—two tons is a baby—and no small boat's safe. Their shells will up under a smack and over she goes and the next instant the water'll be running red. I saw more than one man eaten alive by turtles. And man-eating dogs cover the islands. Do you know wild dogs are the fiercest animals on earth?"

Dan Field nodded. "I've read something to that effect. What about the Wandering Jew?"

"I didn't say he was the Wandering Jew," the tramp contradicted. "I told you, I am not certain. This man was a slave trader on Madagascar. There were no white women on the island and during the time I was there just four other white men—the Jew, two Frenchmen, and a Portuguese—all four slave traders. The Portuguese had a native wife. He'd really married her, took her aboard a ship and had the skipper perform the ceremony. Her face was sour as a baboon's ass and the Portuguese made her keep her body covered but her arms and legs were straight and slim like ebony arrows. Well, anyhow, the Jew and the other three men went out in the bush and rounded up niggers, men, women, and children (the natives didn't have any firearms, so it was easy), and once a month a ship came along and took the catch to Zanzibar, where there's a market. It's the biggest slave market in the world. You can smell the stench a mile off shore, if the wind's blowing right."

Dan Field nodded. "Very interesting. But what made you think this certain slave trader might be the Wandering Jew?"

The tramp shrugged. "That's the point. I said I didn't know if he was or if he wasn't the Wandering Jew."

Dan Field concealed a smile and looked at Ray Stoddard. Ray wasn't more than seven but his alert eyes were fixed upon the tramp as if hypnotized.

Mr. Williams had begun pondering aloud, "His father was a hunchback and his mother was a midget, jest three feet eight inches tall, and he ain't the Wandering Jew. His father was a ——"

The tramp ignored Ray's eyes and Mr. Williams's words. "Of course," he addressed Dan Field again, "there is no doubt about the existence of the Wandering Jew. You heard what I said about life in infinity being immortal because it is regulated by space time, which is eternal. Well, I'll tell you another thing: any time the Deity so chooses He can make a human being abide by space time instead of earth time, thus making him immortal. As a matter of fact the reason I said I am not the Wandering Jew is because my life is also regulated by space time."

What the tramp had seen in Daisy and what Daisy had seen in a crazy tramp no one around Mudtown could understand. But Dan Field realized what Daisy had seen in the tramp—release, new horizons. He could hear the tramp's thin dark voice saying words which entered Daisy's veins, making their meager white fluid rich red blood. Yet what the tramp had seen in Daisy—mad though he might be—to make him take her, as well as five children, along was another thing. Now Dan Field thought, The love of a man passes all understanding.

The evening train whistled again before the station and across Dan Field's mind's eye flashed a picture of the tramp, Daisy, and the five children moving along the track on their way to— infinity, no doubt; he smiled.

But your theories may possess more wisdom than madness, tramp, he thought and not for the first time. Today the mind of man was comprehending forces which never had been more than nibbled upon before. And schools were taking up the cry. At the new Johns Hopkins University in Baltimore certain professors were trying to extract a compound science for youth to carry on—an interrelated philosophic and physical truth. Someday it might be proven that what man thinks and feels and is and will be are ruled by some law as exact as the mathematical formulae which explain the system of the orbits. If I'd a whit of ambition, Dan Field told himself, I'd go to Baltimore and find out what those fellows at Johns Hopkins are doing. I could catch the morning train; Brown Walsh is always glad enough to take over my practice and earn an extra few dollars.

Ackley entered the room. "How soon you all gonna be ready foh dinnah, suh?"

Dan Field poured another drink. "About fifteen minutes, I guess."

Ackley snapped his fingers. "I forget, suh. Matt Williams bring—say, Mr. Doc, Matt he say Gabe run off ovah to Kinton's Knob."

Dan Field mentally patted Bert on the back. Smart little monkey, he thought; without his suggestion it wouldn't have occurred to me that Matt mightn't keep his mouth shut.

He said, "Matt probably knows what he's talking about. What did he bring?"

"Yes suh." Ackley nodded. "I's coming to that. Matt he bring a lettah. I don't know who it's from. Matt he didn't say, suh, and I nevah opens youh mail."

Dan Field nodded. "I must say, Ackley, I appreciate your delicacy no end. Where is the letter?"

Ackley thrust a hand into a pocket and handed over the letter. "Thar you am, suh. I'll announce dinnah in fifteen minutes, suh."

He left and Dan Field opened the note. Seeing the handwriting, he thought, Pris, and read:

DAN:
I'm in fear and trembling that you might forget the reception tonight. . . .

Jesus! he swore to himself. I had completely forgotten the damn thing. He frowned slightly as again the events of the last twenty-four hours flashed across his mind.

And today, he meditated, the preachers' wives have been trying to brighten up their old shabby best dresses and have been brushing and pressing the preachers' old shabby best suits. Poor little Minnie Jennings has been fixing over the dowdy thing she has worn to every big Albright and Sargent party these last ten years. And tonight promptly at eight they will all enter the Albrights' to meet the new principal and his wife.

Pris and Lou, looking like fashion plates, the two grandmothers, haughty as reigning queens, and George and Rufus in custom-made tails (their breaths colored by George's twenty-year-old rye sipped before the early guests arrive), will all, despite the best of intentions, make everyone uncomfortable. The preachers, who are supposed to help the Albrights and the Sargents save their immortal souls, and the preachers' wives and Minnie Jennings will become conscious of the shabbiness of their own clothes and aware of the aridity of the lots they have chosen.

But after their bellies have been stuffed with chicken salad and rolls and ice cream and cake the preachers and their wives and Minnie Jennings will feel brighter and, taking leave, they'll tell the Albrights and Sargents what a wonderful time they've had and believe they're telling the gospel truth.

Then the best families will begin to arrive—Chan and Madge Taylor, Hart and Peggy Martin, Billy and Virginia Price (what a recruit the world's oldest profession lost when Virg, with her pink hair and transparent skin, had been born an aristocrat), and the Berkleys and the rest.

Dan Field yawned. And after a few winks of sleep I'll drop by. Miss Fisher will be playing the piano, her phenomenal face wearing a tortured expression (Miss Fisher disapproved of cards and dancing and simply played at the Albright and Sargent parties because to refuse might offend). But the dancing would be going on as the older crowd played whist in the sitting room.

Dan Field's eyes dropped to the note again.

. . . I have discovered the most beautiful waltz. Its purpose is to interpret lilting lovely blue water. It's called "The Blue Danube." . . .

"The Blue Danube," Dan Field repeated to himself. He remembered the Danube, Vienna, Paris, Rome. He'd known them all before he met Pris. He had been a boy then but he had dreamed of bringing the woman he would someday love back to it all.

But here I am. He shrugged. And tonight, my Pris, you will be in my arms and for a few minutes out of all time there will be nothing else in the whole wide world except the two of us and music. And then I will come home and dream you are in the next room and that all I have to do is open the door to see you stretched upon the great white bed, the bride's bed, the bed I have sworn to myself no one shall ever occupy again unless I can put you upon it. . . .

Yet at the time Dan Field had bought the great white bed he had not known it was called the bride's bed. Its history was another of Ackley's reminiscences.

"The fi'st Massa Ackley who buys my fi'st gran'pappy off a ship in No'folk ha'boh have the bride's bed made and painted white foh his bride. And aftah that day, suh, every Ackley bride sleeps in that bed. When my mammy lay ailing, Old Missus say, 'Liza, you gotta get well. You fixed me to get in the bride's bed, and you gotta fix Young Massa's bride to get in the bride's bed.' But my mammy she dies and Young Massa and my pappy didn't come back from the wah. Reckon Old Massa nevah would evah sold the bride's bed if Young Massa come home."

Johns Hopkins hell! Dan Field swore to himself. Here I am and here I'll stay. I'm too old a dog to teach new tricks.

He read on:

And, Dan, tomorrow is Lillian's eleventh birthday. If you want to make her completely happy come to dinner—two o'clock as usual.

PRIS

Dan Field chuckled; Lillian eleven years old. Miss Muffet, he thought, you're growing up.

Part 2

AUTUMN

Chapter One

$\mathcal{J}$F THE Willowspring *News* gave but a paragraph describing Professor and Mrs. Phelps's background and culture, the Albright and Sargent reception introducing them to society rated headlines and a full column. "SOCIAL TRIUMPH," the headlines began, and the column, after eloquently portraying the decorations and refreshments, and Mrs. Lillian Albright's and Mrs. Priscilla Sargent's regal grace, not forgetting by any means Mrs. Rufus Sargent's apparel and "irresistless" appeal, concluded:

Whereas Willowspring Society is renowned for its unusual and scintillating functions this last affair might be called the *coup de maitre* of a long and glorious record, the *chef d'œuvre* of the evening being when the talented Mrs. George Albright, looking her loveliest, wearing a French model of crushed blue satin, sat down at the piano and in her own inimicable way introduced a bewitching new waltz, "The Blue Danube."

Ralph Pettigrew frowned. Of course the fact that Tracy Whitlock had to continually borrow money from the bank in order to keep his sheet alive had nothing whatsoever to do with his opinion. But Dan Field smiled about Lou's irresistless charm and Pris's inimicable way.

However, excepting Rufe, who was utterly miserable, Margaret Taylor, whose heart was really truly broken (she knew it was) because Ralph Pettigrew had turned his back upon her, Dorothy suffering sympathetically, Laird Culver quaking in his boots, and Dan Field, who held his own private opinion, all the participants agreed afterward that the reception certainly was unprecedented. The preachers and their wives took themselves off replete, Mr. and Mrs. Culver enthralled because their Laird had been invited to stay on with the society set. And Minnie Jennings basked in a seventh heaven when Pris remarked how Lillian and Alexander enjoyed playing together. Lillian and Alexander! Minnie's heart thumped, her poor timid little mind sufficiently stimulated to picture a rosy future for her offspring.

Excepting the young folks and Dan Field, the whole assembly, including the grandmothers, was perfectly charmed by the Phelpses. The Phelpses weren't what you could call good-looking—he was short, rotund, thin-haired, pale-eyed, past forty, and she really appeared older, her skin, hair, eyes, and dress drab—but their poise! And his accent! His Harvard accent!

Virg Price, pink hair falling over the transparent skin of her brow, yellow eyes rolling under their dark lashes (lots of people thought Virg dyed her lashes), whispered to Pris, "I could listen to Professor Phelps's voice all night."

Consequently Dan Field found the usual order of these affairs completely disrupted. Instead of the dancing and whist and Miss Fisher upon the piano stool, the picture of misery, Miss Fisher and both the older and younger sets were gathered in the parlor listening agog to Professor Phelps's Harvard accent. Mrs. Phelps sat beside him, wearing an indelible, enigmatic smile which suggested that she and she alone had access to some secret sacred lore the professor possessed.

Introductions over, the professor continued, "Of course I belong to the old school, class of '61, eight years before Charles Eliot became president of Harvard."

"I understand Dr. Eliot is something of a radical," George put in.

Professor Phelps raised what should have been eyebrows. "My dear Captain Albright, you can't realize the situation. To call Dr. Eliot 'something of a radical' smacks of heresy. Believe me, Charles Eliot's venture at Harvard is no less dangerous to the doctrines of our educational system than the secession of the Southern states was to the Constitution of our country."

An amazed murmur ran around the room and George said, "I'd no idea he was more than a minor agitator."

"A minor agitator indeed!" Professor Phelps exclaimed. "What he has done at Harvard is nothing short of sacrilege. Believe me, Captain Albright, the Harvard catalogue today reads like a political handbook—economics, sociology, political science, logic.

All mere theories, of course, but dangerous theories, which if not stamped out of our schools and colleges will ruin the characters of our young people as surely as their souls would be destroyed by teaching them Darwin's *Origin of Species.*"

"But, Professor," Rufus said, "there's no need to worry about Darwin. His ideas were never considered by anyone with a whit of sense. Don't you think?"

"Would such were the case, Mr. Sargent," Professor Phelps answered. "But what about this new college in Baltimore— Johns Hopkins? Can an institution of learning dedicated especially to science, ignoring religion, be anything save a propounder of evolution?"

"What, may I ask, is evolution?" Gramma Sargent queried haughtily.

"To speak brutally, madam," Professor Phelps explained, "a man named Darwin, Charles Darwin, wrote a book trying to prove that human beings descended from monkeys rather than from Adam and Eve."

Both grandmothers and most of the others gasped, Virg Price giggled, Miss Fisher choked, Pris's jaw dropped, Lou shrugged, and Channing Taylor guffawed.

Dan Field said, "Professor Phelps, I understood that, although Johns Hopkins is dedicated especially to science, the word 'science' means not only physical science but the science of philosophy too."

Mrs. Phelps's indelible, enigmatic smile deepened a shade as the professor again raised what should have been eyebrows. "In this instance, Dr. Field, the science of philosophy means nothing more nor less than a vain groping by a few atheists to find a substitute for religion. However, there never has been and there never will be a real philosopher save Jesus." The professor gave Dan Field a kindly smile. "You know, Dr. Field, Jesus was also a doctor."

Dan Field returned the kindly smile. "Yes, Professor Phelps, Jesus was also a doctor."

Channing Taylor murmured, "Seems to know what he's talking about, don't you think, Dan?"

Dan Field nodded. "He surely does seem to know, Chan."

Channing put a hand over his mouth and whispered, "Dan, hear about Miss Gunther's latest novelty?"

Dan Field nodded again and smiled faintly. But he was thinking that, outside, men with faces and bodies and horses covered by sheets of white cloth were riding through the darkness. He looked at Pris, who was nodding approvingly. *You, too, know there is nothing left for the mind of man to comprehend. But these youngsters who are growing up today . . . His glance* fixed upon Rufe and Laird, Meg and Dot, all the picture of abject misery. *I'd give more than a picayune to know what they're thinking this minute. . . . All right, my good professor, have your say now because your time grows shorter by the* minute. *Remember how short my time is: wherefore hast thou made all men in vain?*

The professor was indeed having his say. "What we must all do is fight these modern innovations with every fiber of our beings. Only by so doing will it be possible to keep our educational system on the same sacred plane, a plane whereupon youth can be taught the beauty of literature, Greek, Latin, with the necessary smattering of mathematics, and an abundance of religion. Surely what was good enough for our fathers, as well as for the Continental fathers who founded this great republic, is good enough for our children."

Came a ripple of applause and George said earnestly, "You're just the man we need around here, Professor Phelps."

The professor bowed. "Thank you, Captain Albright, and now I believe I have occupied the floor sufficiently. Didn't I hear a promise of music?"

"Indeed you did, Professor," George assured. "Pris, my dear, are you ready?"

Pris gave George a nod, flashed Dan Field a smile, arose, and went to the piano. She sat down and her fingers touched the keys . . . *lilting lovely blue water . . . Dan Field closed his eyes . . . the Danube, Vienna, Paris, Rome, long ago . . . but perhaps again someday with you, my Pris . . .*

The following Monday on the dot of nine the new school opened per schedule and, excepting Lillian, Prissy, the Taylor girls, and Ginny Price, all the Willowspring children of proper age, including five Stoddards, two Lawlers, and forty-five young Negroes attended.

Laird Culver was a senior; Rufe, Tom Leonard, Ben Smith, and

Jack Sturdevant among the sophomores; Sammy, Alexander, Mollie Reynard, Bertha Richards, and Helen Boyd in seventh grade; and Bert in fourth.

But regardless of race, age, or accomplishment, all the Mudtown element was segregated and clustered in a back corner of grade one. Of course the colored children sat together, as the white children sat together, which was the proper arrangement, although not for what it seemed. Because where the bones of the Stoddards and Lawlers were covered by dirty rags and their heads unkempt and lousy, the colored children looked spick-and-span. But after the first day Ella and Wilbur Lawler never returned to school.

As Mr. Williams, who had been appointed truant officer, put it, "Soon's I knowed what happened to them poor little young'uns, when it ain't no fault of theirn, I jest didn't have no heart ter make 'em go back ter school no more."

However, before Ella and Wilbur came out of school that first afternoon the initial exodus included Sammy and Alexander; Mollie, Bertha, and Helen; Bert, Shad, and Ray.

Sammy made off fairly fast en route to the livery stable, but Alexander shot over the yard and up the street like a sheet of greased lightning.

Alexander was in a hurry. The girls had half a dozen water closets down basement but the boys' privy was nothing more nor less than a small, two-compartment doorless outhouse near the back of the schoolyard. During the first morning recess (and during every subsequent recess) the outhouse was not merely constantly occupied, it was surrounded. Many of the boys, rather than wait a turn, wetted the ground, not a bit embarrassed, rather the contrary.

Watching the scene, Alexander had wondered what he'd ever do if a time came when he couldn't wait. The other boys certainly wouldn't let him take a turn inside the outhouse and he'd never have the courage to bare himself before the crowd. Moreover, to excuse himself from the room was unthinkable. By midafternoon Alexander thought his time had come but he managed to control himself until he reached his own front yard. There the deluge broke. Wretched and ashamed, he tried to steal into the house but Minnie heard the door open and met him.

She moaned, "Oh, Alexander, did anyone see you pee your pants?"

"No," Alexander choked. "Nobody saw me, not a single soul."

Minnie's face brightened. "Then don't you care, baby. Don't you care a bit. If nobody saw you it don't matter a bit. Come along and I'll help you change your clothes and you can run over and play with Lillian and forget all about it."

"I can't forget all about it," Alexander gulped.

"Yes, you can, baby. If nobody saw you pee your pants you got nothing to be ashamed of. You were just nervous about your first day in public school, that's all. Sometimes big men pee their pants if they're nervous. Once Papa did, baby, right in the pulpit. Papa was nervous, baby. But you know how he always said if you trust in God there is nothing to fear. He trusted in God and nobody ever did find out what happened. He had on a big heavy black suit and nobody could tell if the pants was wet. Come along now, baby, and I'll help you change your clothes and you can run over and play with Lillian. Mrs. Albright told me Lillian loves having you play with her."

Finally Alexander smiled. "Honest, Mama, did Mrs. Albright say that?"

"Yes, she did, baby. She really did."

About the same time Helen was walking out of the school gate ahead of Mollie and Bertha, and, reaching the corner, she turned without a backward glance.

Mollie's eyes followed Helen and then she said, "Somehow, Bertha, I don't like treating Helen mean. It must make her feel bad."

Bertha nodded. "I know it makes her feel bad and Helen can't help being a Jew."

"Still," Mollie speculated, "if Lillian Albright's and Priscilla Sargent's folks think it's right not to let them play with anyone it must be right if our folks won't let us play with someone."

"I suppose our folks do know best," Bertha agreed.

Going home, Helen kept telling herself, I don't care, really I don't. All I want to do today is practice, really it is.

However, Bert, Shad, and Ray still hung around the schoolhouse as Ella and Wilbur came out of the door and started across the now teeming yard. Their dirty little faces beamed. Ella and Wilbur liked school. Excepting Bert and Shad and a very occasional little Negro, no one ever went to see them, and being near other children all day long had made them very happy. And they had almost reached the gate before Buzz Standing spied them.

Buzz's mother, the village seamstress, was a widow and Buzz was the only child, so naturally she thought the sun rose and set in Buzz. He was Sammy's age but a half head taller and at least five pounds heavier. Both Buzz and his mother were easy enough to look at, with their brown wavy hair, bright black eyes, and blood-red lips. Mrs. Standing did quite a bit of sewing and mending for the best families and her chief topic of conversation among her own friends consisted of what she'd said to this or that best-family member. Mrs. Standing herself naturally always supplied the *bons mots* which invariably left this or that best-family member totally foiled. Buzz, on the other hand, established himself among his contemporaries by bragging and bullying. He took particular pride in the fact that he'd never been licked and dared any bastard who thought he could lick him to put his fists up.

Spying Ella and Wilbur, Buzz yelled, "Hey, Ella and Wilbur, your mama's a whore."

Ella and Wilbur stopped and turned toward Buzz, their faces still beaming. This wasn't the first time they'd heard their mother called a whore and they had liked school and had done what Mr. Williams said. After Mr. Williams had explained how every child must go to the new school he had added, "Yer try bein' jest as nice as yer kin ter everybody, Ella and Wilbur, and see if'n folks ain't jest as nice ter you."

So Ella smiled at Buzz and said, "We was jest as nice ter everybody, wasn't we, Wilbur?"

Wilbur didn't have a chance to answer. Before the words were more than out of Ella's mouth Buzz grabbed a pebble and threw it. The pebble hit Ella over the left eye and the blood oozed. Ella screamed, grabbed Wilbur's hand, and the two of them tore through the gate. Several other boys followed Buzz's lead and pebbles and hoots followed the fleeing children.

"Your mama's a whore," Buzz screamed.

"Your papa's a traveling man's convention," Pete Sturdevant, Jack's twelve-year-old brother, cried.

"Hey, Wilbur, did your mama ever let you do it to her?" yelled Chick Hubbard, a thirteen-year-old edition of buttery Fat.

During the fracas Bert, Shad, and Ray had not moved.

Finally the clamor died down and Bert asked, "How come Ella and Wilbur and Cal's mama's a whore?"

Shad answered this easily. "See, Bert, if a whore gits young-'uns, then them young'uns gits a whore fer a mama."

Bert shook his head thoughtfully. "Mighty likely. 'Cept how come some ladies is whores and some ain't?"

Shad answered this question with equal facility. "Whores is jest naturally whores, Bert, and ladies what ain't whores jest naturally ain't whores."

Bert sniffed. "That ain't any reason. Things can't be things just naturally. There's got to be a real reason. Don't you think, Ray? Don't you think there's got to be a real reason why things is things and not 'cause things is just naturally things?"

"Sure, Bert," Ray answered. "They ain't only gotta be a real reason why things is things. They *is* a real reason why things is things."

"Know what it is, Ray?" Bert inquired.

Ray shook his head sideways and the long tousled hair swung like a mane. "Not yit I don't know, Bert, but I's figgerin' fer ter larn. Do yer like ter go ter school, Bert?"

Bert shrugged his square shoulders. "I guess so. I never did think. You like school, Ray?"

Ray's alert black eyes flashed. "School's the very best thing I ever knowed, Bert. See, Bert, 'fore I goes ter school I never seen the insides of a book and that thar primer Teacher give us has got three pitchers right on the very first page. They was a cow and a hen and a pig and the spellin' was right 'neath. And, Bert, I kin spell them words a'ready."

"Let's hear you," Shad commanded unbelievingly.

Ray grinned. "C-o-w, cow. H-e-n, hen. P-i . . . p-i . . . p-i-g, pig."

Shad hawked derisively but Bert said, "That's good, Ray."

"It's good all right," Ray agreed, ignoring Shad's ridicule. "Sure, it's good all right, Bert, 'cept it's slow. See, Bert, if'n I kin larn only three words a day it's gonna take me a mighty long time ter larn everythin' in the world what thar is ter larn."

The conversation was interrupted by another exodus; the high school students were coming. Tom Leonard, Ben Smith, and Jack Sturdevant rushed ahead of the others, hurled the fence, and made for town. Pretty soon Rufe came, also hurrying. Laird Culver followed.

Laird called, "Wait a minute, Rufe. What you going to do this afternoon?"

Hurrying toward home, Rufe didn't hear Laird, his mind being bent upon its own subject. During afternoon recess Rufe had gone to the small reference library adjoining Professor Phelps's office, selected a book at random, opened it, and begun to read. He read until the bell rang, and all the rest of the afternoon he could hardly wait to get back and read the rest. God! God! he kept thinking. I didn't know there could be such a thing in the world. After school Rufe fairly flew to Professor Phelps's office, where he found the professor behind his desk.

"There's a book in the library I'd like to take home and read, please, sir," Rufe said.

"You're Rufus Albright, aren't you?" the professor inquired. "Yes sir."

The professor nodded. "I suppose it will be all right if you take a book home. Of course we can't let just anyone borrow books."

"Thank you, sir."

The title of the book was *The Building of the Parthenon* and, rushing home to the playroom, where he'd not be disturbed, again Rufe thought, God! God! I didn't know there could be such a beautiful thing in the world—a building made all of marble.

Back in the schoolyard Shad was saying, "Come on, Bert, come on. What's we waiting fer?"

Bert, however, knew why he was waiting. Across the street Uncle Doc stood, talking to Judge Hart Martin. Soon's Judge Hart left he'd better go tell Uncle Doc 'bout how the boys had stoned Ella and Wilbur 'cause they might likely be hurt bad.

Miss Fisher's pupils were crossing the street. The Taylor girls and Ginny Price turned over Linden but Lillian and Prissy walked past the school, their little noses high, looking neither right nor left. Prissy prayed silently that Lillian didn't see Bert standing 'longside a colored boy and that dirty filthy white boy who delivered washes all over town.

Catching sight of Lillian made Ray's heart jump to his throat. I wisht . . . I wisht . . . oh, I wisht Miss Lillian knowed I kin spell "cow" and "hen" and "pig," Ray Stoddard was thinking.

The day at Miss Fisher's had been an ordeal all the way through. First, Miss Fisher couldn't help being worried half to death. Excepting seven piano students and a few extra dollars earned playing at parties, the school was the only source of income. However could ends be made to meet now the boys were attending public school!

Miss Fisher had a fine education and through her veins coursed rich red blood. After graduating from the old Willowspring School, class of '47, two years were spent at the Moravian Seminary. Mrs. Fisher, who had been a seamstress, actually sewed her eyes out earning the wherewithal.

By 1880 Miss Fisher was nearing fifty yet she had lost none of her accomplishments and little of her animal allure. Besides being an accomplished musician she could still rattle off the names of all kings and presidents, the capitals of every country and state, the dates of battles from Caesar's conquests through the Civil War, and she could read Latin more readily than the average mortal did English. And Miss Fisher's titian curls were still without a gray hair and her eyes the shade of aquamarines. Her complexion was like an apple blossom and her mouth cherry-red over pearllike teeth. Miss Fisher's breasts, while always amply covered, could not be ignored and reminded Dan Field of huge round hard melons. Her arms and hips curved gently.

One day when Miss Fisher was ailing, her mother had opened the front door and told Dan Field to go on upstairs. Consequently he walked into the bedroom unannounced. Miss Fisher lay upon the bed, only a white gown over her. The lovely curls fell to her bare shoulders; her gown stretched taut across her breasts and thighs, and below the gown her feet peeped out like small white birds. She was terribly embarrassed and pulled the sheet up quickly. But she made Dan Field recall a certain woman of Sparta.

> *Was this the face that launch'd a thousand ships,*
> *And burnt the topless towers of Ilium?*
> *Sweet Helen, make me immortal with a kiss! . . .*
> *And none but thou shalt be my paramour.*

But what sort of system was this where a woman, from whose breasts sufficient milk might flow to suckle a multitude, was fated to live and die a virgin?

Miss Fisher was a virgin both mentally and physically, the word "virgin" here being a precise description. A posthumous baby, Miss Fisher didn't know the meaning of a man around the house. She had never tried to picture anyone she knew, especially herself, carnally touching a member of the opposite sex. That she must have been conceived according to the usual procedure was a subject Miss Fisher ignored. Surely the action perpetrating her birth was the single solitary time her mother had acquiesced, to have a baby. Miss Fisher never doubted that all decent people were innocent of intercourse except for the one purpose of acquiring progeny.

However, Miss Fisher's vitality found outlets. Her devotion to her mother was a combination of innocent incest and actual adoration; the two of them slept nightly with arms and legs locked. Other emotional channels were religion, the temperance movement, music, and her school.

Next to her mother the school was nearest Miss Fisher's heart. Home from the seminary, still unaware of her mother's impending blindness, she had given music lessons merely to help out. To her surprise the income during the first few years was substantial. In those days Willowspring possessed more best-family children than ever afterward. Soon there were twenty piano pupils, one of whom was Pris Albright, née Sargent, aged six.

Mrs. Fisher's sight grew gradually worse. Even before she became completely blind the piano pupils had dwindled to ten. The situation was critical. Then the idea of the school occurred. A young man named Lance Wolfe, from Philadelphia, tutored the Albright and Sargent children. A few of the other best-family boys attended public school, and the rest of them and the girls were taught by their mothers. Consequently the idea of a private school in the Fishers' big parlor was hailed enthusiastically.

George the First and Rufus the First had equipped the school, lending the money on extremely easy terms. Among the first twenty-six students were Pris Sargent, who'd reached the age of thirteen, and Tim Albright, neither of them having made progress under their tutor.

How Miss Fisher had loved every one of those first students, particularly Tim Albright! He was seven then. No one could have called the little thin dark fellow good-looking and Tim was not a scholar. But he'd been so eager and so appreciative. The least attention made his little thin dark face glow. Always after a recitation he'd stand with his head up, fairly beseeching approval, his face looking like a tiny thirsty elf's gazing toward the skies in hopes of rain from heaven. Miss Fisher had never been able to understand why Tim ran away.

He'd seemed such a happy little boy, truly the happiest little boy she'd ever known. Everybody said, too, that Tim was his mother's favorite, and even if Mr. Albright must be severe about the way Tim ran with riffraff and lost himself in the mountains, the father really thought the sun rose and set in the boy. Naturally Tim's daydreaming made Mr. Albright think Tim's poetry something to be discouraged. Yet unto this day Miss Fisher had one of Tim's poems pressed between the pages of her Bible. Across a now parched sheet in Tim's scrawl the poem read:

> *The world is a very big place,*
> *There is not just you and me and this*
> *little town and the crick.*
> *Over the mountains there are crowds*
> *and cities and rivers,*
> *And there are seven seas where the*
> *ships are thick.*

Likewise, down the years Miss Fisher had kept many souvenirs: a drawing by Tertius Martin, a four-leaf clover, a note Pris had sent her from the Boston Conservatory of Music, a post card, a ribbon, or more often merely memories. For unto those breasts, which according to Dan Field might have suckled a multitude, every pupil had figuratively been pressed. But Miss Fisher didn't have it in her to be demonstrative, excepting toward her mother. Not a single solitary soul so much as suspected that Miss Fisher had ever given any one of them more than a kindly tolerance.

Thus stood Miss Fisher at the close of school on the first afternoon during the autumn of 1880, as she faced the big empty room in which the five lone pupils seemed to rattle like five lone peas in a giant pod. The girls had been unusually restless. A fear clutched Miss Fisher's heart. What if she should lose these last five pupils? What would happen then?

Mrs. Fisher entered the room, groping her blind way along until she reached her daughter's side. "How did school go today, deary?"

"Fine, deary, fine."

"I guess we'll make out all right, don't you think, deary?"

"Of course we'll make out all right, deary. Haven't we always? And perhaps Lillian and Prissy will start taking music lessons soon."

As it happened, the girls had been unusually restless. Even the lunch hour didn't relax them. But it wasn't Miss Fisher's fault —the girls had their own troubles. Meg simply couldn't forget Ralph Pettigrew's treatment, Dot couldn't help worrying about Meg, Ginny Price hated school because Sammy wasn't there any more, and both Lillian and Prissy were distrait.

Of course Lillian's trouble was all Prissy's fault, Lillian knew. Yesterday had been Lillian's eleventh birthday and it had been wonderful. She'd got the loveliest presents. And Uncle Doc came to dinner. But after dinner Uncle Doc had a sick lady to see and Rufe and Sammy disappeared and Papa took his nap and Mama and Gramma Albright went over home to see Auntie Lou and Gramma Sargent, the way they did every Sunday afternoon.

"What'll we play, Prissy?" Lillian had asked.

"Nothing." Prissy shrugged, wandering out of the house and seating herself under a maple tree.

Lillian followed suit, perplexed. "Don't you want to play anything, Prissy?"

"No." She shook her head. "I don't want to play. I want to think."

"Can't you think when you're playing?"

"No; maybe Alexander might come over and play though. Alexander surely does seem to like you a lot, Lillian."

Lillian could barely believe her ears. Prissy sounded as if she didn't mind a bit if Alexander liked her.

"You're not sick, are you, Prissy?" Lillian demanded.

Prissy didn't answer. She just smiled, the way she smiled if she had a secret. But what could it be? Always before if Prissy had a secret Lillian could guess it almost right away, the way Prissy could guess Lillian's secrets almost right away. Because each one always knew the secret wishings of the other's heart even if neither one wanted to admit the other knew. But this secret Prissy had now was something different, a new kind of secret Lillian couldn't guess.

But Prissy's secret kept her torn between ecstasy and terror. Since Saturday evening she had thought of hardly anything except Gregory Beamer. Gregory's lips brushing hers like a butterfly wing, Gregory's golden hair, Gregory's eyes, Gregory's voice. Gregory, Gregory, Gregory. And Saturday night, after Mama had tucked her in bed and all the grownups, including Maggie, had gone over to the party at Uncle George's, Prissy thought about Gregory upstairs in Maggie's bed and about the girl Gregory said went swimming bare with fellows. And once Prissy had believed it would be wonderful to run barefoot on a big lawn 'side Alexander. She sniffed. . . . 'Magine me ever thinking *that* was wonderful! She closed her eyes and could feel cool water running over her and over Gregory, both of them bare. Yet there was the terror too. In the midst of dreams it would clutch her. What if Mama found out? What if Mama or anybody found out?

Before Bert came to tell Dan Field what had happened to the Lawler children Judge Hart strolled along the pavement and stopped beside Dan.

Judge Hart was a big, blond, stately man nearing fifty. (Dan Field liked to picture him wearing a white wig.) He and Peggy, his wife, had never traveled over five hundred miles from Willowspring and knew nothing of Paris save by hearsay. They heartily disapproved of their twenty-three-year-old son, Hart the Third, gallivanting around that city studying art! But they weren't disciplinarians and had finally given Tertius his own way, according to long-established custom. Still Alec at Princeton and Wayne at Lawrenceville seemed to be doing all right, despite early spoiling.

"Dan," Hart said, "I suppose you've heard that all hell broke loose here Saturday night?"

"Do you mean the night riders?" Dan Field asked.

Hart nodded. "I heard over fifty of them were abroad, hellbent for heaven. They fine-combed Mudtown and the mountains. An old farmer named Pensyl—maybe you know him, lives over near Kinton's Knob—has a couple of bloodhounds he uses to track cattle. The mob got the old man out of bed in the middle of the night and made him get up and dress and set his dogs on Gabe's trail. How the hell, Dan, do you think Gabe ever escaped?"

Dan Field shrugged. "His time probably hadn't come."

Hart laughed and gave Dan Field a mighty slap between the shoulder blades. "Old fatalist. There may be something in it though. That's the Presbyterian idea, you know, predestination. And of course George and Rufus don't think such a thing as a lynching could happen here in our lovely little village paradise."

Dan Field smiled. "Maybe it couldn't. It didn't."

Hart winked knowingly. "It didn't this time. But, Dan, let me tell you, there is a bubble in this town which has been ready to burst these many a day. Ralph Pettigrew is a dangerous man."

Dan Field said, "Hart, I honestly don't believe Pettigrew had anything to do with the fracas Saturday night."

"No?" Hart's tone changed. "And I suppose you don't honestly believe the fact that Gabe is, or was, George Albright's hired man has anything to do with the fracas either?"

"I wouldn't like to think so."

"I wouldn't like to think so either, Dan. But the truth remains, George and Rufus aren't as popular as they once were by a hell of a sight."

" 'Uneasy lies the head . . .' "

"You're right," Hart agreed. "This town is turning on a pivot."

"The whole world is."

"What the rest of the world is doing doesn't concern us. We've enough to do looking after our own affairs. Dan, I'd not be surprised if before long we'd have a war between capital and labor bloodier than the War Between the States. That is, if steps aren't taken to stop it."

"What steps do you think might be taken?" Dan Field asked.

"First, every man who was involved last Saturday night should be arrested and brought to justice."

"How?"

Hart snorted. "How? There you have a perfect picture of conditions today. Democracy, hell! Mob rule! Why, granting it was possible to find out who the members of the gang were and arrest them, by what statute could they be convicted? No law was ever made forbidding men to ride around the mountains wearing sheets."

Dan Field laughed. "I guess the only thing we can do, Hart, is pray the revolution won't come until after our time. Maybe these youngsters who are growing up today will have a different way of handling situations."

"There's only one way to handle things, Dan, the right way. How did you like Professor Phelps?"

"He seemed to know what he was talking about."

Hart gave Dan Field another vigorous slap between the shoulder blades. "Now you're talking. He's the kind of educator this country needs. Of course we all agree about educating the masses. But from the legal as well as the scholastic standpoint, Dan, trouble starts the minute little minds are fed subjects they can't possibly understand. Political science, bah! All right for you and me, Dan. But look what happens if a fellow like Ralph Pettigrew starts thinking too hard. All he does is stir up trouble. Not one of the hoi polloi has brains enough to realize it's George Albright and Rufus Sargent who butter their bread."

"A certain one of the hoi polloi agrees with you," Dan Field said.

"So?"

Dan Field chuckled. "Yes, one of Lem Stoddard's boys made the remark that it'd take a mighty sight more'n Mr. Ralph Pettigrew gitting 'lected mayor to make him the likes of Captain George or Mr. Sargent."

Hart roared. "That's damn good. So one of Lem Stoddard's boys said that, did he? 'Out of the mouths of children and fools . . .'" Hart sobered. "By the way, Dan, we'd another letter from Tertius yesterday."

"I intended asking if you'd heard lately. No doubt he's still enthusiastic about the life."

Hart nodded. "More so than ever. Of course you know, Dan, neither Peggy nor I approved of Tert going to Paris. Seemed like he could have studied art just as well right here. But Tert's the kind who never says die till he gets his own way. Matter of fact, Alec and Wayne are equally headstrong. Perhaps Peggy and I have spoiled them. Confidentially, Dan, though such a thought would never enter Peggy's head, I can't help wondering if Tert's behaving himself. What would you think, Dan?"

Dan Field smiled. "What I would think depends entirely upon what you mean by behaving himself."

Hart waved a hand. "Come, Dan, I'm not trying to act like an old fogy. I know Tert's bound to sow his wild oats. But the very thought of him getting mixed up with a French whore makes my blood run cold."

"Contrary to the common consensus," Dan Field said, "French whores are not *sui generis* either by attraction or accomplishment. Like members of any other race or profession, the status quo depends upon the individual. The Left Bank offers nothing which can't be duplicated upon Unter den Linden, Drury Lane, the Bowery, not forgetting good old Chestnut Street."

"What about disease, Dan?"

"Unfortunately—that is, for us—the French have no monopoly upon social disorders either. One of the acute forms is believed to have been imported into Europe by certain members of Columbus' returning crew. Jesus! Hart," Dan Field swore, "take the conditions under our own noses. Not a man who enters the Widder Woman's shanty has a Chinaman's chance of coming out clean. And you wouldn't believe me if I told you the number of young girls around town, not to mention many on farms, who are a menace."

"You're right. Of course you're right, Dan." Hart spoke earnestly. "But we've a habit of overlooking what's under our noses, if the picture isn't pretty."

"Another thing, Hart," Dan Field went on, "Tert may have a better chance in Paris than he would have here. There a spade is called a spade. Tert will probably learn how to take care of himself (not run blindly into the trap, the way boys here are forced to do through ignorance), even if the cures *are* mostly experiment."

"I wish I'd had a talk with Tert before he sailed."

"You could make a start by having a talk with Alec and Wayne the next time they're home," Dan Field suggested.

"I suppose I could, Dan," Hart agreed. "Still, on the other hand," Hart sighed, "discussing the subject might put ideas into the boys' heads. After all, maybe the best course is just to impress upon them the sacredness of womanhood, the way we were impressed. There's a lot in what Professor Phelps said about what was good enough for our fathers should be good enough for our children."

"No doubt you're right, Hart."

Watching Judge Hart's stately figure moving away, Dan Field was thinking, *Having eyes, see ye not? and having ears, hear ye not? and do ye not remember?*

Bert came beside him. "Know sumpin, Úncle Doc? Some big fellows stoned Ella and Wilbur. I thought you'd want to know 'cause mighty likely they're hurt bad."

"You're right, Bert. Thank you for telling me. I'll go over and see them right away."

But before turning Nervy's head toward Mudtown Dan Field drove uptown and stopped at Strock's to buy a bag of candy.

Because the Willowspring *News* was a weekly the issue containing the account of the reception didn't appear until the following Friday. So around ten o'clock Monday morning the young man, Tracy Whitlock, owner and editor, sat upon one of the Albright parlor's massive chairs awaiting Pris.

Tracy Whitlock was a town boy who belonged to Willowspring's middle class—that is to say, to the class whose members, although not socially recognized by the best families, had acquired a certain amount of prosperity or prestige. Broadly speaking, this middle class included men who owned their own businesses and their families, while the lower class embraced the hired help and their wives and children. The Mudtown populace had no rating.

Tracy Whitlock was twenty-five years old, of medium height, very thin and narrow-faced. He had stiff tow hair sticking out every which way, small gray eyes, and a struggling beard. When he was a baby his mother died. Aunt Tillie Whitlock, his father's sister, had taken her brother and the infant to live with her in a sizable old house on West Horsechestnut Street which, with an annual pittance, she'd inherited from a grandmother.

Aunt Tillie worshiped and spoiled her nephew but the senior Whitlock had never displayed the slightest spark of affection. At best he had treated the boy indifferently, at worst he'd beaten him unmercifully. More than one person had seen Tracy Whitlock thrashed upon the streets. He loathed his father, cringing at the very sight of him, but no other person had ever seemed to make him knuckle under.

Tracy wasn't popular with boys and most men found him irritating, all of which he either didn't notice or ignored. But from childhood he had possessed an adult poise and what the ladies called "such beautiful manners." Most of the ladies succumbed. His teachers adored him. He was a fair student, too, and during high school days continually talked about becoming an author. The teachers, not to mention Aunt Tillie, believed him a genius, and he agreed. Tracy, he'd say to himself, you'll be a great man.

Someday he'd get plenty of money; where, he wasn't sure, but he'd get it. Then he'd find a suitable environment and start the book.

Finishing high school, waiting for the windfall, he found a job with Joshua Beemiller, owner and editor of the Willowspring *News* since the days of George the First and Rufus the First. Six months later Tracy's father dropped dead and, although he'd been a fairly shrewd lawyer, his estate netted less than four hundred dollars. An office cupboard disclosed what practically the whole town excepting Aunt Tillie had suspected—secret drinking. Tracy's intense hatred made him want to dig a hole in Aunt Tillie's garden and dump the body there but Aunt Tillie insisted upon a proper funeral, burial, and marker, which left Tracy with what facetiously he referred to as his seventy-five-dollar patrimony.

Tracy continued working at the *News* and two years later Beemiller made up his mind to retire and Tracy approached the bank. The bank not only loaned the initial capital but had granted several subsequent amounts, facts which made the town wonder, as Tracy produced no collateral except the press and the bank usually demanded that a note be backed by twice its face value.

Tracy told himself this venture was merely an interlude until the windfall presented an opportunity for bigger and better things. But during the interim he accepted Aunt Tillie's spoiling and adoration graciously, paying her goodly sums often and again, and these last two years Tracy'd been courting Jean Leonard, Tom's nineteen-year-old sister.

Awaiting Pris, Tracy lolled comfortably, his eyes moving about the luxury of the big parlor. Every time he visited the Albrights, or the Sargents either, he thought the same thing: With all the money they possess, it shouldn't be hard to find some way to secure a share. And they'd never miss it.

Pris entered the room and Tracy arose, bowing after a fashion any courtier might have done well to emulate, and smiled. "My lady."

Pris returned the smile. She'd known him all his life and had always liked the boy. Certainly no one could call Tracy good-looking, the way his hair stuck out every which way, and that awful moth-eaten-looking beard. But his manners were charming, really old-school, and he often said the nicest things about her; in fact he often said the nicest things about all the Albrights and the Sargents in his paper. Before he left, Pris told herself, she must mention that yesterday had been Lillian's eleventh birthday. He'd given Rufe quite a nice little notice when she had met him on the street last August and had happened to remark that Rufe was going to be fifteen on the fifteenth. That was the way the notice began: "Fifteen on the fifteenth."

"Sit down, Tracy," Pris said, using her most gracious tone.

Tracy bowed again. "After you, Mrs. Albright."

"No." Pris shook her head. "Before I talk there's something I want you to hear. It's a brand-new waltz—at least it's brand-new to Willowspring—and, Tracy, I think you'll agree it's truly the loveliest waltz ever written."

He seated himself and she went to the piano. She turned on the stool and flashed a smile and then her fingers touched the keys and Tracy was forgotten. Dan's arms around her . . . floating on lilting lovely blue water . . . She finished.

Tracy cried, "Bravo! Bravo!"

He was thinking, How she must love music! Her eyes are as misty as if she was a young girl in love.

Nor did Tracy Whitlock neglect Lou. After hearing Pris's last word he stopped by the Sargents'. Tracy considered Lou attractive, although his private opinion was that she couldn't hold a candle to Mrs. Albright.

Tracy, nevertheless, was not one to be found wanting, and when Lou entered the Sargent parlor he arose, smiled, and bowed regally.

"Good morning, Mrs. Sargent."

"Good morning, Tracy. Sit down."

"After you, Mrs. Sargent."

They seated themselves, Tracy carefully waiting until Lou settled herself before taking a chair.

"Mrs. Sargent, if you please, I'd like to have a description of the gown you wore Saturday night and anything else you care to tell me about the reception. Weren't the flower arrangements your inspiration?"

Wreathed in smiles, Lou began, "Well, if I do say so myself, I've never seen lovelier flower arrangements in the Albright house. Asters were the basic . . ."

George and Rufus arrived home for lunch, feeling very well satisfied with the world, and found both wives, not to mention the grandmothers, still walking on a cloud. And this exaltation survived and buoyed up all their spirits until about a quarter past six that evening, when Lou experienced a terrific shock.

Rufus hadn't come in. But, hearing Bert open the front door, Lou met him and stood a moment, gazing adoringly down upon the sleek black head.

Suddenly Lou gasped, rushed to the front door, and cried, "Charlie, come here. Charlie, Charlie, come running."

Charlie Raub came running. "What's wrong, Mrs. Sargent?"

"Charlie," Lou panted, "run fast as you can and find Dr. Field. Tell him he must come right away. Tell him it's Bert. Run, Charlie, run."

Charlie ran.

Approaching the Widder Woman's shanty, Dan Field heard shrieks of laughter pealing over Limestone Avenue through the sunlight and the shadows and among the swarming little Negroes. Reaching the Lawler shanty, he saw the cause of the hilarity. Lottie, briefly clad in a gauze shirt, corset, and drawers, was hurling herself to and fro upon a small hammock which was stretched from one corner of the shanty to a tree. Shrieking with laughter, she rollicked, violently tossing herself first right, then left, to and fro, always catching herself just in the nick of time to keep from falling out. Ella, Wilbur, and Cal watched, convulsed by their mother's alcoholic antics.

Whence the Widder Woman hailed and wherefore she selected Willowspring as her hunting ground no one ever knew. Probably she didn't know herself, her memory and deduction being limited, to put it mildly. And not only was Lottie a whore and an alcoholic but she was absolutely devoid of shame, carrying on her licentious trade actually under her children's very eyes. Many a night upon the streets of Willowspring Lottie walked, Ella, Wilbur, and Calvary trudging wearily along. Why she took the children on these pursuits was a mystery, unless it might be she enjoyed their company. For after her own fashion she must have loved the little creatures. Never were they deserted. Even the time Lottie was forced to leave town she took Ella and Wilbur along and when she returned there was not only Ella and Wilbur but Calvary as well. Sometimes, too, she'd shower hugs and kisses upon the children, calling them her own darlings, and if a windfall came (which happened once in a blue moon) Lottie would buy toys and candy and fill the cupboard. At other times she beat them cruelly and often days would pass wherein the children were fortunate if they'd a crust to chew.

The Widder Woman had first appeared upon the streets of Willowspring some nine years ago, pregnant. This condition did not prevent her renting the last shanty on Limestone Avenue, where she carried on her business as usual. And one winter dawn Dan Field was awakened by the office bell and, going downstairs, he found Mr. Williams outside.

"Mr. Doc, sir," Mr. Williams explained, "mighty likely yer ain't gonna like what I come fer. And I knows that thar woman what's in the last shanty ain't worth shucks. But, Mr. Doc, sir, yer knows the Good Book says fer him what's 'out sin ter throw the first stone. And, Mr. Doc, sir, that woman she's been a-hollering and a-shrieking the livelong night."

So Dan Field delivered the Widder Woman of Ella and later of Wilbur but not of Cal, who was an import.

Nevertheless, the Widder Woman wasn't titled thus until several months after Ella's birth. Then one day she had appeared upon Limestone Avenue wearing widow's weeds. Dan Field happened to be on the spot and saw what took place. Lottie wasn't drunk that day. She walked up and down Limestone Avenue, wearing the weeds and with tears streaming down her painted cheeks, telling everybody around, including Dan Field, how her husband, Mr. Lawler, had died the day before in a city "horsepital." All the Negroes were laughing their heads off, except Mr. Williams, who was nodding sadly, because none of them believed that Lottie ever did have a husband. Dan Field thought that if a Mr. Lawler had been unfortunate enough to have existed he'd been lost long since in an obscure past. But afterward Lottie was jocosely labeled the Widder Woman—and though the Negroes started it, the name was taken up all over town before you could say Jack Robinson.

Dan Field wondered why Lottie had put on the show, unless in an attempt to make the town believe Ella was legitimate. But Lottie being as she was, why would she care about such a thing? Could it be possible that beneath the sewage of her mind there was another mind, a clean if hidden spring which now had sent forth one tiny bubble? And when Dan Field first saw Cal—Cal with his silver head and wide blue eyes and the pallid skin which miraculously appeared almost clean—he'd wondered again. I may have questioned the possibility of a mind behind the mind, Dan Field told himself, but actually through the refuse of these loins has come a child who looks almost divine, and is this not proof of a body behind the body?

"What a beautiful baby, Lottie. What's his name?"

"Calvary," she told him.

"Calvary?" Dan Field echoed.

"He's called Cal fer short," Lottie said.

"But how did you happen to name him Calvary?"

Lottie shrugged. "How do yer happen ter name anybody?"

There it was again—from what obscurity did that name ascend? Calvary, he thought . . . And if behind our minds there is another mind and if behind our bodies there is another body, then it must necessarily follow that behind our souls another soul exists. And someday men will know.

"Hiya, Doc, hiya, Doc," Lottie shrieked, her furious rollicking accompanied by the children's spasms of mirth.

Dan Field got out of the buggy and said to her, "You'd better go inside and finish dressing. Look at yourself."

She stopped rocking, glanced down, and roared, "Chew my tail, chew it clean off if'n I didn't clean fergit my wrapper." She crawled to her feet, staggered toward the shanty door, but before going inside snickered, "Come 'long, Doc. Come on 'long, Doc."

She disappeared and Dan Field turned his attention upon Ella and Wilbur. The cut over Ella's eye was deep and on both children's necks and arms were bruised spots.

Dan Field opened his bag and took out what was needed. "Does the cut on your forehead hurt, Ella?"

"Not so bad now," she answered.

"I'd like to fix it so it will get well quickly, may I?"

"Don't hurt me no more, will yer?"

"I'll try my very best not to, Ella."

He drew her toward him gently and dressed the cut and took care of the bruises.

"How about you, Wilbur?" Dan Field asked then. "Are you cut anywhere, son?"

Wilbur shook his head. "Me jest gits black and blues."

"Let me make them feel better, will you, son?"

"A' right."

While he attended Wilbur, Ella said, "Them stoned Wilbur and me, and us was jest as good ter ever'body like Mr. Williams says."

Dan Field pulled the bag of candy out of a pocket. "See what I've brought you." He handed Ella the bag. "Be sure and divide it equally, Ella, and Cal gets first pick."

Cal gurgled and grabbed the biggest piece. Dan Field dropped on his knees and took hold of Cal's tiny shoulders. Calvary, Dan Field thought, they say your papa was a preacher but the way you look he might have been an angel. He pressed an ear against Cal's tiny chest. The wheeze was worse. A year, two years at the most, baby. If I'd the guts of a worm I'd put you to sleep before the agony begins.

He patted Cal's silver head. "You're a fine fellow, Cal."

"Wi' yo' bwing us candy some mo'?" Cal lisped.

"You bet your life I will, fellow."

He started toward the Tatem shanty on foot, Nervy dutifully following. Red sat on the steps smoking his corncob pipe, Duke snoring at his feet. Red looked the picture of contentment which verily he was. After leaving Broad Street Saturday evening he'd rolled home, passed out on the porch, and hadn't even come to when the night riders stormed Mudtown. Red had slept right through until Sunday noon, and now his spleen was as serene as a spayed seraph, after the spree, its aftermath, and a good night's rest.

Reaching the steps, Dan Field said, "How are Duke's sores, Red?"

Red took the pipe out of his mouth. "Fine. Jest fine. Bert he fixed 'em. First he puts some blue sa've on 'em, then he puts some yallow sa've on 'em. Think the blue sa've done the work though."

"No doubt," Dan Field answered, remembering the blue salve had been Lou's vaginal jelly.

"I declare, Doc," Red continued, "times I thinks that thar Bert he knows a heap sight more'n the quacks knows. Not meaning you, Doc, but look-a thar . . ." He indicated a wide jagged scar which spread over the greater part of his left palm. "Look-a thar, Doc; an Injun arrow went clean through oncet and when I pulls the dogged thing out part didn't come and the flesh growed over the flint. It give me a lot of trouble. Sometimes my hull arm'd ache. But Bert he says he could cut it out easy and he done it by gorry! Had a little real sharp knife and he jest ripped 'r open."

"After Bert removed the flint your arm stopped aching of course," Dan Field said soberly.

"By gorry! It did. Course my hand was sore a spell. But Bert he made me soak it every day in hot water and lye soap. And by gorry! Bert he seen I soaked it, too. Every dogged day he'd drop by and say, 'Mr. Tatem, did you soak yer hand yet?'" Red guffawed. "Bert he give Duke a bath oncet too."

Chuckling to himself, Dan Field entered the shanty. Dolly and Belle sat in the kitchen, Dolly's face still swollen and blue.

"How do you feel, Dolly?" Dan Field asked.

She shrugged. "All right, I guess. I don't mind."

Belle sniffed. "She's a-frettin' her heart out over Gabe."

"Gabe's all right, Dolly," Dan Field assured.

Dolly choked. "Yeh. Maybe Gabe he's all right but maybe, too, I ain't ever a-gonna see him agin. And I don't mind what folks thinks about me. I loves Gabe. He was the only feller ever treated me decent in my hull life."

"When are you girls going back to the hotel?" Dan Field demanded.

Belle spoke eagerly. "Do you think Mr. Leonard'd want the likes of us back?"

"Of course he'll want you back. But just to make sure I'll stop by the hotel and see him on my way home."

"Promise, Mr. Doc," Belle pleaded.

Dan Field held up his right hand. "I promise. And you go to work tomorrow, Belle, and you, Dolly, when your face heals. Sitting around home brooding won't do any good. Your father's all over his temper now, isn't he?"

Belle snorted. "Sure, Pap's sweet as a tit now. Likely don't even recollect why he beat Dolly up. That's how the old bugger is."

Nervy was once more trotting along the avenue when against the horizon loomed the twelve-year-old figure of Willie Stanwick—short, stocky, pompous, the spit and image of Ackley.

Dan Field never failed to be amused at the sight of Willie. "Hello, Willie," he called.

Willie bowed ceremoniously before returning the greeting. "Evenin', Mr. Doc, suh, evenin'."

Dan Field sobered, however, passing the Stoddard shanty. Lem, Harry, and Rita sprawled upon the porch watching Ray split kindling. Poor little beggar, Dan Field thought, not one of those lazy louts ever lifts a hand to help him.

Myrt's harangue came from the kitchen: "Fer Gawd sake, Ray, can't yer hurry up? I ain't gonna wait all day fer that thar kindlin'."

Mr. Williams called, "Wait, Mr. Doc, please, sir."

Dan Field said, "Whoa."

"Mr. Doc." Mr. Williams came beside the buggy. "I don't rightly know how I knows but I's overly certain it was you git my Gabe off. And I can't rightly thank you, Mr. Doc, sir. Thar ain't enough words ter say what's in my heart. But, Mr. Doc, if'n the good Lord'd seen fit ter make all white men the likes of you thar'd be no trouble in this here world. Mr. Doc, know what they done Saturday night? They goes in my place and tears everything up and they smashes my pulpit and tears my high hat and my long tail suit ter shreds. And I's not only a preacher of God's word, Mr. Doc, I's supposed ter uphold the law in this here town. And know what happened this afternoon, Mr. Doc? Them poor little young'uns, Ella and Wilbur, gits stoned out'n school."

"I really can't see what's to be done about the high-hat situation," Dan Field said. "Matter of fact I've possessed no such embellishment since my salad days. However, I do own an extra long tail suit which, I believe, with a very little alteration would fit you like a glove. I'll have Ackley bring it this evening. And it's a gift. I can't use two."

Suddenly down the deep dark furrows of Mr. Williams's face

the tears again coursed. "The Lord will provide. Veriiy the Lord
will provide."

"The Lord will provide," Dan Field repeated, and drove on.

Ten minutes later he entered the Grand Central. Mr. Leonard,
behind the desk, was the sole occupant of the office. In the dining
room Mrs. Leonard and Jean were helping out until new waitresses could be found.

Mr. Leonard, a worn edition of Tom, also possessed a tall
figure, sandy hair, and honest blue eyes.

"Hello, Doc," he said pleasantly.

"Hello, Nard."

"What can I do for you, Doc?"

Dan Field rested against the counter. "No doubt you've heard,
Nard, about Red beating Dolly to a pulp Saturday afternoon."

Mr. Leonard nodded. "Yeh, I heard."

"She's still about as pitiful a looking object as I ever set eyes
on. Both she and Belle have been afraid to stick their noses outside the shanty door. Belle asked me to stop on the way home and
see if she could return to work tomorrow."

Mr. Leonard frowned. "I don't know if I want neither back,
Doc. You know me, Doc. You know I'm an honest law-abiding
citizen and I think what happened in this town Saturday night is
a disgrace. What's more, I ain't ever going to let Red Tatem in
my bar again. And whether Gabe raped Dolly or whether he
didn't, I don't know. But I do know an awful lot of people
around town are saying whatever happened wasn't all Gabe's
fault. I can't see how it'd do my place any good having neither
of them girls back."

"No doubt you're right," Dan Field agreed. "Certainly no one
else would employ them now. Still"—he shrugged—"the excitement will blow over in a jiffy. Red has already forgotten what
raised his wrath. In a few days Dolly and Belle should have no
trouble finding plenty of places. Competent help's certainly not
easy to find these days, although I don't suppose I'm breaking any
news to you, Nard."

Mr. Leonard frowned again. "You certainly ain't breaking any
news to me. Even the farm girls'd sooner go to a city and work in
a mill or factory, and starve to death, too, by God! And plenty
girls these days got an idea that cooking and waiting table ain't
respectable, even helping out their own folks. Take my own

girl now; I got Jean right this minute helping the missus and she's hot as a hornet. Matter of fact, Doc, ever since Jean started going with Tracy Whitlock her head's been chock-full of nonsense. Maybe Tracy's all right—the missus likes him—but all his fine talk and good manners don't set on me none too good."

Dan Field seldom smoked but the counter displayed a number of cigar boxes, contents plainly marked from three for a penny to a dime each.

Putting down twenty cents, he said, "May I have a couple of those ten-centers?"

Mr. Leonard stuck the change in a pocket. "Help yourself."

Dan Field selected two of the cigars and handed one to Mr. Leonard. "Have a smoke on me."

Mr. Leonard smiled. "Don't mind if I do."

They bit off the cigar ends, lighted up, and puffed away.

"Good smoke." Dan Field smiled.

Mr. Leonard nodded. "I don't make a cent's profit on cigars. Sell them for just what I pay. Good business. More'n one commercial has told me he stays here, rather than go on to the next stop, because he can get a good smoke cheap and the food's plenty."

Dan Field moved away from the counter. "Guess I'd better be getting along. Ackley's going to Mudtown later and I'll have him tell Belle you won't be wanting her back. Hope you don't have too much trouble finding new help."

"Wait a minute," Mr. Leonard instructed. "I haven't made up my mind what I'm going to do yet. Of course I could probably find plenty of country girls if I knew where to put my hand on them, but you never can tell how they're going to turn out. And I will say Dolly and Belle's real good workers and broke in. . . . I tell you what, Doc, have Ackley tell Belle, anyhow, she can come back."

"Whatever you say, Nard. Be seeing you."

"Wait a minute. How about a drink on me, Doc?"

"Don't mind if I do." Dan Field smiled.

They went through the office door to the bar. Ralph Pettigrew was downing a half tumbler of rye.

"Hello, Pettigrew," Dan Field said.

"Hello, Doc," Pettigrew answered.

Shorty pushed the bottle of rye and a glass along the counter to Mr. Leonard. "What's yours, Doc?"

"Bourbon."

Shorty opened a new bottle, saying, "Seldom have a call for bourbon unless you come in, Doc."

When the drinks were poured the men tossed them off. Pettigrew's eyes followed Dan Field out of the bar. He had become convinced that Dan Field was responsible for Gabe's escape. Sunday morning Floyd had brought back a story from the depot. The conductor had told him that Gabe boarded the Saturday evening train at Mount Pallas, going on through to Altoona.

It was a fine thing for Doc to do, a fine thing, thought Pettigrew. I wish I could have a talk with Doc sometime, a long talk maybe. I'd like to find out what Doc makes of a lot of things. Maybe we might talk about Margaret Taylor. But I wouldn't hurt a hair on that girl's head. I wouldn't put a hand on that girl, so help me God! I wouldn't, Pettigrew concluded.

Dan Field found Jake, Fat, and Sammy lounging before the livery stable, one of Jake's pups in Sammy's arms. Why the devil was Sammy hanging around the stable all the time lately? For more than a month now, every time he passed the place Sammy was evident. And it couldn't be the pup because one morning at dawn, on the way home from an all-night case, he had seen Sammy scuttling through the door.

Unlike any other child he'd ever known, however, Sammy was inscrutable. He was friendly enough, always blinking his round blue eyes and smiling. Yet from babyhood he had kept his own counsel. If questioned, no matter how tactfully, he'd withhold any direct information. Exactly like George in this respect, and exactly like George he held his small duplicate figure aloof. Sammy the inscrutable, Sammy the nonchalant, and Sammy who's exactly like George—Dan Field chuckled to himself often and again—but Sammy who belonged to Pris. So now, seeing Sammy before the livery stable, he drew up and stopped.

"Good evening, gentlemen," Dan Field said. "Anything new around town today?"

Jake spat. "The school's new. Fat and me was just discussing the subject. Do you know, Doc, they's got Latin and Greek in the new school? Guess they won't hurt the boys none but if'n my girls wasn't growed I'd not be having them larn foreign languages. Look what just one foreign language done to Miss Fisher. Good-looking woman, but with her head full of Latin, what man'd want her? Why, she ain't never had a feller in her life."

Fat adjusted his fly. "What's the sense'n boys being larned Latin and Greek neither? What good'll it do they? Let me tell you, if'n the English language was good enough for Jesus Christ it's good enough for anybody. What do you think, Doc?"

"It seems perfectly obvious," Dan Field said soberly, "if the English language were good enough for Jesus Christ it should be good enough for anybody." He turned to Sammy. "Want a ride as far as I go, Sammy?"

Sammy blinked his round blue eyes, smiled, hugged the pup closer, and said, "I ain't going home yet, Uncle Doc."

Dan Field was hardly on his way again before Charlie Raub came running up to the buggy, crying, "Mrs. Sargent says hurry, hurry, Mr. Doc. It's Bert."

Charlie jumped onto the seat beside him and Dan Field flapped the reins and flapped them again until Nervy was trotting top speed. Before the Sargent gate he sprang out of the buggy, raced up the walk, leaped the steps, flung open the door, and burst into the hall.

Lou and Bert were still standing there, Lou's face chalk-white.

"What is it?" Dan Field panted.

Bert frowned. "I don't know, Uncle Doc. Mama she just wouldn't let me move till you got here."

"What is it, Lou?" Dan Field repeated, still panting.

Lou gasped, "Dan, Bert's got lice. His head's fairly crawling."

Dan Field couldn't keep a straight face. He threw back his head and laughed until the tears ran down his cheeks.

Lou fairly shrieked, "Stop that laughing, Dan! Stop it, do you hear me? You must do something about Bert right away."

Presently Dan Field stopped laughing, told Lou to stay where she was, and took Bert upstairs. In the bathroom he had Bert hold his head over the basin, found Rufus's razor, soap, and brush, and after shaving the scalp clean struck a match and set fire to the shorn locks, vermin *in medias res*.

"Now, my good fellow," he chuckled, "if you wish to spare yourself further annoyance, from this day forward keep your hieratic head aloof from the proletarian pates of your Mudtown preceptors. In other words, when you have business with the Stoddards or Lawlers, don't get too close."

Bert took a look in the mirror and one of the occasional smiles stole across his face. "Know sumpin, Uncle Doc? What you just did to me is gonna pretty near bust Mama's heart."

Dan Field kept a straight face and asked, "How did you know that soaking Red's hand in hot water and soap was the proper treatment after such an operation?"

Bert again became serious. "See, Uncle Doc, if Mr. Strock or Mr. Butler get bit at a hog butchering they soak the bite in hot water and lye soap. Know sumpin, Uncle Doc? I ain't gonna be a banker after I grows up. I'm gonna be a doctor."

Dan Field sighed. "What I'd not give to be in your boots! By the time you're old enough to go to college, Bert, things will be known about the body, and mind, too, which have not been dreamed today."

Bert had no time to answer.

Outside the bathroom Lou was calling, "What's that awful smell? What are you doing to Bert, Dan? I'm coming in."

Chapter Two

$\mathcal{T}$HENCE in Willowspring—besides the town clock booming the hours and the half hours all day and all night, and the church bells pealing Sundays and for Wednesday evening prayer meeting—the new schoolhouse bell rang out upon the air every weekday, except during vacations. The first bell was at eight-thirty, the second at nine, the first bell after the noon hour at one, and the second at one-thirty, not forgetting the 11:00 A.M. and the 3:00 P.M. recess bells. Now for a whole week another bell would be heard, a bell whose tolling was a harbinger, orotund or ominous, forewarning even life and death. Because now had come November.

Through weeks past, however, over all the valley the fields had been dotted, as a dish of red pepper sprinkled, by farmers and hands, wearing red flannel shirts to the last man, busy harvesting. And if a number employed mowing machines not a few still whetted scythes. Some of the farmers had heard tell of such contrivances as mechanical threshers, reapers, and binders, but they all moved grain by hand cradles and threshed it with flails on the barn floors.

By November the grain had been hauled to the gristmill. Family flour, stable stock bran, and poultry middlings returned. The corn was stored in cribs; in silos the green fodder was beginning to brew. Meanwhile the farmers' wives dried fruit and preserved vegetables. Beside outside fires they stirred huge copper-lined kettles wherein apples, cider, and brown sugar bubbled aromatically to make apple butter. Across Willowspring crops had been garnered and cupboards stocked against the coming winter.

The valley with its shorn fields appeared drab, except where a patch of buckwheat stubble glowed; and the town gardens

looked bare as a bone; the mountains in November were also
stripped, seeming to lower under a no less lowering sky, the
sun's effect an effort at best.

Yet first had come October, with the valley and mountains
and every Willowspring street, even unto Limestone Avenue,
a sudden galaxy, and the whole of earth wearing light like
a halo. The air took on a crackling coolness like ice tinkling in
a glass on a summer day. Grapes ripened and hung heavy and
purple on the vines. Great green pods dropped from the horsechestnut trees or were shaken down by boys high among the
branches, and children collected nuggets of pure brown gold.
Old men put these nuts in their pockets to stave off rheumatism.
The leaves fell and after being raked into huge piles a match
sent sweet smoke sailing. Quail called and hunters started off
across the hills before daybreak. But pretty soon the quail were
silent and all the other birds except the sparrows, jays, and
cardinals migrated. Overhead almost any day could be seen wild
geese winging.

Then the rains came. Windows were put down, doors kept
closed, the weather turned raw, roads became bogs, winds were
high, furnaces and stoves blazed, and those best families who
possessed fly screens had them taken down and stored. The days
grew shorter and the nights longer, and so came November.

During its entire first week this new bell tolled morning and
afternoon. It was the courthouse bell. This was court week, like
six Saturdays all in a row, with people driving to town from all
over the county—not only prisoners and witnesses but spectators
as well. The streets of Willowspring were lined all day long with
buggies and wagons and even oxcarts. The sidewalks were
thronged with people.

A trial here meant what the theater did in some places, and the
courtroom benches were continually crowded. The first afternoon of the 1880 session a heavily veiled woman wedged herself
between a fat woman and a small redheaded girl who held a
baby no bigger than a doll.

Proceedings had not begun, and voices buzzed of politics,
preserves, crops, hard times, and the winter ahead. A boy and a
girl made unabashed love. A goodly quota of bare breasts suckled
infants. A little boy wanted to go out but his mother was afraid
their seats might be lost and told him to wet his pants. A man

reeking of alcohol wandered up and down one aisle. A veteran on a wooden leg pegged up the other, transferring a quid of tobacco from his mouth to a pocket. Practically all the men were chewing or smoking, spitting on the floor. Any number of women knitted, their needles clicking, the way long ago other needles clicked beside a guillotine. Behind the bar lawyers and out-of-town police chewed and smoked and spat around huge brass cuspidors, talking, swearing, and laughing.

Mr. Williams, wearing the red helmet with "Police Chief" across its front, stood alone soberly. Tracy Whitlock buzzed importantly.

Presently the jurors were called. The alcohol-reeking man was one, the wooden-legged veteran who had the quid stored in a pocket was another. A butcher, a baker, a candlestick maker . . . "Hold up your right hand. No, your right hand." Twelve honest men and true.

"There they come. Knight's the dark one," the fat woman cackled loudly.

The prisoners were brought through a door back of the bar: Rudolphe William Knight, alias John Williams, and Albert Long—two thin, well-dressed, and well-groomed young men.

Judge Hart, more stately than ever in his robe, made an imposing entry. Perfect protagonist.

The audience stood up. The audience sat down. There were no sounds now save coughs and rattling papers. The play was on.

"The Commonwealth versus Rudolphe William Knight, alias John Williams, and Albert Long, for larceny of eggs, tools, and a buggy, from three different places in August 1880."

The counsel for the defense, Attorney Ralph Pettigrew, had been appointed by the Court to defend when there was no defense. Knight and Long, their whispers barely audible, merely denied all charges and never took the stand again. And the convicting testimony was as homely as the smell of wood smoke.

After a storekeeper from East Everett swore eggs in an old basket had been sold him by Knight and Long, farmer Roy Wonders took the stand—witness for the Commonwealth.

QUESTION: Mr. Wonders, was a basket of eggs stolen from your barn?

ANSWER: Yes sir.

(*A basket is displayed.*)

QUESTION: Is this the basket the eggs were in at the time they were stolen?

ANSWER: Yes sir.

QUESTION: Where did you get this basket?

ANSWER: I bought it from Charley Feathers twenty-two years ago.

QUESTION: How are you going to be able to identify it?

ANSWER: When a man owns anything for twenty-two years it ain't hard to identify it.

The theft of the tools was as easily proven. They had been taken from a shed at the Waterside Plant of the East Everett Stone and Lime Company, and had been found hidden on the land of farmer George Mowry where Knight and Long had worked. Carpenter T. A. Roberts took the stand.

QUESTION: You are a carpenter employed by the East Everett Stone and Lime Company, are you not?

ANSWER: That's right.

QUESTION: Do the recovered tools belong to the company?

ANSWER: No sir, they belong to me.

(*Some tools are displayed.*)

QUESTION: Are these your tools?

ANSWER: Yes sir.

QUESTION: How do you know they are your tools?

ANSWER: When a fellow has worked with tools for nigh eighteen years there are certain little marks you become accustom' to.

Ralph Pettigrew sprang to his feet. "Your honor, I object. This is the second time this afternoon that a witness has claimed ownership of evidence—first the basket and now the tools—merely by acknowledging said evidence was his."

Judge Hart said, "Objection sustained."

Pettigrew reached among the set of tools, took one out, and, holding it behind his back, spoke to carpenter Roberts.

QUESTION: By what certain little marks can you identify the hammer which I hold in my hand?

ANSWER: There's a small split near the end of the handle and the head's wore off some on the right.

Pettigrew looked the hammer over and sat down again.

A short recess was announced. The knitting needles clicked

again. A few people wandered out. The little redheaded girl put the baby over a shoulder and followed.

The fat woman turned to the heavily veiled woman, saying, "Bet your life I ain't gonna miss *her* case."

"Whose case?" the veiled woman asked.

"The redhead's. The one who was setting next to you with the baby. Ain't you heard about her?"

"No."

The fat woman went on, her eyes sharp as an owl's at night, looking as if she could see things nobody else could see. "She's pretty near fourteen now but she was only twelve when it happened. Mind that, only twelve when it happened. And she's swore it on this fellow, name of Ed Timmons. He's seventeen now but he swears he never touched her. She alwuz slept in the same bed with her sister and brother-in-law. Mind that, in the same bed with her sister and brother-in-law, and nobody can't tell me it wasn't the brother-in-law knocked her up. But see, she —I mean the redhead—is crazy about Ed Timmons, and she's trying to prove Ed knocked her up so the law'll make him marry her. Mind that."

The veiled woman made no answer and those who had gone out came back, including the little redheaded girl and the baby.

The little redheaded girl said to the veiled woman, "I had to fetch her a clean didie. I'm glad nobody got my seat." She turned the tiny bottom up.

Again the veiled woman made no answer but again everybody stood up and sat down because Judge Hart was on the bench once more. Now a respectable-looking, middle-aged woman took the stand—this and the next being the only witnesses Pettigrew had been able to secure for the defence.

QUESTION: Are you the aunt of Rudolphe William Knight, alias John Williams?

ANSWER: I don't know what you're talking about with your al-ali—or whatever that word was, and your John Williams. But if you want to know if I'm Rudy Knight's aunt, I am. And a better boy never lived and anybody who says Rudy stole anything is a liar.

The audience roared. Judge Hart pounded and there was a threat of contempt-of-court action before Knight's aunt was dismissed and Albert Long's father took the stand—a wizened bit of a man with tears in his eyes and voice, who'd worked on the railroad tracks sixteen years and never been laid off one day or ever been in trouble in his whole life, so he testified. And he knew Allie didn't steal the eggs and the tools and as for the buggy—why, the night the buggy was stolen Allie stayed with his mother, who'd been took by a stroke.

QUESTION: Was Allie with his mother the night of August 13, 1880, when the buggy was stolen?

ANSWER: He must have been. Yes sir, he was. I told you once his mother was took by a stroke and I was workin' night shift. And I told you once, too, I worked on the tracks sixteen years and I ain't never been laid off oncet and I ain't ever been in trouble in my whole life.

But on the morning of August 14, 1880, one Peter Dibert of East Everett testified that when he went to his barn the door was open. His team stood in the barn all right but covered with lather and wearing broken harness, while his buggy was gone. And his buggy wasn't found until two days later on the Clayton mountain. It was smashed to pieces with an old torn jacket Peter Dibert had never seen before, on the seat.

Farmer Mowry, upon whose land Knight and Long worked, took the stand, the old torn jacket on display.

QUESTION: Is this your jacket?

ANSWER: It is.

QUESTION: When was the last time you saw this jacket before it was found inside the broken buggy?

ANSWER: About ten o'clock on the night of August 13 I was settin' in the kitchen with my wife when Knight and Long come in. They'd both been drinkin'. Knight said him and Long was goin' to town and he wanted to know if'n he could get the loan of my jacket there, as it was startin' to rain. Next mornin' about six both Knight and Long come back to the farm. I see Knight didn't have my jacket on and ast him where it was. He says he'd lost it but he'd pay me. I told him never mind because the jacket was near gone. If you hold it up you can see both elbows is out and the right front's ripped.

After the usual proceedings the jury filed out to be back in ten minutes.

"Guilty."

An old egg basket, worn carpenter tools, a torn jacket, evidence homely as the smell of wood smoke—six to ten years in Western Penitentiary. Outside was November in a mountain hamlet, inside was autumn requiem.

The town clock struck four.

The heavily veiled woman started, pulled herself from between the fat woman and the little redheaded girl, pushed past knees to the aisle.

As she was going out the door Tracy Whitlock poked Ralph Pettigrew. "Look, if that isn't Margaret Taylor's back I'll eat my hat."

Pettigrew's eyes widened.

Tracy snapped his fingers. "I'm going to run after her and find out for sure."

One of Pettigrew's big hands took hold of one of Tracy's thin arms. "You're going to stay right where you are and not waste time."

Nevertheless, when the heavily veiled woman reached the street, instead of going down Linden toward the Taylors' she turned south on Oak. Presently she entered an alley. Behind a bush she removed the veil, stuffed it in her blouse, and, quickly returning to Oak, rushed down Linden. Before quite reaching the corner, however, she stopped abruptly and gazed anxiously toward Miss Fisher's. For the woman who'd worn the heavy veil was Margaret Taylor and now she must wait until Dot joined her before going home.

But if Miss Fisher's pupils were nowhere in sight, the public school spilled forward upon and over the corner. Tom Leonard, Ben Smith, and Jack Sturdevant loitered near the gate and Rufe and Laird appeared in the doorway. Meg fervently hoped Laird wouldn't spot her. She felt, right then, that the sound of his croaking voice would be unendurable! The little Jewish girl who used to be at the Reynards' so much was walking by herself a bit ahead of Mollie and Bertha Richards. Poor Alexander Jennings streaked across the yard, Sammy, Buzz Standing, and some other boys hooting "Sissy" after him. Bert Sargent strutted between a colored boy and that filthy white boy who delivered washes.

(Meg wondered if she oughtn't tell Mrs. Sargent about Bert.) But finally Miss Fisher's pupils appeared and Meg sighed, relieved.

She quickly crossed the corner and, catching Dot's arm, took her out of earshot of the others. "Was Miss Fisher all right?" she demanded.

Dot nodded. "She was just fine. I told her exactly what you said—how you had an awful headache and were going to stay in your room all afternoon. And she wasn't to let on to Mama because Mama was having a party this afternoon and you weren't going to let her know you were staying home as it might spoil the party. Miss Fisher thought you were real sweet being so considerate of Mama. But, Meg, I can't wait another minute to hear. Was he wonderful?"

Meg sighed. "Wonderful. You've no idea how wonderful, Dot. But oh, Dot, I heard the most terrible things too. Things you'll hardly believe are true."

"What, Meg?" Dot gasped, agog.

"I can't tell you now, Dot," Meg choked. "I really can't tell you now. Let's hurry home."

The new school had progressed normally. By the first of November not only the slats of the boys' outhouse but the walls enclosing the girls' basement water closets, had been adequately decorated with pornographic symbols and pictographs, four-letter generalities and phallic personalities, the latter making no bones whatsoever concerning what Paul had done to Mabel or what Agnes wanted Bud to do to her, et cetera.

Classrooms now took as a matter of course the smell of chalk dust, squeaking slate pencils, rustling papers, shuffling feet, dropped books, spilled ink, teacher's pet, the dunce, and the bright boy or girl.

Laird Culver held first place in senior class because, besides having a good mind to begin with, he studied his head off. Rufe led the sophomores for the same reasons. Yet Rufe had no avidity, merely being too proud not to know his lessons. Tom, Ben, and Jack skimmed over the crust, exerting a minimum of effort. Mollie stood at the head of grade seven easily, Helen and Alexander (both by dint of real labor) ran a nip-and-tuck second, with Bertha somewhere around the middle, and Sammy taking a nonchalant place at the foot of the class. Bert easily outranked every other child in fourth, Shad was baby-room dunce, and on the first Monday in November Ray had been promoted from first to second grade.

Leaving school this afternoon, Rufe, Laird at heel, approached the gate where Tom, Ben, and Jack stood talking. As usual when Rufe came near the conversation ceased abruptly and the other three boys made off.

Laird said, "You know, Rufe, the reason they quit talking if anybody gets near is because they're talking stuff about girls. Terrible stuff."

Rufe had come to this decision some time ago, yet the truth croaked by Laird infuriated him. Suddenly he felt as if he hated Laird Culver more than he'd thought it possible to hate anybody in the world.

"You go to hell," Rufe snarled, swinging out the gate.

But what the hell? Rufe asked himself on the way home. Laird was nothing. Nothing. And what difference did it make how Tom and Ben and Jack acted, or Mollie either? He had his book. Rufe had kept *The Building of the Parthenon* a whole month, reading and rereading every word until he knew the script verbatim. Besides, he'd carefully copied every illustration. And now Rufe was working on a book of his own, *The Building of a City*, a whole city to be built of marble like the Parthenon.

Bert, Shad, and Ray strode jauntily toward Broad, Ray's alert black eyes shining happily.

"Bert, did yer hear how I git promoted ter second grade?" Ray asked.

Shad hawked derisively but Bert said, "That's good, Ray."

"It's good all right," Ray agreed. "But see, Bert, Teacher in second she makes me set off side like Teacher done in first. Only now, see, I gotta set off side myself 'cause they ain't no other Mudtown young'uns in second. How come Teacher makes me set off side myself, Bert?"

Bert shook his head, upon which at last a black bristle was sprouting. "I wouldn't go to hurt your feelings, Ray."

"I ain't got no feelin's, Bert," Ray informed.

"See, Ray," Bert explained, "Teacher she makes you sit off side 'cause you got lice and stinks."

"I guess likely," Ray nodded, not a whit embarrassed.

By this time the trio had reached the corner of Broad.

"What you doing, Ray?" Bert asked.

Ray shrugged. " 'Spect Mam she's got plenty chores fer me ter do."

"Yeh," Bert said. "But Mr. Strock and Mr. Butler's mighty likely butchering."

Ray smiled. "Mighty likely."

Besides being court week, the first of November was official butchering time and on farms and in town most any moment hogs could be heard shrieking and cattle moaning. However, the town killings, compared to the slaughterhouse massacres, were as a cockpit to an arena. During this season Mr. Strock, ably assisted by Mr. Butler, not only slashed the throats of his own stock but accommodated many of the best families by executing their fatlings.

What Mr. Stock called his slaughterhouse was a lot sloping to the creek, with a pen where the doomed animals waited their turn to one side, and the dippings barrels on the other, completely surrounded by a rail fence. After an animal was stuck and bled the carcass was thrown into one of the barrels, where water had been brought to the scalding point by dropping in red-hot stones. As soon as the bristles were sufficiently soft to be shaved it was dragged out. When Bert, Shad, and Ray arrived and perched themselves on the top fence rail, already a dozen clean corpses, stiff and upright—looking like so many erections from loins of roughhewn clay—loomed to one side. The middle of the arena was a gory mess and bloody rivulets ran down to the Juniata, whose blue, around the spot, had taken on the gentle shade of a pink pastel. Mr. Strock and Mr. Butler, themselves studies in scarlet, at the moment struggled with a shrieking, terrified hog.

"Know sumpin?" Bert said. "I don't see how come a hog couldn't be clouted 'fore it's stuck. See, then they wouldn't fight and squeal."

Shad cackled. "Thar's the fun, Bert. Whar'd be the fun, Bert, if'n old hawgs don't fight and squeal?"

Ray answered seriously, "I don't see neither, Bert, how come a hawg couldn't be clouted 'fore it's stuck. But I'll find out. See, Bert, I's figgerin' fer ter larn everythin' what thar's in the world ter larn."

"There ain't nobody in the whole world knows everything, Ray."

"They could, Bert," Ray informed. "See, Bert, that thar tramp gentleman Mrs. Tatem run off with he says anybody what know'd nuff 'bout numbers kin find out anythin' in the world."

" 'Bout numbers?" Bert wrinkled his brow. "You mean numbers, Ray?"

"Numbers," Ray insisted. "See, Bert, the tramp gentleman he says if'n yer knowed half 'bout numbers yer kin find out how fur it is 'round the world, how many miles ter a star, whar the North Pole is at, whar a ship what's still in the middle of the ocean's gonna land and——"

"I guess likely," Bert interrupted. "Know sumpin, Ray? I got a uncle what's a doctor on a boat and he must know how to find out where he's going. See, Ray, if my uncle didn't know how to find out where he's going, how'd he know where he was going?"

Ray nodded. "Sure, Bert. And that ain't all. That thar tramp gentleman says if'n yer knowed nuff 'bout numbers it'd be as easy fer ter me-measure the dep-depths of a soul as it is fer ter weigh the pounds of the body."

Bert grunted. "Hump! What good'd it be to measure the—the depths of a soul?"

Ray smiled. "It took me a long time fer ter figger that un out, Bert. But see, if'n yer weighs a body yer kin tell if'n it's fat or lean and if'n yer measures a soul yer kin tell if'n it's good or bad."

"Yippy, yippy, yippy," Shad began screaming. "Looky, Bert, looky, Ray, old hawg bite Mr. Butler. Old hawg bite Mr. Butler's arm clean through."

Chapter Three

THIS FIRST Monday of November Margaret Taylor, Sr., called Madge, the mother of Meg and Dot, was entertaining—a luncheon with whist to follow—for her own mother, Mrs. Kimbell. Besides Mrs. Kimbell's friends, Mrs. Albright and Mrs. Sargent, Mrs. Dr. Berkley, Mrs. Harley, and Mrs. Judge Martin, Madge had invited Pris, Lou, and Peggy Martin to make up a table of whist for herself.

Madge Taylor was a short, slight woman with ash-colored graying hair, warm blue eyes, and a lovely gentle mouth. Meg and Dot had inherited their buxomness and brown hair and eyes from their father. About five o'clock in the afternoon, watching the departing guests moving away, Madge patted herself on the back. She always worried before every party and became awfully upset afterward if every detail wasn't just right. But today the whole affair had moved like clockwork. The food was truly delicious. Annie, of course, could never be depended upon, one day serving a dish fit to suit the queen's taste and the next time making a perfect botch of it. Gertrude, the new second maid, from soup to nuts had performed like a trained hand. How Pris and Lou managed the way they did, keeping only one girl, never failed to amaze Madge. Although Nellie and Maggie were perfect treasures if one overlooked their plain appearances and the habit the grandmothers fussed about of saying, "Supper's ready" instead of "Dinner is served." You would think Pris and Lou might remedy that.

Still, both Pris and Lou had looked like perfect pictures today, wearing the latest outfits brought home from Philadelphia. It really was about time Chan realized Meg and Dot were quite old enough to wear ready-made clothes, instead of having Mrs. Standing make their every stitch. Of course, not ready-made underwear. . . . Madge flushed properly, remembering the story Chan had told her about Miss Gunther's latest novelty. She turned into the parlor and started picking up cards, thinking, as she had thought before, If I ever happened to be in Miss Gunther's when no one else is shopping I might want her to show me the . . . Madge sighed. On the other hand, she hoped Dot and Meg hadn't heard about the ready-made drawers. But bless their hearts! Madge's lovely gentle mouth curved in a smile. They're innocent as the day is long. Then it dawned upon Madge she'd not heard the girls coming in after school. She picked up her skirts and tore up the stairs.

Arriving home, Meg and Dot slipped up the back stairs to their room, where Meg threw herself across the bed, weeping silently.

Dot couldn't understand the situation. Meg had told her Mr. Pettigrew was wonderful, perfectly wonderful. But Dot did what she believed was expected.

She sat down beside Meg. "Darling sister, dearest of sisters, would that I could bear it for you."

Meg's weeping ceased abruptly and she sat erect. "Don't!" she commanded. "The very thought of beautiful characters like Elsie and her friends is truly unendurable after what I've—I've been through."

"What, Meg?" Dot asked anxiously. "What have you been through? You told me Mr. Pettigrew was wonderful."

Meg sighed from the depth of her being. "He was, Dot, wonderful! Perfectly wonderful! Yet his agony must be excruciating now. If you could ever know what Judge Hart did. If you could ever know, Dot."

"Tell me, please tell me," Dot pleaded.

"I don't know whether you could bear it, Dot."

"Yes, darling sister, dearest of sisters," Dot began, then, catching herself, "Yes, I can bear it all right, Meg."

"Well, Dot," Meg began, her tone truly tragic, "there were these two young men, hardly more than boys, who had faces pure as angels'. And they were well dressed but modest too. Why, Dot, their voices were so modulated you could hardly hear a word they said. But they had been arrested!" Meg stopped emphatically.

"Arrested?" Dot cried. "Why, Meg?"

"Why?" Meg sniffed. "Indeed ask me why. They had been arrested because a lot of the commonest-looking people you ever saw said they'd stolen. And stolen what? Nothing more or less than some eggs, a set of tools, and a buggy."

Dot shook her head unbelievingly. "And those two perfectly lovely young men were arrested for stealing *those* things?"

"The point is, Dot, they didn't even steal *those* things. It was just *those* common people said they did. Rudy and Allie—those were the young men's names—said themselves they didn't steal a thing. And Rudy's aunt said never a better boy than Rudy ever lived and anybody who said Rudy stole anything was a liar. She said 'liar' right out and Judge Hart was furious and pounded and pounded."

"What did he pound, Meg?" Dot inquired.

"The desk. Judge Hart sat behind a big high desk and he had a hammer and every time he got mad he pounded the desk. And then he wouldn't let Rudy's aunt say another word but Allie's father—oh, Dot, he was a wonderful old man. He'd worked sixteen years on the railroad tracks and never been laid off a day and he'd never been in trouble in his whole life. Think of that, Dot, he'd never been in trouble in his whole life."

Dot sighed. "He must be a perfectly beautiful character, Meg."

Meg sighed. "He is, Dot. And he was almost crying and he said Allie didn't steal anything and the night the buggy was stolen Allie stayed home all night taking care of his mother who had a stroke. And oh, Dot, Mr. Pettigrew was perfectly wonderful to Rudy and Allie."

"What did he do?" Dot demanded.

"He took a personal interest in those boys, a personal interest is what he took. He sat beside them all the time and every once in a while he'd whisper to them. And he made the most wonderful speech to the jury—that's the men in court who decide if people are guilty or not—and he told the jury it would be mud on the skirts of justice if two boys whose aunt and father had sworn under oath that they were fine characters . . . Well, that's what it would be if they were found guilty."

"So they let Rudy and Allie go free?" Dot chirped.

"No," Meg groaned. "But they would have let them go free if it hadn't been for Judge Hart."

"Judge Hart?" Dot echoed.

"Yes, Judge Hart. You'll hardly believe me, Dot, but after Mr. Pettigrew's speech Judge Hart practically told the jury they weren't to let Rudy and Allie go free. And what could a poor jury do except listen to Judge Hart? And, Dot, you'll hardly believe this either, but Judge Hart sent Rudy and Allie to the Western Penitentiary for from six to ten years."

Dot groaned. "Judge Hart did that! So Judge Hart did that, did he? Why, do you know, Meg, I don't feel like I ever wanted to speak to another member of the Martin family again, even Tertius. Do you suppose Mama and Papa have any idea the kind of person Judge Hart really is?"

"I don't know what Mama and Papa know about Judge Hart," Meg said. "But I do know something they know that they never let on to us."

"You do?"

"I certainly do."

"What?"

Meg shuddered. "Oh, it's too terrible to tell even to you, Dot."

"Please tell me. Please," Dot begged.

Meg whispered, "Dot, girls—even girls not fifteen years old— can have babies without being married."

Dot's eyes practically popped out of their sockets. "How did you ever find out?"

Still whispering, Meg recounted the fat woman's story about the little redheaded girl and the baby.

". . . And she slept in the same bed with her sister and her brother-in-law," Dot repeated incredulously, "and the fat woman said no one could tell her it wasn't the brother-in-law who—what was it nobody could tell the fat woman the brother-in-law didn't do to the redhead, Meg?"

"Knocked her up."

"What's 'knocked her up'?"

"I don't know," Meg had to admit. "But it's something. The redhead had the baby right there beside me and——"

"You mean she *had* the baby right there beside you?" Dot cried.

"Don't be silly! She didn't *have* the baby right there beside me. She'd already had the baby but—she and the baby sat right beside me."

"Oh . . ."

Meg meditated an instant before continuing. "You know, Dot, for a long time I've been wondering how a marriage ceremony could make a girl have a baby." Suddenly Meg blanched. "Dot, you don't think . . . ?"

Dot blanched. "Meg, you don't think . . . ?"

They were both remembering the same scene. A few years before they'd had a cook who'd lasted only a few days, but she'd remained long enough to point out some dogs in the back yard and tell Meg and Dot, "They's makin' puppies."

Madge entered the room, her warm blue eyes anxiously scanning her daughters. She saw their eyes shining and their cheeks flushed. . . . They were getting to be real beauties, but innocent as the day is long.

Assured that they were safe and sound, after chatting a few minutes Madge went along to her own room.

No sooner was she out of earshot than Meg said, "Dot, I simply have to see him alone and talk to him. I'll die if I don't. I know he must love me. I know it. What's more, I'm going to see him alone."

"Darling sister, dearest of sisters, if I might——" Dot began.

"Stop!" Meg commanded. "Elsie Dinsmore was all right when I was a child, before I knew what I found out in court. Life isn't like they write it in books like that. Dot, I've got to see him and talk to him."

"How could you, though, Meg?" Dot demanded.

Meg's eyes flashed. "I know how. I've been thinking about it. I'm going to write him a note and take it straight up to the post office. He'll get it tonight right after dinner. I'll tell him to meet me—well, to meet me . . ." Meg racked her brains to find a safe place and time for the rendezvous. "I know," she went on finally, "I'll tell him to meet me in the trees by the creek across from Ma Woodward's. At midnight Mama and Papa will be asleep, and then I'll slip out and down the back road."

"Meg, you wouldn't dare," Dot gasped.

Meg didn't answer. She found a pen and paper and wrote the note.

She started toward the door. "Don't you worry, Dot. I know what I'm doing. And Mama and Papa never wake up nights."

On their way home after Madge's party Pris, Lou, and the two grandmothers fairly caused the passing townspeople to gape.

Saturday night they'd returned from the fall trip to Philadelphia. This afternoon, besides being costumed according to the latest city fashions, a foreign atmosphere lingered about them, their nostrils still remembering city air and their eyes still full of city spectacles—crowds, sights, shopping, the theater. Pris wandered in the clouds; she'd had the loveliest experience with Dan's mother.

Pris never failed when in Philadelphia to call upon Dan's parents. In the parlor of the old mansion on Rittenhouse Square she'd sit upon an Adam chair, near the marble mantel, with Dan's father and mother, sipping tea out of a fragile colonial cup. But this time Dan's father had not as yet come home and Pris and Dan's mother were alone quite a while.

"He's well, of course?" Dan's mother said.

She had deep-set black eyes like Dan's and the same white skin and, too, her long thin white hands twitched a bit, holding the fragile cup. But she will never drop it, Pris had thought. . . . Like Dan, she couldn't drop a precious thing.

Pris had smiled. "He's very well. Well in more ways than one. I often think he's the most splendid person I've ever known."

Dan's mother smiled and nodded. "Yes, Dan is splendid. From the time he was born I can't remember a single person who wasn't fond of him. But no wonder. He was always, even as a very small boy, doing things for others, and he still is."

Pris nodded. "Yes, he is."

Dan's mother shook her head. "I worry about him sometimes. Do you think he is happy?"

"Happy?" Pris echoed. "Why, I have never thought of such a thing as Dan not being happy. I'm sure he's happy, Mrs. Field. He must be."

"I hope so," Mrs. Field sighed. "But Dan should have married, a man who loves children the way he does." She leaned forward and Pris felt her long white fingers pressing hers. "My dear, I wish Dan had a wife exactly like you."

This afternoon, turning the corner by the school, Pris saw Dan crawling out of his buggy. He saw her and the others, crossed the street, greeted them. He left Pris until last but presently his hand pressed hers, lifting her . . .

He released his clasp and smiled. "Did you see Mother and Father?"

"Of course. And they both looked splendid."

"Fine," he said. "I'll be along one of these days to hear all the news."

He bowed and recrossed the street.

"Why a gentleman would ever want to be a doctor, I don't know," Gramma Albright said, "running around all over the country day and night, hobnobbing with townspeople and riff-raff."

"I suppose somebody has to doctor the townspeople and riff-raff, don't you think, Mrs. Albright?" Gramma Sargent inquired.

Gramma Albright sighed. "I suppose so. And certainly Madge did her best today. But there never fails to be some little thing, nothing you can put your finger on exactly, but some little thing that's not quite right when either Madge or Mrs. Kimbell enter-tains. Of course Mr. Kimbell's a gentleman to his finger tips, but Mrs. Kimbell was a——"

"Pritchard," Lou put in.

"But Mr. Pritchard made a fortune," Gramma Sargent said, "and Mrs. Kimbell had everything a girl could wish for."

"Of course Mr. Pritchard made a fortune," Gramma Albright agreed. "But have you forgotten how, Mrs. Sargent? Out of a railroad. And do you think for an instant that money made out of a railroad would be able to give a girl who'd the proper back-ground everything she could wish for?"

"Now you two know the party was lovely and you enjoyed yourselves thoroughly," Lou said.

Pris hadn't heard a word. Dan, she was wondering, why haven't you married? And if it hadn't been George and I it would most certainly have been you and I—you and I married, Dan . . . No! No! Pris told herself. I mustn't ever think of such a thing. I could never have loved anyone but George. Suddenly she remem-bered the man who'd come in with Dan's father and who'd sent George a message. Why was it she couldn't remember to give George the message? I must tie a string around my finger. . . .

Across the street went Miss Fisher, leading her blind mother around the corner of Horsechestnut. Poor Miss Fisher, Pris thought, beautiful and kind and who's never known the touch of a man or the feel of little hungry lips, and who's had to strug-gle all her life earning a bare living. I should be the most con-tented woman in the world, Pris told herself.

Miss Fisher and her mother were on their way to visit Aunt Tillie Whitlock by request. Yesterday afternoon Miss Fisher had met Aunt Tillie in Strock's Market and she'd asked her to bring Mrs. Fisher and come over tomorrow afternoon as there was a subject Aunt Tillie wished to discuss with them.

Reaching the door of the sizable old house on West Horse-chestnut, Miss Fisher lifted the knocker and let it drop and Aunt Tillie opened the door, greeted them, and ushered them into the parlor.

The Whitlock parlor was opened only for a weekly cleaning or for what Aunt Tillie considered auspicious occasions, and the air reeked of must. Furniture, pictures, and what Aunt Tillie termed her art objects—vases, china statues, a wax angel under glass, and a bunch of paper roses—all appeared not quite settled, the way things in a seldom occupied room are doomed to look.

Aunt Tillie insisted upon the Fishers taking the most comfortable rockers as she seated herself upon a stiff straight-legged chair.

Aunt Tillie was a plump, kindly faced, white-haired old lady and she folded her plump, work-worn hands over her plump abdomen.

"I guess you two been wondering what I wanted you to come over for," she began. "Well, I'll tell you. It's about Tracy. Now you know I'm not one to talk about my own flesh and blood neither. But ever since poor Mr. Meeker got lured uptown into that saloon (and you know he must have got lured or he'd never of done what he did after signing the pledge) I've been worrying my head off about Tracy going with Jean Leonard. Of course I don't think a moment that Tracy'd marry Jean. But it's just about been killing me to think of my own nephew, who's like my own son, going with a girl whose papa sells liquor."

Miss Fisher and her mother nodded sympathetically.

"I know what you mean," Miss Fisher said. "And I'm positive also that unless some influence had been brought to bear Mr. Meeker would never have succumbed."

Mrs. Fisher sighed. "If Dr. Walsh could just find something to cure his indigestion. He suffers that bad. I do feel so for Mrs. Meeker and Mrs. Diggers. If Mr. Diggers was only still alive to help them."

"That's right," Aunt Tillie agreed. "And now getting back to

Tracy. As I was saying, I'm not one to talk about my own flesh and blood, but this thing's been brooding in my mind so long seems like I'd go crazy, and I thought if I could talk it over with someone I'd feel better. And I thought you two'd be just the ones because I know you'll never breathe a word I tell you."

Mrs. Fisher said, "You know you can trust us, Aunt Tillie."

Aunt Tillie nodded. "Yes, and I thought, too, maybe you could help me think up something to do. I don't suppose anything'd stop Tracy going with Jean till he's good and ready but it seems to me something could be done in the meantime."

"Did you tell Tracy how you feel?" Miss Fisher asked.

"Land sakes! No." Aunt Tillie threw up her hands. "If I said a word to Tracy, or he knew I said a word to anybody, he'd get madder'n a wet hen. But it seems like something ought to be done."

"Maybe we might influence him to sign the pledge," Miss Fisher suggested.

"He don't drink. Never touched a drop in his life. What's more, he never will. Tracy's not the drinking kind. Don't smoke or chew neither."

Both Miss Fisher and her mother rocked backward and forward, meditating.

Finally Mrs. Fisher spoke. "Even if Tracy don't drink it might be real nice if he signed the pledge. It would make people know he's never going to drink."

"That's so," Aunt Tillie agreed.

Miss Fisher supplemented her mother's suggestion. "You might get Tracy to sign the tobacco pledge too. If he were to sign both pledges everyone would know he couldn't go wrong no matter how long he went with Jean."

"If we only could get him to sign them," Aunt Tillie sighed.

"Don't you think he would if you were to ask him?" Miss Fisher inquired.

Aunt Tillie had no time to reply. There was a sound at the back of the house, a door opening.

"Aunt Tillie," Tracy called.

"Land sakes! There's Tracy now. Don't let on what we been talking about. He'd be madder'n a wet hen." She called, "Tracy, I'm in the parlor. Miss Fisher and Mrs. Fisher's visiting."

He came and stood in the doorway, bowing, smiling, saying, "What mischief are you three little ladies up to?"

Aunt Tillie stammered, "We were just talking about—well, about——"

Miss Fisher came to her rescue. "I wanted to tell Aunt Tillie" —and Miss Fisher felt she was not telling an untruth because she had really wanted to tell someone about Meg—"what a thoughtful girl Margaret Taylor is. She had such a severe headache today she couldn't come to school. But she stayed in her room and didn't let her mother know a thing. Mrs. Taylor was entertaining and Meg was afraid if she knew about the headache it might spoil the party."

"Then Margaret wasn't in school this afternoon?" Tracy inquired.

Miss Fisher smiled. "No. Meg——"

Tracy didn't hear the rest of Miss Fisher's sentence. He was thinking, I'd give more than a hat to know what Margaret Taylor was doing in court, and why Pettigrew didn't want me to go after her.

A few minutes after six o'clock Ralph Pettigrew finally left the courthouse, and if he were not suffering excruciating agony, as Meg believed, his mood was anything but sanguine. Moving toward the hotel, he speculated bitterly upon the Knight-Long trial. Both had been indicted before; their guilt concerning the present charges was obvious. The only defense Pettigrew could muster was the Knight aunt's lame testimony about his character and the Long father's perjury, swearing Albert was home attending his sick mother the night the buggy was stolen. But what irritated Pettigrew was that the Court had appointed him counsel. A direct slap, Pettigrew considered the appointment, the precedent being that young lawyers who'd little practice received such assignments. And Pettigrew knew the power behind the insult: Judge Hart. That august gentleman never failed to belittle him if possible. Oh well, Pettigrew shrugged, dismissing the matter.

However, he could not put Margaret Taylor out of his mind so readily. He knew the veiled woman Tracy Whitlock had pointed out was Margaret. He could never mistake the curve of those hips. And he knew why she'd been there: to see him. But after his fingers had gripped Fat's butter neck a change had come over Pettigrew. Suddenly the very thought of being free with the girl became obnoxious to him. I wouldn't touch that girl, I wouldn't hurt a hair of her head, I wouldn't put a hand on that girl, so help me God! he kept swearing to himself. And always after that if he met the girls on the street he'd keep his eyes upon Margaret's face and merely nod. . . . What was the sense in anything else? he'd ask himself. Maybe the girl would marry him but he wouldn't marry her. What chance would there be for happiness, what with her own family and the rest of the God damn best families sticking up their noses, the way they would if she married him?

Out of the livery stable Sammy Albright darted, the pup in his arms. With Nigger Harry's return at last, Pettigrew supposed Jake was letting Sammy take the pup home. Jake'd certainly got his money's worth out of Sammy! Much as the Albrights and the Sargents galled him, he couldn't help admiring Sammy's guts —the way the boy'd gotten up before dawn, week after week, and shoveled and sweat, scooting home at daybreak. Jake fairly split his sides telling how Sammy must reach home before the family started stirring.

Crossing the street to the hotel, Pettigrew saw Tracy Whitlock going through the office door. To see Jean, of course, and I wonder what'll come of that? Pettigrew speculated. Jean is a sweet kid and head over heels in love, and Tracy's a squirt if ever one lived.

He entered the bar, crowded as on a Saturday night because of court week. Shorty immediately pushed the rye and tumbler toward him. Yet by the time he reached the dining room Belle was the only person left. Belle had returned to work shortly after the uproar, although Dolly had never shown up. Several times Pettigrew inquired about Dolly. All Belle'd say was, "Dolly she's pretty good."

Tonight, however, he inquired again.

Belle narrowed the eyes so much like Dolly's. "You keep astin' all the time how Dolly is. Do you mind, Mr. Pettigrew?"

"Of course I mind," Pettigrew answered earnestly.

Belle shook her head. "Then I'll tell you, Mr. Pettigrew. Dolly's she's near crazy. I's plumb skeered she might likely kill herself."

"No!" Pettigrew exclaimed.

"You don't know, Mr. Pettigrew," Belle moaned. "You don't know."

"What is it, Belle?"

"Dolly she's knocked up."

Pettigrew didn't say anything for a minute and then he asked, "Has she heard from Gabe?"

"No," Belle said, "nobody hear a word from Gabe, not even Mr. Williams. That's what's near killin' Dolly. She's skeered she'll never see Gabe no more. She keeps saying if'n she jest had some money to go after Gabe she knows she could find him. . . . We got chicken hash, fried sausage, and hard-boiled eggs. Coffee, milk, and buttermilk."

After supper, as Pettigrew passed through the office, Jean and Tracy were sitting there. Jean was a rather plump girl. She was sweet-faced and, like her father and Tom, had sandy hair and honest blue eyes.

"Let me tell you something funny, Jean," Tracy whispered. "This afternoon in court I saw this woman going out and I said to Pettigrew . . ."

Pettigrew went out of the hotel and over to his office. There he found an envelope, put a twenty-dollar bill inside, sealed and addressed it to Dolly Tatem. What the hell difference Dolly's plight could make to him he didn't know. But it did make a difference. And what the hell else could she do now except marry Gabe? Pettigrew asked himself. Poor little devil, he kept thinking, and that poor dumb black buck nigger.

He took the envelope to the post office and after sliding it into the chute drew the mail out of his box and thumbed through the envelopes. They were all business letters except one. The writing made Pettigrew draw his brows together: a woman's, evidently. Pettigrew slit the envelope, withdrew the sheet, and read:

I simply must see you alone and talk to you. Tonight at twelve everyone will be asleep and I'll slip out of the house and down the back street to the creek. I'll be in the trees across from Ma Woodward's. Please, please don't fail me. You know who this is from.

Yes, Pettigrew knew who the letter was from all right—Margaret Taylor. The little fool, Pettigrew thought, the damned little fool. If there was just some way to stop her. But how? How? He couldn't go to the Taylor house, and a note sent there would surely be intercepted by the girl's parents. God damn! Pettigrew swore to himself. If Sammy Albright hadn't taken his pup home today he'd probably be at the livery stable and could have slipped a note to Margaret Taylor.

Like their wives and mothers, around Captain George and Rufus upon this day there lingered a foreign atmosphere. And the trip to the city this time had particularly exhilarated Rufus. He'd spent hours in John Wanamaker's store examining and discussing with Mr. Wanamaker the windows' four arc lights operated by five Brush dynamos which a certain writer called "miniature moons on carbon points, held captive in glass tubes." Mr. Wanamaker had also shown Rufus facts and figures concerning the practicability of lighting whole cities with arc lights.

Going home this day, Rufus said to George, "Mr. Wanamaker has figures proving that it costs eight hundred dollars a year less to light Wabash, Indiana, by electricity than to light it by gas."

"We've no gas," George laughed. "And the point happens to be how much more will it cost to light Willowspring by electricity than by coal oil. Incidentally, Rufus"—George gave a sly look—"how soon do you expect your dynamos?"

Still laughing, George turned in at the gate. He found his family, excepting Sammy, gathered under the sitting-room lamps. Rufe looked a bit less glum than usual, he noted. They greeted him and Lillian jumped to her feet, pirouetting, twirling a red ruffled skirt.

"Look, Papa," she laughed, "isn't this the most beautifulest dress you ever saw? Of all the clothes you and Mama brought me, this is my very favorite."

"Most beautiful, not most beautifulest," George corrected, seating himself and spreading the *Ledger* across his knees.

There he goes, Lillian thought darkly. This was the first moment since the folks returned that she'd not been ecstatic. In truth both Lillian and Prissy were so thrilled about all their lovely new outfits that neither of them had had another thought over the week end.

Pris snapped her fingers. "George, by the way, before I forget again. You remember I told you some college friend of yours happened to come in the day I was calling on Dan's parents. What did I say his name is?"

"Percy Parrish," George told her.

Pris nodded. "That's right, Percy Parrish. Well, he sent you a message but for some reason I've never remembered to tell you. He was a funny-looking, little, bald-headed man. He really did look years and years older than you, George. I did tell you that, you know."

"What about the message?" George inquired. "Don't forget it again."

Pris smiled. "I won't. Mr. Parrish said he'd happened to run across an old friend of yours a little while ago and she'd inquired if he knew what had become of you."

"She?" George smiled.

Pris smiled too. "Yes, George, it—or rather, she—was a she. Her name is Viola, I believe. Anyhow, Mr. Parrish said, 'Tell George Vi was inquiring about him.' Do you remember anyone named Vi, George?"

After an instant George answered, "The name sounds somewhat familiar."

The front door flew open, banged shut, and Sammy burst upon the family circle, holding a half-grown hound before him. George noted the pup's sex and frowned.

Lillian gurgled, "What a precious little dog. Where did you get him, Sammy?"

Sammy grinned proudly. "Spotty's mine, Lillian. My dog, Lillian."

"What do you mean, your dog, Sammy?" George demanded. "You can't keep that animal around here."

Sammy blinked his round blue eyes. "You don't understand, Papa. I gotta keep Spotty. She's my dog."

"You take that dog straight back to where you got it," George commanded.

"I can't, Papa," Sammy insisted. "You don't understand, Papa. Spotty she's my dog. See, Papa——"

"George!" Pris pleaded.

George whispered in her ear.

"Oh . . ." Pris said.

"Sammy"—George's tone had become severe—"take that dog straight back to where you got it and right this minute, too."

"I won't!" Sammy shrieked.

George sprang to his feet, grabbed Spotty, and threw her out the front door.

Returning to the sitting room, he faced Sammy irately. "Now, young man, you go upstairs and get to bed. And the next time your father tells you what to do perhaps you'll have sense enough to obey."

Sammy tore out of the room, up the stairs. Go to bed, huh! Sammy choked. He'd never go to bed in this old house again as long as he lived. He shot through his room, over the back porch, and down the post.

Slipping around the house, he kept calling softly, "Here, Spotty. Here, Spotty, Spotty . . ."

Presently through the dusk Spotty came wiggling and wagging and bouncing, and, choking, Sammy gathered the pup into his arms. Then like a streak he dashed down Maple Street. Before the new schoolhouse he met Bert, on his way home from the slaughterhouse.

"I'm running away from home like Uncle Tim did, Bert," Sammy announced.

"How come?" Bert inquired.

"Papa he won't let me keep Spotty. And Spotty she's my dog. I worked to get Spotty. And I ain't never coming back, like Uncle Tim. And I ain't never going to wash or comb my hair and I'm going to sleep with all my clothes on and I ain't never gonna change them neither." ·

"Where you gonna go?" Bert demanded.

"Up the railroad track."

"Where you gonna sleep?"

" 'Longside the track."

"Know sumpin?" Bert said. "It'll mighty likely be cold sleeping 'side the track this kind of weather."

"Mighty likely," Sammy agreed.

"And mighty likely you'll get hungry, too, this kind of weather. Know sumpin, Sammy?" Bert had a sudden inspiration. "If you didn't run off you could keep Spotty in Shad's woodshed."

"In Shad's woodshed?" Sammy repeated.

Bert nodded. "Yeh. I kept a little rabbit there oncet. It's a good place. And see, Sammy, Spotty could sleep with me tonight. I can slip her under the covers easy and Mama'll never know. And tomorrow morning 'fore light we could go over and fix a little pen in the woodshed. It's a good place, Sammy. And after school every day you could take swill over and feed Spotty. You got nuff good swill to feed plenty of dogs, Sammy."

By the time Pris slipped up the back stairs, carrying Sammy's dinner on a tray, she found him fast asleep, a smile upon his lips.

"God bless you, darling," she whispered. "I'll make your father buy you the most beautiful puppy in the world, maybe a little hunting dog, darling."

Nights, if a patient lived within a reasonable distance, Dan Field left Nervy in her stall. And about ten o'clock on the evening of this November's first Monday found him walking toward Limestone Avenue to make a delivery. The prospective mother, Pansy Ferris, an eighteen-year-old flashy yellow girl, and her husband, one Ed Ferris, a twenty-year-old huge black boy, were comparative strangers to Mudtown, having been residents less than a year. But though they'd arrived a bride and groom, according to rumor Mr. Ackley proved a constant visitor. And when at dawn upon this November's first Tuesday Pansy brought forth a nine-pound daughter (who was later christened Little Flower) Ed's bulk sagged and his face sagged.

"I ain't the fussy kind, Mr. Doc," Ed sniffed. "Still I al'ays figgered I'd kinda like to know fer sure if'n my wife's first young-'un belonged to me."

"She's a fine baby, Ed," Dan Field assured. "And remember what the Good Book says: 'It's a wise father that knows his own child.' "

Ed's expression brightened considerably. "I guess likely it's best to 'bide by what the Good Book says."

Chuckling to himself, Dan Field left the shanty and started over Limestone Avenue. What peace, he thought, with all of Mudtown sleeping, and what loveliness, with the faint line of dawn over the shanties. He saw two small figures scooting along to enter the Stanwicks' woodshed—Bert and Sammy. So Sammy, too, has joined the Mudtown contingent. . . .

He crossed the bridge against a stiff wind. But over the creek not a breath seemed astir and before Ma Woodward's Dan Field stopped still. From the woods across the street came the sound of someone crying.

Dan Field crossed the street and stepped into the trees and as he did so a woman threw her arms around his neck and clung to him, sobbing.

"For Christ' sake, Meg!" he swore. "What are you doing here at this hour?"

"Dr. Field," she choked, "help me, please help me."

"Of course I'll help you, child. But you must pull yourself together. There's a good girl."

Ralph Pettigrew kept telling himself all evening that he'd not meet Margaret Taylor. If she can get herself down to the creek at midnight she can get herself back, he kept telling himself. But a few minutes before midnight he stepped into the trees across from Ma Woodward's. She was already waiting.

"What do you want?" he asked brusquely.

"I . . . I . . ." she faltered.

"Don't you know you're a damn little fool to do a thing like this?" Pettigrew demanded.

He meant to tell her to go on home, to get to hell home, when suddenly his arms went around her and she felt his great strength pressing her back, down, down. . . . The world went black for them both, then white, then crimson. . . .

"Meg," Dan Field pleaded, "don't make any more noise. Someone will hear you. Be a sensible girl and tell me quietly what's happened."

She stifled her sobs and tried to speak calmly. "I wrote him and asked him to meet me here at midnight. I thought nobody would see us here and I could slip down the back road."

"You wrote whom?" Dan Field asked.

"Mr. Pettigrew."

Dan Field could hardly believe his ears. "Ralph Pettigrew? Have you ever met him before, Meg?"

"Just on the street. But he'd look at me and I'd look at him and I thought—I guess I thought I was in love with him."

"Have you been here since midnight?" Dan Field demanded.

Meg nodded. "Yes. He—he left right after it happened. I really, though, don't know what did happen, Dr. Field. He threw his arms around me and that's all I can remember now. After a while I found he'd gone and left me and I just lay on the ground. I was afraid to move. I just started crying when you came along."

Dan Field patted her on the shoulder. "All right, Meg, all right, everything's going to be all right. You don't need to be afraid any more. I'll slip you home the back way and no one will ever know a thing about this unless you tell. Pettigrew will keep his mouth shut, I'm sure. And I want you to promise me that you'll never mention what has happened to anyone, least of all to Dot. Promise?"

Meg nodded. "I promise, Dr. Field."

"And, Meg," Dan Field went on, "if you find you're going to have a baby come straight away to me."

"How'd I know?" she asked.

He told her.

"Come along, child," he said.

At the door of their room Dot met her, wide-eyed and fearful. "Meg, it's morning, tell me where you've been. What happened?"

"Nothing happened," Meg said. "Nothing at all."

Dan Field went into his parlor, lighted a lamp, threw his overcoat and hat down, poured himself a stiff drink, and sank into a chair.

Jesus! What a night, he swore to himself. And what would have been the outcome if someone else should have discovered Margaret Taylor in the bushes? He downed his drink and poured another stiff one. And Ralph Pettigrew of all men. Dan Field shook his head. And God help the poor child if Chan finds out.

Ackley appeared from the room where he slept back of the kitchen, wearing a peaked nightcap and a long nightshirt, his big black feet bare.

"Ready foh some breakfast, suh?" he inquired.

Dan Field downed the second drink and poured a third. "No breakfast at the moment, thank you. But let me tell you something, Thomas Jefferson Ackley, one of these fine days some great big black buck is going to pound you to a pulp."

Ackley blinked. "Pound me to a pulp, suh? What'd any great big buck black—I means any great big black buck—pound me to a pulp foh?"

Dan Field sipped his drink. "Well, Mr. Ackley, I'll tell you. I have spent the entire night delivering Mrs. Daisy Ferris of a nine-pound daughter and Mr. Ed Ferris seems anything save pleased over the event."

Ackley drew himself up to his full five feet four. "Suh, down Vi'ginny Old Massa used to say to ma pappy, 'Jeff, you all bettah git busy with them field wenches and 'culcate quality.' What you 'spect I's doing in Mudtown 'cept 'culcatin' quality? It'd shu' nuff be a mighty meany husband not to 'preciate ma se'vices."

Dan Field threw back his head and roared. "Thank God for you, Ackley."

Ackley threw back his head and roared. "Yes suh, thank God foh me, suh."

Some time later Dan Field heard that, despite Little Flower's mama's husband (as Ackley expressed it) displaying displeasure, Ackley fairly showered Little Flower with attention and gifts.

Once Dan Field asked, "How's Little Flower Ferris, Ackley?"

Ackley beamed proudly. "Dat Little Flowah's the onliest young'un I evah 'bided."

Chapter Four

*T*HE FROST bit the pumpkins. Prissy's eleventh birthday and Thanksgiving came and went, the Albrights entertaining the Sargents on the latter date, as it was their turn this year. Now it was the second Wednesday of December, with the temperature down near zero. For over a week upon the creek men and women and boys and girls had skimmed along on what seemed like silver skates. At Elm Bank cutters hoisted great slabs of ice from frozen pools and finally hauled them off to icehouses where, safely stored under sawdust, they'd last the livelong summer. Yet there'd not been a flake of snow to date and everywhere you went someone queried, "Think we'll have snow by Christmas?"

The town had long since stopped talking about Dolly Tatem —whom rumor had with child—taking the train one evening last November; and this December Wednesday the weather lost precedence, hardly anybody being able to think of anything save the circumstances surrounding Old Man Meeker's death.

During the past month Dr. Walsh had been called oftener than usual to relieve, as Mrs. Meeker and Mrs. Diggers put it, "one of Papa's indigestion attacks." Dan Field would think, Poor old devil, sitting day in and day out with those sensitive, skillful fingers which never idled an instant during the most of a long lifetime now as inert as pinioned wings, and with the once mellifluous being desiccated, its every cell parched and panting. And contemplating the situation, Dan Field wondered what treatment he might prescribe were he the doctor.

He asked Brown Walsh, "What are you giving Old Man Meeker?"

"Laudanum."

"Do his wife and daughter know?"

Brown Walsh hawked and spat. "I explained the situation so clearly that there could be no possible doubt in their minds."

"Jesus!" Dan Field swore.

Brown Walsh was a heavy, bearded man who'd come to Willowspring some ten years before, married the blacksmith's oldest daughter, and sired three children. Dan Field considered him a first-rate physician. Certain best-family members, however, complained of his abrupt manner when they'd been forced to call him during Dan Field's annual vacations.

Brown hawked and spat again. "Jesus, hell! Sometimes, Dan, I think so-called good women are the devil's own inventions. If there was nothing but whores on earth a man'd know where he stood. Take those Meeker women: they'd sooner have the old man poisoned than have him touch a drop of alcohol. And they can watch him suffering the agony of the damned, feeling smug as a couple of archangels. Well, the laudanum gives him temporary relief. I'd like to administer an overdose some night."

"I probably would," Dan Field said.

Now Old Man Meeker was dead. Early Tuesday morning for the second time he'd eluded his wife and daughter and got himself uptown. This time, however, he did not make for the Grand Central Bar but stumbled into Heckshire's Drugstore where, in the window among the medicinal jars still stood that other jar which contained the seemingly immortal carcass of the two-headed squirrel preserved in wood alcohol. Mr. Heckshire and several early customers saw Old Man Meeker open the door, stumble over the sill, and face the window. But before anyone could realize what was happening the sensitive fingers discerned among the medicinal jars that which they sought. Exactly one hour later Old Man Meeker breathed his last.

"A bad indigestion spell," his wife and daughter sobbed.

Passing the Meekers' residence during the morning on the second Wednesday of December, Dan Field saw Ma Woodward and Mr. Williams (who sometimes assisted Ma on such occasions) carrying one of Ma's seasoned pine board caskets, held together by wooden pegs, toward the Meeker door, hardly discernible behind voluminous crepe hangings. Dan Field thought, Old Man Meeker, wherever you are today I hope those fingers are busy once more and the thirst of your desiccated being is quenched forevermore. Amen.

Eating breakfast that morning, Pris said, "Truly, George, I don't know how I'm going to get along without Old Man Meeker."

George smiled. "You've been managing to get along without him more than a year now, my dear."

"I know." Pris nodded. "But I always hoped his sight might be restored. You know, George, there's never been another person in town who could fix anything halfway."

Sammy blinked his round blue eyes. "Wonder what happened to that squirrel."

"What squirrel?" Lillian demanded.

"You know that squirrel, Lillian," Sammy told her. "That squirrel what had two heads in a jar up at the drugstore. It was the alcohol off that squirrel Mr. Meeker drunk."

"Was that what he drunk?" Lillian gasped.

Gagging, Rufe arose. " 'Scuse, please."

"Wonder if Mr. Meeker took that squirrel out," Sammy continued, " 'fore he drunk the alcohol."

"Please, Sammy . . ." Pris shuddered.

"Yes, Sammy, no one wants to hear a thing about the squirrel," George instructed.

"I should say not." Gramma Albright frowned. "What's more, I don't believe a word of the story about Mr. Meeker. I've know Mr. Meeker forty years and anyone I've know over a number of years wouldn't think of committing such an outrage."

Sammy stuffed his mouth with what remained upon his plate, pushed back his chair, muttered, " 'Scuse, please," dashed to the hall, grabbed his cap and coat, and tore through the front door.

Outside he saw Bert plodding toward school and joined him. "Bert, know what happened to that squirrel?"

Bert nodded. "Yeh. Mr. Heckshire give it to me. Soon as I heard 'bout Mr. Meeker yesterday noon I went uptown. Know sumpin, Sammy? Nobody thought a thing 'bout that squirrel. When I asked Mr. Heckshire if he knew where that squirrel is at he says, 'For God sake! No!' And when I asked could I have that squirrel he says, 'For God sake! Yes!' "

"How'd you find that squirrel, Bert?" Sammy demanded.

Bert shrugged. "Easy. I just goes up 'side the window and there that squirrel is on the floor. Guess Mr. Meeker he threw that squirrel out 'fore he drunk the alcohol."

"A mighty good thing he did throw that squirrel out," Sammy informed. "It sure'd been too bad if Mr. Meeker he'd swallowed that squirrel. Two-headed squirrels ain't easy to find, let me tell you."

Bert agreed. "Two-headed squirrels ain't easy to find. Know sumpin, Sammy? That squirrel's soft. When I pick that squirrel up the tail pretty near come off. Had to put that squirrel back in alcohol."

"Where'd you get the alcohol?"

"See, Uncle Doc he'd of let me have some if he was home, 'cept Uncle Doc wasn't home. So I put that squirrel in a jug of Papa's whisky. Jug got great big cork and that squirrel goes in easy. But you can't see it and Uncle Doc'll give me nuff alcohol and a jar, mighty likely."

Sammy and Bert had reached the schoolhouse and made their way around the building to the outhouse, this prodigiously popular rendezvous being more crowded and surrounded than ever because of the freezing weather. And after exploiting mother earth Sammy and Bert joined the company of Buzz Standing, Pete Sturdevant, and Chick Hubbard.

As Sammy and Bert joined them Pete and Chick nodded pleasantly. Buzz eyed the city caps and jackets Sammy and Bert wore; their families had brought them, as well as the girls, new duds from Philadelphia.

"Look what Sammy and Bert's wearing," Buzz sneered. "I wouldn't be saw dead in things like them. And if you-uns don't like it put your fists up and I'll lick both you-uns."

Bert remained silent.

Sammy nodded. "That's all right, Buzz. Sure, Buzz, that's all right."

"Bet your life it's all right," Buzz agreed. "All right with you, too, Bert?"

"All right with me, too, Buzz," Bert said.

"Better be," Buzz went on, "or I'd just lief stone you-uns like I stoned Ella and Wilbur." Suddenly Buzz pointed across the yard. "Look what our Alexander's up to."

Everybody within earshot looked. Also affected by the weather, Alexander had determined not to be afraid any more. He resolved to make straight for the outhouse and await his turn and when his turn came he intended taking it. But walking across the yard, Alexander kept telling himself, I am trusting in God and there is nothing to fear. I am trusting in God . . . He'd come beside the outhouse. Shad jumped out of one of the compartments. Alexander stepped inside. Buzz Standing stepped in back of Alexander and behind Buzz on the lawn Sammy and Bert and a whole crowd of other boys pushed.

Buzz loomed over Alexander, grabbed his pants and pulled them down, twisted Alexander around, and thrust him back upon the seat.

"If you gotta pee, you gotta pee sittin' down, sissy," Buzz shrieked.

Behind Buzz on the lawn Sammy and Bert and the whole crowd of other boys hooted and laughed.

All day Miss Fisher'd wondered if she could see the day through. First Miss Fisher felt weak from hunger. The school netted exactly twenty-five dollars a month, five dollars per pupil, and the piano pupils netted exactly seven dollars a month (there were three other music teachers in town these days). Besides, coal had to be bought and taxes paid. Prices being what they were, Miss Fisher could hardly afford to buy enough food to nourish her mother, let alone herself. Of course she'd the savings account, one hundred and thirty-seven dollars and fifty-one cents, but the very thought of drawing a penny from the bank made Miss Fisher's blood turn cold. If she became ill or died, whatever would her mother do then? And to top all of Miss Fisher's personal worries came Mr. Meeker's sudden demise.

Nevertheless, Miss Fisher remained positive that the awful story about Mr. Meeker drinking the wood alcohol couldn't be true. Hadn't Mr. Meeker signed the pledge? Still, Miss Fisher wished Aunt Tillie'd not dropped in and repeated the gossip to her mother. For some reason Miss Fisher kept remembering an evening not long before when she had visited the Meekers, and the way Mr. Meeker was sobbing and moaning had just about broken her heart.

Today, for the first time since her school began, Miss

Fisher regarded her pupils analytically. Meg and Dot took piano
lessons, of course, but this season they didn't seem to be able
to keep their minds on their lessons; Ginny Price was a spoiled,
insufferable little creature, Sammy Albright being the one person who'd been able to make Ginny behave (and Sammy of all
people, Sammy who'd never before seemed interested in anything except Sammy); and as for Lillian and Prissy—well, if
their parents saw fit to allow them music lessons it would mean
better than four dollars a month more. . . . Miss Fisher tried not
to visualize the amount of food better than four dollars a month
could provide.

Sighing, Miss Fisher dismissed the girls at the noon hour,
hurried to the kitchen, heated some leftover vegetable soup,
spread her mother a bread-and-butter sandwich, fixed the table,
and called Mrs. Fisher. When her mother finally groped her way
into the room Miss Fisher poured her a large bowl and herself
a small cup of the soup.

Miss Fisher said, "There's another helping of soup if you
want it, deary."

Mrs. Fisher smiled. "We are making out all right, aren't
we, deary? Although how you manage on the little you make I
don't know."

Meg and Dot rushed along the street toward home, the way
they always rushed of late, as if pursued. What was more, they
never walked uptown any more, nor went anyplace if they
could help themselves. Reaching home, they'd go to their room
and stay there, and no matter how hard she tried, Dot wouldn't
be able to make Meg talk. Only if their mother came into the
room would Meg start a conversation, making believe they'd been
talking all the time.

Dot knew something terrible must have happened to Meg on
the night she'd met Ralph Pettigrew down by the creek. But
Dot couldn't imagine what. That night when Meg had crawled
back to their room she'd tried to question her but Meg would
say nothing, nor had she told her anything since. Meg just
acted like she might be going crazy. She'd sit and stare into
space, her eyes looking as if she was seeing something terrible.
Often in the night Dot would hear Meg sobbing. Sometimes Dot
wondered if she hadn't better tell their mother. . . . But what

could she tell Mama? Dot asked herself. She couldn't tell her that Meg had sneaked out of the house in the middle of the night and met Ralph Pettigrew down by the creek.

At the same time Lillian and Prissy were on their way home, Prissy still acting as she'd acted ever since Lillian's birthday, like she didn't mind about anything, Lillian thought. Of course, for a few days after the folks brought them all the beautiful outfits home from Philadelphia, Prissy'd seemed like she used to seem, bragging about a new dress or hat or coat: "Mine's better'n yours, Lillian." Then again Prissy started behaving as if nothing interested her, not even Alexander liking Lillian best. Lillian simply couldn't understand the situation.

Prissy herself couldn't understand the situation. Since the day Gregory Beamer had kissed her and told her about the girl who went swimming bare with fellows there'd been no chance to talk to him again. But Prissy saw Gregory going in and out of their house and his eyes looking at her made Prissy know Gregory liked her better'n anybody else in the world. And knowing the way Gregory felt made Prissy not care whether anybody else liked her a bit.

However, this noon, passing the public school, the little girls heard a howling mob. A whole crowd of boys, including Sammy and even Bert, shrieked and laughed after Alexander, who streaked out of the yard and passed Lillian and Prissy without a glance.

The rest of the way home neither Lillian nor Prissy spoke. And when Prissy went along Lillian waited until Sammy reached her. Bert was with Sammy but Lillian didn't care if Bert did hear.

"I hate you, Sammy Albright," Lillian flared.

Sammy blinked his round blue eyes. "Hate me? How come?"

Lillian choked. "How come? I'll tell you how come, Sammy Albright. It's how mean you are to Alexander."

Sammy shook his round yellow head. "I wasn't mean to Alexander, Lillian. It was Buzz Standing was mean to him. All I did was laugh. Wasn't that all I did, Bert?"

Bert vouched, "Sammy didn't do nothin' 'cept laugh, Lillian."

Lillian choked, "What did you laugh for? If Buzz Standing was mean to Alexander why didn't you make him stop, Sammy Albright?"

"What for?" Sammy demanded.

"Course you couldn't see what for," Lillian sniffed. "You wouldn't know, Sammy Albright, that Buzz Standing being mean to Alexander and all you boys calling him sissy and laughing makes Alexander feel bad."

Lillian fled toward the front door.

Sammy scratched his yellow head thoughtfully. "Think Alexander does feel bad, Bert?"

Bert nodded. "He feels bad all right, Sammy."

Again Sammy scratched his head. "I never did think 'bout Alexander feeling bad, Bert."

When Bert opened the Sargents' front door Prissy flared at him, "As if it isn't bad 'nough having the town boys laughing at Alexander 'out you and Sammy too."

Bert made no response but, remembering the look on Sammy's face, he'd a pretty good idea Alexander's troubles were 'most over, even if Buzz Standing was a whole lot bigger.

Chapter Five

PRIS WAS about beside herself. To begin with, she'd not told George about Sammy's report cards and they'd been simply terrible. When she saw the first one, with the highest grade seventy-five, Pris tried to explain that little boys must study and make good grades or they'd never amount to a row of pins after they grew up and Sammy had blinked his round blue eyes and grinned and told Mama she was mighty likely right, the result being that the second report card boasted no grade higher than sixty-five. And oh, Pris sighed, she'd felt so encouraged about the way Sammy behaved last fall, up every morning and into the tub and out before anybody else had stirred. But again the awaking of Sammy became a siege and to make him take a bath was a major operation. Then this afternoon Mrs. Standing had burst through the front door and sobbingly accused Sammy of beating her Buzz almost to death.

"To think anybody could be so cruel to my fatherless boy," Mrs. Standing had sobbed.

Sammy, round blue eyes black, nose bloody, lips bruised, and knuckles torn, strutted toward Mudtown accompanied by the admiring glances of Bert, Ray, and Shad. Ray, unfortunately, had not been among those present around the ringside; hence as they moved along Shad obligingly recounted the fight.

"Sammy he walks up to Buzz and he says, 'Stop being mean ter Alexander,'" Shad began. "That Buzz he says, 'What fer?' Sammy he says, ' 'Cause I says.' Buzz he says, 'Want ter fight?' Sammy he says, 'Yes.' Buzz he says, 'Come 'hind the poop house if yer ain't yeller.' Sammy he says, 'Come 'hind the poop house yerself.' They goes 'hind the poop house. Buzz socks Sammy's right eye. Buzz socks Sammy's left eye. Buzz socks Sammy's nose and the blood squirt out'n. Then Sammy he gits mad."

Shad let out a shriek and started hurling his arms, upon whose ends fists clenched, in and out after the manner of a fighter.

"Yippy, yippy, Ray," Shad bellowed, "ought ter see ol' Sammy when he git mad. Ol' Sammy he beat that thar Buzz till he hollered and cried. 'Spect ol' Sammy he'd be beating that thar Buzz yet 'cept Tom Leonard says ol' Sammy gotta quit or he'll mighty likely kill that thar Buzz."

"Think yer might likely of killed that thar Buzz, Sammy?" Ray demanded breathlessly.

"Mighty likely," Sammy admitted loftily.

They were entering the Stanwicks' woodshed and Spotty ran toward Sammy and wiggled and wagged and bounced. From his pockets Sammy pulled several great hunks of beef, upon one of which Spotty began to nibble daintily. Ray's eyes grew ravenous.

There was a shuffling outside and Ray said, "Thar's Ella and Wilbur and Cal. They come early today."

"What they want?" Sammy asked.

"After yer goes home, Sammy," Ray informed, "they come times ter pick up what Spotty ain't et."

"How come?" Sammy inquired.

"They's hungry," Shad said.

Sammy blinked his round blue eyes. "You mean hungry?"

Ray nodded till his long unkempt locks swung like a mane. "Yep, they's hungry. Their bellies is clean empty."

"You hungry, Ray?" Sammy demanded.

Again Ray nodded vigorously. "Sammy, I ain't hardly had a full belly oncet in my hull life."

Sammy turned to Bert. "Think they are hungry, Bert?"

Bert vouched, "They's hungry all right, Sammy."

Sammy indicated Spotty's leavings. "Help yourself, Ray."

Smiling gratefully, Ray gathered Spotty's leavings and began gnawing loudly. Sammy watched thoughtfully.

Finally Sammy spoke. "I never did think 'bout nobody being hungry, Ray. But nobody's gotta be hungry no more, nobody a-tall. You tell everybody what's hungry that starting tomorrow I'll be over every morning 'fore light wheeling a barrow full of swill. And it's good swill. Ain't our swill good, Bert?"

Bert agreed, "It's good swill all right, Sammy."

"Think there'll be nuff swill fer ter feed our young'uns 'long-side the Widder Woman's?" Ray inquired.

"Sure, Ray, sure," Sammy answered.

"I's hungry," Shad announced, " 'cept I ain't hungry enough ter eat swill."

"I is," Ray admitted, unabashed. He called, "Ella, Wilbur, and Cal, 'fore light termorrow Sammy gonna wheel a hull barrow full of swill, good swill."

The only answer was a scuttle, and Bert said, "Mighty likely Mr. Thornhill's digging Old Man Mr. Meeker's grave."

Like a single shot the four of them started off, Spotty trotting at Sammy's heels. When the boys finally arrived at the Greenhill Cemetery Mr. Thornhill was digging the grave, or trying to dig it. Big, ox-shouldered man that he was, he had to use an ax to break the frozen sod and he sweat like a horse despite the bitter weather.

"Mr. Thornhill," Bert inquired, "how come dead folks has to be buried?"

Mr. Thornhill ceased laboring and, finding a red handker-chief, wiped his beady brow. "What else could you do except bury 'em, Bert?"

"Keep 'em in wood alcohol, maybe, or stuff 'em like birds," Bert informed.

Sammy stood apart, his gaze wandering over the Greenhill Cemetery, which looked anything save green during this season. But the tombstones looked white and pretty as ever, Sammy decided. Sometimes when Mama and Auntie Lou came to put flowers on the graves Sammy rode along and the stones always impressed him, from the great big ones like Grampa Albright's and Grampa Sargent's to the teeny ones. Sammy's favorite happened to be Baby George's marker, the figure of a little lamb under which stood what Sammy termed "the writing":

BABY GEORGE ALBRIGHT
One of God's Little Lambs

Today, surveying this stone, Sammy thought, Mighty likely a tombstone could have any kind of animal on it, even a two-headed squirrel. Sammy guessed he could have a two-headed squirrel on his tombstone. And the idea of his demise assumed a rosy aspect as Sammy visioned his bones resting throughout eternity marked by a two-headed squirrel.

Arriving home this evening, George thanked God (reverently) that the day was over. What a trial it had been! A situation which had been worrying him for some time was finally settled but without Rufus's knowledge and with Judge Hart's disapproval. Unfortunately Hart had to be brought into the matter, the transaction having to be according to the law in every respect. George had granted Tracy Whitlock another loan, out of his own pocket of course; Rufus from the first had never permitted the boy a bank cent. To cap a climax, upon entering the hall, Pris, looking as if she'd lost her last friend, met him carrying a sorry tale about the terrible report cards Sammy'd had and the Standing woman's claim.

"What possible difference can it make if Sammy killed the Standing boy?" George frowned. "As for the reports, what you want me to do—have Sammy's teacher dismissed?"

Pris didn't answer. What a help he is, she was thinking. All right, George, all right.

But when Sammy arrived and she saw his battle scars she forgot everything else. "Sammy, oh, Sammy darling, what did that awful Standing boy do to you?"

Sammy blinked his round, blue, blackened eyes. "You mean Buzz, Mama? Did Buzz do sumpin to me, Mama?"

Pris called to Rufe, who was in the sitting room. "Rufe, run right away and find Uncle Doc." She took Sammy by the hand. "Come on upstairs, darling. I'll try and make you as comfortable as possible until Uncle Doc gets here."

"I'm comfortable, Mama," Sammy insisted.

Upstairs Pris said, "Sammy darling, how would you like to have Papa buy you the most beautiful puppy in the world, maybe a little hunting dog?"

"No, thanks, Mama, I don't want the most beautiful puppy in the world, maybe a little hunting dog."

"You mean you don't want it?" Pris demanded.

"No, thanks, Mama."

Sammy Albright, Pris thought, if you're not the other end off the piece your father was cut from I'm very much mistaken.

Downstairs in the sitting room Lillian beamed happily. She

knew why Sammy beat up that awful Buzz Standing, 'cause he'd been mean to Alexander. Wonderful Sammy!

Going after Dan Field, Rufe hadn't an idea why the fight had taken place, yet Rufe's heart was full of gratitude. He'd not seen the excitement himself but as he came out of school Tom, Ben, and Jack had met him.

"Rufe," Tom laughed, "Sammy damn near kilt Buzz Standing. If I hadn't pulled him off he might of kilt him. God! What Sammy didn't do to that Buzz."

Ben and Jack laughed, too, and started talking about the fight and before Rufe realized what was happening he was walking uptown with the other three boys, all laughing and talking the way they used to do. Presently Jack made a remark about a passing girl and when the other two looked at Rufe he quoted Jack and laughed.

"Ever know any country girls, Rufe?" Jack inquired.

"No," Rufe admitted. "I'd like to all right," he added.

"We might fix it up," Ben said. "See, Rufe, us three fellows don't worry much about town girls; it causes too much gossip."

Jack snickered. "And what them country girls won't do ain't worth doing."

"We go out to the country sparking every month," Tom explained. "We each got a girl. These girls go to school together and are good friends—they're all sixteen—and there's another girl who's good friends with them. Her name's Fanny Rhimer. Maybe we could get Fanny to take Rufe on."

"Know how to get took on, Rufe?" Ben snickered.

Tom and Jack went into stitches.

"Damn right I know how to get took on," Rufe snickered.

As Dan Field settled himself in the parlor after dinner the front door opened and Judge Hart strode through.

Entering the parlor and seating himself, he said, "Don't get up, Dan, I can't stay a minute. Simply want to tell something strange which happened this afternoon—something very strange."

"So?" Dan Field queried.

"Of course this must be absolutely confidential between us," Hart cautioned.

"Absolutely."

Hart continued, "No doubt, Dan, you've your own opinion

of George Albright, but the fact remains, most people believe where his heart should be is adamant."

Dan Field nodded. "No doubt you're right, Hart."

"Certainly I'm right. But I'm here to tell you if it weren't that Rufus held the guiding rein the bank, let alone the Albright estate, would be in the hands of a receiver."

"Who would know better than you, Hart?"

"Truthfully speaking, Dan," Hart admitted, "the reason I came along tonight is because I'm worrying about George's mind."

"Are you speaking seriously?"

"I am." Hart was emphatic. "You are aware of the fact, certainly, that the church gives Minnie Jennings a thirty-dollar pension. But do you know George Albright owns the house where the Jennings live, pays the taxes, and charges no rent?"

"That's news to me."

"What is more, today George did the damnedest thing!" Hart swore. "It seems Miss Fisher and her mother have been on his mind. Even if Miss Fisher's school is earning practically nothing this year, why in the name of God should George care? But today—without Rufus' knowledge, you can bet your bottom dollar—he had me transfer certain securities to the Fishers which will assure them fifty dollars a month for life. On top of this largess the papers were so drawn as to make it appear that Mr. Fisher left an endowment fund payable at this time."

Smiling inwardly, Dan Field said, "Who'd ever have imagined George in the role of philanthropist."

Hart shrugged. "Old adamant George. You've not heard the whole story by a long shot, Dan. George, out of his own pocket, has loaned Tracy Whitlock nearly three thousand dollars. Now I'll grant you, Dan, a man might become sentimental about a widow or a beautiful old maid, but seriously, Dan, what man could become serious over Tracy Whitlock's affairs unless he's addlepated?"

Dan Field also shrugged. "You have me there, Hart. However, I honestly believe George's mind is perfectly clear."

"Keep an eye on him anyhow," Hart instructed. "Seen him lately?"

"This evening." Dan Field laughed. "Sammy was the patient. A few minor cuts and bruises, but the other fellow, Buzz

Standing, was fit to be poured out, and by the time I arrived at the Standings' his mother was hysterical."

Hart smiled. "Did Sammy lick Buzz? Didn't think Sammy had it in him."

"Sammy's just like George," Dan Field said. "They are both unpredictable."

"By the way, had a letter from Tert this morning," Hart changed the subject. "Has a new friend by the name of Sargent. No relation, though, Tert says, to our folks. That's all right, but wait till I read you some of the rest of the letter and see what you make of it." Hart took the letter out of a pocket and skimmed through it. "Here it is." He read aloud:

" . . . gotten friendly with another American fellow, born in Italy though, name of John Sargent—no relation but his family's all right. He had an exhibition at the Paris Salon last year and has no end of ability. Studied under Duran too. Only I'm not under Duran any more. I've joined a group of artists who call themselves Impressionists. No use me trying to explain what we're doing as neither one of you could possibly understand. . . ."

Hart stopped reading and demanded, "What would you think of that?"

Dan Field smiled. "I might think Tert is not studying under Duran any more and has joined a group of artists who call themselves Impressionists and there is no use of his explaining what they're trying to do as neither one of you could possibly understand."

Hart didn't smile. "It's no joking matter, Dan. Why can't boys these days follow in their fathers' footsteps? By the way, remember those two boys last court session, named Knight and Long, convicted of grand larceny?"

Dan Field shook his head. "I seldom follow court proceedings."

"Well, anyhow, I sentenced them to from six to ten years in Western Penitentiary. Last week Knight tried to escape and a guard shot him in the back, killed him outright."

At least, Dan Field thought, no one will be worrying because Knight stopped studying under Duran and joined a group who call themselves Impressionists.

Outside the prayer-meeting bells began to ring.

Hart arose. "Guess I'll drop in on prayer meeting this evening and forget my worries. You keep an eye on George, Dan."

Chapter Six

$\mathcal{I}$T WAS Christmas Eve and still no snow. By this time eyes fairly ached for the sight of Mother Carey's feathers fluttering from her bed, and ears fairly ached to hear sleigh bells jingling on the air. Still the wind whistled and the church bells rang and on Broad Street the store windows gaily wore, among what was left of the gift suggestions, trimmings of evergreen and cranberries—Strock's boasting a whole suckling pig whose waxen jaws held a round red apple. All over town holly hung on doors and mistletoe over them, candles burned in windows and little children pinned stockings to mantels, because their mamas told them Santa Claus would really come, snow or no snow.

The big Albright and Sargent parlors stood ready to greet the dawn, tall trees bedecked and wrapped gifts piled high upon the floor. Now all the Sargents, accompanied by Dan Field, were entering the Albright place—it being the custom of the two families to take turns entertaining each other, Dan Field included if possible, every Christmas Eve.

The Sargents and Dan Field opened the Albright door and swept in, taking a bitter blast along. Pris closed the door quickly and after greetings were over and wraps off Rufus ceremoniously presented George with a gallon of twenty-year-old rye, the jug handle wearing a red bow and a sprig of holly.

"Let's sample it now, George," Rufus suggested. "And if you don't consider it ten per cent smoother than your brand I'll be very much mistaken."

George, Rufus, and Dan Field saw the ladies, accompanied by Rufe, settled in the parlor and then went to the dining room, followed by Sammy and Bert. George found an empty decanter, placed it upon the table, uncorked the jug, and tipped its nose slightly over the decanter. A few drops trickled out . . . suddenly there was a gurgle, a splash, and across the decanter, down upon the table, a bunch of sodden fur splotched.

"What in the name of heaven!" George exclaimed. "Is this some sort of practical joke?"

Rufus seldom swore but now he said, "Practical joke hell! What could it be?"

Dan Field took a pencil from a pocket and with an end spread out the bunch of sodden fur.

George threw back his head and laughed. "It looks like Old Man Meeker's two-headed squirrel."

Rufus swore again. "How in the name of God could Old Man Meeker's two-headed squirrel get in a jug of my whisky?"

Dan Field had a vague recollection of Bert at one time saying he was coming around to get some alcohol and a jar to keep a two-headed squirrel.

"That's a bat if ever I saw one," Dan Field said. "How many nips have you gentlemen had tonight?"

"Well, how would a bat get into a jug of my whisky?" Rufus demanded.

Dan Field smiled. "Bats have a way of getting into things, you know."

George roared, "So, Rufus, you'll be very much mistaken if I don't consider your rye ten per cent smoother than my brand." He called into the kitchen: "Nellie . . ."

Nellie put her head through the door. "Yes sir?"

George pointed to the table. "Nellie, burn that thing—it's a bat. And empty this whisky out—it's poisoned." He roared again. "Now, gentlemen, I'll give you a nip of rye which, if not as smooth as you've been accustomed to, at least won't kill you. Ha! Ha! Ha!"

Nellie found a dustpan and departed, bearing the fur and jug. She dumped the remains of the two-headed squirrel into the stove and dumped the whisky outside. She'd been on her way over to see Maggie when Mr. Albright called her. Mrs. Sargent had given Maggie permission to keep Gregory all night this Christmas Eve. It was the first Christmas Eve Gregory had ever spent with Maggie. She had got a little tree and set it up on the kitchen table and trimmed it with cranberries and rings of colored paper. Nellie herself had bought Gregory a ball because it took practically every cent Maggie earned to buy material to make Gregory's clothes, let alone her own.

After the men had downed their drinks and gone to join the ladies, Sammy looked at Bert and Bert looked at Sammy.

Bert sighed, "Too bad I forgot that squirrel, Sammy. Two-headed squirrels ain't easy to find."

Sammy sighed, "Too bad you did forget that squirrel, Bert. Two-headed squirrels ain't easy to find."

However, upon this night nothing could down Sammy's happiness. He'd five whole dollars in his pocket, and they were all his to do with as he wished. Mr. Ralph Pettigrew had given the money to him. And Sammy was grateful, though he couldn't understand why Mr. Pettigrew had given him such an amount for just doing a little favor and promising not to tell anyone. This afternoon Sammy had been staring into Carl's window when Mr. Pettigrew came along and stopped.

"See anything in there you'd like, Sammy?" Mr. Pettigrew asked.

Sammy'd blinked his round blue eyes, smiled, and nodded.

"What?" Mr. Pettigrew inquired.

"A couple of things, Mr. Pettigrew."

"How much?"

"I just got through figgering—about four dollars and six cents' worth."

"Listen! Sammy," Pettigrew said, "if you'll do a little favor for me and cross your heart never to tell I'll give you five dollars."

"Five dollars!" Sammy cried.

"Shh!" Pettigrew cautioned. "Now cross your heart and hope to die if you ever tell."

"Cross my heart and hope to die if I'll ever tell, Mr. Pettigrew."

Pettigrew had a big box of candy under an arm and he handed it to Sammy. "I want you to take this and give it to Margaret Taylor but I don't want anybody to know. Do you suppose you can slip it to her some way without her family finding out?"

"Sure I can, Mr. Pettigrew. Sure I can."

"How?"

Sammy blinked. "I ain't thought of how yet, Mr. Pettigrew."

"Then listen!" Pettigrew instructed. "You hang around the Taylor place this afternoon till you see Mrs. Taylor go out. She'll be sure and have something to buy at the last minute on the day before Christmas. After she gets out of sight you ring the bell. If anybody but Margaret answers you ask for her. When you give her the candy say, 'You know who this is from.' Now what are you going to say?"

"You know who this is from."

It happened that Meg answered Sammy's ring. He handed her the candy and delivered the message.

"Was it Mr. Pettigrew?" she asked.

"I crossed my heart and hoped to die I wouldn't tell," Sammy said and ran. . . .

"Come on, Sammy and Bert," Mama was calling from the parlor, "we're going to sing the carols now."

They sang the carols, according to custom, and George read from the Bible the part beginning, " 'And she brought forth her firstborn son . . .' " Both grandmothers remarked the way they always did that it didn't seem more than yesterday that their children were small and Mr. Albright and Mr. Sargent still with them. And they'd hardly finished lighting the candles on the tree when the front door knocker sounded.

Lillian ran but as the door opened a cold blast made her shiver.

"Come in quick," she said before she banged the door.

Out of the darkness and into the light Ray Stoddard stepped, his eyes fairly blinded: never had he ever dreamed of anything like this—the big room beyond the hall and the big lamps and the tree all over silver and gold balls and stars and wax angels and candles burning, and Miss Lillian standing there beside him.

Lillian knew who'd come in, that dirty filthy white boy who delivered washes all over town. But his eyes—Lillian thought she'd never in her life seen anything shine like his eyes, not the candles on the tree nor stars even. And Lillian smiled at Ray.

Dan Field stood beside them. "Looking for me, Ray?"

"Yes sir, Mr. Doc. Mam she's took."

"I'll be right along."

Ray opened the door and was gone.

Lillian fussed, "I'm just not going to let you go, Uncle Doc."

Prissy fussed, "Uncle Doc, if you go it's just going to spoil our whole Christmas."

Gramma Albright said, "It seems to me, Dan, a gentleman like you could have chosen another profession."

Dan Field smiled. "Perhaps, but I didn't."

He found his coat and Pris was suddenly holding it for him. "It is going to spoil our whole evening if you go, Dan," she whispered. "Is it so important?"

Dan Field slipped into the coat and, turning, looked down at her. "I don't know whether it's important or not. What's another Stoddard going to mean to the world? Not much, one would think. And yet remember, 'And she brought forth her firstborn son, and wrapped him in swaddling clothes, and laid him in a manger; because there was no room for them in the inn. . . .'"

Her eyes looked up into his. "Dan," she whispered again, "Dan, there's never been anybody else like you since the world began."

Darling, darling, he thought, turned, and said good-by to the others and went out.

At the office he picked up his bag and started on foot toward Mudtown; he wouldn't take Nervy from her warm stall in weather like this unless it was positively necessary. Passing the corner, he wondered about Margaret Taylor. Pettigrew evidently hadn't got her in trouble or she would have been to see him before this.

Several times since the night Dan Field had found Meg beside the creek he'd met Pettigrew on the street. Pettigrew's not the kind who'd rape a woman, Dan Field thought; there must have been co-operation.

"What is it, Doc?" Myrt asked weakly.

Dan Field put the baby to her breast. "A girl."

Myrt sighed as the little lips took hold. "Girl, huh? Wonder what's left ter name her?"

Outside a cock crew.

Dan Field smiled. "Call her Noel; it means Christmas."

Upon arriving at the shanty Dan Field had found Lem soddenly stretched across the kitchen floor—drunk upon my whisky, Dan Field thought. That afternoon Ackley had arrived in Mudtown bearing two huge baskets of food to brighten the Stoddard and Lawler Christmases. But the baskets also included a jug of whisky each because Dan Field knew full well that otherwise the turkeys would be bartered by Lem and the Widder Woman to secure the needful. Besides Lem, the children, covered by filthy blankets and sacks, lay upon the kitchen floor, some of them sleeping peacefully and others fretting or crying.

"I'll git the water hot in a jiffy, Mr. Doc," Ray promised.

Dan Field went into the shanty's one other room where Myrt tossed upon a rickety bed. All the night long by lantern light he worked over her intently, but every so often he'd feel a presence behind him as Ray or one of the other children wandered around, curious about their mother's progress. With Noel at Myrt's breast, Dan Field became conscious of an alien presence, and turned, only to gasp, "Where under the heavens did you come from?"

"From home," Bert answered. "I come over right after Mama tucked me in bed. Know sumpin, Uncle Doc? I always did want to see a baby getting borned."

Dan Field reached for his bag. "Well, my young friend, your ambition has been fulfilled. Come on."

Ray followed them to the door. "Bert, if yer gits a chanct tell Sammy he don't have fer ter bring the swill terday. We got victuals." He smiled at Dan Field. "Mr. Doc, sir, I's mighty 'bliged fer the victuals."

"That's all right, Ray." Dan Field returned the smile. "Merry Christmas, son."

He and Bert went outside. The ground was white and the snow was still coming down. Snow at last.

They walked along.

Bert said, "Know sumpin, Uncle Doc? Ray's figgering on learning everything in the world what there is to learn."

"Just how?"

"By numbers. See, Uncle Doc, the tramp gentleman Mrs. Tatem run off with told Ray if you know nuff 'bout numbers you can find out anything in the world you want to know."

"Ray couldn't have been more than seven years old at the time the tramp was here," Dan Field said, yet again he remembered how Ray's eyes had fixed upon the tramp as if he understood his strange philosophy.

"Ray's awful smart, Uncle Doc," Bert vouched.

Dan Field shook his head. "I'm going to have a talk with Ray one of these days. What did he mean about Sammy not having to bring the swill over tomorrow?"

"Sammy he takes a barrow full of swill over every morning 'fore light," Bert informed.

"Why?" Dan Field inquired.

"See, Uncle Doc, if Sammy didn't take it 'fore light Uncle George or Auntie Pris'd catch him."

"But why does he take the swill over at all, Bert?"

"See, Uncle Doc, Sammy he found out 'bout the Stoddard and the Widder Woman's young'uns being hungry."

Dan Field could barely believe his ears. "You mean to say, Bert, that Sammy gets up every morning before light and wheels a barrow of swill to Mudtown in order to feed the Stoddards and the Lawlers?"

"It's good swill, Uncle Doc."

"Imagine Sammy doing a thing like——" Dan Field began.

"Know sumpin, Uncle Doc?" Bert interrupted. "Sammy he's tough. He's tough all right. See, Uncle Doc, Mr. Smith told Sammy if he'd come mornings and clean out the stalls till Nigger Harry got back he'd give him Spotty. And every morning 'fore light Sammy got up and cleaned the stalls out, and when Nigger Harry got back, Spotty she was Sammy's dog and then . . ." Bert hesitated an instant.

"Then what, Bert?" Dan Field asked.

"Then, Uncle Doc, Uncle George he wouldn't let Sammy keep Spotty and Sammy run away from home."

"He couldn't have gone very far."

Bert shook his head. "No, not very far, just as far as the school and he met me and I says he could keep Spotty in Shad's woodshed. But know sumpin, Uncle Doc? Sammy he really is tough. He really was going to run away and sleep 'side the railroad track and he wasn't never going to wash or comb his hair and he was going to sleep with his clothes on and he wasn't never going to change them."

"You don't say," Dan Field put in.

"Yes sir," Bert went on, "Sammy he really is tough. But know sumpin, Uncle Doc? Things make Sammy feel much badder than they make other fellows feel, things like folks being hungry and having their feelings hurt and things like that, if Sammy knows 'bout them. See, Uncle Doc, the reason Sammy beat up Buzz Standing was 'cause he made Alexander sit down to pee and Lillian told Sammy it made Alexander feel bad."

"Bert, Bert, I couldn't live without you," Dan Field chuckled.

But soberly he put an arm around the square young shoulders and held the boy close to him. A minute they stood there, the snow falling over them. Now across the street was the Catholic Church and lights shone through the windows full upon the snow. People were going into the church and as the door swung open Dan Field could hear the words falling from Father Callahan's lips, " '*Ave Maria* . . .' "

Bert, Dan Field was thinking, you will do those things which I have left undone, your soul will be my soul marching on.

Aloud he said, "Bert, it's Christmas. And it's a white Christmas. And it's a pretty good old world after all."

The day dawned clear and crisp and white with sleigh bells jingling on the air. "A good old-fashioned Christmas," people said. With perhaps the exception of Mrs. Standing and Buzz, both of whom still smarted spiritually from Sammy's outrage, all over town everybody seemed to believe there really was "on earth, peace, good will toward men."

Madge Taylor was happy because Meg seemed more like herself than she'd been these many days and Dot was happy for the same reason. Christmas Eve as they trimmed the tree Meg had actually smiled several times. But Meg hid the candy that Pettigrew sent her, even from Dot. She was afraid if Dot saw the candy she'd try questioning again and Dr. Field had told Meg not to tell anyone anything, although what she could actually tell Dot Meg didn't know. Since the night down by the creek Meg had been in a trance. What had happened all seemed like a dream, terrifying and wonderful. Dr. Field had told her she might have a baby. But she wasn't going to have a baby, she knew, because the doctor had explained how she could tell, and that hadn't happened. No, she wasn't going to have a baby; only at times Meg wished she was. Maybe if there was a baby Ralph Pettigrew wouldn't hate her the way he must. . . . Although now that he'd sent her the candy she began to feel that he couldn't hate her so very much. . . . The first thing Christmas morning Meg slipped out of the house and mailed a note to Ralph Pettigrew. About ten o'clock he found the note in his box, slit the envelope, pulled out a sheet, and read:

DEAR MR. PETTIGREW:

Thank you very much for the candy. Chocolate is my favorite kind and the box is so pretty with the apple blossoms design. Thank you very much, too, for thinking of me.

You know who this is from.

Pettigrew put the note in a pocket, took out a big handkerchief and wiped his eyes. It was a crazy thing to send her the candy, he knew. He was sure he'd not gotten her in trouble, and the best thing to do was let her forget him. Ralph Pettigrew wasn't the kind of man who felt a girl who'd known a man was ruined. He had sent the candy and she'd written him . . . "You know who this is from." Yes, Pettigrew knew who the note was from all right. Poor little girl, he thought, poor sweet little girl. He wondered now why he'd been such a damn fool as to send the candy.

That night he'd purposely left her lying on the ground among the trees. When he came to his senses he had realized that, if he left her without a word, someday what had happened would seem like only a bad dream. He also realized what the result would have been if he'd stayed. He would have pulled her to her feet and taken her in his arms and told her he loved her, and then what? What the hell? he asked himself. Now he'd sent the candy and she'd written him a note.

Oh well, Pettigrew shrugged, strolling toward the office. Alexander Jennings and his mother came along. Out for a walk on Christmas morning, Pettigrew imagined. Pettigrew had heard about the Albright-Standing fight but he didn't know the reason, and now, seeing Alexander, he wondered what made him look so perky. The boy looks as if he'd got a new lease on life, he thought.

At the corner across from the hotel Tracy Whitlock stopped him, laughing. "Merry Christmas, Pettigrew. Hear about me signing the pledges?"

"Two of them?" Pettigrew asked.

Tracy laughed again. "Yep, two, liquor and tobacco. And of

all the darn fool things, me signing those pledges when I never drank or used tobacco in my life. But Aunt Tillie begged me to do it for her Christmas present. It sure made the old lady happy. Cheered up Mrs. Meeker and Mrs. Diggers a lot, too, not to mention the Fishers."

"Regular little ray of sunshine, aren't you, Whitlock?" Pettigrew drawled.

Tracy missed the sarcasm. "Not that the Fishers need much cheering up these days," he continued brightly. "Funny thing about Mr. Fisher leaving an income not payable until fifty years after his death, don't you think? What's more, do you realize fifty years ago was 1830, the year old George and Rufus founded the bank?"

Pettigrew didn't answer. He shrugged and moved along. Still, he thought, since Whitlock mentioned the fact, there did seem something funny about the Fisher business, and not only funny but suggestive of a dead rat having been buried in the bank's vault since its founding. If there is a stench, trust Tracy to find the stink, Pettigrew concluded, entering the office building.

As he disappeared Tracy was thinking, I'll bet my hat there is more than can be seen by the naked eye between Pettigrew and Margaret Taylor, her being in court and him acting the way he acted when I was going after her. If he could discover the truth Tracy felt a pretty penny might be forthcoming. Crossing the street to see Jean, he hummed brightly, feeling very much in harmony with the universe upon this bright Christmas morn. By signing the pledges today he'd really made Aunt Tillie and the other old ladies happy (and making anyone happy always gave Tracy a sense of his own power), and last night he'd finally had his way with Jean. It had taken a long time but . . . Tracy hummed a bit louder.

Entering the hotel office, he saw Tom, Jack, Ben, and Rufe Albright huddled together, whispering and snickering. Tracy knew what happened to be upon the first three boys' minds. Tonight they intended going out in the country to have a peck at some farm girls. Could it be possible, Tracy thought slyly, that Rufe Albright would join them? If so, what would the information be worth to George Albright? Or maybe he could secure enough evidence about Rufe's misconduct as well as any other irregularity committed by an Albright or Sargent . . . For instance, there might be some reason why Dr. Field had never married and spent so much time at the Albrights'. There was the Fisher income too. If he passed the information along to Pettigrew's henchmen they'd realize what a valuable asset having Tracy Whitlock on their side would be and make Pettigrew pay handsomely—especially if the Taylor truth could be unearthed. Pettigrew himself, Tracy speculated, felt too pompous now to be approached directly; doubtless he still believed he might become mayor under honest steam. Tracy smiled, anticipating; he didn't mean to spend all his life in a hick town living on money borrowed from a hick bank. Certainly anyone who'd a mind might make a small living with the printing press and the newspaper but Tracy wasn't one to watch pennies. Pretty soon big money would come and then the proper environment, perhaps New York City, and he'd begin his book. Tracy, he promised himself, you'll be a great man. The long-awaited windfall seemed near.

Jean came down the stairs, her honest blue eyes sparkling at the sight of him.

George and Rufus, however, totally forgetful of the fact that there was alive upon the face of the earth a man named Tracy Whitlock, were particularly enjoying the day. George awakened in a rare holiday mood and, kissing Pris laughingly, asked her if she'd ever known anything funnier than the bat in the whisky Rufus had given him. And Rufus received a letter Christmas morning saying the Brush dynamos would be along before another month. Besides, on December 17 Brush lamps had been installed along Broadway for three quarters of a mile. The letter went on to say, furthermore, that in the city of New York prospective customers were the Steinway Ware Rooms, the Park Theatre, the Brunswick and Sturdevant hotels, and Koster and Bial's Music Hall. It was also believed that before long incandescent lamps would be available. Enclosed was a clipping from the New York *Herald* telling what had happened a few nights before at a place called Menlo Park. The clipping read:

A Delegation from the New York Board of Aldermen made a pilgrimage to Menlo Park last night to form an opinion of the resident wizard's work. Stretching away on either side and intercepting the Park at intervals ran long lines of lights. There were illuminated spaces above all these gleaming points and the prospect was very beautiful as the visitors looked out upon it.

But at a sign from the wizard all changed. A workman's finger pressed the key and in an instant Menlo Park was in darkness. A ripple of applause involuntarily ran through the onlookers, but before it had subsided the finger was applied again, and the landscape was illuminated in a twinkling.

Santa Claus brought every member of both the Albright and Sargent families enough presents to make half a dozen individuals grateful. The men received new gold cuff links and studs as well as ties, handkerchiefs, socks, and sundries galore. Pris, Lou, and the grandmothers, among countless trinkets from family and friends, got a thousand dollars each from George and Rufus. And the children found so much underneath the trees they didn't know which gift to tackle first—there were balls, bats, new skates and new sleds, knives, blocks, new wax dolls big as live babies and more, the boys' big presents being gold watches and the girls' big presents being gold rings. Dan Field had a dozen giant red roses shipped from New York to each grandmother and Pris and Lou, and he gave each one of the children a five-dollar gold piece, which Pris and Lou promptly confiscated to put in their savings accounts. Both families showered Dan Field, himself, with ties, socks, and handkerchiefs. More, George the First, Rufus the First, and Baby George could not be forgotten. Early Christmas morning Pris, Lou, and the grandmothers drove to the Greenhill Cemetery and placed giant wreaths of palm leaves and pink roses (ordered from Philadelphia) upon the graves.

It was the Sargents' turn to have the dinner this year and, as on Sundays, at two o'clock both families and Dan Field gathered around the great Sargent table. Through later years the children loved telling about those dinners. "There's nothing like it today," they'd say. "Food doesn't taste like that any more. We had everything from a twenty-five-pound turkey and green-gage jam to the fruit cake and plum pudding with rum sauce. Enough would be thrown away to feed a dozen others."

Having stuffed until they could hardly breathe, the ladies, including Lillian and Prissy, and accompanied by Dan Field, returned to the parlor. Rufus went upstairs to write letters, and George, Rufe, Sammy, and Bert left the house, George on his way home to take a nap.

Before George reached the Sargents' gate Rufe stopped him. "Papa, will you listen to me, please? You always said I could play with the town boys till I grew up, didn't you?"

George nodded. "That's right, Rufe."

"Well, Papa, Ben's going to get one of their two-seated sleighs and a team this evening and take Tom, Jack, and me on a long ride out in the country. It's liable to be a long ride, too Papa. Maybe we won't get home till maybe—well, maybe till te; or eleven o'clock. Is that all right, Papa?"

George nodded again. "I suppose so, Rufe."

Rufe dashed toward the hotel and George sauntered home.

Behind the Sargent house Sammy and Bert lingered, waiting until Maggie dumped the swill into the barrel. The five dollars Pettigrew had given him still rested in one of Sammy's pockets. Hanging around the Taylors' waiting till Mrs. Taylor came out, Sammy could hardly wait to get back to Carl's, but once the candy had been delivered he couldn't bear to spend the money. Never before had Sammy possessed such a staggering sum to do with as he pleased, and what's more, Sammy decided, mighty likely he'd never again have such wealth. That was yesterday, however, and this Christmas afternoon the money fairly burned a hole through his pocket. He couldn't imagine what under the sun he'd spend it on, though, since he'd found everything he wanted under the tree. Sammy sighed deeply; life seemed particularly difficult at the moment. Suddenly an inspiration presented itself: he'd have Ma Woodward build Spotty a kennel, a five-dollar kennel, all for Spotty.

Gregory Beamer came out upon the back porch and eyed Sammy and Bert. He wondered again why he darsn't talk to them or play with them. Still, Gregory was happy. He'd had a Christmas tree and a ball and it was the first Christmas tree and present Gregory'd had during his whole life.

Husbands and sons having departed, Pris said, "Aren't husbands and sons strange? Wouldn't you think on Christmas afternoon that George and Rufus might enjoy chatting a bit?"

Gramma Albright said, "Mr. Albright and Mr. Sargent were never chatterers."

"Take the boys," Pris continued, "what with all their presents, you'd think they'd enjoy staying around." She gazed under the tree where Lillian and Prissy played happily. "Girls are so different."

Dan Field laughed. "Men must wage and women must wonder."

Lou said, "I was so afraid Bert had stopped believing in Santa Claus. But this morning I slipped into his room before light and there he stood all dressed. I asked, 'Why up so early, dear?' and Bert said, 'Looking for Santa Claus, Mama.'"

Dan Field kept a straight face. "How about *the* nocturne, Pris?"

She smiled. "Of course, Dan."

She went to the big square piano, her piano, the piano she'd had as a girl; the feel of these ivories always meant so much more to her than the keys of the Albright piano. I wish I'd known Dan when a girl, she was thinking. She began to play.
. . .

Dan Field closed his eyes. He remembered the morning. He'd stopped by and said Merry Christmas to the Boyds. Helen had played *the* nocturne. Little girl with lovely gentle Jewish eyes and fingers like white doves flying, he had thought. The child was really gifted, and he'd told Vera and Eli and they'd laughed and seemed proud and happy. But on the way home he met Mollie Reynard and Bertha Richards. . . . And passing the Martins', he'd heard shouts from within and knew the younger boys were home on holiday, even if Tert *had* joined a group who called themselves Impressionists. Dan Field remembered the story Hart had told about the boy he'd sentenced to from six to ten years and who'd been shot through the back trying to escape from Western Penitentiary. *The blessings of liberty to ourselves and our posterity* . . . As for me, Dan Field told himself, I emphatically don't want George to die but . . .

Mudtown also brimmed with Yuletide spirit. There wasn't a single colored family who'd not at least a chicken in the pot. Lem Stoddard and the Widder Woman remained gloriously drunk the livelong day and the bellies of their children bulged beatifically. Red started off through the snow before dawn after rabbits, his musket over one shoulder, a gunny sack over the other, a jug of whisky in a hand, and Duke following. During the morning Mr. Williams entered the Tatem shanty and read Belle a letter which finally had come from Gabe.

The letter ran:

DEAR MR. WILLIAMS,

i am writin to tel you and Mrs. Williams and the rest a mary christmas. Dolly wants you shuld tell Belle she found me. Dolly says i alays says if i left Willowspring id come to Johnstown and work in a mill and thats whar i come. me and Dolly got married.

GABE

Mr. Williams stopped reading and looked at Belle and Belle looked at Mr. Williams, then suddenly both laughed and laughed. Even the news that Gabe and Dolly were married couldn't lessen the joy of having heard from them.

About five o'clock, Sammy's pockets finally stuffed with turkey for Spotty, he and Bert headed toward Mudtown. On the bridge they met Ray.

"How's Noel?" Bert inquired.

Ray smiled. "Suckin' and sleepin'. And Mam she's been sleepin' most all day. Hardly waked up even when I gives her her victuals."

"I'll tend Noel and your mama this afternoon, Ray," Bert proffered. "And I shinnied up Sammy's pole on the way home this morning and told him 'bout the swill."

Ray nodded. "Mighty 'bliged, Bert. But, Sammy, we'll mighty likely need swill by termorrow."

"You'll get it all right, Ray," Sammy promised.

Ray nodded again. "Mighty 'bliged ter yer, Sammy."

Sammy and Bert continued across the bridge and Ray kept on toward town. Reaching Broad Street, he turned west and strolled along until he reached Carl's Novelty Shop. Never during his whole life had Ray received a Christmas toy but for the last few years he'd come over town Christmas afternoon and figured out what, if he could have a present, he'd choose from Carl's window. Last year he'd picked a pair of skates and today, staring at the window's marvels, he guessed mighty likely he'd take a pitcher book. Wonder what the insides of a pitcher book's like? he meditated. Then suddenly Ray saw something he wanted more than he'd ever wanted anything before in his life, and as afterward he described it: "It was a gold watch and it had leetle red stones

—rubies, the lady says they was—and the rubies wound round and round and makes a four-leaf clover on the gold. But it was marked plain as terday with a little tag what says twenty-four dollars and seventy-five cents. And let me tell yer, twenty-four dollars and seventy-five cents is a heap of money fer ter git."

Still, seeing the watch there in the window for the first time, Ray thought maybe he could earn the money. Maybe I kin, he choked to himself. I could git out'n bed earlier and maybe shovel folks' snow or tend furnaces.

All at once the snow began falling again and Ray Stoddard stood covered only by great downy flakes and a few filthy rags. Yet Ray was not conscious of the cold. Again he was seeing the big room and the big lamps and the Christmas tree all over silver and gold balls and stars and wax angels and the candles burning bright, and Lillian was standing there beside him, smiling at him.

"Maybe if'n I kin git that money," Ray thought out loud, "and buy that thar watch fer Miss Lillian she'll smile at me agin."

Part 3
WINTER

Chapter One

$\mathcal{I}$T HAD hardly stopped snowing an instant since Christmas, and snow was piled everywhere, except upon some walks which had been diligently shoveled. Willowspring's main streets stretched shining from the smoothing of constant cutters. The wind had kept right on blowing, too, and over most rural roads deep downy drifts bound the country people to farms and firesides. Came Saturday, and hardly a handful made town.

But at last a fair night shone and the wind merely murmured while at midnight the tollings of the church bells and the school bell and the court bell pealed throughout the town and resounded toward the welkin as the old year died and 1881 drew its first breath.

When the last bell died away Dan Field, glass in hand, seated himself upon a chair where long ago crinoline had rustled, and quoted:

> "O warblings under the sun—ushered as
> now, or at noon, or setting!
> O strain, musical, flowing through ages—
> now reclining hither!"

Upon another chair where long ago crinoline had rustled, Father Callahan, also holding a glass, quoted:

> "As God comes a loving bed-fellow and
> sleeps at my side all night and close to
> the peep of day,
> Leaving me baskets cover'd with white
> towels swelling the house with their
> plenty . . ."

Dan Field refilled the glasses. "No baskets covered with white towels for us, Padre. It's these children growing up today whose houses will be swelled. You and I, Padre, are merely the little nooks bordering the rapid stream. It was Washington Irving, I believe, who put it: '. . . those little nooks of still water which border the rapid stream, where we may see the straw or bubble riding quietly at anchor, or slowly revolving in the mimic harbor by the rush of passing torrent.' Which reminds me, how is your Gregory Beamer?"

Father Callahan shook his head. "With the roads what they are, I've not seen him since Christmas; and what's more, with what the roads may likely be, I probably won't see him many times until spring. Gregory is not what might be termed a scholar, and it takes very little reason to make him miss Latin lessons. Sure and I've a good mind to send the lad away to school."

"Still bent on saving his soul, Padre?"

"Sure and why not? At my age, Dan, a man who has no children might do worse than to find a boy to—to——"

"To do those things which he has left undone," Dan Field supplied the phrase. "Padre, I'm beginning to comprehend your enthusiasm. There is a certain lad about whom I'm more than ordinarily concerned."

"Who might that be?" Father Callahan inquired.

Dan Field's eyes twinkled. "Bert Sargent. He's a born doctor. You probably heard that Christmas morning another Stoddard entered the teary vale. I named her Noel. Bert, unobserved by me, slipped into the shanty and watched the whole procedure."

Father Callahan's eyes twinkled. "Bert Sargent did that?"

"He did. What's more, he's taken it upon himself to attend Noel's welfare somewhat. The other day I dropped by the Stoddards' and found Bert at the helm. 'Know sumpin, Uncle Doc?' he said. 'Noel's bottom looked 'zactly like a hunk of raw meat. And Ray he says you say to keep Noel's bottom dry and use corn meal. Uncle Doc, you can't keep that Noel's bottom dry and the corn meal didn't do no good.' How would you think Bert handled the situation, Padre?"

Father Callahan chuckled. "Sure, I wouldn't be knowing."

Dan Field chuckled. "Bert said, 'Know sumpin, Uncle Doc? If Mr. Strock's and Mr. Butler's hands get like hunks of raw meat butchering they uses lard and I puts lard on Noel's bottom and it makes it well.' "

Dan Field roared and Father Callahan roared.

"That's what I mean, Padre," Dan Field roared. "These children today use their heads. Certainly I know grease ameliorates chap. It simply never entered my senile skull to apply lard to a baby's bottom."

Still laughing, Father Callahan arose. "Much as I dislike tearing myself away from your charming society, not to mention the bourbon, Bert would likely prescribe a few hours' sleep before six o'clock mass. And a little rest might put you on your feet again, Dr. Field."

Dan Field followed him to the door and outside. He stood upon the veranda and watched Father Callahan crossing the street. Rufe Albright hurried past the school. Getting to be a big boy, Rufe—Dan Field smiled—old enough to watch the New Year in. His eyes followed the boy home. A light burned in a window —George's and Pris's bedroom.

Sighing, Dan Field turned, entered the house, and mounted the steps. In the second-story hall he halted a minute before the one closed door. Perhaps someday I shall actually open that door and see your golden body stretched upon the bed, the bride's bed, he was thinking. Darling, darling . . .

Pris and George retired about ten o'clock but Pris never closed her eyes, and as the bells began their pealing she arose and lighted a lamp.

George rolled over, blinked his round blue eyes, and sat up. "What under the sun? Oh yes," he yawned, "it's New Year's. Infernal nuisance, those bells." His white teeth flashed. "Happy New Year, Pris."

Pris returned the smile. "Happy New Year, George."

His gaze fixed upon her fondly. In that ruffled gown, the curls falling over her shoulders, she looked no older than Lillian.

"Come on back to bed, dear," he urged. "You're liable to catch your death of cold standing there."

Pris nodded. "All right. But do you mind if I leave the lamp burning awhile? Rufe's not home yet."

George shrugged. "All right, leave the lamp burning. Only for heaven's sake don't worry. Rufe's all right. Can't keep him tied to your apron strings forever, my dear."

He fell back upon the bolster and closed his eyes. Pris crept in beside him, more wide awake than ever. Probably it was foolish to worry about Rufe—he'd told her exactly where he'd be tonight and what he intended doing—as it certainly had been foolish worrying about him Christmas night when he'd just been sleigh riding out in the country, even if he'd not reached home till after midnight. Still, Pris told herself, she simply could not approve Rufe's friendship with Tom, Jack, and Ben, despite George's insistence that mingling with the town boys would do Rufe good.

The bells stopped tolling. He should be getting home now. Still, it seemed an interminable period before she heard the front door open and close softly. A second time Pris arose, took the lamp, and went to the head of the stairs.

Coming before her, Rufe stopped still. "Aren't you asleep yet, Mama?"

"I can't sleep until you're home, Rufe."

Rufe sighed. "Mama, I told you exactly where I'd be and what I intended doing. And everything was exactly like I said. Tom gave the party in the Leonards' private parlor and we played card games and had popcorn and gingerbread and milk. Then at twelve o'clock us fellows went over to the courthouse and rang the bell. What's there about that to worry anybody, Mama?"

"Nothing, I suppose, dear. Did you enjoy yourself?"

"Yes, thank you, Mama."

Pris kissed him. "Good night, dear, and a happy New Year." He didn't return the kiss. "Happy New Year, Mama."

She watched him enter his room. A stranger in the house, she thought. But she ascertained that Gramma Albright, Lillian, and Sammy had not been disturbed; and she tucked the covers closer around all three before blowing out the lamp and returning to George's side. It was dawn before sleep came to her. All through the night she was remembering again the first time Rufe's soft little lips had found her breast and Dan was there leaning over her, closer, much closer than George had ever been.

Rufe's eyes did not close for quite some time either. Why, he couldn't go one place, he fretted, without having Mama waiting when he came home, looking as if he'd done something terrible.

Also Rufe felt particularly righteous at the moment, because the party tonight had been exactly what he claimed. Besides Tom, Ben, and Jack there'd been Jean Leonard and Tracy Whitlock; and Tracy, Rufe decided, was really a perfectly wonderful person. The moment Rufe arrived Tracy focused attention upon him, telling Rufe he'd always wanted to know him better. As a matter of fact Tom had told Rufe previously that Tracy had asked to be invited, because he wanted to know Rufe better.

Then, aside from the others, Tracy whispered, "Bet the fellows regretted taking you along out in the country Christmas night, Rufe. Bet after those farm lassies got a good look at you Tom, Jack, and Ben's noses were out of joint, old boy."

"I'd hardly say that," Rufe answered modestly.

"What was your tootsy's name?" Tracy asked.

Rufe flushed. "Fanny—Fanny Rhimer, Mr. Whitlock."

"Was she something special, Rufe?"

Rufe borrowed a cadence from Jack's repertoire. "What that Fanny ain't got ain't worth having, Mr. Whitlock."

Tracy chuckled. "I bet you had yourself a time, old boy."

Rufe chuckled, if somewhat nervously. "No fellow could help having a time with that Fanny Rhimer."

The truth of the matter happened to be, however, that that Fanny Rhimer, not to mention the other boys' girls—Lena Porter, Carrie Simpson, and Gracie Watts—had proved more than a disappointment, all being buxom (tubs, Rufe thought) and dressed in the funniest-looking clothes. Afterward Rufe asked himself, What else could he have expected? Hadn't he seen country girls on the streets Saturdays often enough to have known what they'd be like? But Tom, Jack, and Ben had given many a flattering description of their respective girls, and during the ride through the country Christmas evening they had extolled Fanny to such an extent that Rufe expected a paragon.

"That Fanny!" Jack had emitted a long whistle. "My God! Rufe, what that Fanny ain't got ain't worth having. There's nothing Fanny don't know. A city fellow twenty years old, name's Earl Foster, comes clear from Huntingdon twict a month to see her. Help me God! Time I first asks Lena could she get Fanny sometime for you Lena said she didn't think Fanny'd notice a fellow wasn't from a city."

Ben had smacked his lips. "I'd just lief take a peck at Fanny myself if Carrie wouldn't be jealous. How about you, Tom?"

Tom had smiled. "Fanny's a peach all right, only Gracie's my girl."

Their destination had been the Wattses' farmhouse, some ten miles distant, and by the time the sleigh bearing the boys drew along the fence, night shrouded the earth. The four girls rushed out of the house, carrying candles, crying greetings, their voices loud and shrill from excitement; and the answers of Tom, Jack, and Ben were equally loud and shrill. After introducing Rufe, Ben hitched the horses to the post and everybody went inside to a parlor where the voices quieted down considerably. Rufe guessed because of Gracie's parents in the adjoining kitchen—although the old people appeared absolutely oblivious of the young people. Through an open door Rufe could see Mr. Watts, a tired-looking lean man wearing overalls, reading a *Farmers' Almanac* by the light of a single candle; and Mrs. Watts, a tired-looking fat woman, rocking backward and forward, her fat hands clasped across the apron covering her fat stomach.

The girls placed their candles over an organ and the boys removed their wraps. Gracie sat down upon the organ stool, opened a hymnal across the rack, and began pumping and playing. The rest gathered around and sang, first one hymn and then another, except Rufe, whose voice simply wouldn't come. He thought he'd never seen such a strange-looking room as this parlor, the carpet worn threadbare, the furniture shabby, and against the streaked and faded walls were two framed mottoes—"IN GOD WE TRUST" and "MIZPAH," whatever that meant. Above the mantel hung a chromo of a young man in a Union uniform, probably the homeliest young man Rufe had ever beheld, who was probably Mr. Watts at the time of the Civil War.

After playing and singing for more than an hour, Gracie abruptly sprang from the stool and she and the other girls dashed into the kitchen.

Tom followed them. "Hello, Mr. and Mrs. Watts," he said pleasantly.

Without raising his eyes from the *Farmers' Almanac* Mr. Watts grunted.

Without stopping her rocking Mrs. Watts nodded. "Howdy, Mr. Leonard."

Pretty soon Tom and the girls returned, bringing cider and

sand tarts. Refreshments gone, Tom, Ben, and Jack, with Rufe following, donned their wraps, and silently sauntered outside. It was snowing again, and Ben took the robes from the sleigh and blanketed the horses.

"What you doing that for, Ben?" Rufe asked. "Aren't we going home?"

The three other boys went into stitches.

"Home?" Tom roared.

"God! You pretty near kill me, Rufe," Jack roared.

"You don't think we come all the way out here just to get cider and sand tarts, do you, Rufe?" Ben roared.

Presently the girls, wearing topcoats but no hats, rejoined the boys and each one grabbed an arm of her respective beau and pulled him through the snow to the barn. Inside the barn it was pitch-dark, but Rufe could hear animals stirring, probably seeking some warmth, and he could smell a blend of cattle and manure and fodder dust. All the days of his years Rufe never smelled cattle and manure and fodder dust without remembering this night.

"Come on, Rufe," Fanny instructed.

Through the darkness she pulled him along to what proved to be a wagon and, shoving him up onto a long wide seat, climbed beside him. From different parts of the barn came the sounds of the others whispering and giggling. Then there was silence. Suddenly Rufe felt Fanny's arms, fat and furious, go around his neck, and her lips, hot and wet, pressing against his. A terror seized him. He wanted to tear himself away from those fat, furious arms and those hot, wet lips. He wanted to run somewhere, anywhere. But he knew if the other boys suspected his fear he'd never live it down.

Finally Fanny's arms and lips loosened. "Oh, whatever's the matter, Rufe? Don't you want to do nothing?"

Under the night Rufe could feel the blood rushing to his face. "No," he choked.

"Don't you like me, Rufe?"

"I like you all right," Rufe lied like a gentleman.

"What's wrong then?"

"Nothing's wrong. It's just . . . it's just . . ." Rufe tried to find an excuse. "It's—well, it's this way. I got a steady girl and she'd be jealous if I did anything."

"What's her name?" Fanny inquired.

Rufe heard his voice saying, "Mollie——" He caught himself. "Mollie Baylor. She don't live around here. She lives in Philadelphia. She's a city girl and she's twenty years old."

Fanny giggled. "Ain't that funny? I got a city fellow lives in Huntingdon, name's Earl Foster, and he's twenty years old."

"I heard about him," Rufe said.

Fanny continued giggling. "Earl he'd be jealous if he knowed how nice I'd be to you, like your girl'd be jealous. Only what neither of them don't know won't hurt them. Come on. . . ."

Again Rufe felt her arms around his neck and her lips upon his. Just hugging and kissing can't be a sin, Rufe told himself. And that's all there'd be, just hugging and kissing. Fear flew and a burning breathlessness entered him.

After what seemed hardly any time Rufe became aware of voices calling him. He pulled away from Fanny. His eyes, having become accustomed to the darkness, could see figures moving toward the barn door. He jumped from the wagon and followed the others, Fanny following him. Besides the Wattses' gate everybody said their good-bys. Fanny, Lena, and Carrie, who lived some distances apart, were spending the night with Gracie.

Going home, even though the snow kept falling and the wind blew bitterly, Rufe felt snug, the memory of Fanny's arms and lips supplying a psychological warmth. Funny, though, Rufe kept thinking, how a fellow can have fun hugging and kissing a girl he don't like. And Tom, Jack, and Ben, also lost in memory, hardly uttered a word the whole return trip.

Nearing town, however, Jack shivered. "Oncet it's all over, I don't know if it's worth the long ride back this kind of weather. What do you think, Rufe?"

Rufe shrugged. "Got to pay a price for everything you do in life, you know. What do you think, Tom?"

Tom laughed. "I like old Gracie good. I'd ride twict as far any kind of weather to see Gracie."

"God sake! Tom," Ben swore, "don't you go falling in love and spoiling all the rest of us's fun."

Tom's good nature deserted him. "Shut your mouth, Ben," he snapped.

Rufe really paid a price. He tried to slip noiselessly into the house, only to find his mother, holding a lamp, waiting at the head of the stairs. She questioned him and he answered her. "Mama, I just went out in the country on a long sleigh ride. What's there about that to worry anybody, Mama? And Papa said I could go." Still, the sight of her and the sound of her voice made his very soul cringe. Just hugging and kissing, he defended himself, yet he felt, like Hester Prynne, that a scarlet letter burned across his breast.

During the following week Rufe swore to himself over and over that never again, no matter how long he lived, would he ever have a thing to do with a girl like Fanny. He spent most of his time in the playroom working upon the plans for his city to be built all of marble. He didn't see Tom, Jack, or Ben till Tom came around and invited him to the New Year's Eve party.

"No women invited except Jean," Tom told him. "Just us four fellows and Jean and Tracy. Tracy he asked me to invite him and Jean 'cause he always wanted to know you better."

In the dark of the new year's early morn, Rufe lay awake upon his bed and finally his conscience ceased smarting. Hadn't Tracy Whitlock, Rufe asked himself, who was really a wonderful person and twenty-five years old, acted as if me having fun with Fanny was something worth bragging about? Yet right before Rufe fell asleep he thought, Wonder how it'd feel to hug and kiss a girl you really liked, a girl who'd maybe black curls and blue eyes and slim legs and slim arms? Wonder how . . . Rufe slept.

Most of Willowspring, like the Albrights (excepting Rufe) and all the Sargents (including Bert), lay snugly in bed when the bells began their pealing. A goodly number slept right through the processional. After the manner of Gramma Albright, Sammy and Lillian, Gramma Sargent, Prissy, Bert and Lou, too, never heard a sound. Under the Sargent roof only Rufus's eyes opened. What will this year bring? He answered himself—arc lights, incandescent lamps, the telephone, perhaps the beginning of electric railways. Right now among the other wonders at Menlo Park was a train operated by dynamos. A good time to be alive, this year, Rufus thought. A good time . . . Still beside him, beneath the knell of yesterday, he could hear Lou's breathing. A great loneliness engulfed him. He moved a hand and the fingers closed around one of her small full breasts, yet gently lest he waken her. She cares about no one except Bert, he told himself again, and Bert seems to care about no person or thing. And poor little Prissy should have a mother's love. If there were anything he could think of to make Prissy's life richer; but they had grown so far, far apart. Lou stirred and Rufus's fingers relaxed. The bells tolled on and on and on. Long after they'd stopped, and Rufus slept once more, his ears still heard the tong—otong—otong—tong, tong.

Revelry ran rife at certain points, however. In the steeples the bell ringers cried banteringly. Around the Grand Central Bar many a man had more than he could rightly hold. Against a wall slumped Mr. Williams, his red helmet pushed farther back than usual upon his white wool, his eyes often closing tranquilly and his mouth sometimes opening stertorously. Mr. Williams desired the peace and quiet of his own bed but he never dreamed of deserting his line of duty until the last man left the bar. Twice already this evening Mr. Williams, ably assisted by others (there usually being plenty of eager hands willing to help upon such occasions), had dragged a fighting drunk out of the place and into jail. Because, try as they might, Mr. Leonard and Shorty Clapp couldn't keep the bar orderly.

Across the street around the red-hot potbellied stove of the livery stable's combined office and harness room gathered Jake Smith, Floyd Shires, Fat Hubbard, and Ralph Pettigrew. A gallon jug of rye rested on the floor and they'd been drinking, smoking, and talking a great part of the evening.

Hearing the first clang of a bell, Jake raised his cup. "A toast to the next mayor of Willowspring, Mr. Ralph Pettigrew."

Pettigrew smiled and the other three men tossed off their drinks, Floyd allowing his to slide past the inevitable straw sticking between his turtle jaws.

Fat Hubbard said, "What us's got to do next time ahead the election is get a newspaper on us's side. A feller 'crost to the hotel yesterday—feller lives way West, place called Chicago, and him says Chicago's a real big place—wall, see, this feller him sells sewing machines and him goes all over and him tells I nobody can win an election if him ain't got a newspaper on him's side."

Pettigrew emitted one of his bull roars. "That's a hell of a brilliant idea. Get a newspaper on our side—that's all we got to do. Did this fellow lives in Chicago and sells sewing machines and goes all over tell you how to get a newspaper on our side if there happens to be just one in town and the bank owns it?"

Floyd blinked his little round black beady turtle eyes. "Mightn't be so hard. T'other day I be setting out front in the hack and 'long come Tracy Whitlock. He stops and he says, says he, 'Don't you think it's funny 'bout Mr. Fisher leaving an income to be paid fifty years after he's dead? Why,' says Tracy, 'fifty years ago was the very year the bank got founded.' "

"What about it?" Jake demanded.

Floyd shrugged his humped shoulders. "Wall, the way Tracy says what he says sounded like he be thinking thar's something crooked a-going on at the bank, and ever since it be founded. Sounds like Tracy he don't think too much of George Albright and Rufus Sargent or thar fathers 'fore 'em. Looks to me like if we could get the money and pay off what Tracy owes the bank he'd be on our side."

Pettigrew sniffed. "Personally, I'd rather never be mayor of Willowspring than have Tracy Whitlock on my side."

"What be the matter of Tracy?" Floyd demanded.

Pettigrew spat. "If ever a squirt lived he's one."

"Tracy's all right, Ralph," Jake said. "I'll tell you something he says to me too. You knows how Ben, Tom, and Jack been going out'n the country after tails. Now them girls they got's all right, never knowed city fellers. But Christmas night they takes Rufe Albright along and gets him a girl named Fanny Rhimer. Fanny she's got a city feller, lives in Huntingdon, and he goes after her a couple times a month. Tom tells Tracy how he meets this city feller, name's Earl Foster, out to the country oncet and how Earl tells Tom 'bout all the cat houses he's been at. Now Tom'd hardly think 'bout what'll mighty likely happen to Rufe; Ben and Jack'd hardly think 'bout it neither. But Tracy he says, wouldn't it be funny if'n Earl'd pepper Fanny and Fanny'd pepper Rufe Albright?" Jake's fat sides shook mirthfully and Fat and Floyd chortled. "Don't you think, Ralph," Jake continued, "that thar sounds like Tracy he don't like George and Rufus so good neither?"

Pettigrew didn't crack a smile and, ignoring Jake's question, he arose, donned his wraps, and left.

Fat spoke sadly. "Ralph ain't like he a-tall no more. Him don't come round we hardly a-tall. 'Member that day him chokes I 'cause me was a-gonna ask the Taylor girls if'n them seen Miss Gunther's latest novelty?"

Floyd's little black beady turtle eyes brightened. "Tracy he tells me sumpin else. He says, says he, last court he seen a woman going out'n. She'd a black veil kivering her face, but Tracy knowed her all right. It be Margaret Taylor."

"How'd Tracy tell if'n he couldn't see her face?" Jake demanded.

Floyd cackled. "Tracy he says he'd of knowed that tail this side hell. And that ben't all. Tracy tells Ralph it be Margaret Taylor and starts after her to find out how come she's thar and Ralph grabs Tracy and won't let him go."

Jake's fat head shook sideways. "Sumpin sure has got into Ralph these days. Maybe he's fell in love with that Margaret Taylor. Maybe she's in love with him." Jake chuckled. "Wouldn't that be a stinkin' kettle of fish for the best families? What we better do is talk to Tracy Whitlock. Maybe he can tell us what to do 'bout the way Ralph he's acting lately. Ralph he's got aplenty; he could easy enough pay the bank what Tracy owes 'em."

Outside upon the pavement Ralph Pettigrew stopped, drawing a full breath, and the cold clean air seemed an ablution, washing his lungs of the harness-room stench—dung and urine-soaked straw, sweat-rotted leather and fetid fodder, smoke, whisky, and the seldom-washed bodies of Jake and Floyd and Fat. If there could just be a way to clear your ears as a deep breath clears your lungs, Pettigrew thought. He smiled wryly; strange the difference a few months can make. A few months ago he'd have despised a man whose nose minded a stink, and the idea of Rufe Albright becoming polluted would have tickled his ribs. What's more, Pettigrew knew that Jake and Floyd (regardless of his Sunday afternoon interludes) and Fat (despite the fact his wife supported him) were stolid citizens, honest as the day is long and kind to their families. Which was a lot more than could be said about many members of the best families. Yet lately Pettigrew despised the sight of his one-time cronies. Why? Pettigrew wondered. Why?

The bells stopped their tolling and the bar's clamor came across the street. No use thinking of sleep over that brawl. He made his way to his office, lighted a lamp, regulated the stove damper, removed his hat and coat, and sat down at the desk. Maybe he could get some work done. Maybe. Since he'd sent Margaret Taylor the candy and she'd written him the note he'd been unable to concentrate upon anything. That was the reason he'd gone to the livery stable tonight, because he couldn't work and there was no place else. . . .

No place else . . . Pettigrew leaned back in his chair. His family were most of them dead and the rest scattered. He'd not had a word from any one of them these many years. And there'd never been a girl Pettigrew wanted to marry. He'd known enough women, though, before he hung his shingle out here, and then . . . Then what? he asked himself. Suddenly the answer flashed across his mind. There'd been no woman here because he couldn't have the kind he wanted. Although he'd not realized the fact until this moment, since coming to Willowspring, always in the back of his mind had been the idea that someday he'd be able to marry a girl like Margaret Taylor—a girl who could be queen when he'd made himself king. But after all these years he still wasn't king, the aristocracy still regarded him as part of the kit and crew. And that was why, he realized, that Jake and Floyd and Fat, and his other henchman, had become despicable. Because he wasn't part of the kit and crew, he was the leader, the leader of lesser men, yet the leader; and the sole difference between him and any best-family male was the fact that he'd been born poor, had to work his way up from the bottom. By God! Pettigrew swore, I'll show them. I'll make so much money I'll outbid George and Rufus every time, if that's the only way to a throne. He clutched a batch of papers. . . .

Not until five o'clock that morning did Pettigrew return to the street. The only sound breaking the stillness of that hour dusting dawn was the town clock booming five. A single small shadow slipped through the darkness.

The figure started past him and Pettigrew said, "Wait a minute, Ray. What you doing around town this early on New Year's?"

Ray stopped. "Tending furnaces. What yer doing up yer-self?"

Pettigrew laughed. "Tending furnaces, too, except a different kind. Listen! Ray, tell me why you don't like me."

"I ain't got nothing agin yer."

"You like George Albright and Rufus Sargent better. Why, Ray?"

Ray shook his tousled head. "I wouldn't go fer ter hurt yer feelin's, Mr. Pettigrew."

"Sometimes it does people good to have their feelings hurt, Ray. Go ahead."

"It's kind of hard fer ter say, Mr. Pettigrew. It's—wall, see, it's like this. I thinks it'd take a mighty sight more'n yer gittin' 'lected mayor of Willerspring fer ter make yer the likes of Captain George and Mr. Sargent."

Ray tore down the street and Ralph Pettigrew stared after the fleeing shadow.

The morning following the Christmas night that Ray resolved to find work so that he might buy Lillian the watch in Carl's window, he tapped the Fishers' front door knocker lightly.

Presently Miss Fisher opened the door. "What can I do for you, Ray? You are the one named Ray, aren't you?"

Ray nodded. "Yes ma'am, I's the one named Ray. I's trying fer ter git work and I figgered long's yer ain't got no man round the house, mighty likely yer'd like me fer ter tend yer furnace and shovel snow."

Miss Fisher shook her head. "You're so small, Ray."

Ray crooked his skinny little arms, trying to show muscles under the ragged sleeves. "See thar, ma'am. Mighty likely I's mean fer ter look at but I's mighty strong. And I aims fer ter work cheap. I'd tend yer furnace 'fore light mornings and din-nertimes and afternoons and I'll bank it last thing at night fer fifty cents a week. And I'll shovel yer walk every time it snows fer a dime. Please, ma'am, won't yer give me a chancet?"

Miss Fisher gave him a chance and later that same day Mrs. Meeker and Mrs. Diggers gave him a chance. Ray figured it wouldn't do any good applying elsewhere because every other

family over town had a man or boy around the house or else kept
a hired man. Besides, considering all the chores, and Noel an
added burden, and what with school starting again pretty soon,
Ray felt he'd tackled about enough. Bert alone gave him a hand,
often minding Noel. Ray couldn't understand why Bert bothered minding Noel. Ray tended the baby because someone must
perform certain tasks and it seemed easier to do them than to
have them hanging overhead. But Bert often held Noel and he
fixed her bottom and pretty nearly put an end to her squalling.
After the first day of her life Noel had squalled every minute
she wasn't sleeping or nursing; even a sugar-tit didn't shut her
mouth. Until Bert made her a tit from a little piece of Spotty's
meat. Noel grabbed hold of it the way she grabbed hold of
Myrtle's breast, and sucked most of the day, hardly ever crying.

"Know sumpin?" Bert addressed the assembled Stoddard family.
"I figgered if meat's good for puppies it'd be good for babies.
See, babies they don't get nothing 'cept milk and sugar-tits
till they ain't babies and they cries most the time and they's mostly
sick. And know sumpin? Puppies they eats meat 'most soon as
they's born and a puppy it never cries 'less it's penned in or penned
out and you hardly ever hear tell of a sick puppy."

Lolling across a chair, Lem emitted a long spiral of brown
juice which missed the coal pail. "Mighty likely yer got sumpin
thar, Bert. It's meat what puts the meat on ter human bones right
nuff."

Wringing clothes, Myrt sneered. "If yer'd quit yer drinkin' and
git yer ass off'n itself likely we-uns'd git a bit of meat oncet
in a blue moon."

Lem let out a guffaw. "Listen ter the old slut. One of these
here days I's gonna own a farm, a vegetable farm, and thar's
gonna be stock, cattle and hawgs."

"God damn black liar," Myrt swore. "Git a move on, Ray,
and hang these here clothes on the line."

However, no matter how busy Ray happened to be every
afternoon, some time or other would find him standing before
Carl's window, eyes glued upon the watch. It was his wafer,
his wine, the Holy Grail which he'd live or die to possess. And
the thought never entered Ray's mind that someone else might
buy the watch before he had time to earn the money.

"If'n it jest keeps on snowing," Ray would think aloud, "it

won't take me hardly more'n three months fer ter git that thar twenty-four dollars and seventy-five cents."

New Year's morning during breakfast Pris said, "Rufe, I forgot to tell you, the Martins are having a party this afternoon and because Alec and Wayne are home they've invited you and the Taylor girls and Laird Culver. Isn't that nice?"

Rufe sighed. "Do I have to go, Mama?"

"Certainly you have to go. You'll have a perfectly lovely time. What's more, while Alec and Wayne are home I'm going to invite them and the Taylor girls and Laird and give you a little party."

"Mama, please," Rufe pleaded, "don't do anything like that. If I have a party I want Tom, Jack, and Ben and Tracy Whitlock."

"I never heard of such a thing, Rufe," Gramma Albright put in. "No Albright or Sargent ever thought of such a thing before."

"Papa told me I could play with the town boys till I grew up, didn't you, Papa?" Rufe defended himself.

George nodded. "That's right, Rufe, but inviting them to a party in your own home is a different matter. There's reason in all things, you know."

Rufe turned toward Pris. "Anyhow, Mama, please don't have that other crowd here to a party."

Pris sighed. "All right, Rufe. But I want you to come along this afternoon."

Rufe sighed. "All right, Mama."

"Mama, will you give me a party?" Lillian chirped.

Pris smiled. "Of course, darling, this very afternoon. You may invite Prissy and Alexander, if you want him, and I'll have Nellie make ice cream and cake."

"Goody, goody," Lillian cried.

"Not so much noise, Lillian," George instructed.

Sammy gulped his last mouthful. " 'Scuse, please."

Glory Ned, Sammy thought, rushing through the front door, hope Mama don't get any old idea of giving me a party! Mighty glad my birthday ain't till summer.

Prissy skipped into the Albright dining room, her eyes sparkling and her cheeks crimson.

"Prissy," Lillian gurgled, "Mama says we may have a party and have ice cream and cake and Alexander."

Prissy ignored the tidings. "Lillian, guess what? Papa says I may take piano lessons. Do you hear, Gramma Albright and Auntie Pris and Uncle George and Rufe? Papa says I may take piano lessons."

"How very nice, dear," Pris said.

Lillian spoke eagerly. "Mama, if Prissy takes piano lessons, can't I?"

"Of course." Pris looked at George. "I've been meaning to speak to Miss Fisher about Lillian taking lessons. By the way, George, you never told me how it happened Mr. Fisher left that income not to be paid until fifty years after his death."

George shrugged. "There is no answer to why men do certain things."

Pris shook her head. "Fifty years is such a long while, though. Why, fifty years ago was the year the bank was founded. How would Mr. Fisher know that in fifty years both his wife and daughter'd not be dead and buried?"

George pushed his chair back. "I couldn't say." He arose, started toward the door, turned back. "Pris, what do you do with Sammy's old clothes?"

"Put them in the missionary box, of course."

"It might be a good idea to give the Beamer boy a few. I met him on the street not long ago and he looked frozen, and Bert's things are too small, I'd imagine."

"I think it might be a splendid idea," Pris said.

She was thinking, What under the sun would make George notice Gregory Beamer?

Anticipating Christmas, the day itself, and the full following week with all their lovely presents made Lillian and Prissy unmindful of other matters. Alexander became a remote personality somewhere in Lillian's past. To Prissy, Gregory Beamer would have seemed, had Prissy been able to analyze her emotions, as colorless as a long-forgotten flower pressed between the pages of a book.

These days, however, Alexander felt anything save remote. Since the fight, if the boys still did not make him one of them, they let him alone, and Alexander walked the street, his feet feeling firmly set on ground instead of skimming over its crust. Although Alexander knew he still loved Lillian better than anyone, Sammy had become his hero. Terror-stricken, Alexander had watched the fight between Sammy and Buzz, but since that day he'd spent hours daydreaming about Sammy maybe coming to play with him, or maybe asking him to his house. And one night Alexander really dreamed that Sammy and he walked together along Broad Street while the whole town watched breathless. Minnie never heard that Alexander was the cause of the fight, but of course she noticed her offspring's change and her own poor timid little heart assumed a mite of courage.

There was no courage, nor fear either, in Gregory Beamer's being—simply a mystification. After mass Christmas night Mr. and Mrs. Beamer took Gregory back to the farm. Long snowbound weeks followed wherein Gregory was held away from school as well as town. Every morning before light and every evening before dark Gregory and Mr. Beamer shoveled and waded and fought their way to the barn, tended the stock, and struggled back to the house. The rest of the time during those long weeks Gregory stayed within the cold, dark, silent house where the old man and old woman he called Papa and Mama never spoke to each other and seldom to him. Sometimes he bounced his ball and always he speculated concerning certain facts.

He wondered again why his mama and papa were so old, why Maggie treated him nicer than Nellie, why he dasn't speak to or play with Bert and Prissy. And there was a brand-new wonder. Why did Bert and Prissy get a great big tree and more presents than could be counted when all he got was a little tree and a ball? Because late Christmas afternoon Maggie had gone upstairs and, not hearing a sound downstairs, Gregory tiptoed out of the kitchen, through the wide hall. He stood on the edge of the huge parlor, staring awe-stricken at the big tree and the pile of toys beneath.

Gregory understood now why Father Callahan made him take Latin lessons. The father wanted Gregory to become first an altar boy and later a priest. . . . And this to Gregory Beamer was the wonder of wonders: Why would the father want this?

To wait until summer came, then to feel the warm air and walk beside the creek, to pull off his pants and jump into the

water, perhaps a girl swimming with him—those were Gregory
Beamer's ambitions on New Year's morning in the year 1881, as
well as through many months to come.

By New Year's morning, the holiday spirit suddenly departing, Lillian and Prissy felt quite let down. Until Mama told
her she could have a party, Lillian had been wondering what
she could do today, while during breakfast an empty feeling
filled Prissy's soul. Mama talked to Bert and Gramma Sargent,
and Papa didn't talk, and the house and the whole wide world
seemed lonely. What was more, Prissy knew if she went over
to see Lillian, where they'd all act nice, everybody'd like
Lillian best.

Suddenly Papa looked at her. "Prissy, this is New Year's Day.
Can you think of anything you'd particularly like to do during
the coming year?"

Prissy nodded. "Yes, Papa, I'd like to take piano lessons."

Thinking the matter over later, Prissy couldn't understand
how she'd come to say piano lessons. She'd never really thought
about taking piano lessons; all she'd felt was that whenever she
heard music a shiver ran through her, and specially if Auntie Pris
played.

"Why, Prissy," Mama spoke to her finally, "it never dawned
upon me that you had any musical talent."

Prissy's face fell. "Maybe I haven't, Mama."

"Lou," Gramma Sargent said, "after all, her name is Priscilla
and I played very well in my younger days and Pris is an
artist."

Mama shrugged. "All right, if she wants music lessons."

Papa smiled. "I think piano lessons are a very wise choice,
Prissy. Good luck, my dear."

"Thank you, Papa." She beamed. She could hardly wait to
tell Lillian. " 'Scuse, please."

Prissy having departed, Lou turned back to Bert. "Bert, can
you think of anything you'd particularly like to do during the
coming year?"

"No, Mama."

"Perhaps you can think of some very nice present you'd
like."

"No, Mama."

Lou smiled. "Last fall your auntie Pris said something about getting Sammy a beautiful little hunting-dog puppy. How would you like one, dear?"

Bert swallowed what he'd been chewing. "No, thanks, Mama. Sammy he didn't want one neither."

"Why not?" Lou inquired.

"Guess me and Sammy we don't like beautiful little hunting-dog puppies."

That boy, Rufus was thinking, doesn't seem to have a spark of feeling throughout his whole being. I suppose Lou knows where he spends his time but it's beyond me; he's never here except at mealtime.

Returning home, after wheeling the swill to Mudtown before the New Year's dawn, Sammy had left his barrow among the tombstones displayed before Ma Woodward's workshop. Right after breakfast Sammy retraced his steps, entered the workshop, and, excepting the lunch hour, spent the whole day until five o'clock that afternoon perched upon a seasoned pine-board coffin, swinging his feet.

"Don't you go kicking your heels agin that coffin," Ma cautioned immediately.

"No indeed, Mr. Ma," Sammy promised. "I'd never do a thing like kicking my heels against a coffin."

Ma, his corncob pipe a little yellow smoking knob against his full white Santa Claus beard, sawed and hammered away, building what would eventually become Spotty's five-dollar kennel. The workshop smelled of pipe smoke and pine wood and sawdust and nails. Through a window Sammy could see the barrow entirely surrounded by tombstones, and a half-dozen impressively framed pictures of such bedecked the workshop's walls. If on this New Year's Day Sammy hardly noticed the atmosphere, through later years the sight of a tombstone never failed to bring to his nostrils a nostalgia for the smell of pipe smoke and pine wood and sawdust and nails.

The better part of the day Ma attended his work and Sammy attended Ma's progress, the stillness broken only by the saw and hammer, Ma cautioning Sammy about kicking his heels against the coffin, and Sammy's defenses. About midafternoon Sammy began engaging Ma conversationally.

"Reckon you like building a kennel better'n making a coffin, don't you, Mr. Ma?" Sammy inquired.

Ma shook his white head. "No, Sammy, coffins is my specialty. Now don't you go kicking your heels agin that coffin."

"I'd never kick my heels against a coffin." Sammy shook his round yellow head. "How come coffins is your specialty, Mr. Ma?"

"Wall, Sammy, coffins is a benefit to humanity. There's no law saying a dog's got to have a kennel but a corpse ain't a corpse without a coffin."

Sammy drew his brows together. "I never did know there's a law saying a corpse ain't a corpse 'out a coffin."

Ma hammered and sawed a bit, then admitted, "It ain't a legal law, Sammy, it's one of the Good Lord's laws. No Christian'd bury an unincarcerated corpse, like no Christian'd not get a baby baptized."

"Is it one of the Good Lord's laws that babies got to be baptized, too, Mr. Ma?" Sammy inquired.

Ma stopped working a few minutes, took the corncob pipe from his beard, refilled and relighted it, and reburied the stem amid the snowy hirsuteness. "Sammy, an unbaptized baby goes to hell. Sad but true, Sammy; poor little unbaptized souls are burning in everlasting fire all over hell."

Which horrifying revelation made Sammy cogitate mournfully the better part of an hour, his eyes drifting from the real tombstones outside to the pictured ones inside, back outside and in again.

Finally, however, Sammy spoke again. "Do folks who don't have tombstones go to hell, Mr. Ma?"

Ma meditated before answering. "Not having a tombstone'd hardly damn a soul, Sammy. Stop kicking your heels agin that coffin."

"I'm not, Mr. Ma. How come folks have tombstones if they can go to heaven 'out them?"

"I'll tell you, Sammy," Ma proffered, his tone lowered reverently. "During the sad days following the passing of a dear one to the great beyond the bereft longs to bestow a gift upon the deceased and a tombstone is the only thing worth a hoot to a corpse."

Sammy grasped the idea. "Like folks want to give a Christmas present or a birthday present if you ain't a corpse, Mr. Ma?"

"You hit the nail on the head, Sammy. Stop kicking your heels agin that coffin."

"I'm not." Sammy nodded thoughtfully. "I always did like the looks of tombstones. I'd sure like having a pretty tombstone over my grave. They must be awful dear, though, ain't they?"

"Fifty dollars and on up to any price," Ma informed.

Sammy whistled. "From fifty dollars on up to any price. . . . Glory Ned! They are dear. How much'd one what has a little lamb on cost?"

"Around about a hundred dollars."

"Glory Ned! Around about a hundred dollars. What'd one cost if it had a two-headed squirrel on it, Mr. Ma?"

Ma laughed until his round belly really shook like a bowlful of jelly. "Never did hear tell of a two-headed squirrel on a tombstone. It'd be dear all right, Sammy, probably about two hundred dollars. It'd have to be made special—wouldn't be in stock."

This staggering announcement silenced Sammy as reluctantly he dismissed the idea of having a two-headed squirrel mark his last resting place. Mama and Papa'd never spend two hundred dollars buying him a stone. What's more, they mighty likely wouldn't spend fifty dollars. Morbidly Sammy pictured his bones resting throughout eternity under untended, unhallowed, and unmarked sod.

Around five o'clock that afternoon, however, Sammy reached a conclusion which brightened him considerably. If he couldn't have a tombstone there might be an alternative.

He pointed to the walls. "How much'd one of them pictures cost, Mr. Ma?"

Ma gave the final tap, dropped the hammer, took the pipe from his beard, and laid it down. "They ain't stock, Sammy. The tombstone company just sent them along to show their goods."

Sammy's tone became hopeful. "Think the tombstone company'd send me one along?"

"Hardly, Sammy. How's it you want one?"

Sammy cleared his voice. "See, well, see, Mr. Ma, it's like this. You can't hardly tell till you die if you'll get a tombstone. Maybe after you die nobody'll want to spend a lot of money on a tombstone."

"That's right, Sammy," Ma agreed sadly.

"And see, Mr. Ma," Sammy continued, "long as I can't hardly tell if I'll get a tombstone I thought—well, see, I thought I'd like having a picture of a tombstone hanging over my bed till I died."

"Not a bad idea, Sammy," Ma admitted. "And these are really nice pictures, good gold frames. Tell you what, Sammy, if your heart's set on one of them pictures I'd just lief give you one. Stop kicking your heels agin that coffin."

Sammy beamed. "I'm not, Mr. Ma. I'd never do a thing like kicking my heels against a coffin. And thank you very much. I'll take mighty good care of that picture." Sammy frowned slightly. "I'll have to fetch it later, though, 'cause I got to wheel the kennel on the barrow now." He pulled the five dollars Pettigrew had given him from a pocket. "Here's your pay, Mr. Ma. Would you mind giving me a hand onto the barrow?"

Ma didn't mind giving him a hand onto the barrow and some minutes later Shad didn't mind giving him a hand off of the barrow, as they placed Spotty's kennel behind the Stanwicks' woodshed.

Hearing Sammy's voice, Spotty came trotting forward, wiggling and wagging and bouncing.

"See your new home, Spotty," Sammy gurgled. "No more old woodshed, Spotty."

Shad's eyes were popping. "Never did see the likes, Sammy. How much did yer pay fer it, Sammy?"

Sammy never batted an eye. "Two hundred dollars."

"Two hundred dollars, yippidy, yippidy!" Shad shrieked.

Sammy shrugged nonchalantly. "If you think this kennel looks good now, Shad, wait till I get her painted. Wonder what Spotty's favorite color'd be, Shad?"

Shad rolled his round eyes. "It'd be hard ter say, Sammy, real hard ter say. Mighty likely Bert he'd know."

"Mighty likely. Where's Bert at?"

Shad pointed toward the Stoddards' shanty. "Ray fetched him ter put the lard on Noel's bottom. Ray says Noel's bottom it don't do so good if'n somebody 'sides Bert puts the lard on. Here he come now."

Bert left the Stoddards' and crossed a lot, joining them. "That's a good kennel, Sammy."

"That thar kennel it cost two hundred dollars, Bert," Shad informed.

Bert whistled. "That's a lot of money to get a kennel made."

Sammy sniffed. "Not to get a kennel like this made, Bert."

"Where'd you get the two hundred dollars at, Sammy?" Bert asked.

Sammy meditated a moment. "A man gave it to me for a tombstone."

"Whar did yer git the tombstone at?" Shad demanded.

"That," Sammy replied loftily, "is something I crossed my heart and hoped to die if I ever told." He remembered. "Bert, what would you think Spotty's favorite color'd be?"

Bert answered quick as a wink, "Liver color like Duke's spots. 'Cause know sumpin, Sammy? Spotty and Duke's been playing together the livelong day and the way they was playing Spotty'll mighty likely get pups."

"Pups!" Sammy gasped. "You mean Spotty's going to get pups, Bert?"

Bert nodded. "Mighty likely."

Something must have got in my eyes, Sammy thought, wiping away the tears with a sleeve.

"Glory Ned!" he choked. "Glory Ned! I sure got to get a hurry on me and paint this kennel 'fore Spotty she gets her pups."

Which exigency completely absorbed Sammy during many days to come. He even forgot to go back to Ma Woodward's to claim the picture, until some weeks later when a real emergency arose.

About the time Sammy heard Bert's prediction concerning Spotty's probable fecundity the three senior Albrights, Rufe following meekly, accompanied by the three senior Sargents, moved along the school pavement toward the Martins' party.

At the corner Laird Culver waited and Pris whispered, "Rufe, please be nice to Laird, dear."

Consequently, greetings over, Rufe walked by Laird's side down Linden Street. Passing the Reynards', he wished fervently that Mollie would appear so he could cut her dead. Mollie, however, was nowhere to be seen, but next door Mr. and Mrs. Taylor, Mrs. Kimbell, and the Taylor girls appeared, Meg and Dot wearing what Rufe considered the craziest greenest-looking hats and coats. My God! Rufe swore to himself.

Greetings over again, Pris told the young people to skip on by themselves, took hold of Madge's arm, and drew her a few steps behind the others.

"The girls look perfectly beautiful today, Madge," Pris said. "Where did you find those outfits?"

Madge flushed proudly. "I told Chan it's high time Meg and Dot wore ready-made clothes and he agreed. I wrote Wanamaker's and it just happened they sent along hats and coats which are becoming."

Pris smiled. "Girls are so much fun."

Madge nodded. "They are indeed. But, Pris, Meg hasn't been a bit like herself these last few months; nothing seems to interest her and she doesn't eat enough to keep a bird alive. She couldn't help losing weight. I wanted to take her to Dan but when I suggested it she burst into tears. Of course, unless she's downright ill, any young girl's embarrassed if a doctor examines her and Meg's unusually modest. Really, it's a problem to know what to do with children these days. Though Meg's been brighter since Christmas."

Pris sighed. "It certainly is a problem to know what to do with children these days. Rufe isn't a bit like himself either."

According to Rufe the party exceeded his dourest foreboding. All the best families and Professor and Mrs. Phelps attended, and the old and older people talked, talked, talked, drinking eggnog and eating cakes; the young people, eating ice cream and cake, hardly uttered a sound. Alec and Wayne, dressed like a couple of monkeys, were exceptions, buzzing here and there and making damn fools of themselves by spluttering about "exclusive clubs" and "running up to Philly" and "these girls we know on Rittenhouse Square." . . . Bla, bla, bla, Rufe sniffed inwardly.

Rufe didn't want to find his tongue and Dot couldn't find hers, Alec and Wayne having simply fascinated her. Laird suffered silently because Meg ignored him. Meg was thinking how handsome Alec and Wayne were and remembering how long ago she'd thought she was in love with Tert but now no one, not even her mother and father and Dot, meant anything to her but *him*.

Pris was asking Peggy Martin, "Isn't Dan coming?"

Peggy shook her head. "You know Dan, Pris. He forgot my birthday party last year."

Suddenly there he was, calling "Happy New Year" to everybody.

Hart tried to hand him an eggnog. "None such for me, thank you, Hart. Haven't you a nip of bourbon tucked away somewhere?"

When he'd his bourbon he moved from this person to that, finally reaching Pris. "The rest of the ladies are beautiful tonight. But you, my dear Pris, look like a hag."

"Dan, Dan," she laughed.

Chapter Two

$\mathcal{T}$HE DAY AFTER New Year's the snow started falling again and hardly stopped an instant all the rest of January and a part of February. The country people continued bound to farms and firesides, and Willowspring Saturdays boasted no more flurry than Mondays through Fridays. Eyes which once yearned for the sight of Mother Carey's feathers, and ears which had ached for the sound of sleigh bells, had long since felt enough's enough. These days everywhere you went someone queried, "Think this weather'll ever end?" Tom, Ben, and Jack fretted fitfully because they couldn't visit their girls, although Rufe felt relieved about there being no immediate prospect of another rustic rendezvous. And Dan Field's rural patients caused him considerable concern. Probably the one person who relished the seemingly everlasting drift was Ray Stoddard, every flake meaning another bit of change to store in the little bag tied around his waist under his pants. Yet despite the work, by February Ray'd been promoted to third grade.

Pris's thirty-eighth birthday fell upon February's first Saturday. Awaking, she looked at George, expecting a greeting. George merely yawned, stretched, and smiled. He's forgotten, Pris thought. All right, George, she resolved, next time I'll forget your birthday. Also the rest of the family seemed oblivious of the occasion until sometime after lunch, when Rufe, Sammy, Lillian, and Gramma Albright, accompanied by Prissy, Lou and Gramma Sargent, suddenly burst upon her, all bearing gifts.

Lillian giggled, "You thought we'd forgotten your birthday, didn't you, Mama? And we planned surprising you this way and it was me thought up the idea."

"You darling!" Pris hugged her close.

But Pris'd finished dressing for dinner before hearing George downstairs calling, "Pris, where are you?"

"I'll be down in a minute."

She found him in the parlor and he said, "It's stopped snowing, Pris."

Pris shrugged. "What am I supposed to do about that—clap my hands?"

He looked down at her and she saw his blue eyes twinkling and his white teeth flashing. He reached into a pocket and pulled out a small box.

He handed her the box. "Funny thing, Pris, this afternoon coming home I found this on a pavement. Haven't an idea what's in it."

She opened the box. "George, oh, George, I've never seen anything so beautiful!"

He took a ring from the box and slipped it on her finger. "It's a star sapphire, Pris."

She threw her arms around his neck, pulled his head down, and kissed him. "I thought you'd forgotten."

George kissed her and laughed. "Never, my dear."

She let loose of him, laughing too. "It's the most beautiful stone I've ever seen, George. A star sapphire—how did you ever come to think of such a thing?"

George shrugged. "Happened to see it at Bailey, Banks and Biddle's when we were in Philadelphia last fall and told them to put it away."

She looked up at him. "Sometimes I believe you really do love me, George."

George's brows came together. "Sometimes you believe . . . What do you mean by sometimes?"

"Well, in all the years we've been married you've never said so."

George blinked. "Haven't I? Well, perhaps I haven't. It never occurred to me that it was necessary." His white teeth flashed again. "So you like the ring, my dear?"

Her eyes shone. "I adore it, George."

Dan Field strode through the front door, calling, "Pris."

"We're here, Dan, in the parlor," she answered.

He joined them and handed her a long box. "Happy birthday, Pris. Hello, George."

George nodded and Pris opened the box, exclaiming, "Oh, how lovely! Red roses. Thank you, Dan. You never forget my birthday, do you, Dan?" She left the room and returned an instant later, bringing a vase. Arranging the flowers, she talked. "There, aren't they magnificent? What a birthday I've had. Look, Dan. . . ." Her hands left the flowers and she showed him the ring. "A star sapphire. . . ."

"Spoiled woman," he smiled.

But he was thinking, A star sapphire indeed! Would that I could bring all the gems of earth and lay them at your feet. Her eyes shone upon George, though, and his white teeth were flashing. They're happy enough and thank God! Dan Field told himself.

Pris pointed to a table. "Look at all my other presents, Dan. George, you haven't seen them either. Everybody remembered, even Sammy." Her laughter rang. "Wait till you see what Sammy gave me. I could hardly keep my face straight."

Since New Year's night Sammy's life had been a dilemma. First thing the next morning he'd presented himself at Morgan & Sons.

"What can I do for you, Sammy?" Mr. Morgan inquired.

"Got any liver-color paint, Mr. Morgan?" Sammy inquired.

"What you mean—liver color?"

"Why—er—liver color. Like on a hound what's got liver-color spots. Like on Duke, Mr. Tatem's dog."

Mr. Morgan shook his head. "No, might give you some red paint and some yellow paint and you could mix it together and get the right shade. How much'd you want?"

Sammy speculated. "Let's see. . . . Well, maybe a couple of quarts and a brush. It's to paint a kennel four—I mean four feet, Mr. Morgan, four by three and a half by three."

"That'd take two quarts easy, Sammy," Mr. Morgan agreed.

"How much'll it cost?" Sammy inquired.

"The paint'll be a dollar and you said you wanted a brush, too, and it'll be a quarter. Want to take them along, Sammy?"

Sammy cleared his throat. "See, it's like this, Mr. Morgan: all I got's a quarter. I can buy the brush all right, only I ain't got a dollar and I simply gotta have that paint, Mr. Morgan."

"Why don't you ask your papa to give you a dollar?" Mr. Morgan suggested.

Sammy frowned. "He never would give me that much; the most Papa ever give me's a quarter and that just some special time. Ain't there some little favor, like sweeping out the store or shoveling snow or tending your furnace or nothing, I could do round here to earn a dollar?"

"No, Sammy, I've all the help I need. Give me the quarter and you can have the brush and when you got a dollar come back and get the paint."

Sammy handed over the quarter and took the brush, his round blue eyes fixed upon Mr. Morgan. Skinny, mean-looking old man, Sammy sniffed inwardly, not fat and kind-looking like Mr. Smith.

Some time later, squatted beside the kennel holding Spotty, he told Bert and Shad his troubles. "That old Mr. Morgan he's mean, he really is mean. He wouldn't let me have any paint 'out paying him a dollar."

"Know sumpin, Sammy?" Bert said. "What you ought of did was have Mr. Ma build you a hundred-and-ninety-nine-dollar kennel and kept a dollar to buy paint."

Sammy nodded mournfully. "Mighty likely. Only see, Bert, I thinks Mr. Morgan'd let me work out the paint like Mr. Smith he let me work out Spotty. And all he says is he got plenty of help."

Shad rolled his eyes around. "That old Mr. Morgan he sure must be a mighty mean old man. Mighty likely yer could git som'un else ter let yer work, Sammy, maybe shoveling snow or tending furnaces like Ray he git."

"Think maybe I could, Bert?" Sammy spoke hopefully.

Bert shook his head from side to side. "Hardly likely, Sammy. See, Sammy, Ray he say if the snow stops he'd like to get some more furnaces to tend 'cept there ain't a chance. Know sumpin, Sammy? Ray he says everybody 'cept the Fishers and Mrs. Old Man Meeker and Mrs. Diggers got a man or boy round the house or else keeps a hired man."

During the following lagging weeks Sammy racked his brains trying to think of some way to obtain a dollar. Dismissing the idea of being able to secure work, he contemplated trying various tactics upon George, telling Papa someone was starving or dying and needed money. But Sammy knew Papa'd never give him a lot of money, and if he did the lie would surely be discovered.

Sammy even approached Pettigrew one afternoon as he stood before the office building. "Mr. Pettigrew, I crossed my heart and hoped to die I'd never tell you know what. I never will tell, Mr. Pettigrew."

Pettigrew smiled. "I know you won't, Sammy."

"Don't have any other favor maybe I could do, do you, Mr. Pettigrew?"

"Not at present, Sammy. But if I ever do I'll remember you."

"Anything else you'd like done, I'd do cheap. All you'd have to give me'd be a dollar. Can't think of nothing you'd like done now, can you, Mr. Pettigrew?"

"Not a thing right this moment, Sammy."

The earth and the skies seemed futile and lowering to Sammy during this period. Until a certain Saturday morning, after Mama went upstairs, Papa called Rufe and Lillian and Sammy aside and handed each one a dollar.

"Don't let your mama know I reminded you," Papa'd said, "but today's her birthday. Buy her a present, each of you. And, Lillian, you run over and see the Sargents haven't forgotten."

"Goody." Lillian clapped her hands. "We'll have a s'prise party this afternoon. Rufe and Sammy, don't you dare forget to come."

Sammy thrust his dollar in a pocket and strolled outside. That old dollar'd buy the paint, he thought, that old dollar'd buy the paint. . . . And he had to get Mama a present. Then like a bolt from the blue an inspiration came. He could buy the paint and still get Mama a present, and a present that'd mighty likely cost a lot more'n a dollar if Sammy had to pay for it.

Shortly before noon Sammy gave the kennel the last stroke of the brush, observed by Bert and Shad.

"Know sumpin, Sammy?" Bert said. "You got that kennel pretty near 'most the color of Duke's spots."

Shad rolled his eyes around. "That old Mr. Morgan he sure must be a mighty mean old man. Sammy, that old Mr. Morgan he sells yer nuff paint ter kiver a hull house."

"This kennel it's got to have two or three coats, Shad," Sammy replied loftily.

"Take mighty sight more'n two or three coats ter use all this paint up, Sammy," Shad informed. "What yer 'spect ter do with what's left over?"

Sammy shrugged. "Mighty likely I'll be wanting to paint something else 'fore long."

Glory Ned! he speculated suddenly. I better be getting Mama's birthday present 'fore I go forgetting it.

He started along, cautioning, "Shad, don't you let none the young'uns go near that wet paint till I come back."

Pris's laughter rang. "Look what Sammy gave me." From among the gifts she took one. "The picture of a tombstone"—she could hardly talk because of laughter—"framed in gold."

George and Dan Field looked and roared.

"Where do you suppose he ever got it?" Pris still laughed. "And why under the sun would he ever select such a thing?"

The knocker sounded and Pris replaced the picture and opened the front door.

Tracy Whitlock entered. "Good evening, Mrs. Albright." He bowed, removing his hat. "If I am not mistaken this is your birthday. I dropped around to wish you well and find out if you're entertaining."

Pris smiled. "How nice of you to remember, Tracy. Come in and sit down a few minutes, won't you?"

"Thank you." He followed her into the parlor. "Good evening to you, Captain George and Dr. Field."

The men greeted him and as they all found chairs Tracy continued, "Are you having a party tonight, Mrs. Albright?"

Pris shook her head. "Just a family dinner, unless Dr. Field will stay. How about it, Dan?"

"Sorry," Dan Field said, "I'm having a dinner guest myself this evening."

"But I've had such a lovely day, Tracy." Pris nodded toward the table. "All those gifts this afternoon and"—she held out a finger—"my husband gave me this star sapphire and Dr. Field brought me these exquisite roses." She indicated the flowers.

Tracy smiled. "You really have had a lovely day, Mrs. Albright. And, your permission granted, I'll take a few notes to grace the next edition of my unworthy sheet."

"Certainly, Tracy."

Jotting, he remembered the last time he'd called upon her and she'd played "The Blue Danube" waltz and when she'd finished he'd thought the expression in her eyes like that of a young girl in love. With the good doctor here I might find out a thing or two, Tracy told himself.

He finished the notes. "Mrs. Albright, would you think me presumptuous should I ask you to play 'The Blue Danube' again? Remember you were gracious enough to play it for me last fall?"

"I'd enjoy playing it again, Tracy."

She went to the piano and her fingers found the keys. Tracy watched Dan Field's expression. Nothing written there, Tracy thought. Yet, the last chord dying away, she turned and the look was in her eyes again and the eyes fixed upon Dan Field. She's in love with him all right, Tracy gloated inwardly. This will be my *pièce de résistance*, not to be employed unless all else fails, he concluded.

He arose. "You are an artist, Mrs. Albright. Thank you. Good night, gentlemen."

Tracy departed and pretty soon Dan Field followed. Gramma Albright came downstairs and Lillian returned from the Sargents'. Pris showed them her ring. Gramma Albright exclaimed and Lillian clapped her hands.

"Bet Uncle Doc brought you the roses, didn't he, Mama?" Lillian asked.

"You're right, dear," Pris answered, smiling.

Sammy burst through the front door.

"Wonder where Rufe could be," Pris thought out loud.

"I forgot to tell you, Pris," George explained. "He's gone out in the country sleigh riding again this evening."

Pris frowned. "On my birthday, George, and with the roads what they are?"

George shrugged. "Rufe came to the office about four o'clock and said it had stopped snowing and they wanted to go out in the country sleigh riding again. I forgot it was your birthday when I told him all right. As for the roads, if they're not passable he won't be gone long."

It was almost dawn before Pris heard the front door open and close quietly and she'd not slept a wink. But she didn't meet Rufe at the head of the stairs this morning. What good does it do? she asked herself. And she remembered the star sapphire on her finger and crept closer to George's warmth.

Leaving the Albrights', Tracy Whitlock moved down the street, mentally patting his own back. Matters seemed to be shaping themselves better than he'd dared dream. Even if the Fisher business still remained obscure, the Mrs. Albright-Dr. Field affair looked as plain as a printed page, and if Rufe Albright wasn't already peppered he'd probably get a dose tonight. Every evening Tracy scrutinized the hotel registry, seeking an entry interesting enough to make news and not long ago one met his eyes which had whetted his scent: "Alvin Cosgrove, Huntingdon, Pa." Looking around the lobby, Tracy spotted his quarry by the process of elimination.

Alvin Cosgrove proved to be a bald-headed, squint-eyed, fat-jowled tobacco chewer who represented the Home Builders Supply Company, Mr. Leonard told Tracy. Also Mr. Cosgrove proved to be a man of few although pertinent syllables.

Introducing himself, Tracy took a seat at Mr. Cosgrove's side. "I've heard considerable concerning your company and your valuable contribution to its success," he lied.

Mr. Cosgrove spat, skillfully striking the cuspidor's bull's-eye. "So?"

"Huntingdon is certainly quite an up-and-coming town."

"So?"

"Ever know a young fellow who lives in Huntingdon named Earl Foster?"

"Yep."

"What sort of fellow is he, Mr. Cosgrove?"

"Chippy chaser," Mr. Cosgrove grunted, scoring a second bull's-eye.

Now, passing the school, Tracy happened to glance across the street in time to see Dan Field's front door open and Ralph Pettigrew step across the lighted portal. So Pettigrew's the dinner guest the good doctor's expecting. Tracy smiled. That would be another item the harness room's ears should relish. Since New Year's Tracy had enjoyed several promising conferences around the potbellied stove.

These snow-sodden days, if Dan Field must neglect his rural patients, ailing town bodies kept him busy enough. Following a crowded morning, this first February Saturday, his sleigh reached home about noon only to find Wilbur Lawler waiting on the curb.

"What is it, son?" Dan Field asked.

Wilbur trembled. "Cal him cough. Mam says hurry, Doc. Cal him——"

"Jump in, son. I'll let you drive Nervy."

The Widder Woman opened the shanty door, practically sober, probably from fear, Dan Field speculated.

"Cal," she sniffed, "he's chokin' ter death. Love o' Gawd, Doc, don't let my own poor leetle darling croak."

Ella whimpered, "Cal him cough."

Dan Field pushed by them. The shanty's front room, combining kitchen and Lottie's theater of operations, contained a stove and a pot, a table with several cracked plates and cups and a few battered knives, forks, and spoons, two chairs, a water bucket, and a sagging couch whose original green plush covering had become a threadbare splotched saffron. The family followed Dan Field into the shanty's single other room which possessed a foul overflowing slop jar and a filthy bed where Cal writhed, his tiny body racked and his tiny face purple. Despite a faint fire in the stove, both rooms held no more warmth than the outdoors; but only a ragged shawl covered Cal. If I'd the guts of a worm I'd put you to sleep, baby, before there's any more suffering, Dan Field thought.

"Haven't you a blanket or quilt, Lottie?" he demanded.

"Nary un, Doc. Love o' Gawd, Doc, don't let Cal croak."

Dan Field removed his overcoat and covered Cal. "Lottie, hurry and heat some water and fill half a dozen whisky bottles." Working over Cal, he instructed Wilbur, "Run and see if you can find Bert Sargent, son, and tell him I want him right away."

Her mother and Wilbur gone, Ella whimpered, "Doc, Cal cough all night. Mam hain't here, and me and Wilbur's skeered, awful skeered, Doc."

"Of course you were scared, Ella, and the next time Cal starts coughing, whether your mama's here or not, you send Wilbur right after me, no matter what time it is. Will you?"

Ella nodded. "Me'll send Wilbur."

Presently Cal's coughing ceased and the purple of his face became a faint blue. Lottie brought the whisky bottles filled with hot water and Dan Field placed them around Cal.

Bert, followed by Wilbur, entered.

Bert's eyes fixed upon Cal. "What's wrong, Uncle Doc?"

"Lungs, Bert." He took a pad and pencil from a pocket and wrote a note, handing it to Bert. "Bert, take the sleigh and drive to my house. Read this note to Ackley; he probably couldn't make it out himself. Have him put the things I've written down in the sleigh and you get them back here on the jump. Make Nervy trot the whole way, please, Bert."

"Nervy'll trot, Uncle Doc," Bert promised.

By the time Bert returned Cal's breath came easily and his face looked white as usual.

"Want me to bring the things in the shanty, Uncle Doc?" Bert asked.

"Thank you, Bert. Wilbur and Ella, run along and help Bert. And, Ella, empty this slop jar and please keep it clean, dear."

"Gawd bless yer, Doc. . . . Gawd bless yer," Lottie choked. "If'n thar's evir any favor I kin do fer yer, Doc . . . Thar's no favor I wouldn't do fer yer, Doc."

"I'll tell you the greatest favor you can do for me," Dan Field said, "and that is look after this baby until he's up again. Bert's brought blankets, firewood, and plenty victuals to feed all of you until tomorrow. What's more, I'll see you all receive enough food and wood to keep comfortable as long as you stay sober, keep off the streets, and mind Cal properly."

"Help me Gawd, Doc, I'll never tetch 'nither drop nor never whore no more," Lottie sobbed. "All I'll ever do is ter mind my own leetle darling."

Dan Field called, "Bert, please bring the blankets." Bert brought the blankets and, lifting his overcoat, Dan Field tucked them closely around Cal. He handed Lottie an envelope. "Give Cal one of these pills every hour, or if you haven't a clock give him seven before morning, keep him covered, the bottles hot, and feed him all the soup he'll take. You brought the soup, didn't you, Bert?"

Bert nodded. "Ackley says fetch the pot back, Uncle Doc."

"The pot must wait." Dan Field spoke to Lottie again. "And I'm warning you, Lottie, unless you follow instructions to the letter Cal will die and nothing on earth will save him."

Leaving the shanty with Dan Field, Bert asked, "How soon's Cal really going to die, Uncle Doc?"

"In from six months to a year, Bert."

"Cal seems mighty little to die even in from six months to a year, Uncle Doc. Know sumpin? They says Cal's papa's a preacher."

Dan Field shook his head. "I've always thought Cal looked as if his father were an angel."

"Maybe he is, Uncle Doc, maybe the preacher's an angel now and that's how come he don't look after Cal."

They were walking along Limestone Avenue, Nervy following.

"Thought I'd better take a look at Noel, seeing I'm here," Dan Field changed the subject. "I've not seen her these many a day. How is the young lady doing?"

"Noel she's doing fine, Uncle Doc," Bert informed. "Noel's bottom it's fine. Know sumpin, Uncle Doc? I fixed Noel a tit out of a little piece of Spotty's meat and——"

"You what?" Dan Field interrupted.

"Know sumpin, Uncle Doc? See, I figgered if meat's good for puppies it'd be good for babies and it is. Wait till you see Noel."

Among various crawling whimpering young ones upon the Stoddard kitchen floor Noel lay contentedly sucking her meat-tit. Dan Field could barely believe his eyes. The other Stoddard children's bodies were sound enough but each and every one of them, until grime overtook him or her, had possessed skin the color of paste. Noel looked almost rosy.

"Well, well," was all Dan Field could say. "Well, well."

Myrt stopped ironing. "Noel she looks good, don't she, Doc? Ray, git a move on yer and fix that thar fire. My flat won't heat half."

Lem emitted a long spiral of brown juice which missed the coal pail. "Since Bert he bring Noel a meat-tit every day Noel she hardly squalls none."

Jesus! Dan Field swore to himself. Maybe Bert's got something here. Anyhow, he'd a baby near Mount Pallas whose blood seemed like water and whose death looked inevitable unless . . . Jesus! I'm going to try it, Dan Field decided.

He chuckled, "I can't see a single reason why I shouldn't resign my practice and turn my patients over to Bert."

Across Bert's serious young face one of the occasional smiles passed. "Know sumpin, Uncle Doc? I used to think soon's I was a real doctor I'd get on a boat and be like Uncle Bert. Only I ain't. I'm going to be 'zactly like you, Uncle Doc."

You will do those things which I have left undone, Dan Field was thinking; your soul will be my soul marching on. Bert, Bert . . .

Aloud he said, "By the time you're a doctor, Bert, men will know more than is dreamed of on earth today. Riding along home, boy?"

Bert shook his head. "No, thanks, Uncle Doc. I better hang round watching if the Widder Woman she's minding Cal."

Crossing the bridge, Dan Field remembered he'd had no lunch, and breakfast before seven, yet at Broad Street he turned Nervy's head west, meaning to see Mr. Strock about delivering daily provisions to the Lawlers.

Before the market Ralph Pettigrew hailed him. "Wait a minute, Doc." Pettigrew came beside him. "Doc, I'd like to have a talk with you sometime. Some evening if you're not busy could I drop by your place?"

Dan Field smiled. "Certainly. How about tonight? Why not come and have dinner with me?"

"Dinner," Pettigrew echoed. "Sure, Doc, thanks. What time?"

"A little past six, if that suits you."

Dan Field felt sure Pettigrew wanted to talk about the Margaret Taylor situation, either directly or indirectly.

Since the dawn of New Year's morning Ralph Pettigrew's mind had been chaotic. Ray Stoddard's dictum might be an ultimatum, he considered. What if in spite of his education there was something which marked him as part of the kit and crew? What if it wasn't that he'd been born poor and had to work his way up from the bottom that made the aristocracy snub him? What if, no matter how much money he earned or how far he rose politically, there was an innate quality, or lack of quality, which would foredoom marriage to a girl like Margaret Taylor? But if there was, Doc Field would know and one of these days he meant to ask Doc to tell him. The day had finally arrived.

They ate as the lights from the candelabra flowed across linen and plate and silver, but every time the kitchen door opened the candle flames flickered and dimmed an instant. Dan Field chuckled to himself; this evening the spirits of the South were no doubt arising in holy horror to blow breath across the lights because white trash, as Ackley put it, sat breaking sacred bread.

During dinner they talked about this or that, the weather, crops, community health; and having eaten their fill, they settled upon chairs.

Ralph Pettigrew looked around the room admiringly. "Brought these here things up from Virginia, didn't you, Doc?"

Dan Field nodded. "And the pillars out front, not forgetting Ackley."

Pettigrew shrugged. "There's no reason why a man shouldn't have what he wants, especially if they're as pretty as all you got, Doc."

Dan Field smiled. "Except most people think it's strange that I should prefer Southern elegance to Northern grandeur."

Ralph Pettigrew smiled. "People will think, if that's what you call what they do. Personally, I wouldn't be able to guess. You did fight on the North's side, you know, Doc."

"Yes," Dan Field said, "I did fight on the North's side but I fought to preserve the Union and not to destroy the South. And I've always respected the Confederate principle. Any country or group or state who admits slavery is well on the way to salvation. One poet put it:

> *"Virginia, mother of greatness,*
> *Blush not for being also mother of slaves,*
> *You might have borne deeper slaves—*
> *Doughfaces, crawlers, lice of humanity—*
> *Terrific screamers of freedom,*
> *Who roar and bawl, and get hot i' the face,*
> *But were they not incapable of august crime,*
> *Would quench the hopes of ages for a drink—*
> *A dollar dearer to them than Christ's blessing."*

Pettigrew's brows came together. "It never occurred to me before that anything could be said in defense of the South. You're correct, though, Doc, there's plenty right here in this town, not to mention the whole North, who scream freedom when a dollar's dearer to them than Christ's blessing."

"However, the line is so very fine between black and white and between white and black," Dan Field continued. "Years ago while traveling abroad I went to a brothel in Marseille. Sailors from all over the world traded there and the girls were about as depraved and sordid a lot as you'd find anywhere. During the evening a stretcher was borne in from outside and upon it lay what was supposed to be a man. His legs were off at the hips, his arms off at the shoulders, and part of his face was gone. Anyhow, the litter was carried upstairs and one of the girls followed. I knew the girl's name—Fronnie." Dan Field hesitated.

"What happened?" Pettigrew demanded.

"Some time later the litter was borne downstairs again and out. But Fronnie didn't appear. From curiosity I asked one of the other girls where she might be. I was told that Fronnie was certainly being sick. It seemed the cripple visited the establishment often but Fronnie was the only girl who would touch him, although after every contact she became violently nauseated. When Fronnie finally appeared I called her to my table and asked why, if the cripple were loathsome to her, she tolerated him. Did he pay more than the others? No, he paid the regular fee. 'Then why?' I asked. Fronnie said, '*La vie a déjà tant arraché de lui que je ne pouvais pas prendre davantage.*' Which, translated loosely, means, 'Life has already taken so much from him I could not make it more.'"

Pettigrew took a cigar out of a pocket. "Mind if I smoke?"

"Not at all. If you've an extra cigar I'll join you."

Pettigrew found a second cigar and handed it to Dan Field. "Never knew you smoked, Doc."

Dan Field laughed. "I do everything at times."

Pettigrew didn't laugh and he lighted the two cigars before speaking. "That's a story to make any man think. I suppose if you'd know where to look a fair speck could be found in everyone and everything."

"Yes." Dan Field nodded. "We could find a fair speck even in the money-changers and the temples. Pettigrew, I'm going to tell you something, although I must rely upon your word not to repeat it. You've heard, of course, about the Fishers' recent income. What you and the rest of the town haven't heard is that George Albright gave the money himself and had papers so drawn that it appears Mr. Fisher left money payable at this time."

"God damn my soul!" Pettigrew ejaculated.

Dan Field lifted the decanter and filled two glasses. "Know you prefer rye, Pettigrew, but maybe a spot of my bourbon will slip down all right this evening."

Pettigrew downed the drink, reached for the decanter, and

poured another. "I'm not such a damn fool as to think there's not plenty of good specks in George Albright and Rufus Sargent, too. Not to mention their henchmen, especially his honor, Judge Hart. Listen! Doc, now I'm going to tell *you* something and I must rely upon your word not to repeat it. Matter of fact that's why I come here this evening. Remember I told you I wanted to have a talk with you? And the reason it's you I wanted to talk with is because you're the only man I know who could understand what's on my mind and would be able to give me the right answer. Look, Doc, I was raised out here in the country on a farm. Those were the days George the First and Rufus the First were kings. Saturdays we come to town and I'd see them on the street and I'd think someday I'd be walking along holding my head high; and I made up my mind right then that when I was king I'd treat everybody right, be friendly with everybody the way Tim Albright was. I knew Tim."

"Did you really?" Dan Field asked. "I've always wondered about Tim. The family never mentions him and nobody else seems to remember him except vaguely."

Pettigrew sniffed. "The family wouldn't mention Tim. He wasn't like the other Albrights. He was a little skinny dark fellow and he talked to everybody, white and black. I used to hear stories about him going up in the mountains and getting lost. Tim never got lost, Doc. He knew the mountains good as he knew the town here. What Tim was trying to do was get away from something here."

"I see." Dan Field nodded.

Pettigrew poured himself a third drink. "The day I heard he run away I wasn't surprised. He was about my age, maybe a year's difference one way or the other, but not half my size. I was fourteen or fifteen the Saturday we come to town and heard everybody along the streets wondering why Tim Albright left home."

Pettigrew downed his drink and Dan Field refilled both glasses. "How's the bourbon?"

"Good. As I was saying, I wasn't more'n fifteen but I knew why Tim run off. Doc, people don't remember Tim except vaguely because nobody but me knew how he felt. Funny thing, too, I can't remember a single word he ever said. It was just intuition made me understand that Tim run away for the same reason he pretended to get lost in the mountains; this town made him feel like he was in jail."

Dan Field nodded. "I've always suspected that was the reason."

Pettigrew nodded. "You'd know, Doc, the way I'd know but nobody else'd even suspect. Well, going on, the bank held a mortgage on our farm and the whole lot (there was nine of us counting Mam and Pap) worked from dark till dark trying to make ends meet and paying interest on the mortgage. We had plenty to eat and not a God damn thing more except one rag to cover our hides summers and a few more winters to keep us from freezing."

"Didn't you go to school?" Dan Field asked.

"Yeh," Pettigrew answered, "there was a school six miles off. The other young ones wouldn't bother walking that far. I went till I was ten, four years, then Pap told me I must quit and work on the farm. The last day I went I didn't tell Teacher I wasn't going back and I took what books I could lay hands on—a speller, a history, a geography, and a Bible."

Dan Field smiled. "A Bible, huh?"

At last Pettigrew smiled. "That's another thing about you, Doc, makes people wonder. You're always quoting the Bible and you never go inside a church."

"There's no law against a man who never goes inside a church quoting the Bible, is there?"

Pettigrew shrugged. "No law, it's just odd."

Dan Field put out his cigar. "It's merely that if any passage comes to mind, from the Bible or elsewhere, which I believe fits an occasion, I quote."

"You must read a lot."

"Not any more. I merely have what is called a retentive memory."

"I don't." Pettigrew spoke emphatically. "I had to work my fool head off to learn anything. I used to stay up hours after the rest of the family was asleep reading the books I had. When I was sixteen Mam died and I run off too. I went to State College and clerked in a grocery store days and studied nights. Finally I got myself through law school and I come back here." He laughed hardly. "Yeh, I come back here. All the time, all those years I was growing up and studying, I kept thinking about why

Tim Albright left home and believing I could come back here and show the town."

Dan Field filled the glasses again. "Exactly what did you want to show the town, Pettigrew?"

"That this place don't have to be a jail. That a boy from a family like Tim Albright's has a right to be friends with a boy off a farm and a boy off a farm has a right to be friends with an Albright or a Sargent or a Martin. This is a democracy, every man's supposed to be created free and equal. That's what the history books teach us, don't they?"

Dan Field shrugged. "Don't forget, though, that at the time the Constitution was drawn about one third of the population of these United States was either Negro slaves or bond servants. Also that the vote was given only to men who held property. We're struggling in the right direction, though, our theory is equality."

Pettigrew's cigar had gone out and he chewed upon the butt as he talked. "Sure, our theory is equality. Any boy has a chance to become President, any boy has a chance to become mayor of Willowspring. Sure, Abraham Lincoln got to be President and maybe someday I'll get to be mayor of Willowspring. But what about the Catholics and the Jews and the niggers? Think we'll ever have a Catholic President? Then take the Boyds—no finer folks ever lived than the Boyds, and Eli and Vera haven't a friend and Helen don't either any more. And Gabe Williams didn't rape Dolly Tatem but he'd have been lynched if you hadn't sneaked him away."

Dan Field's brows raised. "What gave you the impression it was I who sneaked Gabe away?"

Pettigrew winked. "My intuition again, Doc. And here's another thing the town don't know and I must rely upon you not to repeat. Belle tells me Gabe wrote Mr. Williams and him and Dolly's married. What do you think about that?"

"I don't know," Dan Field admitted.

"Listen!" Pettigrew ejaculated. "I don't know neither, Doc. But Gabe was the only fellow ever thought Dolly was fit for anything except to paw. What chance did the poor little devil have, raised in nigger town with a bum for a father and her mother running off with a crazy tramp? And what chance did that big black dumb buck nigger have against her white skin and that red hair and those eyes the color of purple pansies? Sure, the idea of them getting married goes against any man's grain, but when Dolly was knocked up (I guess you heard that story, Doc) what else was there for her, unless she and Gabe got married?"

"Probably nothing else, Pettigrew."

"That's how I figured it and, Doc, I was the one sent Dolly the money to go find Gabe."

"I suspected it."

"Why, Doc?"

Dan Field winked. "My intuition."

"See, that's what I mean." Pettigrew spoke earnestly. "If we can help people who can't help themselves . . . You feel the same way."

Dan Field nodded. "Certainly I feel the same way. And paradoxical as it may seem, George Albright and Rufus Sargent, as well as many others of the present ruling class, also feel the same way. I told you about the Fisher income and I could cite many another case proving the point. But at present everyone's power is so limited. A strong arm, a crust, a bit of succor, a friendly nod, and that's about all during the days of our years, Pettigrew. It may take many generations to evolve a democracy wherein a Catholic may become President and Jews will not suffer ostracism and persecution, and miscegenation won't be considered an abomination as revolting as sodomy."

Pettigrew sniffed. "Yeh, and it may take many generations, too, to evolve a democracy wherein a boy born rich and a boy off a farm can meet equally, and wherein a fellow like me who's worked his way up from the bottom won't be treated like scum by the present ruling class. But see, Doc, ever since I can remember I believed there wasn't any difference, except as individuals differ, between me and any best-family male. I felt all I had to do was educate myself, earn enough money and become politically important, and the snottiest'd realize I'm his equal."

"Have you changed your mind?"

"That's one reason I come here tonight, to find out what you thought about it. There's a little Mudtown beggar—Ray Stoddard, Doc—and he set me thinking. What do you make of that little beggar, Doc?"

Dan Field chuckled to himself: So Ray enters the picture. "The boy's smart as a whip," he said.

"He's smart all right," Pettigrew agreed, "and sassy. Last summer he stops before the livery stable and stands staring at me. The expression on his face made me feel he didn't have too high an opinion of me and I gave him a quarter. He threw the money back and says, 'If'n it's a sin fer ter buy votes it's a sin fer ter try and buy someone ter like yer.' I couldn't help wondering what he had against me and I concluded probably he didn't dislike me but thought more of George Albright and Rufus Sargent. Before daylight New Year's I met him on the street and asked him the reason he liked them better than me. Know what the little beggar says, Doc?" Pettigrew answered his own question. "He says, 'It'd take a mighty sight more'n yer gitting 'lected mayor of Willerspring fer ter make yer the likes of Captain George and Mr. Sargent.' "

Dan Field brought his hands down upon his knees. "There's the trouble in a nutshell, Pettigrew. Why would you want to be the likes of them?"

Pettigrew took the cigar butt from his mouth. "It's the boy's inference which has all but upset my applecart. And here comes the cat out of the bag, Doc. Do George and Rufus, as well as the rest of their breed, have certain qualities which sets them above me?"

"Assuredly they have certain qualities which set them above you and you've certain qualities which set you above them. Were you thrown together socially, their very qualities would stifle you as your very qualities would strangle them. Pettigrew, the matter with you is you're trying to reap a harvest others have sown instead of scattering your own seed."

"Maybe," Pettigrew muttered. "Maybe."

"Not maybe, Pettigrew," Dan Field continued, "actually. Upon a few cottages and a single store George the First and Rufus the First formed a thriving town and a far-flung community. Their sons are carrying on. A great deal of this world's woe is caused by people striving to secure status or estate which if obtained brings very little if any satisfaction. Life would be so much more purposeful if we could realize our limitations as well as our possibilities. Granted, you may eventually defeat George and Rufus but you may find the throne uncomfortable. For, faulty as the present regime may be, what better will you have to offer the people?" Dan Field hesitated.

"Go on," Pettigrew commanded.

"Pettigrew, you're the stuff which made this country. Not a George Washington or a Thomas Jefferson, with their inherited fortunes and powdered wigs and satin breeches, nor a George Albright or Rufus Sargent either. Essential as this type of ruler has been or may be to the nation, you're of the stuff which made probable the thrones where the kings were to sit; you're like the pioneers who felled the first trees, who dug the first ditches, who raised the first walls, and who planted the first gardens."

"What you driving at, Doc?" Pettigrew demanded.

"You asked for it, Pettigrew, and I'm giving it to you straight from the shoulder. George and Rufus and the rest of their breed will never accept you as one of them, no matter what. Even were you to marry one of their daughters . . ." Dan Field shrugged. "But there's no reason why you can't find an environment where your possibilities can be used to create rather than destroy, where you can scatter your own seed and reap your own harvest. To-day out West cities are crying to be born, empires waiting until prophetic hands shall shape their spires. With a girl who loves you enough as wife, Pettigrew, your children should inherit a kingdom."

Pettigrew's lips curled. "Not many women would have the guts to face life in a wilderness, and as far as one of your so-called best-family girls goes, bah!" Pettigrew spat.

Dan Field chuckled. "Inheritance plays a great part in so-called guts, whether the girl's from the streets or a palace. There's a story told concerning a certain great-grandmother. On a summer afternoon she was alone, excepting her baby in its cradle, when an Indian stalked across the threshold and started toward the cradle. Great-grandmother Taylor grabbed an ax and split the Indian's skull straight through the scalp lock."

Pettigrew gasped. "How did you know?"

Dan Field winked both eyes this time. "My intuition again, Pettigrew. What's more, I've an idea Margaret Taylor's the paramount reason you're here tonight."

"That's right," Pettigrew admitted. "The whole business is too involved for me to explain. But I've wanted to marry her a long time now and I'm pretty sure she would. I felt the way things are here at the moment that marriage'd hardly work out, though. Still, Doc, the back of my mind'd been carrying the idea that I was equal to any of her class and maybe someday . . . Then that little beggar Ray Stoddard . . . Oh well." Pettigrew shrugged. "And, Doc, if I should go West, do you think I could run off with the girl?"

"Undoubtedly you could run off with the girl," Dan Field told him, "but I believe that might be a great mistake. Why don't you go West alone and look the situation over, stay away six months, and see how matters really are? After six months . . ."

Pettigrew interrupted. "Six months is a long time, Doc. Almost anything can happen in six months. Maybe in six months she won't want to marry me."

"Maybe not," Dan Field agreed. "And maybe in six months you won't want to marry her either. In either case you'd both be well shut of one another. But if at the end of such time your minds are still unchanged, I'd take the girl and tell her father your plans. Unless I'm very much mistaken Meg will stand right beside you and face him."

"Meg . . ." Pettigrew's tongue lingered over the word. "Meg's what she's called." He laughed. "Isn't that a joke, Doc? Here I'm thinking about marrying the girl and never knew what she's called."

"Have another nip?" Dan Field asked.

Pettigrew got to his feet. "I've had enough. Thanks, Doc, I appreciate you giving me all this time. I'll think over what you've said. Listens pretty sound all right, worth careful consideration anyhow." He laughed. "Don't think I like George Albright and Rufus Sargent a whit better, though. Which seems to be another pretty good reason why I should skip town; just the other day I was hating their God damn guts so much I contemplated buying votes myself. Only when it comes to the point it just don't seem to be in me to fight foul. Guess that line in the poem you says about describes me. What kind of crime wasn't they incapable of?"

" 'But were they not incapable of august crime,' " Dan Field supplied the line.

"Yeh, I guess I am not incapable of august crime. See, some of my henchmen made a couple of discoveries they believe'll make good campaign material. One of them was that the Fisher business looked like a rat in the bank's vault. The other . . . Doc, Rufe

Albright's been fooling around a country girl who's doused. He's there tonight."

Dan Field got to his feet and held out his hand. "Thank you for telling me, Pettigrew."

Pettigrew shook Dan Field's hand. "You're all right, Doc." He started toward the door, looked back over his shoulder, and grinned. "Guess Tim Albright found something to his liking across the mountains or he'd been back long ago."

Chapter Three

$\mathcal{T}$HE NEXT Friday night, a few minutes past seven o'clock, Rufe strode jauntily down Maple Street on his way to Linden. Funny, he was thinking, how a few days can change a man's complete outlook. Tonight he hadn't a care in the world and less than a week ago he'd been worrying his head off.

In the first place last Saturday he hadn't intended taking another country trip. He'd meant to tell the other boys it was Mama's birthday, which would be a good enough excuse, until Tracy Whitlock took the words out of his mouth.

Tracy happened to be lounging around the hotel office at the moment the snow stopped falling, alone excepting Rufe, Tom, Jack, and Ben.

"Look." Tom pointed through the big glass window. "It's quit."

Tracy laughed. "Bet you fellows'll be trying to get through to see your country girls tonight. Must have been hard on you going all this time without a peck."

Tom said, "Maybe we could get through. We could go round and pick up the other girls on the way to Wattses'."

(Rufe knew now the Wattses' was always the meeting place because Mr. and Mrs. Watts didn't snoop about the barn the way the other girls' parents did.)

"We could get through some way," Jack assured.

"We better take shovels along in case we get stuck," Ben suggested. "You're coming, ain't you, Rufe?"

"It's Ma——" Rufe began.

Tracy took the words out of his mouth. "Sure, Rufe's going. Rufe Albright's not a blade to pass up any high time. How about it, Rufe, old boy?"

"I'll—I'll—well," Rufe faltered, "I'll have to go over to the bank and tell Papa I'm going."

Tracy sprang from his chair. "Rufe, old boy, I'll walk along far as my atelier." Outside he asked, "Rufe, did your father ever happen to say anything to you about me?"

"No, Papa he——" Rufe began.

Then he remembered.

New Year's morning as he left the house his father had come out behind him and asked, "Rufe, why did you say if you'd had a party you'd want to have Tracy Whitlock invited?"

Rufe had answered, "Why, he was at Tom's party last night."

"How do you like him, Rufe?"

"Fine."

"In the course of the conversation did Tracy happen to mention a book he's writing?"

"Don't think he did, Papa."

Remembering, Rufe corrected himself. "Yes, Mr. Whitlock, come to think of it, Papa did talk about you. He asked me how I liked you and if you'd happened to mention a book you're writing. Are you writing a book, Mr. Whitlock?"

Tracy slapped Rufe's shoulder. "Old boy, you are walking beside a man whose name'll be indelible upon the pages of history. Long after everybody else who now exists about this minute speck yclept Willowspring is forgotten I shall be remembered." They'd reached the printing office. "Good-by till next time, Rufe, and give Fanny an extra peck from yours truly."

The ride both going and coming proved a terror. The snow reached the horses' bellies most of the way and they fairly crawled, and half a dozen times on the way out and as many times returning the boys had to shovel away great drifts before the team could budge the sleigh. The sky kept clear but hoofs and the wind pelted the boys' faces with stinging snow. By the time they'd collected the other three girls, carrying them on their laps, and reached Gracie's, the Wattses had retired. Tom called and Gracie stuck her head out of an upstairs window and said she'd be down pretty quick. Considering the late hour, hymns and refreshments were omitted (although the boys had had no dinners and Rufe, if no one else, felt starved) and the entourage made straightway for the barn. Fanny's fat furious arms around him and her hot wet lips on his, Rufe forgot his belly hunger.

. . . Just hug and kiss is all I'm ever going to do, Rufe promised himself again, and hug and kiss was all Rufe did. But that Fanny . . . What Fanny did revolted Rufe yet it paralyzed his mind, too, and if he'd not suddenly heard the other boys calling him anything might have happened. He writhed wretchedly, recalling.

Through church service the next morning Rufe's every muscle ached and his very soul cringed. He didn't dare look at Mollie in the choir. No wonder she hated him, Rufe thought bitterly. Mr. Lanning hurled texts warning, *"For the wages of sin is death"* and *"There is no peace, said the Lord, unto the wicked."* Why couldn't there be a merciful God the way poor old Mr. Yates believed? Rufe moaned inwardly.

Going home, however, Uncle Doc came along, greeting everybody, and ended, "Rufe Albright, I've not had a talk with you since Hector was a pup. How about having a bit of dinner with me? It's about ready. You don't mind, do you, Pris?"

Ackley served fried chicken and everything, but Rufe forced himself to the little he managed to swallow. Uncle Doc kept asking him questions: how he liked the new school and what lesson he most enjoyed and things like that. Pretty soon they went into the office and seated themselves.

Uncle Doc leaned back and smiled. "Rufe, you used to draw remarkably well. Ever do any drawing these days?"

Rufe nodded. "I've been drawing a lot lately."

"Mind telling me what?"

Rufe flushed to the roots of his cowlick. "If you'll not tell anyone else I'd not mind, Uncle Doc."

"Certainly I'll not tell anyone else."

"Uncle Doc, did you ever hear of a building called the Parthenon?"

"I've seen the Parthenon."

Rufe could barely believe his ears. "You've seen the Parthenon?"

"Several times."

Rufe's eyes burned. "Uncle Doc, I found a book in the school library called *The Building of the Parthenon*. I never knew before there could be such a wonderful thing in the world as a building made all of marble. I took the book home and copied every picture, the whole Parthenon and each separate part and the statues they think a man named Phidias hewed. Then I got to thinking, if a building could be made all of marble, a whole city could be made all of marble and I started planning it. I'm almost through."

"When you've finished I'd like very much to see the work, Rufe."

"I'll bring it down the minute it satisfies me. And, Uncle Doc, lately I've decided to draw a whole world built of marble."

"A whole world of marble . . . Good! Rufe, it's such ideas running through minds which have produced the treasures of art. Let me tell you about the first time I saw the Parthenon. I wasn't much older than you. . . ." Uncle Doc talked on and on and on, describing not only the Parthenon but the other wonders of Athens.

Rufe heaved a great sigh. "If I just could see it all with my own eyes someday!"

"You will, Rufe." Uncle Doc chuckled. "It's about time you were finding yourself a girl, Rufe. At your age I'd adopted a little strumpet named Ruby."

Rufe's eyes popped. "You'd adopted what?"

"A little strumpet. Don't you know what a strumpet is? The dictionary defines the word something like this: 'Strumpet—a woman of low moral character.'"

Rufe stammered, "You—you mean—you mean . . ."

"Sure. Every boy passes through the strumpet stage sooner or later. I'm rather inclined to think the sooner the better."

Rufe gasped, "You don't think it's a sin, Uncle Doc?"

"Some persons consider it a sin, Rufe. Still, since the time of man no power on earth has ever stopped boys from adopting strumpets. And I believe a day will eventually arrive when a fellow's fiddling will be considered as natural a function as his breathing."

Rufe's muscles and soul relaxed. "I wish I'd known that a long time ago, Uncle Doc."

"The trouble today is a boy takes such a tremendous chance that the game's never worth the powder."

"What kind of chance, Uncle Doc?"

"Disease. You'd be surprised the number of girls around town, not to mention many in the country, who would pollute any boy who'd touch 'em."

"Uncle Doc," Rufe cried, "could you get a disease just hugging and kissing?"

"Hardly."

"Uncle Doc, I'm going to tell you something. I been a couple times sparking a country girl named Fanny Rhimer."

"Like her, Rufe?"

Rufe sniffed. "She makes me sick. She's a tub. What I can't understand is why I have fun hugging and kissing her when I don't like her."

"That's another masculine proclivity which the world may eventually acknowledge. Tell me some more about this girl."

"I tell you, Uncle Doc, she's a tub. Honest, all I ever did was hug and kiss her but what she didn't do to me last time . . ." Rufe felt like crying. "See, Uncle Doc, she's got a city fellow twenty years old, name's Earl Foster and he lives in Huntingdon, and he shows her stuff to do."

"Sounds to me, Rufe, as if you're a lucky fellow to have limited your sparking. Eventually girls and women who've a communicable malady will be segregated and doctors will know how to handle their cases as well as the cases of the men they've polluted previously. Today we know practically nothing. . . . Sometimes if a sufferer sees a doctor immediately there's hope. Rufe, I want you to promise me if you ever happen to go the limit you'll come straight here."

Rufe threw back his head. "Uncle Doc, I'll never go the limit. I'm not going to give that Fanny Rhimer, or any other strumpet, a chance to start stuff again."

"Why don't you find yourself a nice girl, Rufe? One you could love. Nothing can touch love, Rufe. Haven't you ever seen a girl you thought you could love?"

Rufe nodded sadly. "Yes."

"Do I know her?"

"It's—it's Mollie Reynard."

"She's a beauty, Rufe. Why don't you spark Mollie?"

Rufe scowled. "She hates me."

"How do you know?"

"She said so."

"That doesn't mean a thing. Did you ever tell her you liked her?"

"I told her I detested her."

"There you are, Rufe, you didn't mean what you said and no doubt Mollie didn't mean a word she said either."

"But what could I do, Uncle Doc?"

Uncle Doc handed him two silver dollars. "Take these and buy a big box of candy tomorrow. After dinner go down to the Reynards' and tell Mollie you brought her the candy because she's the prettiest girl you ever saw."

"Don't you think she'd get mad?"

Uncle Doc laughed. "Hardly mad, Rufe. I've yet to see a young lady of Mollie's age who could resist a box of candy, and there never was and never will be a lady of any age who won't succumb to flattery."

"I'll try it, Uncle Doc, only there's a thing bothers me. See, I know if Mollie'd like me I'd want to marry her sometime. And what do you suppose Papa and Mama'd do if they knew I wanted to marry a girl whose father's a carpenter and whose mother does her own work?"

"Rufe, by the time you and Mollie are old enough to consider marriage the Albrights may be paupers and the Reynards lords of all they survey. Stranger things have happened. Boy, don't cross your bridges till you come to them."

Rufe arose, smiling. "Thanks a lot, Uncle Doc. Thanks a lot for everything. You've made me feel a lot better this afternoon." The smile faded. "There's one more thing I'd like to ask you, though. Uncle Doc, do you think it might be possible that there could be a merciful God?"

Uncle Doc got up and put his arm around Rufe's shoulder. "I not only think it might be possible but I know no God could be anything but merciful."

Mollie herself opened the Reynards' door next evening.

Rufe took the bull by the horns. "Mollie, I want you to have this candy because you're the prettiest girl I ever saw."

Mollie took the candy and her blue eyes danced. "Why, Rufe, thank you. Won't you come in?"

He stayed an hour. They talked and ate candy and Mollie played and sang.

Before he left she said, "Rufe, I didn't mean what I said about hating you."

"I didn't mean what I said either, Mollie."

"Let's don't ever fight again, Rufe."

"We won't, Mollie. Good night."

And this Friday night Rufe strode jauntily toward the Reynards', not having a care in the world. This afternoon Mollie'd asked him to come around again tonight and Rufe meant to tell her he wanted to go with her steady. That'd fix that Fanny Rhimer. All he'd need to do was tell Tom, Jack, and Ben, and Tracy Whitlock, too, he was going with Mollie Reynard steady and no more strumpet sparking.

A little before eight this evening the Fishers sat in their sitting room and on a table stood a huge chocolate cake and five teacups.

Mrs. Fisher said, "I can smell that cake, deary. My! It does smell good, deary."

Miss Fisher smiled. "Doesn't it seem fine to be able to invite friends in and be able to afford refreshments, deary?"

Mrs. Fisher sighed happily. "How you ever managed the way you did before on the little we had I'll never know, deary."

Miss Fisher sighed happily. "It's all over now, deary."

The Fishers had accepted their gratuity gratefully and, if astonished completely, they did not speculate, blindly believing a miracle had been wrought. They'd always held complete confidence in Captain George and Rufus Sargent, as they'd implicitly trusted their fathers before them. And since Lillian and Prissy had started music lessons four more dollars every month swelled the family pocketbook. Besides, these days Miss Fisher often pressed Prissy figuratively against her ample bosom, as she'd pressed Pris Albright long ago. For Lillian accepted instruction passively but Prissy, like Pris, had music in her finger tips. Even the very first scale sounded rhythmic under Prissy's touch. Miss Fisher's rife rich red blood surged happily.

Presently the knocker tapped. Miss Fisher opened the door, and the guests entered: Mrs. Meeker, Mrs. Diggers, and Aunt Tillie Whitlock.

The ladies greeted each other, settled themselves, and chatted about this and that the greater part of an hour. Then Miss Fisher excused herself, made the tea, and, returning to the sitting room, served the refreshments.

Aunt Tillie smacked her lips. "My! This cake's delicious, tastes just like my recipe. I must make Tracy a chocolate cake tomorrow. Never saw a boy like chocolate cake like Tracy."

"How's him and Jean coming along?" Mrs. Diggers inquired.

Aunt Tillie wrinkled her nose. "Since Tracy signed the pledges I don't worry a scrap. And I always told everybody I'd never had any idear Tracy'd think of marrying a girl whose parent sells liquor."

"Know what's been worrying us?" Mrs. Meeker demanded, nodding toward Mrs. Diggers. "Mame and me have been wondering if it's right we should hire that Ray Stoddard when his papa's drunk most the time. Likely Lem takes Ray's money and buys liquor with it."

Mrs. Fisher, Miss Fisher, and Aunt Tillie gasped.

Mrs. Diggers said, "Mama and I didn't think about Lem time we hired Ray and we'd not keep him around the place a minute if he didn't work so cheap and do his work so good."

Miss Fisher nodded. "Ray doesn't charge much and no man could do better. He's such a skinny little fellow, too, nothing but skin and bones. Oh, I do hope he doesn't give Lem his earnings. Couldn't I pass someone else another piece of cake or a drop of tea?"

The ladies said they'd had sufficient and Miss Fisher collected the cups and saucers and placed them beside what remained of the chocolate cake.

From down cellar came the sound of a scraping shovel and Mrs. Fisher blinked her sightless eyes. "There's Ray now, banking the furnace."

Aunt Tillie folded her plump hands across her plump abdomen. "Maybe if we called him up here and talked to him we could influence him to persuade Lem to sign the pledge."

Miss Fisher sprang toward the hall, called down the cellar steps, "Ray, come up here a minute."

She returned to her chair and in an instant Ray stood at the door, his eyes fixed ravenously and hopefully upon the remains of the chocolate cake. "Did yer want sumpin, ma'am?"

He'd addressed Miss Fisher but Aunt Tillie spoke. "Ray, do you know what it means to sign the pledge?"

"Yes ma'am, like Mr. Old Man Meeker done."

The ladies nodded.

Mrs. Meeker said, "Ray, wouldn't you like to have your papa sign the pledge?"

"No ma'am."

"Ray," Miss Fisher admonished, "you know you want your papa to sign the pledge. Think how happy it would make your mama."

Ray shook his tousled head. "Mam she likes a swig oncet in a blue moon herself."

The ladies gasped.

"Ray, you love your mama and papa, don't you?" Aunt Tillie asked.

"No ma'am."

The ladies groaned.

"Ray," Miss Fisher admonished again, "you know you love your mama and papa and your sisters and brothers, don't you?"

"No ma'am."

The ladies at this point were too utterly horrified to do anything except look at each other and back at Ray.

Mrs. Diggers finally spoke. "Ray, what do you do with your earnings?"

"I's saving 'em, ma'am."

"Ray, are you sure you don't give any of your money to Lem?" Mrs. Meeker demanded.

"No ma'am. I's saving 'em, ma'am."

"In the bank, Ray?" Miss Fisher inquired.

Ray became conscious of the moneybag, around his waist and under his pants. "In *a* bank, ma'am."

"You may go now, Ray," Miss Fisher instructed.

Giving the remains of the chocolate cake a last ravenous but not hopeful look, Ray departed.

"Well," Mrs. Meeker sniffed, "if he didn't work so cheap and so good we'd not keep him around the place a minute, would we, Mame?"

"Not a minute," Mrs. Diggers agreed.

"We wouldn't either, would we, deary?" Mrs. Fisher queried.

"Of course not," Miss Fisher assured.

Aunt Tillie refolded her plump hands across her plump abdomen. "Did it ever strike you Fishers funny that Mr. Fisher left an income not to be paid till he'd been dead over fifty years?

Tracy says how'd Mr. Fisher know both of you wouldn't be dead after fifty years?"

All day Dan Field had been visiting his rural patients. One whom he'd seen was the baby near Mount Pallas whose blood seemed like water and he'd advised the parents to give him a meat-tit daily. He'll die anyhow, Dan Field salved his conscience. Arriving home shortly before nine, dead tired, he'd had a few drinks, dinner, and taken himself off to bed.

He'd hardly touched the bed, however, before the office knocker banged and, throwing on a robe, he lighted a lamp and, carrying it downstairs, found Wilbur Lawler at the door.

"Come in, son. What is it?"

Wilbur entered trembling. "Cal him cough blood. Blood all over Cal. Cal him cough blood all over. Cal him——"

"I'll be right back, son."

Dressing, Dan Field wondered what had happened. Just yesterday when he'd seen Cal he was sitting up in bed playing with a few broken clothespins.

Cal had smiled. "They's so'jers, Doc."

Also Bert had reported, "Uncle Doc, the Widder Woman she's been minding Cal fine."

Walking toward Mudtown, Wilbur beside him, Dan Field asked, "What happened, Wilbur?"

Wilbur whimpered, "Mam her take Cal's blankets and go over town good spell back. Ella her keep whisky bottles hot. Mam her git ter home soused. Cal him cough blood. Cal him——"

"All right, son, let's walk a bit faster."

The Widder Woman, a fresh bottle in hand, followed by Ella, came from the bedroom as Dan Field and Wilbur entered the kitchen.

Ella shrieked, "Doc, me keep whisky bottles hot."

Lottie moaned, "Lov' Gaw', Doc—hic—don't le' Cal croak. Yer quits Cal croakin' oncet—hic—and yer can keep Cal 'live agin. Lov' Gaw', Doc."

Yes, Dan Field was thinking, I quits Cal dying once and I can keep him alive again, for six months or perhaps a year, while you sell all the blankets which might be given him to buy drink and he spits his tiny lungs out bit by bit, bit by bit. . . . Yes, I can keep Cal alive.

He found a cup, water, and a spoon. "All of you stay here," he told Lottie and the children.

He went into the other room. Cal's tiny shattered body was lying in a pool of blood, the broken clothespins scattered through the gore.

"Good-by, Cal, little so'jer," Dan Field whispered.

He took a bottle out of his bag and, pouring some liquid into the cup, stirred the mixture.

He leaned over the bed. "Cal, can you hear me?"

Cal's white lids fluttered.

"Cal, it's Doc. If you can swallow something to please me you'll never hurt any more."

Please, God, Dan Field prayed.

And as he dropped the laudanum upon Cal's tiny tongue Dan Field thought: *The blood of our Lord Jesus Christ, which was shed for thee, preserve thy body and soul unto everlasting life. Drink this in remembrance that Christ's Blood was shed for thee, and be thankful.*

Across the splotched saffron-colored couch Lottie sprawled, the children huddled near. She didn't hear when Dan Field said Cal was dead but Ella and Wilbur shrieked. Dan Field left the shanty and walked along Limestone Avenue, knocking upon Mr. Williams's door.

Ella had come outside and was shrieking the same words, over and over, "Doc, me keep whisky bottles hot. . . . Doc, me keep whisky bottles hot. . . . Doc, me . . ." Her voice rent gashes through the black, bitter air.

Presently Mr. Williams opened his door, carrying a candle and covered by his red flannel underwear. "Want me, Mr. Doc? Is that thar Ella hollering?"

"Cal's dead," Dan Field said.

Mr. Williams moaned, "Poor little unbaptized soul. Poor little unbaptized soul."

"He's lying in a pool of blood," Dan Field continued, "Lottie is dead drunk and Ella and Wilbur terrified." He handed Mr. Williams a five-dollar bill. "Will you go over and take charge?"

"Jest soon as I kin git my pants on, Mr. Doc."

"I'll stop by and tell Ma Woodward to make a coffin and I'd be grateful if you'd have a couple of your boys dig the grave and bury Cal."

"I'll tend the burial myself, Mr. Doc. But yer can't put a little white feller in a colored cemetery and the white folks'd hardly let the likes of Cal in the Greenhill. What yer think'd be a likely place ter dig the grave, Mr. Doc?"

Dan Field shrugged. "Probably a ways up the mountain. It really doesn't matter."

"No, Mr. Doc, it don't matter much. Poor little unbaptized soul."

Trudging home, ravenous and weary, Ray wondered why the ladies wanted Pap fer ter sign the pledge 'cause signing the pledge didn't stop Mr. Old Man Meeker drinking the wood alcohol off'n the two-headed squirrel. Ray wondered also why the ladies seemed to think he ought ter love Mam and Pap and the young-'uns. How come they'd 'spect me fer ter love the likes of 'em? Ray asked himself. Miss Lillian was the only person during his whole life Ray had ever dreamed of loving. The moneybag jogged against his side and Ray hoped fervently it would start snowing again. I wisht—oh, I wisht Miss Lillian knowed I got promoted ter third grade.

Turning toward their place, he saw Mr. Doc and Wilbur hurrying along. Early this evening Ray had met the Widder Woman on Broad Street, some blankets over her arm. 'Spect she sell the blankets Mr. Doc give Cal, fer ter git drink, Ray speculated now, and Cal he's coughing agin.

Entering the Stoddard shanty, Ray heard his mother snoring in the bedroom and the young'uns, excepting Noel, snoring or whimpering around the kitchen stove. But his father sat upon a kitchen chair, bloodshot eyes wide awake.

Lem emitted a long spiral of brown juice which missed the coal pail. "Ray, I hears sumpin over town this evening. I hears yer been tending furnaces and shoveling snow and earning money."

Ray's black eyes blazed. "What's it ter yer?"

Lem's tone became honey-sweet. "It like this here, Ray, I wouldn't go fer ter see no son of mine git in bad with the law. Ray, the law it says 'fore a boy gits ter be of age the money what he earns belongs ter his pap. If'n yer don't give yer pap what yer earns it'll be my duty fer ter turn yer over ter the law."

"Turn me over ter the law and be God damned," Ray yelled.

"It was me works fer ter git that thar money and yer ain't ever a-gonna tetch a penny."

"I ain't, ain't I?" Lem snarled.

He sprang toward Ray. But Ray sprang quicker, grabbed the coal pail, and, mustering more strength than he knew he possessed smashed the pail, coal included, mightily across Lem's face. Lem recoiled, groaning, dust stinging his eyes and his nose a bloody pulp.

Ray spread his skinny legs apart and shook his small grubby fists. "Yer better mind me, Pap. Yer seen what I jest done ter yer. And if'n yer ever tetches a penny of my money I'll git me the loan of Mr. Tatem's musket and I'll fill yer God damn stinking hide so full of shot yer won't know what hit yer. I'll kill yer, Pap."

Quailing, Lem stumbled into the bedroom and flopped upon the bed beside Myrtle and Noel. Ray sank among the other children around the stove. He thrust a small grubby hand inside his filthy ragged pants and stroked the moneybag. Pap he won't worry me no more, he sighed contentedly. Pap he's skeered I'd kill him and I would. I wisht—oh, I wisht Miss Lillian knowed I gits promoted ter third grade. . . . Ray slept.

Dan Field didn't sleep, however, until morning. He sat and downed one glass of bourbon after the other. He kept remembering Cal's tiny shattered body lying in the pool of blood, the broken clothespins scattered through the gore. He kept remembering Lottie's sodden body stretched across the splotched saffron-colored couch and Ella and Wilbur shrieking, terrified. He kept hearing Ella's voice rending gashes through the black, bitter air, screaming the same words over, "Doc, me keep whisky bottles hot. . . . Doc, me keep whisky bottles hot. . . . Doc . . ." He kept telling himself, I did the right thing, I know I did the right thing, I know . . . The lamp went out.

Finally dawn touched the windowpanes. Dan Field poured a last drink and staggered to his feet.

His long thin white twitching hand raised the glass. "Good luck, Cal. Good luck, little so'jer."

About eight o'clock Friday evening Rufus Sargent joined the assembled Albright family, excepting Rufe, in their sitting room.

"Sit down, Rufus," Pris said.

Rufus sat down, beaming. "They're here, George."

"What?" George asked.

"The dynamos. I'd been notified they were arriving but didn't let you know until I drove over to the depot tonight and made sure."

"What are dynamos?" Gramma Albright inquired.

Pris answered. "They are little engines used to make electric lights. Like the lights we saw in Wanamaker's windows. You remember."

Gramma Albright shook her head. "What's going to be done with them here?"

Rufus laughed. "Broad Street will be lighted first, then as soon as enough dynamos are available the whole of Willowspring will be electric-lighted."

"Why?" Gramma Albright demanded.

George's white teeth flashed. "That's what I think, Ma, why?"

Gramma Albright sniffed. "Mr. Albright and Mr. Sargent never thought Willowspring needed electric lights."

Rufus smiled at her. "But during Pa's and Uncle George's day there weren't such thing as electric lights."

Gramma Albright frowned, perplexed. "Then why, if there weren't such things as electric lights in Mr. Albright's and Mr. Sargent's day, do they have them now?"

Rufus nodded toward Sammy and Lillian. "Before these children are grown there will not only be electric-lighted streets but electric-lighted houses and trains, perhaps horseless buggies, too, run by electricity. Probably every home will have a telephone."

"What is a telephone?" Gramma Albright inquired.

Rufus explained, "A telephone is an instrument by which someday you may be able to hear voices a hundred miles away."

Again Gramma Albright sniffed. "Seems to me we've enough racket right around without hearing voices a hundred miles away."

Smiling to himself, Rufus arose and took his departure.

Pris laughed. "Rufus always did have a preposterous imagination. I remember well when he wasn't more than ten years old he said that someday men would be able to fly."

George shrugged. "He'll learn his lesson in good time. Pris, invite Professor and Mrs. Phelps to dinner soon. We've not had them here since the reception and his ideas are sound. Remember his conviction? 'Surely what was good enough for our fathers, as well as for the Continental fathers who founded this great republic, is good enough for our children.' "

"I remember, George. I'll invite them to Sunday dinner."

George continued, "What the school, governed by such a man, will mean to the community is more than may be estimated. Did you ever realize, Pris, that this new school gives every child in Willowspring, including the Mudtown element, the same opportunities which our own sons enjoy? That is democracy. By the way, Pris, did you remember to give Maggie some of Sammy's old clothes for Gregory Beamer?"

Pris shook her head from side to side. "That's the strangest thing, George. I told Nellie the minute I'd a chance I meant to look over Sammy's things and give Gregory a few. What do you think happened? The next day Nellie told me Maggie said she was much obliged but Gregory had all the clothes he needed."

George frowned. "Pride, the root of much evil. We can't help *them* if they won't let us."

Gramma Albright sniffed a third time. "Why would anyone want to hear voices a hundred miles away?"

The country people were coming to town once more, some in rags and some in tags and some in velvet gowns, but practically all to the tune of sleigh bells. By the time dawn touched Dan Field's windowpanes there was not an available hitching post left on one of the main streets. By the time Sammy and Bert trudged toward Mudtown vehicles lined alleys and lanes unto the town's boundaries and Broad Street again had become a teeming, thriving, endeavoring center.

"Ever know anybody lives out in the country, Bert?" Sammy inquired.

"Gregory Beamer. You ever know anybody lives out in the country, Sammy?" Bert inquired.

"Gregory Beamer." Sammy changed the subject. "Bert, you know how long it takes a dog to hatch pups?"

"Never did think, Sammy," Bert admitted. "But know sumpin? It takes ladies nine months."

Sammy's face fell. "Nine months. Glory Ned! Don't suppose it's going to take Spotty nine months, do you, Bert?"

"Let's go round to the livery stable and ask Mr. Smith," Bert suggested. "Mr. Smith he'd know how long it took Spotty's mama to get pups."

They found Mr. Smith in the harness room.

"Mr. Smith, how long did it take Spotty's mama to get her pups?" Sammy asked.

"Around nine weeks, Sammy."

Sammy beamed. "Only nine weeks. Glory Ned! Spotty ought to be having her pups about . . ." He stopped, speculating.

" 'Bout first week in March," Bert came to Sammy's assistance.

"Wall," Jake drawled, "it didn't take Spotty no time to fill her belly."

Sammy grinned proudly. "Mr. Smith, it wouldn't take Spotty no time to fill her belly."

As the boys started past the Woodwards' place, Ma stuck his head through the workshop door and called, "Sammy, you and Bert want to lend a hand?"

"All right, Mr. Ma," Sammy called back.

Inside the workshop Ma indicated the smallest coffin either Sammy or Bert had ever beheld. "I takes the same infinite pains building a little coffin as I takes making a big one. Every one's fashioned out'n sound seasoned pine-wood boards held by hand-made pegs. What if I do get paid more for a big casket? I asks myself. They's all for the same purpose, the incarceration of a deceased. Ain't that right, boys?"

Bert nodded in accordance and Sammy said, "That's right, Mr. Ma."

"However," Ma continued, "I means to make Doc Field a mighty good price on this here coffin. Two weeks back looked like that little Rankin girl was dying and I turns this piece quick as a wink. But mind you"—Ma shook a fat finger—"she ain't dead yet, and what's worst, she'll likely live. So when Doc stops last night I says, says I, 'Doc, I got just what you want right on hand and I'll make you a mighty good price.' See, thar's few calls for children's coffins lately and this one might of been left on my hands for dear knows how long. Now, it ain't heavy and if you boys will carry it along it'll save me a trip."

"Carry it along where, Mr. Ma?" Sammy inquired.

"Ain't you heard about Cal dying last night?"

"Cal!" Sammy gasped.

"Cal he can't be dead. Uncle Doc he said Cal'd live . . ." Bert began and stopped.

"He's dead all right," Ma informed. "Now, Sammy, you take the head here and, Bert, you take the foot thar."

Sammy took the head and Bert took the foot and beyond the bridge Shad's helping hands caught the middle. Crossing the Widder Woman's threshold, the boys set down the coffin carefully beside the door. Lottie, Ella, Wilbur, and Mr. Williams were in the kitchen. The Widder Woman rocked backward and forward upon the couch. From somewhere she'd resurrected the weeds which had been responsible for her title and tears streamed down her painted face. Ella and Wilbur sat at the table eating porridge Mr. Williams had cooked. Mr. Williams stood by the stove, his red helmet pushed back upon his white wool. At first no one seemed aware of Sammy, Bert, Shad, and the coffin.

Mr. Williams said, "Ella and Wilbur, yer had plenty breakfast now, git up." The children got up and he spoke to their mother. "Yer better eat a bite yerself. Might sober yer up some more."

Lottie moaned, "I don't want no victuals. My own poor leetle darling Cal."

Mr. Williams pulled the two chairs which Ella and Wilbur had left closer together and raised the coffin, setting its head on one chair and its foot on the other. He entered the bedroom and returned carrying a little bundle, placing it gently in the box. Sammy, Bert, and Shad stepped forward and looked. Mr. Williams had washed away the blood and wrapped around Cal one of Mrs. Williams's clean sheets, and all to be seen was the tiny white face, whiter than the sheet.

Finally Mr. Williams addressed Sammy, Bert, and Shad. "Guess thar's nothing else kin be did 'cept nail the lid on now. Poor little unbaptized soul."

Sammy's eyes became horror-stricken. "Mr. Williams, ain't Cal been baptized?"

Mr. Williams shook his white wool sadly. "No, Sammy, Cal ain't never been baptized."

"But, Mr. Williams," Sammy cried, "if Cal ain't baptized he'll go to hell. Hell's full of poor little unbaptized souls."

Lottie screamed and Ella and Wilbur sobbed.

"Right yer are, Sammy," Mr. Williams agreed. "But it's too late now."

Bert spoke. "Mr. Williams, do you think just a couple of hours'd make God keep a baby out of heaven? Don't seem to me like it would, Mr. Williams. And know sumpin? Cal he's been dead only a couple hours."

Mr. Williams pondered an instant. "Don't seem ter me neither that jest a couple hours'd make God keep a little feller the likes of Cal out'n heaven."

"Know sumpin, Mr. Williams?" Bert demanded. "If a couple hours don't matter you could baptize Cal 'fore he's buried."

"Likely I could, Bert," Mr. Williams agreed.

He dipped a bit of water from the pail with a cup and set the cup on the table and, removing his red helmet, he said, "Sammy and Bert, yer gotta stand godfathers. Take yer caps off'n." Sammy and Bert obeyed and Mr. Williams instructed, "I's gonna say the service and when I git ter the part 'Name this child' yer both say, 'Calvary.' Understand?"

Sammy and Bert nodded.

Somewhere long ago Mr. Williams had acquired an Engiish *Book of Common Prayer* which he'd employed through the years until he knew many passages verbatim, and if Mr. Williams's conversation were prone to error, quoting a ritual his tongue never slipped.

So over the slain body of Calvary Lawler, certainly borne by Willowspring's one professional whore and probably sired by a preacher, as the whore mother groaned and the bastard sister and the bastard brother sobbed, while a rangy black boy rolled his eyes and two small aristocrats stood godfathers, Willowspring's one colored minister recited the same words which christened the monarchs of the British Empire. And by a lone grave dug from frozen sod upon a bleak mountainside Mr. Williams repeated words with which princes were laid to rest in royal abbeys.

" 'I am the resurrection and the life, saith the Lord: he that believeth in me, though he were dead, yet shall he live: and whosoever liveth and believeth in me, shall never die.

" 'Jesus called them unto him and said, Suffer the little children to come unto me, and forbid them not: for of such is the kingdom of God.

" 'He shall feed his flock like a shepherd: he shall gather the lambs with his arms, and carry them in his bosom. . . .

" 'In sure and certain hope of the Resurrection to eternal life through our Lord Jesus Christ, we commit the body of this child to the ground. The Lord bless him and keep him, the Lord make his face to shine upon him and be gracious unto him, the Lord lift up his countenance upon him and give him peace, both now and evermore. Amen.' "

Mr. Williams put the red helmet back upon his white wool and helped the groaning Widder Woman, her weeds flapping in the wind, down the mountainside, followed by the sobbing Ella and Wilbur. Frank and Fred, two of Mr. Williams's sons, started filling the grave, and Sammy, Bert, and Shad watched mournfully. The earth replaced, Frank and Fred departed, and Sammy, Bert, and Shad seated themselves upon the mound.

Sammy shook his head sadly. "Cal ought to have a tombstone. He really ought to."

"What fer?" Shad demanded.

" 'Cause, Shad," Sammy explained, "when a loved one goes to the—the great beyond the be-be—well, anyhow, when a loved one goes to the great beyond folks want to give him a present and a tombstone's the only thing worth a hoot to a corpse. Don't you think Cal he ought to have a tombstone, Bert?"

Bert agreed. "Cal he really ought to have a tombstone."

Shad had an idea. "Maybe yer could work and git money and buy a tombstone, Sammy."

Sammy sniffed. "Couldn't even work and get a dollar to buy the kennel paint. And tombstones's dear; they cost from fifty dollars on up."

"Yippidy, yippidy!" Shad shrieked. "Tombstones they really is dear."

"Know sumpin, Sammy?" Bert demanded. "What you ought of did was have Mr. Ma build Spotty a hundred-and-fifty-dollar kennel and saved some to buy Cal a tombstone."

Sammy scowled. "How could I know Cal he'd die?"

Bert had an idea. "Maybe, Sammy, you could get that man give you the tombstone 'fore what you sold to get the kennel built to give you 'nother tombstone."

Sammy's scowl deepened. "That man he tells me that tombstone it was the only tombstone he ever had and he wasn't ever gonna get another tombstone."

Morbidly Sammy visioned Cal resting throughout eternity under an untended, unhallowed, and unmarked mound.

While, heaping insult upon injury, when Sammy reached home near lunchtime Lillian met him at the gate.

"It's Alexander's birthday," she announced brightly.

Sammy sniffed. "Bet you're giving him a present."

Lillian tossed her curls. "I'm not either, Sammy. Mama said I could invite him and Prissy over this afternoon and have ice cream and cake. But Alexander says he don't want any presents. Alexander said he justs wants something to happen on his birthday and he'd sooner have it happen than get all the presents in the world."

"What?" Sammy demanded.

"Sammy, Alexander said he'd sooner have you walk uptown and around Broad Street with him than get all the presents in the world."

Sammy's jaw dropped. "Why?"

" 'Cause Alexander says he admires and respects you."

"Glory Ned!" Sammy groaned. "Well, I ain't gonna do it."

"Sammy!" Lillian looked as if she'd burst into tears. "I promised Alexander you would. And it's going to hurt Alexander's feelings and make me break a promise if you don't."

Sammy gnashed his teeth. "What time's he coming over?"

"Right after lunch." Lillian's tone became bright again.

Right after lunch Sammy, with Alexander at heel, dashed uptown, around Broad Street, and back home in less than no time. Dropping Alexander like a hot potato before the gate, Sammy tore toward Mudtown, where all afternoon he meditated mournfully concerning Cal's stoneless state.

Next day after church, however, Sammy, Bert, and Shad visited the grave and Sammy's eyes popped. A small marker graced the mound.

"Whar yer s'pose that thar come from?" Shad demanded.

Sammy shook his head. "Looks like one of Mr. Ma's, Bert. It sure is one of Mr. Ma's and if anybody comes along and finds it, mighty likely they'd think we stole it."

"Know sumpin, Sammy?" Bert said. "You got plenty kennel paint left and if you painted that tombstone liver nobody could tell whose stone it is. 'Sides, hardly anybody comes up here winters, Sammy."

Sammy nodded. "I got some red left, too, and I could put the writing on red."

The liver paint having dried, Sammy's soul reposed once more. The idea of Cal's bones resting under a tombstone the same hue as Spotty's kennel seemed perfect. And with the red paint Sammy inscribed the epitaph:

Chapter Four

THE TEMPERATURE remained near zero and the wind blew bitterly but there was hardly a flurry of snow the rest of the month, and toward the end the mercury shot up and there came what people called a "good old-fashioned February thaw"; March entered like a lamb. First the mountains and the valleys and the village floor stretched under seemingly steadfast slush stacks; then, presently, down the highlands rivers ran, vales became ponds, Willowspring a mire, and the creek a turgid torrent, lapping over the north bank, seeping under the railroad trestle, filling Limestone Avenue. And if only every other person in the town proper had a cold, not a dry nose could be found throughout Mudtown.

Delivering the swill upon March's first Monday, Sammy waded through water to his knees and he could hardly drag himself going and returning; his every muscle ached. Back in his room he fell across the bed and stretched, completely exhausted, until daylight.

Finally, hearing Pris stirring, he called weakly, "Mama."

At sight of him she frowned. "Sammy Albright, have you been out already this morning? And what do you mean lying on the bed wearing those muddy shoes?"

Sammy moaned. "Mama, I'm sick."

"Darling!" she cried. She put her hand on his forehead and called, "George, Sammy's ill. Have Rufe run right away and bring Dan."

She'd undressed him and put him to bed by the time Dan Field arrived and she and George both hovered near.

Dan Field smiled. "Well, Mr. Sammal, what have you been up to? Stick your tongue way out, please."

"I'm sick, Uncle Doc." Sammy stuck his tongue out and in.

Dan Field pulled out his big gold watch, felt Sammy's pulse, and took his temperature.

"Think it's anything serious, Dan?" George inquired anxiously.

"No. Just a bad cold. Keep him in bed a few days and I'll leave some pills to stop the aches. Have Nellie brew a pot of stiff strong beef broth and see our invalid drinks plenty." He put his hand on Sammy's yellow curls. "You'll be all right in less than no time, boy. Every other person around town has a cold."

During the morning Pris never left the bedside but by noon Sammy seemed better and Pris found her mending and, seated near one of his windows, began stitching.

Sammy, however, still didn't feel like himself, although his pains had abated enough to permit some reflection. Wonder if I'm going to die, like Cal? he meditated. Mighty likely I am.

"Mama," he asked, "what did you do with that tombstone picture I give you on your birthday?"

"You gave me on my birthday, Sammy. I have it put away very carefully, darling."

"Why don't you hang it on a wall, Mama?"

Pris threaded a needle. "Well, I don't know exactly the right spot to hang it, Sammy."

"Couldn't you hang it over my bed, Mama?"

"Over your bed, darling? Why?" Pris stitched away.

Sammy shook his head. "See, Mama, I just always wanted a picture of a tombstone over my bed."

Pris could hardly keep her face straight. "Why, Sammy?"

Sammy shrugged. "I just do. Won't you hang it over my bed, Mama?"

"All right, darling, if you want it over your bed the minute Rufe comes home I'll have him drive a nail. But wouldn't you sooner have a picture of a dog or a horse or maybe some kittens?"

"No, Mama, I'd sooner have a picture of a tombstone."

Rufe hung the picture before lunch and when all of the family, except Sammy, were downstairs eating Sammy switched about on the bed and fastened his gaze upon it. The sight reminded him of Cal's marker and events following the discovery.

Returning home the Sunday they'd found the stone, Sammy and Bert had encountered Tracy Whitlock coming out of Ma Woodward's house.

"Hear about the robbery, boys?" Tracy inquired.

"What robbery, Mr. Whitlock?" Bert inquired back.

"Last night someone stole one of Ma's tombstones. Ma's raving, says he's going to run the culprit down and have the law on him if it's the last thing he ever does."

"Know sumpin, Mr. Whitlock?" Bert said. "I bet some country person stole that stone. Anybody round town'd know if he stole it it wouldn't do no good, 'cause if he'd use it Mr. Ma'd find out."

Consequently the next issue of the *News* contained the following editorial comment:

Sometime either late Saturday night or early Sunday morning a crime was perpetrated upon one of our outstanding citizens. A tombstone displayed before Mr. M. A. Woodward's workshop was stolen. Any theft is a blot indelible upon our fair village face but the theft of a tombstone, a symbol of respect for a departed loved one, is the depths of depravity. However, it is the humble opinion of the owner and editor of this sheet that some country man is the guilty party. Anyone in town would realize, were the stone erected, the theft would be discovered.

Now Bert entered the room. "You sick, Sammy?"

"I'm sick, Bert. Say, Bert, who do you really s'pose really put that tombstone on Cal's grave?"

Bert shrugged. "With the liver paint on nobody could tell it was one of Mr. Ma's. Sammy, what you got a tombstone picture over your bed for?"

Sammy told him.

"You mighty likely won't die till you're an old man, Sammy," Bert assured. "Know sumpin, Sammy? I'll wheel the swill to Mudtown 'fore light and tend Spotty till you get well."

But the next morning, wheeling the barrow along, Bert met Ray near the corner of Broad Street.

"Whar's Sammy at?" Ray asked.

"Sammy he's sick."

Ray shook his tousled head. "Might as well take that thar swill whar it come from, Bert. Everybody's ter the depot and all night folkses out'n this side town bring victuals and clothes."

"Why?" Bert demanded.

"Bert, yer niver seen nothing the likes of last night. They says a big ice floe musta come down out'n the mountains. The water jest rush like a dam'd bust, all a sudden in ter everywhar, high as our stove top. Mama and Pap and Harry and me grabs the littlest young'uns. Everybody gits out'n all right 'cept Little Flower Ferris. Little Flower she git drownded."

"Drowned?" Bert gasped.

"Drownded dead, Bert. When we-uns git ter the depot Mr. Doc come and he work and he work hard fer ter make Little Flower breathe. Mr. Ackley he takes on awful. Some folks says God willed Little Flower ter die 'cause she was the only one his young'uns Mr. Ackley evir 'bided. And Mr. Ackley stop by Mr. Ma's a'ready fer ter git him ter fix Little Flower a coffin and he says he's gonna buy Little Flower the biggest tombstone Mr. Ma git and the funeral's gonna be ter the depot this afternoon."

Bert shook his sleek head. "How come Little Flower got drowned?"

Ray explained. "See, Bert, Mr. and Mrs. Ferris and Mr. Ackley was out visiting and I tells yer the water come like a dam'd bust, all a sudden. When Mr. Ackley and Mr. and Mrs. Ferris gits home Little Flower'd washed off'n the bed and was floating round the room. They couldn't git the door open any —water musta been holding it shet—and Mr. Ackley bust a window and climbs in and thar's Little Flower floating round."

"Know where Spotty's at, Ray?" Bert demanded.

Again Ray shook his tousled head. "No, Bert. Right off we gits ter the depot Shad he run back and gits clost ter his place as he kin and he calls and whistles and when he gits ter the depot agin he tells me mighty likely Spotty she git drowned like Little Flower done. Got ter go 'long now and tend my furnaces, Bert."

Bert wheeled the barrow into an alley and left it. He moved down Maple, across the bridge, and waded through thigh-deep water till he reached the beginning of Limestone Avenue. He also called and whistled and whistled and called, until the dawn arose.

No one could ever claim Willowspring wouldn't rise to an occasion. Not more than a few minutes after the flood news reached Broad Street wagons and buggies carrying food and clothing moved toward the depot. By the time Dan Field came upon the scene next morning to inspect conditions the refugees, excepting Ackley and the Ferrises but including Bert Sargent, were lolling upon benches and the floor, wearing donated garments and eating donated food. Mr. Leonard had sent one of the hotel's giant coffeepots and atop the depot's red-hot potbellied stove it boiled, sending forth a delicious aroma. The atmosphere breathed festivity. Even the Lawlers appeared happy, the Widder Woman having acquired a pink jacket and Ella and Wilbur red woolen undershirts which they wore over their dirty rags. Only one corner hinted disaster, where the corpse of Little Flower Ferris lay along a bench, Ackley seated at her head, her mama's husband (as Ackley expressed it) at her feet, and her mother crouched before her.

The previous night Ackley had rushed into Dan Field's parlor, sobbing bitterly. "Mr. Doc, my poo' Little Flowah she's daid. My poo' Little Flowah——"

Dan Field sprang to his feet, grabbed his hat, coat, and bag. "Come on, Ackley, let's hurry. Perhaps I can do something. Where is Little Flower? And you're soaking wet."

Rushing toward Mudtown—or rather, the depot—Ackley had disclosed the story of the flood and Little Flower's drowning. "Mr. Doc," he sobbed, "dat Little Flowah's the onliest young'un I evah 'bided."

Now, entering the depot, Dan Field said, "Everybody all right?" Some said they were and he moved to Little Flower's group. "Feeling better this morning?" he asked them.

Ackley and Ferris looked at each other, nodding sympathetically. Well, Dan Field thought, if Ferris ever resented Ackley's contribution to his lares and penates this common sorrow has made them the way brothers should be.

The mother moaned and Ackley said, "No bettah, Mr. Doc. And, Mr. Doc, kin you all get 'long tonight? Aftah the funeral I'd like foh to spend the night by Little Flowah's mama and heh mama's husband."

Dan Field couldn't help a silent chuckle but he spoke seriously.

"Certainly, Ackley, take all the time off you want. Let me know if you need help." He turned to the Lawlers. "Hello, Wilbur and Ella. How are you?"

Chewing great sandwiches, they smiled and Ella said, "Us git red shirts and us bellies full, Doc."

"Good." Dan Field smiled and started toward the door. Bert sprang after him. "Uncle Doc, Spotty's gone."

"She'll probably turn up, Bert. Dogs are good swimmers, you know."

Bert shook his head. "Hope Sammy he don't hear Spotty's gone. Being sick like Sammy is and hearing a thing like Spotty being gone, it'd be bad, Uncle Doc."

"It'd be bad all right, Bert. There's an old saw, though, that says 'Don't give up hope till hope is dead.' Coming along, boy?"

"No, thanks, Uncle Doc. I'm going over round Mudtown and look for Spotty." The morning train whistled. "Give me a ride far as the trestle, Uncle Doc. Mighty likely it won't hold."

The trestle held, however.

Tracy Whitlock felt very bright this morning. Damn if he hadn't gotten Jean Leonard in trouble and she'd been deviling the life out of him to get married. The only possible way to avoid being tied down would be to skip town, but he'd seen no immediate prospect of securing enough cash for a proper start until last night. Still, he'd had well-laid plans which might mean Ralph Pettigrew would bestow his windfall eventually.

Jake, Floyd, and Fat had suggested the idea that Pettigrew pay the bank in order to have the *News* on their side. Which was all right, Tracy decided, but his mind had stepped forward. There was no sound reason why, if Pettigrew should give him the three-thousand-odd dollars, he, Tracy, must turn such a fortune over to George Albright. Once he'd the money, the few things he could tell Captain George concerning his family would make that potentate gladly release the notes. Then all he himself would do would be to give the notes to Pettigrew and leave town with the windfall safely tucked away. All perfectly legal, too; there'd never been a mention concerning his continuing to edit the *News*. You'll be a great man someday, Tracy, he told himself.

Pettigrew, however, had proved difficult. He decidedly refused to hear anything Tracy might have to say. But yesterday Jake had sent word that at last Ralph was willing to get down to brass tacks.

Around the not-so-hot-at-this-season potbellied stove the five of them finally sat, all smoking save Tracy.

"All right, Whitlock," Pettigrew said, "you've wanted to get something off your chest some time now. Go ahead and spill it."

"What I want you gentlemen to believe," Tracy began, "is the fact that I am being swayed by principle rather than ambition. These many years I've felt the policies of George Albright and Rufus Sargent should be condemned. My hands were tied, gentlemen." He stopped an instant.

"How did they get untied?" Pettigrew demanded.

"They didn't," Tracy confessed. "Pettigrew, you have made a major point of the fact that the Albright-Sargent henchmen buy votes. And mind you, not that they've bought me, but they own the paper and I am little better than a pawn."

"What you want to do about it?" Pettigrew demanded.

"If you paid the bank the *News's* notes the sheet would be yours and loyal to your cause."

"How much do you owe the bank?" Pettigrew asked.

Tracy speculated. "A little over three thousand dollars plus interest. Say three thousand four hundred and some."

Pettigrew smiled. "Sounds reasonable enough. I'm going to be pretty busy the next couple days, though. Let's see, this is Monday. . . . Tell you what, Whitlock, you drop in my office around ten o'clock Friday morning and see what you shall see."

Tracy beamed. "You'll not regret your decision, ever, Pettigrew."

Jake, Floyd, and Fat cackled, well pleased.

"Another thing, Pettigrew," Tracy continued. "It is essential that I deliver the money personally. The bank most certainly wouldn't knowingly place the sheet in your able fingers."

"Certainly they wouldn't," Pettigrew agreed. He chewed the end of his cigar. "You've sure figured out every angle of the situation, haven't you, Whitlock?"

Dan Field paid Sammy another visit about four o'clock Wednesday afternoon and found Pris by the bed.

"Hello, Pris, how's the invalid? Stick out your tongue, Sammy."

Sammy answered, "I'm all well, Uncle Doc. Could I get up?"

"We'll see, Sammy." He felt his pulse and took his temperature. "It won't hurt him to get up, Pris. He's all right. But keep him indoors a few days. Sometimes these colds have repercussions."

When he left Pris followed him out in the hall. "Did you see the picture over the bed, Dan?" she whispered. "He wanted it there. I could hardly keep my face straight. Dan, why would he want a picture of a tombstone hanging over his bed?"

Dan Field smiled. "Some kink in his little brain."

She looked up. "Dan, you're such a comfort. I don't know how I'd live without you."

"You'll never have to live without me, you know, Pris."

As he went downstairs Lillian and Prissy skipped through the front door.

Prissy chirped, "Uncle Doc, don't you want to hear us play our duet?"

"Of course."

Lillian chirped, "Uncle Doc, Prissy plays the bass and I play the treble. It's called 'Pure as Snow.' "

After hearing the selection and being duly appreciative Dan Field paid two more calls and arrived home before six. Thank God! Ackley's here to cook dinner tonight and maybe I can get some sleep, he thought.

But he'd hardly downed his first drink when Bert burst upon him. "Uncle Doc, Uncle George gets home and tells Auntie Pris 'bout how he sees the flood and there's woodsheds and chicken coops and a dog kennel and dead cats and dead chickens floating round and Sammy he hears Uncle George. And Sammy he runs off and finds Shad and Shad says, 'Mighty likely Spotty's drowned.' And, Uncle Doc, Sammy's over there wading round in water up to his belly and——"

Dan Field sprang to his feet, calling, "Ackley, hitch the rig quickly as possible. Come on, Bert, we'll help."

It was pitch-dark when they reached Limestone Avenue but Shad moved in the shadows.

"Did you watch Sammy like I tells you to, Shad?" Bert demanded.

Shad pointed through the darkness. "He's over thar. When yer eyes gits set yer kin see him and if'n yer listens a minute yer kin hear him. Sammy he sound like he's going crazy."

Dan Field crawled out of the buggy and peered over Limestone Avenue and presently distinguished Sammy's vague shape and an instant later heard the screams Shad described as sounding like Sammy's going crazy.

"Sammy," Dan Field called, "it's Uncle Doc. Please come here. Please come here, Sammy, there's something I want to tell you. Sammy, it's Uncle Doc." Sammy paid no attention and Dan Field said to Bert, "I'll have to wade after him."

"That won't do no good, Uncle Doc," Bert informed. "Sammy he can wade twice as fast as you. You couldn't catch him."

"Then what in the name of God are we going to do, Bert?" Dan Field demanded.

"Know sumpin, Uncle Doc? It's a mighty mean thing to do but I gotta do it."

"What, Bert?"

Bert bayed like a hound.

An instant later Sammy crawled up the bank, screaming, "Spotty, Spotty . . ."

Dan Field grabbed him around the shoulders and Bert and Shad each clutched a leg. By the time they'd lifted Sammy onto the buggy seat he was unconscious.

Reaching the Albrights', Dan Field told Bert, "You run ahead and tell your auntie Pris I'm bringing him in and not to worry, he'll be all right in no time."

The next day the news had spread all over town: Sammy Albright was dying—pneumonia.

Late Thursday afternoon Ralph Pettigrew stood staring out of his office window. He was thinking about Sammy Albright, the latest report being that Sammy had sunk into a coma and would probably die before morning. Pettigrew recalled Sammy's yellow curls and his round blue eyes and his grin and the way he'd slaved shoveling all those weeks to get that damned hound bitch. Across the street he saw Ray Stoddard staring into Carl's window and Pettigrew wondered why the hell a boy like

Sammy Albright, who'd every reason to live, had to die and a poor little beggar who'd not a chance in God's world ever to amount to anything, no matter how smart he might be, would probably live to a ripe old age. Pettigrew thought of Rufe Albright, too, keeping steady company with Mollie Reynard. . . . Pettigrew nodded. Doc fixed that up some way or other. Poor Doc, Pettigrew sympathized, Sammy's death would go hard with him. Reports had it he'd not left the boy's side some twenty-four hours now, just drunk one cup after another of black coffee. . . .

There went Helen Boyd along the street, alone, of course. . . .

Meg, he meditated, Meg . . . What was it Doc had said? Oh yes. "With a woman who loves you enough at your side your children should inherit an empire." Guess Tim Albright found something to his liking across the mountains. . . .

Gabe Williams and Dolly came to mind. Could they possibly be making out? Pettigrew wondered. Tonight he must ask Belle if Mr. Williams had had any news since the Christmas letter.

However, after everyone else left the dining room it was Belle who questioned him. "Mr. Pettigrew, mind if'n I asks you something?"

"Of course not, Belle."

"Mr. Pettigrew, you al'ays acted as if'n you liked Dolly real good and you knows what everybody else thinks 'bout Dolly and Gabe, so I thinks maybe you could tell me something."

"I certainly will if I can, Belle," Pettigrew promised.

"See, Mr. Pettigrew, it's like this. Mr. Williams gits another letter from Gabe and him and Dolly's near dying 'cause they's so homesick."

"Homesick!" Pettigrew ejaculated, asking himself, What in the name of God could they be homesick for?

"Seems funny they'd be homesick after how they git treated here, don't it?" Belle went on. "But Gabe says they wants to come back and did Mr. Williams think folks'd let 'em alone if'n they comes back? Mr. Williams he don't know. What do you think, Mr. Pettigrew?"

Pettigrew shook his head. "I don't know. But as long as they're married, people might mind their own business."

Belle's eyes shaded like purple pansies filled with tears the way Dolly's had long ago. "If'n they comes I's leaving town, Mr. Pettigrew. It ain't I don't love Dolly. But you don't know what I've had to put up with. The things men and boys 'long the street says and every new man comes in this here dining room I can tell how he looks me over somebody's told him my sister run off with a nigger."

"Where would you want to go, Belle?" Pettigrew asked.

"Maybe Altoona. I hears thar's work to be got thar in the hotels."

Pettigrew took a twenty-dollar bill from a pocket and handed it to her. "Good luck, Belle."

"Mr. Pettigrew," she gasped. "You oughtn't to . . . Mr. Pettigrew, was it you sent Dolly the money?"

"What money?" He took her hand and pressed it. "Good-by, Belle."

"God bless you," she sobbed. "God bless you, Mr. Pettigrew."

Entering the office, Pettigrew's eyes were moist, but the sight of Tracy Whitlock filled him with silent laughter.

Dan Field sat alone by Sammy's bedside. Downstairs in the big Albright parlor all the Albrights, except Sammy, and all the Sargents, except Bert, marked the minutes. Only Rufe held faith; hadn't Uncle Doc told him no God could be anything but merciful? And a merciful God wouldn't let Sammy die.

Dan Field had told them all to stay out of the room. It was better that way. But George kept coming in and going out and Pris crept back every few minutes and knelt by the bed.

Now she came. "Dan, is he dying?"

"I don't think so, Pris. I'm doing everything I can. If he just arouses from this coma . . ."

I've got to save Sammy for her, he kept telling himself. I let Baby George slip through my fingers but . . .

"Dan," she pointed to the picture over the bed, "I laughed when he wanted it over his bed. Do you think his wanting it over his bed was an omen?"

"Oh, Pris, don't be ridiculous. My dear, my dear. . . ."

If I could just take you in my arms, Pris. . . .

"Dan, I want to tell you something. The morning you put Rufe into my arms I—I felt as if you were his father and I wanted to name him Dan Field. I wouldn't let George call him after him and when Baby George died I felt God might be punishing me. . . ."

He took hold of her shoulders and pulled her to her feet. "Pris, please go downstairs. Please."

"All right, Dan."

She left, and he poured another cup of black coffee and downed it.

I've got to save Sammy for her. I let Baby George slip through my fingers but . . .

Bert came through the porch door. "Uncle Doc, Sammy ain't dying, is he?"

"I hope not, Bert. If he just rouses from this coma."

"What's coma, Uncle Doc?"

"Know what a stupor is, Bert?"

"Yes."

"Well, a coma is a deathly stupor."

"Know sumpin, Uncle Doc? Mighty likely I could rouse Sammy from this coma." He went and stood by the bed. "Sammy, it's me, Bert. Sammy, I found Spotty. Spotty she fixes herself a little nest clear over by the Greenhill Cemetery. Sammy, Spotty she got her pups." Sammy's round blue eyes opened. "Sammy, hear me? Spotty, she got her pups, thirteen of 'em, Sammy, and every last one of them pups is a bitch."

Sammy blinked his round blue eyes and smiled.

Dan Field sobbed.

Sammy closed his round blue eyes and, still smiling, slept.

"Know sumpin, Uncle Doc?" Bert whispered. "Them pups ought to be mighty good hunters 'cause Duke's their papa, and pups what's got a papa owned by a man what shot Indians gotta be good hunters." Bert pointed to the picture over the bed. "Know sumpin, Uncle Doc? I told Sammy he'd live all right. But he thought if he dies Uncle George and Auntie Pris mighty likely wouldn't get him a tombstone. So Sammy he thinks if he ain't gonna have a tombstone after he dies he'd like having a tombstone picture hung over his bed till he does die."

"Bert, Bert," Dan Field choked, "I couldn't live without you."

Next morning the news saying Sammy Albright seemed well on the way to recovery spread around town like wildfire. Until people believed Sammy doomed, no one had considered how much they liked him. Probably the single person not happy over the turn for the better was Tracy Whitlock, Tracy being entirely self-absorbed. He felt certain that at ten o'clock this morning Pettigrew would hand over the windfall, then a little session behind a closed bank door, and over the hills and far away; no wedding bells for Tracy.

Right on the ten o'clock dot Tracy entered Pettigrew's office and stopped short. It was cleaned bare of everything except the furniture and a single sheet of paper on top of the desk.

Tracy took the paper and read:

Dear Whitlock:

I am leaving town to be gone an indeterminate period, maybe six months, maybe six years, and will leave the town at your mercy. Considering the faculty of observation at your command, you should have no trouble getting the whole place in a stew in short order.

Love and kisses,
Pettigrew

Tracy turned red, then blue, then white. The dirty double-crossing bastard, he thought. If he could just have found out what was between Pettigrew and Margaret Taylor . . . Tracy sank upon a chair. What now? he asked himself. There seemed to be but one other chance: he must demand that George Albright not only release the due notes but give him a thousand extra dollars. If he stayed around town much longer Jean's condition would be noticed and Nard Leonard might take a shotgun. . . . Tracy'd not put it past Nard.

Five minutes later Tracy walked into George's office. "Good morning, Captain George."

George sat behind his desk. "Hello, Tracy, what can I do for you?"

Tracy placed his hat upon the desk and sat down. "I've come to settle accounts."

"Pay your interest?" George asked.

"No, this settlement will be in full."

"Good." George went to another department and returned, carrying a few papers. He seated himself again. "Here are the notes. Now let's see. . . . You owe three thousand four hundred and sixty-five dollars and seventy-eight cents. Must have had a windfall, Tracy."

"Not yet, but I intend having one," Tracy said.

George nodded. "Good. I suppose you've the money to pay your notes with you, though."

"No, Captain George, I haven't the money to pay my notes with me, nor do I have any money anywhere this moment. But I want you to receipt my notes and give me an additional thousand dollars."

"If you've no money, may I ask why you expect me to do all this?" George inquired.

"Because I've got a girl in trouble and have to leave town immediately."

George leaned back and placed the tips of his fingers together. "Because you've got a girl in trouble I'm supposed to receipt your notes and give you an additional thousand dollars?"

Tracy sighed. "Captain George, you've always seemed sympathetic before. You are the one person in the village I've believed capable of appreciating my ambition. Can't you understand now that I can't leave town unless you receipt the notes and give me the thousand dollars?"

"What about it?" George demanded.

Tracy leaned forward. "It's this about it, Captain George. If I have to stay here and have a family hanging around my neck my book will never be written. I'm bound to be a success someday, Captain George, and I'll pay you back every cent."

George shook his head. "Sorry, Tracy, you've had every penny you'll ever receive from me."

Tracy smiled. "Oh no, I haven't, Captain George."

George smiled. "May I ask why?"

Tracy's narrow eyes became mere slits. "Because there are certain facts concerning this bank and your family which, if brought to light, would mean ruin."

George raised his brows. "Namely?"

Tracy bowed. "Namely, first, because if the state bank examiners happened to be notified that Mr. Fisher left an income payable fifty years after his death there'd be some thorough going over of your books. Namely, second, if it was made known that your son Rufe is fooling around a country girl who's peppered, his future might be affected. Namely, third, you yourself would experience considerable mortification if the town happened to discover what's going on between your wife and Dr. Dan Field."

George arose, went to the door, locked it, and put the key in his pocket. "I've heard, Tracy, your father thrashed you upon the streets and I've pitied you because of the fact. But at the present moment I feel much the way he must have."

George grabbed Tracy Whitlock by the scruff of the neck, yanked him to his feet, threw him face down across the desk, reached for a giant ruler, and beat him upon his skinny rump until Tracy begged for mercy. Then George lifted him by the scruff of his neck and flung him back upon the chair.

George found a handkerchief and wiped his hands. "Now, my fine fellow, you listen to why you're going to do what I say from this time forward. Namely, first, if I ever hear a breath concerning any member of my family or any one of my friends out of you again I'll break every bone in your body. Namely, second, if you don't get to work and pay every cent you owe me I'll have you jailed on more counts than will be necessary to keep you behind bars the rest of your life. Namely, third, if you haven't married the girl you've got in trouble inside a week I'll see to it that Nard Leonard takes a shotgun to you." George got up, unlocked and opened the door. "Get out."

Tracy Whitlock got out.

When Dan Field reached home around five o'clock that afternoon he found George Albright seated in his parlor, sipping a drink.

"Helped myself to a nip, Dan," George said. "I need it."

Dan Field found a chair. "Don't tell me I'm going to have you on my list now. I've had all the Albrights I can take this season."

"No," George said, "I'm feeling fit but I've had an extremely trying experience today." And for the second time during his life George made a confidant of Dan Field. "Dan, I've loaned that Tracy Whitlock out of my own pocket more than three thousand dollars. Rufus and Hart both think me insane and they are quite correct. I tell you what influenced me, though, Dan. Tracy told me he wanted to write a book and it made me think about my brother Tim. No doubt you've heard the story; he ran away when he was fifteen. Not that Tracy's anything like

Tim, but Tim wanted to be a writer too. Pa would have none of it and I've always thought, had Pa been more understanding, Tim wouldn't have left home. And it seemed to me that were I to help another boy who was trying to write it'd be some sort of recompense. The telling sounds inane, I know."

Dan Field poured himself a drink. "Not inane at all. Your idea seems perfectly logical."

"Anyhow," George continued, "after all I've done, this morning Tracy came to my office and tried blackmailing me. Said he'd got a girl in trouble and wanted to leave town and if I didn't receipt his notes and give him an extra thousand dollars to boot he'd make public certain incriminating facts he knew concerning me and my family."

"What did you do?" Dan Field asked.

George blinked his round blue eyes and grinned. "I turned him over my desk, Dan, and I took a ruler and beat his bottom until he begged for mercy."

Dan Field roared. "Good for you."

George's expression sobered. "But one accusation he made has me a bit worried. He claimed Rufe's been fooling around a country girl who, as Tracy put it, is peppered."

Dan Field shrugged. "Nothing to it, George. Rufe told me the circumstances. He did go out in the country twice but the whole business was practically innocent. He didn't like the girl and stopped seeing her."

George drew a deep breath. "What a relief. Of course, Dan, I've the utmost confidence in Rufe, yet—well, sometimes the flesh is stronger than the spirit."

"You're quite right," Dan Field agreed. "By the way, George, the next time you take a trip to Philadelphia, why don't you take Rufe along? Boys his age are bound to be restless and a change of scenery does us all a world of good."

"Might be a good idea, Dan."

Dan Field refilled the glasses. "Suppose I should keep rye on hand."

George smiled. "I can down this under necessity, if there doesn't happen to be a bat in it."

Dan Field smiled. "I wouldn't vouch for that. You know, I told you bats have a way of getting into things. Seriously, though, I'm glad you stopped by. I've been wanting to see you when

Pris isn't around. George, Sammy's not going to be himself again these many a day."

George winced. "I thought we were going to lose the boy."

"I can tell you now I did too, George. Sammy's recovery was a miracle. And as I said, he's far from being out of the woods yet. What I want you to do is think of some way to keep him contented at home until he's entirely well."

"Any suggestions to make, Dan?"

Dan Field chuckled to himself but spoke seriously. "I know where you can get a hound bitch and thirteen bitch puppies."

George gasped. "Are you serious?"

"Certainly I'm serious."

"Good God Almighty!" George swore for perhaps the first time in his life. "We couldn't have fourteen bitches around the place. Why, I wouldn't tolerate one, with Lillian . . . Such a situation is simply out of the question, Dan. And why fourteen?"

Dan Field chuckled. "I know what I'm saying sounds ridiculous. But do you recall last fall when Sammy brought a puppy home and you threw her out of the house?" George nodded and Dan Field continued. "You just about broke Sammy's heart."

"No!" George exclaimed.

"You did, though. A colored boy in Mudtown has been keeping the dog—Spotty's her name—and recently Spotty became the mother of thirteen pups, every last one of them bitches."

George poured himself a third drink and downed it. "But, Dan——"

"Wait a minute. Spotty and her pups mean more to Sammy at the moment than either you or his mother, not mentioning the rest of humanity. The night I brought Sammy home he'd been wading through the flood trying to find Spotty. And I really believe he'd never have come out of the coma if Bert hadn't climbed up the post, come into the room from the back porch, and told Sammy he'd found Spotty. Of course all this is confidential."

"Of course, Dan. Of course. . . ."

"And there's another thing I'd like you to do: tell Sammy if he does happen to die you'll personally see he has a proper tombstone."

"Are you in your right mind, Dan Field?" George fairly bellowed.

Dan Field roared. "Never since I can remember has my mentality been more lucid. Whether you believe me or not, the reason Sammy wants that picture over his bed is because he's afraid he'll never have a real tombstone."

George sank limply backward. "I've always taken you to be an honest man and perhaps you know what you're talking about. . . . All right, I'll promise Sammy to add a codicil to my will assuring a tombstone. But as far as fourteen bitches are concerned —why, one would probably be in heat every day throughout the year."

Dan Field winked. "That situation can be easily remedied and I'll not charge you a cent. Then you can have Matt build a pen in the far fields, which suggestion is also gratis."

George sniffed. "Your generosity overwhelms me, Dr. Field. But Sammy is your patient. And speaking of Matt, do you happen to know what's become of Gabe? I heard the Tatem tart followed him wherever he may be."

Dan Field shrugged. "I should think that's about all anyone knows."

"Another bit of news, Dan. There's a rumor that Ralph Pettigrew's left town. Suppose it's true?"

"Might be."

George arose. "It's to be hoped so. What greater blessing could the town receive than to have that blackguard gone? All right, Dan, thanks. The news about Rufe's relieved my mind if I can't admit being delighted concerning the fourteen bitches, including their operations."

Dan Field arose. "Another bit of news, George: you better have Matt fix some sort of portable case so Sammy can have those bitches around the house a few hours every day until he's up."

George blinked his round blue eyes and grinned. "Anyhow, there seems a single blessing I could consider—neither Rufe nor Sammy give any indication of wanting to become writers."

Going home, George decided probably Dan was correct concerning Sammy. The dogs would be an infernal nuisance, yet . . . And if Dan knew the insult Tracy Whitlock had directed toward him and Pris, there'd be another thrashing across the skinny buttocks.

While, as Dan Field poured himself a third drink, he was thinking about George. If he could know the part Pettigrew had played saving Rufe. And remembering the thrashing of Tracy Whitlock, Dan Field chuckled to himself. If Sammy with his round blue eyes and grins and reticence and compassion and ready fists isn't a chip off the old block no one ever saw one. And Lillian is exactly like Pris, with her straw-colored curls and shadow-filled eyes and golden skin. Miss Muffet, Dan Field thought, who will love you—and whom will you love?

Part 4
SPRING AGAIN

Chapter One

*A*PRIL BROUGHT sudden showers but the sun, like an eager lover with searching fingers, ran penetrating rays into every crevice of the earth. Mudtown began drying up and over town the mire gradually grew less. The first week every house through the village proper, from the smallest cottage to the Albright and Sargent mansions, was turned inside out for house cleaning. Trees and bushes and shrubs wore a new green fuzz. The woods bordering the creek opposite Ma Woodward's place had long since been cleared, and by April's second Saturday the electric light plant stood there and wire-strung poles lined Maple Street to Broad and up as far as the Grand Central Hotel.

Tonight the lights were to be turned on and the project had been creating so much excitement that otherwise important events, such as Tracy Whitlock and Jean Leonard having to get married, Belle Tatem leaving town, and Gabe and Dolly Williams slipping back, went unnoticed.

Ralph Pettigrew hadn't sent a soul a line since he had vanished, seemingly into thin air. Jake, Floyd, and Fat now regarded him the way some regard the dead, as one who'd been incapable of wrong. These days they were concerned about Tracy Whitlock's attitude. Since Pettigrew's departure Tracy had ignored them.

This afternoon the three lounged before the livery stable and Fat remarked, "Ralph him was right saying Tracy him's a squirt."

Floyd drawled, "Wall, Tracy he sure be wrong 'bout Rufe gittin' peppered. Wonder if'n George Albright know how Rufe and Mollie they be a-going steady?"

Jake shook his head. "Wouldn't hardly know. Ben he says Rufe he won't go out'n the country a-tall no more. Other boys don't go much neither. Funny! Lately Ben, Tom, and Jack they think they gotta do everythin' Rufe does. Rufe he gets him a town gal and they gets 'em town gals. And oncet they didn't even want Rufe 'round."

Floyd's jaw clamped on the straw. "Boys be queer. Men be queer. Only Ralph he ben't queer. Mighty likely Margaret Taylor had sumpin to do with why Ralph goes off."

Jake scratched his head. "Maybe, but I can't see . . ."

"Me neither," Fat agreed.

"Thar be Helen Boyd." Floyd pointed. "Glad Reynard stops his gal a-goin' with the likes. I'd not be lettin' no gal of mine go with a Jew. Or with no Catholic neither."

Jake nodded. "Ain't seen Mollie and Bertha 'round together lately. Maybe Reynard he stops that too."

Fat sniffed. "Likely since Mollie her's a-goin' with Rufe her thinks her belongs to the best families."

Floyd pointed again. "Thar be that Gregory Beamer. Queer how Father Callahan have Gregory takin' Latin lessons. Don't call that thar decent. No minister of the gospel, if'n he do be a Catholic, ought be larnin' a bastard Latin."

Fat hawked and spat. "Looka Ray Stoddard. Every day me see he a-standin' 'fore Carl's window. Maybe him's fixin' to steal. 'Member the day him sass Ralph?"

The other two men nodded.

Floyd chewed the straw and spoke. "What you think 'bout the 'lectric lights?"

Fat belched. "Feller me knowed oncet, him tell I 'lectric lights is immoral. See, this here feller him says 'lectric lights is that bright them shines clean through women's skirts and you kin see they's legs. Us-uns kin look tonight and find out. Thar goes Doc Field. Wonder how come Doc him pretty near al'ays has Bert Sargent 'long?"

Toward the end of the afternoon Rufe and Mollie sat upon the Reynards' front steps, their young heads close together.

"Spring," Rufe sighed. "It does things to you inside. Makes you want to do things you've never done before." He felt older than he had ever felt, no longer a boy but a man.

Mollie's blue eyes met his gray ones. "What, Rufe?"

"I don't know exactly, Mollie." A breeze blew one of her curls across his cheek. He choked, "You know I'll always love you. You know that, don't you, Mollie?"

She choked. "If you don't I'll die, Rufe."

He moved a bit away from her. "Mollie, it's going to be a long time before we can get married."

"It don't matter, Rufe."

He nodded. "I suppose not. Except, Mollie, I've so much to do before I can dream of getting married and raising a family."

"What, Rufe?"

Rufe cleared his throat. "Well, here's one thing: I've only finished the plans for three cities. . . . It will probably take years before my world made all of marble will be finished. And I've a lot of other ideas I want to work out before I settle down."

"I'll wait, Rufe."

He smiled. "Dear Mollie. Of course you'll wait. . . . Of course. What I'm trying to tell you is this: Monday I'm going to Philadelphia with the family and——"

"How wonderful!" she interrupted.

Rufe shrugged. "I don't know how wonderful. Philadelphia probably can offer little that I've not experienced. No doubt I may run across a few new ideas. . . . Of course a fellow my age can't expect any surprises. Life is very much the same, Mollie, whether lived in Willowspring or Philadelphia or Athens."

"You're so wonderful, Rufe," Mollie breathed.

"Not really, my dear. Not really. However, I'm fortunate in having found a girl who can understand my ambitions. Who will wait while I'm away now and through the long years to come."

"Maybe the time won't seem so very long, Rufe."

"Yes, it will, my dear. You've long lonely days ahead. How will you amuse yourself during the days I'll be in Philadelphia?"

Mollie pondered an instant. "Practice the piano . . . Oh, Rufe, do you remember what Professor Phelps said about a concert?" She didn't give him a chance to answer. "Professor Phelps said that the first Monday of May any student who plays a musical instrument can enter a contest. And the student who plays best will be awarded a framed certificate. Wouldn't it be wonderful if I could win, Rufe?"

"You will win, Mollie."

"How do you know, Rufe?"

"Because, my dear, Mama has discovered the most beautiful new waltz. It's called 'The Blue Danube.' . . ."

Helen Boyd's fingers ran along the keys. Vera stood beside the piano, her eyes burning.

Helen raised her hands. "Mother, really I'd sooner not enter the contest. I don't believe I'll win. And I don't care whether I win or not. Really I don't."

Vera smiled. "You're going to win, Helen. I know you're going to win." She touched her breast. "I've a feeling here. It's called intuition."

The front door opened and Eli called, "Vera."

"We're here, dear, in the parlor."

He joined them. "What have you been up to, Vera? You look as if you'd been born again."

She laughed. "The school's having a musical contest the first Monday in May and the student who wins will receive a framed certificate. Helen's going to play *the* nocturne. Won't Dr. Field be pleased, though? Come, Eli, run through the piece with Helen. Your timing is so perfect, dear."

He took his violin off the piano top.

Gregory Beamer had forgotten the long winter behind. On his way to town this day the warm air fondled him. Reaching the pool beside the road, he pulled off his pants and jumped into the cold water. . . . He came out finally and stood on the bank, looking down at the reflection in the still deep pool.

But when Gregory put on his pants again he did not continue along the road. He moved through the bushes edging the creek. He was thinking, Maybe there's a swimming hole hid round here where a girl could go swimming bare.

He remembered Prissy's soft lips. . . .

Course he'd have to confess if he took Prissy swimming bare. . . . Gregory never worried about the future, though.

No one had bought the watch and it was still in Carl's window. Jest two dollars and seventy-five cents more, Ray was thinking. I wisht, oh, I wisht Miss Lillian knowed I git promoted ter fourth grade.

Dan Field had taken Bert to see the Mount Pallas baby he'd put on the meat-tit.

Going home, Bert said, "Know sumpin, Uncle Doc? That baby it ain't gonna die."

"You're right, Bert. That baby it ain't gonna die, thanks to you."

"How come you never did think 'bout giving babies meat-tits, Uncle Doc?"

"Because you and I, Bert, belong to different generations. You children who are growing up today think your own thoughts."

"Ray Stoddard really thinks his own thoughts. Know sumpin, Uncle Doc? Ray got promoted to fourth grade and this is the first year he went to school."

"It's an almost unheard-of thing for a boy to be as smart as all that. I must see Ray soon and have a long talk."

" 'Sides being smart, Uncle Doc, Ray he does the chores round home and he tends furnaces over town and he shoveled snow. Ray's making money, Uncle Doc. Ray he really is making money."

"How does he spend his money?" Dan Field asked.

"He don't spend his money, Uncle Doc. Ray he saves his money. Nobody knows where he keeps it neither. Know sumpin, Uncle Doc? Harry Stoddard he says one night their papa tries to make Ray tell where his money's at. And Ray he grabbed the coal bucket and hit Mr. Stoddard 'crost the face and says he'd get the loan of Mr. Tatem's musket and kill him if he ever touches a penny. Ray he would, too. If Ray gets mad he really is mean, like Sammy."

Dan Field concealed a smile. "Haven't seen Sammy lately. How's he doing?"

"All right now," Bert informed. "He was worrying till Uncle George says he'll get him a tombstone if he dies and I start wheeling the swill to Mudtown. 'Cept I don't wheel, I just pick the best chunks and fill a poke."

Dan Field laughed. "You certainly use your head, boy. Haven't seen Noel lately, either. How's she coming?"

"Mrs. Stoddard she says that Noel's the bestest brat she ever borned. Know sumpin, Uncle Doc? I've been taking Noel apples to suck."

"Apples?"

Bert nodded. "That Noel she just loves apples. Know sumpin, Uncle Doc? That Noel she gets diarrhea and after she sucks a couple apples it stops."

Dan Field roared. "Maybe you've something there too. Bert, Bert, I couldn't live without you."

Nervy stopped before Dan Field's house. He and Bert got out of the buggy.

"Think I'll go have a look at Sammy," Dan Field said.

They found Sammy on the Albrights' back porch, surrounded by Spotty and her thirteen pups.

"Sammy, you're the picture of health," Dan Field said. "And those pups grow handsomer every minute."

Sammy blinked his round blue eyes and grinned. "Spotty's pups they would grow handsomer every minute, Uncle Doc."

Pris thrust her head through the kitchen doorway. "I thought I heard you, Dan. Want me to play *the* nocturne or 'The Blue Danube' today?"

"Let's have 'The Blue Danube.' "

He took one of the big parlor chairs and her fingers found the keys. . . . The Danube . . . lilting lovely blue water . . . Vienna, Paris, Rome . . . Perhaps someday again with you, my Pris. The last note . . .

George entered. "Hello, Dan. Well, tonight's the night. Honestly, though, what do you think about Rufus' arc-light venture?"

"I'd hardly call it Rufus' venture. There *is* a man named Edison."

Pris smiled. "The whole town will turn out, anyhow. Dan, why don't you join us?"

"I should be delighted, unless I've an unexpected call."

Dan Field reached home to find Margaret Taylor waiting in the office. He had never seen her look so beautiful, her eyes shining and her cheeks crimson.

"There couldn't be anything wrong with you, Meg," he said.

"I'm perfectly all right. But, Dr. Field—well, you must remember the night you found me down by the creek, where the electric light plant stands." She laughed. "Tonight the lights will be turned on."

"That's right. Sit down, Meg?"

She took a chair. "You haven't had a letter, have you, Dr. Field?"

He sat on the edge of the desk. "You mean, have I had a letter from Pettigrew?"

Her eyes met his. "Of course."

Here is a miracle, Dan Field was thinking. Meg is no longer a child. Meg is no longer afraid. Great-grandmother Taylor split the Indian's skull straight through the scalp lock. . . . Meg has become a woman, a beautiful unafraid woman.

"No, I've not had a letter," he said. "Have you?"

"No. What's more, I may never have a letter. It doesn't matter."

"It doesn't?"

"No! Dr. Field, we saw each other alone before he left."

"I'm glad."

She threw back her head. "You're glad? How do you think I am? You know the way I've been raised, never allowed to think, let alone to feel."

"Of course I know."

"We met here."

"Here?"

She nodded. "I saw him on the street, quite by accident, and he whispered to come here. Neither you nor Ackley was home."

"Well!" was all Dan Field could say.

"He'll return someday, Dr. Field. But tonight . . . tonight means something, not only to me, though. It means something to all the girls in the world who've never been allowed to think or feel. The thicket, opposite Ma Woodward's where he first took me, seems a symbol."

"I understand, Meg."

"You do understand!" she cried. "He told me you would. He said if I was ever afraid or lonely or doubted his love, to see you. Only today I'm not afraid or lonely nor do I doubt his love. . . . None of those are the reason I'm here. It's the lights. . . . Tonight someone beside the creek will touch a button and way up on Broad Street . . . On the same spot beside the creek he first took me and maybe in years to come there will be other kinds of lights by which girls like me . . . Oh, Dr. Field, I'm expressing myself very badly but you know what I mean, don't you?"

"Of course I know, Meg."

She stood up. "He said, 'Our children will inherit the earth.' "

A high tower had been erected before the Grand Central Hotel, upon which the arc lights were mounted. From this peak most of Broad Street would be illuminated. Before dusk turned to dark the whole town waited. Finally the moment arrived. As the Willowspring *News* recorded the event next day:

People stood overwhelmed with awe, as if in the presence of the supernatural. The strange, weird light, exceeded in power only by the sun, rendered Broad Street as light as midday. Men fell upon their knees, groans were uttered at the sight and many were dumb with amazement.

Rufus laughed. "Well, Captain George, what do you think now?"

George shrugged. "Must I think, Mr. Sargent?"

Eddie Perkins, the lamplighter, stood near. "Temptin' Providence. Temptin' Providence."

"What do you think, Dan?" Pris asked.

Dan Field said, "It's tomorrow."

The rest of the Albright and Sargent families stood speechless.

Dan Field saw Ray Stoddard and moved near him. "What do you make of the lights, Ray?"

"They's sumpin brushed straight out'n heaven, Mr. Doc."

Dan Field heard Father Callahan's voice. "Sure, my good doctor, it is too bad that Mr. Darwin is not among those present here tonight."

"Sure, my good padre, I've an idea that Mr. Darwin is among those present here tonight. Except these days Mr. Darwin needs must travel under another name, which might be—Ray Stoddard."

Chapter Two

IT'S MAY. The same breath which calls the birds from the south and stirs the sap in the trees and brings the flowers out of the earth and stirs the blood of beasts whips human breasts. Today the ruby-crowned kinglet is back, but the robins and other birds have been around for weeks. The arbutus went with the snow, the lilacs are still jade buds and the lilies of the valley tiny jade bells. Every tree wears such tender green and the fruit trees are blown with white froth and pink froth, hardly a petal falling yet. Violets sprinkle the far fields; along roads clover and timothy and redtop wave. Tulips and jonquils border lawns, and beside the now cooing creek mint scents the air. Like narcissus, Gregory Beamer sees a beautiful naked boy reflected in a still deep pool. Prissy Sargent sits under a great sugar maple, remembering . . .

Dan Field walks across Limestone Avenue and the earth yields under his tread. It is the same kind of yield the bricks over town give—a sweet resistlessness after the bitter relentlessness of frozen ground, like the ultimate surrender of a virgin. Hens fly every which way, prodigiously pursued. Duke trots jauntily about, sniffing hopefully. Black boys and girls wander toward the bushes by the creek. Ackley enters the Ferris shanty. The Widder Woman rocks drowsily in her hammock. A cow moos and a bull a quarter of a mile off bawls. Behind the Stoddard shanty Ray counts his wealth—one more dollar and he'd have enough to buy the watch. I wisht, oh, I wisht Miss Lillian knowed I gits promoted ter fourth grade. She stands beside him smiling. . . . There is a little wind and he sees her curls blowing. Really Lillian sits under a great sugar maple, wondering . . .

Through the whole valley the rich red earth is being turned to plant the corn. Red and Lem are planting their corn.

Red calls, "Doc, ever seen a deer-mouse ear? The ιjuns used ter say ter plant yer corn when the oak leaves is the size of a deer-mouse ear."

Lem rests on his spade. "Doc, the flood done good. It washed rich soil down here. Likely this'll be the prime crop come yit. Someday I's gonna own a farm. Gawd A'mighty! I git borned with green fingers. Yer kin hear my corn grow."

Lem's eyes have lost their bloodshot. His face and hands and clothes are still dirty, except this dirt is clean dirt. Over Lem today is good earth, mother earth, such a purifying flame.

"Yer kin hear my corn grow, Doc. Still nights it sounds like rain on a roof. That's how my corn sounds a-growing, Doc."

Tonight before people go to bed windows will be hoisted and outside frogs and crickets will be strumming. Old folks looking out will think the moon and stars are the same moon and stars they saw when they were young. Cats will scream serenades. Come dawn, cock crows will have a shriller tone and nesting birds will call.

There's night and day, brother, Dan Field was thinking, *both sweet things; sun, moon, and stars, brother, all sweet things; there's likewise a wind on the heath. Life is very sweet, brother; who would wish to die.*

Vienna, Paris, Rome, perhaps again someday with you, my Pris . . .

"Mr. Doc, sir," Gabe Williams called.

Dan Field waited. "Hello, Gabe."

"Mr. Doc, mind walking off, so nobody hears us?"

"Not at all."

They walked through the woods into the mountain.

"What's on your mind, Gabe?"

"Mr. Doc, sir, I's been wanting a talk since me and Dolly gets home. I ain't forgot the money I owes you, and the coat."

"Never mind them, Gabe. Captain George took you back, didn't he?"

Gabe nodded. "Yes sir. I got my old job. It's Dolly. . . . She ain't happy, Mr. Doc."

"Few of us are, Gabe."

Gabe shrugged. "Mr. Tatem he lets us live to his place. He don't mind what since I feeds him. Belle's going upset Dolly.

Guess folks wonder why me and Dolly come home. Likely you'd know, Mr. Doc, if'n nobody else would, how when you's born and raised someplace it's part of you. When we was away nights we sees the moon shining over Limestone Avenue and we hears the train rumbling over the trestle. Mornings we could see the sun rising 'crost these here mountains and we hears voices we knowed talking."

"I understand, Gabe."

"Still, Dolly she ain't happy here. . . . When you seen her the other day what did you think?"

"She's probably happier here than she would be anyplace else, Gabe. Many a woman carrying a child is moody. After the baby comes Dolly may be brighter."

From somewhere deep within Gabe a great sob arose. "I knowed all along it wasn't right. But what could I do, Mr. Doc?"

"Nothing, Gabe. Be thankful people are letting you alone."

They had reached Cal's grave.

Gabe pointed. "Do you s'pose that thar's the tombstone what got stole, Mr. Doc?"

The melting snows and the spring rains had washed Cal's marker clean, the liver-color paint and the red epitaph gone.

"I couldn't say if that's the stolen stone, Gabe," Dan Field said.

"Mr. Doc, you knows I's thankful 'bout folks letting Dolly and me alone. What's likely to happen, though, if'n some thinks the Widder Woman stole the stone? Likely they'll run her out'n town again and maybe she feels this here place is her home too. She comes back the other time. . . ."

Dan Field thought, ". . . nights we sees the moon shining over Limestone Avenue . . . Mornings we could see the sun rising 'crost these here mountains . . ." Jesus! Dan Field swore to himself. Jesus! Jesus! *Who would wish to die.* Who would wish to live?

Gabe didn't spread the news. May moved along and others discovered that the stolen stone marked Cal's grave.

Tracy Whitlock told Jean and Aunt Tillie the news during the noon hour of the month's first Tuesday. Tracy had taken Jean to live in Aunt Tillie's sizable old house. And after the first shock of Tracy's sudden marriage to a girl whose father sold liquor had faded, Aunt Tillie regarded Jean as second only to Tracy.

She explained to the agreeing Mrs. Meeker, Mrs. Diggers, and the Fishers, "What if Mr. Leonard does sell liquor? Children can't pick their parents. Mabbe the baby'll come early; most first babies do. And I never see two young people so happy neither. The way Tracy's working these days, too, paying off the bank! Don't seem right them pressing him, with him just got married. But Tracy won't let me say one word against the bank."

"The Widder Woman stole Ma Woodward's tombstone," Tracy told. "Someone found it on Cal's grave. Ma's still sore as a wet hen. She'll probably get run out of town again."

"How are people run out of town, Tracy?" Jean asked.

Tracy shrugged. "Many ways. The last time they merely warned her that if she didn't leave town trouble would start. This time, who knows? The night riders might tar and feather her."

Jean shuddered. "How terrible!"

Aunt Tillie warned, "Tracy, remember Jean's condition."

Toward midafternoon Tracy decided he'd better walk to the woods beyond Limestone Avenue and inspect the stone.

Nearing Maple Street, he met Mollie Reynard and stopped. "Hear you won the musical contest yesterday, Mollie. What did you play?"

Mollie's eyes shone. "The most beautiful new waltz—'The Blue Danube.'"

Tracy smiled. "'The Blue Danube,' eh? Suppose Rufe Albright had something to say about your selection."

Mollie smiled. "Yes, he did, Mr. Whitlock."

"Aren't you afraid a city girl will cut you out while Rufe's in Philadelphia?"

Mollie tossed her curls. "Of course I'm not. Rufe's not that kind. What's more, Mr. Tracy Whitlock, I'd thank you to mind your own business."

Tracy laughed. "Fiery little piece, aren't you?" He remembered the feel of George Albright's ruler. "I'm merely joking, Mollie. My next edition will have quite an article concerning you winning. Rufe will be pleased and proud. Of course you know the Albrights and Sargents are expected home tomorrow evening."

Tracy moved along. Nearing the electric light plant, he saw Gregory Beamer and Prissy Sargent slipping through the bushes along the creek. "When the cat's away," Tracy thought.

After school Prissy sat with Lillian under one of the Albrights' great sugar maples. The air felt warm and the air felt good and, as on the first day of May, Prissy was remembering and Lillian was wondering. Prissy saw Gregory's hair, Gregory's eyes; she heard Gregory's voice. Cool clinging water slipped over her and Gregory Beamer, both of them bare. Lillian kept asking herself, Why before Mama went away did she tell me never to run and jump? Since spring came this year Lillian had felt she must run and jump. To run, run, run, to leap, perhaps to fly, was what Lillian wanted to do. Why couldn't she?

Alexander joined the little girls. Alexander's mien had become more assured than ever since Mrs. Standing and Buzz had left town. Mrs. Standing said her sister had always wanted them to come and live with her. But everybody knew the reason the Standings moved, because after the fight the other boys began tormenting Buzz, the way they'd once tormented Alexander.

Spring made Alexander's breast throb too. "Lillian," he breathed. "Lillian."

Prissy started. "You got to talk, Alexander?"

"Don't you want me to talk, Prissy?"

"No!"

"Why not?"

"I'm thinking."

"Can't you think if I talk?"

"No!"

Lillian frowned. Prissy had started acting again the way she had acted a long time ago, like she'd a special secret Lillian didn't know.

"This is our yard, Alexander," Lillian said. "If you want to talk, don't mind Prissy."

"Lillian," Alexander sighed again. "Lillian . . ."

Prissy sprang to her feet and ran toward home. Beside the back porch she dropped down. Tears fell. She hated Alexander. She hated Lillian. She hated the whole world.

"Everybody likes Lillian best," she sobbed out loud. "Why can't anybody like me best?"

"I likes you best, Prissy."

"Gregory!" She started.

She'd not heard him approaching.

"You're crying, Prissy."

She blinked and smiled. "Not any more. Do you honest like me best, Gregory?"

"Course. That's why I come today. This ain't Saturday, it's Thursday." He whispered, "Yer folks still away?"

She whispered, "Yes."

Gregory still whispered. "Whar's Maggie at?"

"Uptown, I guess," Prissy said. "Maggie buys things afternoons when Mama's in Philadelphia."

He leaned nearer her. "Prissy, I finds a swimming hole clost by. It's hid and girls could go swimming bare and nobody could see nothin'."

"No!" Prissy cried. "No!"

Gregory cocked his beautiful head. "You needn't go swimming bare, Prissy. It wouldn't do no harm if'n you jest looked whar girls could go swimming bare, if'n they wanted."

Bert left the porch overhead, tore down the stairs and outside. From a safe distance he trailed Prissy and Gregory. Finally Prissy started home alone and Gregory moved toward the Catholic Church.

Bert caught him. "Where you going, Gregory?"

"To confession," Gregory answered.

Chapter Three

*T*HE NEXT EVENING, shortly before train-
time, Maggie found Prissy huddled on her bed.

"What's wrong?" Maggie asked.

"No-no-nothing," Prissy chattered.

"Thar must be. You's shaking all over, Prissy." She called,
"Bert, fetch Dr. Field. Prissy's took sumpin."

"No," Prissy sobbed, "no, Maggie. Please don't get Uncle Doc.
Please . . ."

"Thar, thar, Prissy, quiet down. Be a good girl and let Maggie
undress you. Yer mama'll be that mad if'n you won't let me."

Arriving home, the Sargents found Dan Field beside Prissy's
bed.

"What's wrong, Dan?" Rufus demanded.

"Nothing much, I hope. Her temperature's up but I can't find
anything else wrong. And she says she's all right, don't you,
Prissy?"

Prissy choked. "I—I am all right, Uncle Doc."

Gramma Sargent shook her head sadly. "Poor little Prissy."

"Prissy can't be bad," Lou said. "She's never had any serious
illness in her life. You know that, Dan. But I thought we were
going to lose Bert the time he'd the measles."

Dan Field handed Lou a paper of pills. "Give her one of these
every hour. If she's not better tomorrow morning call me immediately." He stroked Prissy's head. "When you're up we'll take
a long drive. Nervy's been inquiring where you and Lillian have
been keeping yourselves."

Bert followed Dan Field outside. "Know sumpin, Uncle Doc?
Prissy she ain't sick, she's scared."

Dan Field stopped. "Scared, Bert?"

"See, Uncle Doc, Prissy she thinks everybody likes Lillian best 'cept Gregory Beamer."

"Gregory Beamer?"

"Know sumpin, Uncle Doc? Gregory Beamer he comes round yesterday and tells Prissy he found a hid swimming hole where nobody could see nothing. It's a little way past the 'lectric light plant. And Gregory he took Prissy swimming bare."

Dan Field cleared his throat. "Let me get this thing straight, Bert. Unless my ears deceive me, Gregory Beamer took Prissy swimming bare."

Bert nodded. "See, Uncle Doc, Gregory tells Prissy he likes her best and he wants she'd just look at the swimming hole. When they's there Gregory he pulls his pants off and jumps in and hollers, 'Come on, Prissy.' And Prissy she takes off her clothes and jumps in."

"I take it you were somewhere near, Bert."

"Couple feet away under a bush, Uncle Doc."

"What happened after the swim, Bert?"

"Gregory he pulls on his pants and Prissy she puts on her clothes. And Prissy she goes home and Gregory he goes to confession."

"To confession?"

"Likely Gregory he thinks he ought to confess quick and get it past. But know sumpin, Uncle Doc? Prissy she acts all right till just 'fore Mama and Papa gets home. That's how I knows she's scared and ain't sick."

"Thank you for telling me, Bert," Dan Field said.

Passing the Albrights', he turned through the gateway. Wonder if this house holds a new story? He smiled. What if George has seduced a Philadelphia virgin?

The Albrights were assembled in the sitting room.

Greetings over, Dan Field seated himself. "Did you visit my family, Pris?"

"Of course, Dan."

"Mother and Father are well, I expect."

"Very well."

"City unchanged, George?" Dan Field asked.

"Practically."

"What kind of time did you have, Mrs. Albright?"

Gramma Albright sighed. "Affairs aren't like they were when I was young, Dan."

Dan Field smiled. "Probably not. How did you enjoy your trip, Rufe?"

Rufe started. "What did you say, Uncle Doc?"

"I asked how you enjoyed your trip."

Rufe raised his eyebrows. "Quite well, thank you. Quite well. We went to the Chestnut Street Opera House and saw Mrs. John Drew. Quite an actress. Quite."

"Quite," Dan Field agreed. "What do you think of Mrs. John Drew, Pris?"

She sighed. "Very charming, Dan."

Dan Field turned to George. "Did you succumb to the lady's allure, Mr. Albright?"

George shrugged. "Hardly."

Something has gone wrong, Dan Field thought, something wrong between Pris and George. But what? Here was one riddle Bert would not be able to unravel.

Later Pris went over home and called Rufus out. "Walk around the yard with me, will you, Rufus?"

He looked surprised but said, "Of course, my dear."

They strolled around back, by the graystone icehouse covered with rambler rose vines, under the Concord grapevines, along the lilac-lined path to the flower garden, where the buds had only begun to show.

"You know, Rufus," Pris said, "alike as they are, this place has always meant so much more to me than the Albright one."

"We were children here, Pris."

"Sometimes I wonder if there isn't something more to my sentiments than that. It was here I waited until George and I would be married. It was here I looked forward to a lover who'd be my husband."

"You found your lover and husband, Pris."

"Did I?" She took hold of his arm. "Wait a minute, Rufus. I want to ask you some questions and I believe you will answer them honestly."

"I'll do my best, my dear."

"Did you ever know a woman named Viola Larsen?"

Rufus started. "Where did you hear of her?"

Pris shrugged. "Never mind that. Did you know her?"

"No, I didn't know her. What are you driving at, Pris?"

"I'm asking questions, not answering. If you didn't know her you certainly heard about her, didn't you?"

"A few things."

"Rufus, there's no sense hedging. I want the truth. I must know the truth. George loved her, didn't he?"

Rufus shook his head. "Why uncover a grave, Pris? If George ever loved her it was years ago."

Her eyes narrowed. "Why didn't he marry her?"

Rufus cleared his throat. "Well—er—well, Pris, you know the understanding between the two families. Since you and George were——"

"Don't!" she interrupted. "I can't bear hearing the formula again. Tell me why George didn't marry Viola Larsen." Rufus made no answer and she went on. "I think I know the truth without your telling me. George's father stopped him. He probably told the Larsens he'd cut George off without a cent."

Rufus grasped her shoulders. "Pris, you're acting like a fool. All that happened years ago. George and you have been happy. Pull yourself to——"

She wrenched away and ran toward the Albright place. Nearing the gate, she slackened her pace. Rufe moved down the street.

"Rufe," she cried. "Rufe, my baby, wait!"

He did not hear her.

Mollie waited before the Reynard place. She caught Rufe's hand and pulled him into the house. Their arms went around each other, their lips clung.

Finally Mollie choked, "The time did seem long, Rufe."

He stood away. "That's the unfair part, my dear. It's the woman who must suffer."

They entered the parlor and seated themselves.

"Didn't you suffer, Rufe?" Mollie asked.

"Quite, Mollie, but my time was full. I must tell you about Mrs. John Drew."

Mollie looked alarmed. "Who's Mrs. John Drew?"

"An actress."

Mollie sighed, relieved. "Oh, Rufe, I won the contest."

"What contest?"

"The musical contest, Rufe. I played 'The Blue Danube' and the judges awarded me the framed certificate. They wouldn't let me bring it home, though. I have to win three consecutive years to keep it."

Rufe smiled. "I'm proud of you, my dear. Are you quite elated?"

Her brow darkened. "I suppose I am elated, Rufe, except . . . Well, Rufe, I couldn't help feeling sorry for Helen Boyd. She played one of Chopin's nocturnes and she played wonderfully. I believe, Rufe, that if the judges really knew what good music is they'd have given Helen the prize."

Rufe shrugged. "Don't worry over that."

Mollie shook her head. "I can't help worrying, Rufe. I don't mind very much if my folks won't let me go with Bertha any more. Bertha has enough Catholic friends, both girls and boys. But Helen don't have a single soul, Rufe. Winning the prize would have meant a lot to Helen——"

"Forget it!" Rufe interrupted. "Listen! Mollie, I must tell you about Mrs. John Drew. One night we went to the Chestnut Street Opera House and . . ."

This evening Dan Field called upon Father Callahan and they discussed this and that until all hours.

Taking leave, Dan Field said, "By the way, my good padre, did you hear any particularly interesting confession yesterday?"

"Sure, all confessions are particularly interesting—human documents so to speak. By the way, my good doctor, I'm sending the boy Gregory Beamer away to school immediately."

Dan Field chuckled. "Still bent on saving his soul, Padre?"

Father Callahan chuckled. "One soul saved may mean a second soul saved, Dr. Field, and sure, perhaps a third and so on ad infinitum."

Dan Field crossed the street and entered his house.

Bert stood in the hall. "Know sumpin, Uncle Doc? Every time I don't get to Mudtown it's bad. Last week oncet I didn't go and another dog bit Duke's right ear clean off and the ear gets lost. And this afternoon I stayed home."

"What happened?" Dan Field asked.

Bert frowned. "Uncle Doc, toward evening some men come and take Wilbur and Ellen to a orphan asylum. And know sumpin, Uncle Doc? A couple hours back the night riders run the Widder Woman out of town."

"Are you sure, Bert?" Dan Field demanded.

"Sure, I'm sure, Uncle Doc. A little while ago Shad he shinnied up my pole and tells me I better come quick. But know sumpin, Uncle Doc? By the time I gets there the Widder Woman's gone and 'they's' gone. Ray says 'they' was terrible. 'They' was wrapped and their horses was wrapped in sheets and 'they' drug the Widder Woman out the shanty. Then 'they' stoned her miles along the road. Uncle Doc, 'they' thinks she stole Cal's tombstone."

Dan Field patted Bert's head. "Don't worry, Bert. Ella and Wilbur will be far better off in an orphan asylum. And where the Widder Woman lives doesn't matter much."

"I ain't worrying, Uncle Doc. 'Cept the Widder Woman didn't steal Cal's stone. I stole it."

"You stole it!" Dan Field exclaimed. "Why?"

"See, Uncle Doc, Cal he wasn't baptized and Sammy he felt mighty bad 'bout Cal going to hell. So I says, I didn't think a couple hours'd make God keep a little feller the likes of Cal out of heaven. Mr. Williams he didn't think so neither and he baptized Cal after he's dead. Sammy and me we was godfathers."

"You and Sammy were godfathers, eh?"

Bert nodded. "Yeh. Then Sammy he got worrying 'bout Cal not having a tombstone. Sammy and Shad didn't know but I goes to Mr. Ma's in the middle of the night. I had to steal the littlest stone, though, 'cause I couldn't lift a big one onto the barrow."

"Didn't you think you might be caught, Bert?" Dan Field asked.

"No, Uncle Doc. See, Sammy he had some kennel paint left and he painted the tombstone liver color and he put the writing on red."

"What did the writing say, Bert?"

" 'Cal, God's best little lamb.' "

" 'Cal, God's best little lamb,' " Dan Field repeated.

"It was all right, Uncle Doc. 'Cept the rains washes the paint off."

Dan Field shook his head. "But, Bert, you shouldn't have stolen the stone."

"Know sumpin, Uncle Doc? Folks can't help what they does. The Widder Woman she didn't want to sell Cal's blankets and buy drink. She felt mighty bad 'bout Cal dying."

"Bert, the Widder Woman and you aren't to be judged by the same standards. She is what the world calls an unfortunate. Probably she can't help what she does. But, Bert, people like you and me can govern our conduct."

Bert's unflinching eyes met Dan Field's. "Know sumpin, Uncle Doc? You says Cal he'd live six months to a year. And Cal he didn't live one month."

You win, Bert, Dan Field thought. You win.

Finally he spoke again. "No use telling Ma now who stole the tombstone. We'd better see him tomorrow and I'll pay the price. Sammy would have a relapse if Cal's stone were removed. We'll have Ma chisel the epitaph—that is, the writing. Tell me the words again, Bert."

" 'Cal, God's best little lamb.' "

" 'Cal, God's best little lamb,' " Dan Field whispered.

Leaving Ma Woodward's workshop the next morning, Bert said, "Know sumpin, Uncle Doc? Mighty likely I ought to pay Mr. Ma 'cause it was me stole the tombstone. Uncle Doc, you could keep the five-dollar gold piece you gives me every Christmas till you saved up fifty."

"We'll think about that later, Bert," Dan Field said.

Bert shrugged. "Might as well keep that old five-dollar gold piece. It never does me no good. Mama she always sticks it straight in the bank."

"How's Prissy this morning?" Dan Field changed the subject.

"She wouldn't eat a bite till Mama made her."

"I'll have a look at her."

Dan Field crawled into the buggy and Bert moved across the bridge.

By Prissy's bed Dan Field said, "What you need is a dose of country air. Put your clothes on and we'll take a long drive."

"No," she cried, "I don't want to take a long drive, Uncle Doc."

Lou spoke. "Do what your uncle Doc says, Prissy."

Pretty soon Nervy trotted by the Albright place.

"Aren't you taking Lillian along today, Uncle Doc?" Prissy asked. "It's Saturday."

"Not today."

"Why?"

"I want you to myself."

"Why?"

"I like having you to myself."

"Why?"

"I like you."

"Why?"

He laughed. "Why, Miss Prissy? I'll tell you why. You're a lovely little girl. That's why I like you."

Tears started. "Am I, Uncle Doc?"

"You certainly are." He handed her the reins. "How about driving? If Lillian's along you're always wanting to drive."

All morning they drove and near noon came across the covered bridge. Dan Field told Nervy to stop before the light plant.

"Come on, Prissy," he said.

Terror filled her eyes. "Where?"

"Prissy, there's nothing to be afraid about. I want to walk with you beside the water where you and Gregory swam, so you may see there is nothing to be afraid about. Come, dear."

Finally Nervy jogged along again.

"There isn't anything to be afraid about, is there, Uncle Doc?" Prissy said.

"Not a thing, Prissy."

After leaving Prissy, Dan Field saw Lillian on the Albright lawn and stopped. "Hello."

Lillian frowned. "Hello."

"What's wrong?"

She came beside the buggy, still frowning. "You wouldn't know what's wrong. No, you wouldn't know—taking Prissy driving and letting me home all alone."

Dan Field chuckled to himself, She's jealous, Miss Muffet's jealous.

He smiled. "I'll tell you something if you promise never to tell."

"Cross my heart."

He stroked her curls. "You need never be jealous of my affections for anyone. Sometimes I think I love you more than anyone in the world, Miss Muffet."

"Miss Muffet," she giggled. "Uncle Doc, you haven't called me Miss Muffet for years and years. 'Member when I was little how you'd pretend I was Miss Muffet and you were Mr. Spider and you'd sit down 'side her? And I'd pretend I really was scared."

"Of course I remember."

Ray Stoddard was passing. "Hello, Mr. Doc."

"Hello, Ray. How does life go?"

"Mighty fine, Mr. Doc."

Ray was thinking, Jest a couple hours more . . .

Miss Fisher handed Ray a dollar. "I'm sorry to let you go, Ray. But we won't need many more fires this year."

"That's all right, ma'am. Mrs. Meeker and Mrs. Diggers they says the same, ma'am."

Miss Fisher closed the door and spoke to her mother. "He is such a poor skinny little creature. . . . I wonder if he does give Lem his pay?"

Mrs. Fisher shook her head. "It seems likely, deary."

They went to the kitchen and Miss Fisher said, "Roast beef today, deary. I can't accustom myself to having such bounty."

Mrs. Fisher seated herself. "Never did see such a change as getting married made in Tracy. I'm going to tell you something now, deary, the way Aunt Tillie talked once made me think Tracy didn't like the bank."

Miss Fisher placed two full plates upon the table. "I noticed myself, deary. It sounded as if Tracy thought the bank had done something dishonest, regarding the money Papa left." She sat down and they began eating. "The weather's kind of cool, deary. Maybe I should have kept Ray a week or two longer. If I could only forget Lem."

"Maybe by next year Lem can be persuaded to sign the pledge, deary. How were the girls this week?"

Miss Fisher helped them both to more beef. "The girls, deary? Lillian and Prissy were fine. Ginny Price surly as usual. Strange, the way Sammy managed her, and Sammy of all people! Meg Taylor's doing the most wonderful work lately, though. Really, deary, I've never seen such a change come over a girl. Dot seems brighter too. Wonder if the Albrights and Sargents got home last night?"

Looking as if they had never been away, George and Rufus moved toward home this Saturday afternoon.

Before Dan Field's place Rufus said, "I'm leaving you here, George. Want to see Dan." He went into the office. "Glad you're here, Dan. Busy?"

"Not at all. Have a seat."

Rufus cleared his throat. "Dan, what's the matter with Prissy?"

"Do you really want me to tell you, Rufus?"

"Certainly."

"She's lonely. Bert completely absorbs Lou and you pay little attention to either one of the children."

"You—mean—Prissy—is—lonely?" Rufus weighed his words.

"She is eating her little heart out."

Going home, Rufus was thinking, Prissy is lonely; then the two of us are lonely.

She stood in the yard when he arrived and he held out his arms. "Come here, Prissy."

Wondering, she came. "Me, Papa?"

He hugged her close, close. "Prissy, do you know I love you? I love you."

"You love me?" she echoed.

"You, Prissy."

Her arms and legs wrapped around him. "Papa, I didn't know," she choked. "I didn't know you loved me."

They entered the house, arms around each other.

Lou met them, frowning.

"What's wrong?" Rufus asked.

"It's Maggie," Lou explained. "She's been sniffing all afternoon. Father Callahan's going to send that boy Gregory Beamer away to school and instead of being grateful Maggie's acting as if the boy was about to die."

Rufus, an arm still around Prissy, went to the kitchen. "I know how you feel about Gregory going away, Maggie," he said. "But I'll see Father Callahan and arrange so that you can visit the boy every so often."

"May the Virgin bless you, Mr. Sargent," Maggie sobbed.

George stood a few minutes upon the walk before entering the gateway. He was wondering how he could explain things to Pris. There had to be certain words which could clear the situation. Pris loved him, he loved her, the Larsen woman meant nothing. Damn that Percy Parrish. Damn him to hell! George swore under his breath.

"Please, Captain George," he heard a small voice say, "would yer respectably give this ter her with my compliments?" Before him stood that filthy boy from Mudtown—Lem's boy—was his name Ray? He held out a package.

George opened the package and took out the watch. "Give this to whom?" he demanded.

"Why, ter her—ter Miss Lillian."

"You mean you want *me* to give *this* to Lillian?" He was incredulous and then angry—angrier than he had ever been in his life.

"Yes sir."

George threw the watch upon the bricks and stamped upon raging, "You filthy little swine, get out of my sight or I'll break every bone in your body."

The boy tore off and George regretted his actions. He'd pay him twice the value of the watch. But of all the infernal nerve, bringing Lillian a present. Life became more confused daily. Why had he ever bothered looking up Vi Larsen? What a disappointment she'd proven—fat and middle-aged. But the whole business would have amounted to nothing except a tea party if Percy Parrish hadn't told Pris, "Your husband's visiting his old sweetheart Vi Larsen this afternoon." Pris had been cold as ice ever since. But maybe the pearls . . . Pris, George thought, you're the one woman I've ever really loved. . . . You're the one woman I ever will love, Pris. . . .

Ray turned and ran, too stunned to think at first. But by the time he reached the bridge his thoughts ran red. God damn ol' bastard, I'll kill him. . . . I'll kill him. . . . I'll git me the loan of Mr. Tatem's musket and . . .

Chapter Four

GEORGE FOUND Pris in the sitting room. He wanted to tell her how much he loved her, make her believe no other woman had ever meant anything to him.

He said, "How are you, my dear?"

She shrugged. "All right."

Perhaps tonight, he thought, when she is getting ready for bed I'll give her the pearls and make her understand.

He went on upstairs.

She thought again what she had been thinking most of the night and all of the day. George had never been in love with her and she had never been in love with him. They had lived together over seventeen years. Over seventeen years they had slept together. He had begotten and she had brought forth four children. But they had never been in love with each other. It was preposterous but it was true. Yet Pris felt no resentment toward George and the woman. She merely envied the brief ecstasy the two had experienced. And if George's father hadn't interfered she would have found a lover of her own. . . . Pris felt the blood fingering through her every fiber. Dan, Dan, I must see you. I must talk to you. I must . . .

Rufe came into the room.

"Rufe," Pris asked, "do you remember how when you were a baby you called Uncle Doc Da-da?"

"No, Mama."

Why under the sun would she ask him such a question? Rufe wondered. What difference could it make whether he remembered such a thing? She was probably worrying about something else. She was forever worrying. Suddenly Rufe began pitying his mother. He pitied his father. He pitied all the older generation, the way they had lived their lives, never having experienced any real suffering nor happiness either. . . . How very different his own life was and would be. . . . Why, the suffering and the happiness he'd already experienced had given him a knowledge of life far beyond comprehension of any of them. Mollie, Rufe thought affectionately, he'd always love Mollie best but . . . Rufe remembered Mrs. John Drew. No man could devote his entire life to one woman. And tonight, Rufe guessed, he'd work upon his world to be made all of marble.

Lillian skipped through the doorway.

"Where have you been, Lillian?" Pris asked.

"You told me I might go with Prissy to gather violets in the far fields."

"Where are the violets?"

Lillian flushed. "I—I guess I forgot to bring them home, Mama."

Pris's eyes fixed upon Rufe again. Who is he, this man taller than I? This man who keeps his thoughts a secret from me. This man who resents my caress. And Lillian, and Sammy, who are they? Strangers all, Rufe and Lillian and Sammy. Children begotten by a man and brought forth by a woman who had never been in love with each other. Dan . . .

Without putting on a hat or coat Pris opened the front door and started down the street.

Rufus had hardly left him when Helen Boyd came for Dan Field. Shortly before six he returned to the office and sank upon a chair. Jesus! he swore to himself. Jesus! Jesus!

Vera Boyd had hanged herself from a cellar rafter. Eli had gone down to fix the furnace and found her dangling. He cut the rope and went back upstairs. Helen had just come home and he told her to run quick and fetch Dr. Field.

He didn't explain what had happened but Helen sensed some tragedy. About two o'clock Vera had told her to go out and stay away all afternoon. Remembering, Helen knew this had been strange; Vera had never done such a thing before.

Eli stood by the gate waiting when Helen brought Dan Field back.

He said bluntly, "Dr. Field, Vera hung herself down cellar. She's dead."

Helen screamed and started toward the house.

Eli grabbed her, then his hands dropped. "Go look at your mother if you want. What difference can it make?"

Helen rushed into the house and Dan Field and Eli followed. Eli had carried the body upstairs and laid Vera on the parlor couch. He'd thrown a red tablecloth over her, the first thing he laid hands on. Through the doorway Helen saw the draped figure. She stopped still, shrieking. Dan Field took her hand and led her along the hall to the kitchen.

"Be a brave girl," he said. "At a time like this no one can do very much to help you except yourself. Please wait here. It will be easier all around."

Helen quieted and Dan Field returned to the parlor.

Presently he said, "She's been dead some time."

Eli began talking, as of some casual happening. "When I got home I couldn't find Vera. I didn't think much of it, though. Supper was cooking—an extra good one like Sunday dinner— a chicken stewing and dumplings on top the oven ready to drop. She'd baked a huckleberry pie, my favorite kind. The table's all set too. But the house felt kind of damp—you know these spring evenings are chilly—and I thought I'd better start a furnace fire. I went down cellar. There she was. . . ." He cleared his throat several times. "I cut the rope. I knew she was dead the minute I touched her but I went upstairs. Helen had just come home and I told her to run fetch you quick. I followed her outside and watched if she was hurrying. Fat Hubbard came along. I thought everybody would know sooner or later, so I told Fat, 'Vera hung herself down cellar. She's dead.' He said, 'Gawd sake!' and went along. Guess everybody knows by this time."

"That's all right, Eli," Dan Field said.

Eli shrugged. "Anyhow, I went back down cellar and brought Vera up. . . . Then I dropped the dumplings. They ought to be done soon. . . ." Suddenly he screamed, "God damn their black souls! God damn their black souls! What harm did she ever do to any of them? My poor sweet little Vera."

Dan Field shook his head. "It's hell, I know, Eli. But you must keep hold of yourself because of Helen."

Eli fairly spat, "Helen! Helen's the cause of all this. Vera could of stood anything as long as she had me if it hadn't been for Helen. The trouble was she couldn't bear seeing Helen suffer. Helen's the cause of all this."

The child stood in the doorway listening but she spoke calmly. "My mother really is dead, Dr. Field?"

Dan Field nodded. "Yes, Helen."

"I was hoping you'd be able to do something, Dr. Field."

"So was I, Helen."

She began choking. "If I just hadn't gone out this afternoon. She made me . . . only I shouldn't have let her."

"Don't think about that, Helen," Dan Field said.

Her voice became calm again. "Remember what you told Mother and me last summer, Dr. Field? That the reason certain people didn't fit into certain groups is not because they are inferior but because they can do things better than others—things like playing the piano or the violin or singing? And you told about all the great people who'd been misfits. Remember, Dr. Field?"

"I remember, Helen."

His eyes followed her glance to the piano, where a book of songs stood open across the rack and Eli's violin lay on the top.

"I kept reminding Mother what you'd said, Dr. Field. And for a long time things were a lot better. Mother spent hours helping me practice. You know, Mother really understands—I mean understood—music, and she believed I'd real talent. Sometimes my father played his violin. Yes, for a long time things were quite a lot better. Really they were, Dr. Field."

"I'm sure they were, Helen."

"I got so I didn't mind the other girls ignoring me. Oh, of course often my mother would get blue, thinking I'd no friends, but I tried to make her know I'd stopped caring. Then they announced about the school musical contest and—and——"

"What, Helen?"

"Well, Dr. Field, Mother felt sure I'd win the framed certificate. She had the idea if I won people would begin liking me again. They'd think after all I really was a worth-while person if I won, was what my mother believed. I played *the* nocturne, too, Dr. Field. . . . But I didn't win. . . . I told my mother I didn't care. . . . She wouldn't believe me. . . . She wouldn't even listen to me practicing. . . . She thought nothing was any use any more."

Helen stopped and Eli spoke, his voice a monotone now. "I wanted to go away, move out of town. She said every place was the same. In the last town we lived a cousin of mine died. When his wife wanted to give him a Christian burial she was told to get a rabbi. There wasn't any rabbi and I read the burial service myself. That was the reason we moved here." He began choking with some kind of laughter. "I don't mean we moved here because there wasn't a rabbi. It sounded like I meant we moved here because there wasn't a rabbi." He kept on laughing.

"Vera will have a Christian burial, believe me, Eli," Dan Field assured. "I'll stop going home and see Mr. Culver. And I'll send Ma Woodward word. Don't you worry about a detail, Eli. Listen! You and Helen go eat some of the chicken and dumplings and pie. Vera would want you to."

Eli groaned. "Funny, isn't it? Vera's dead. She can't move. But out in the kitchen's chicken and dumplings and pie she cooked. A man could go crazy thinking about such a thing, couldn't he?"

When Dan Field left the Boyds' he found Sammy standing outside, a puppy under an arm and his eyes rounder and bluer than ever.

"Uncle Doc," Sammy said, "I hears upstreet Mrs. Boyd hung herself down cellar. Did she?"

"Yes, she did, Sammy."

Sammy tried to say something.

"What is it, Sammy?"

Finally Sammy stammered, "Helen—Helen—how's Helen?"

"Sammy," Dan Field said, "Helen needs a friend more than any little girl I've ever known. Go tell her you're her friend."

Sammy's face grew red to the roots of his yellow curls. "Sure I will. See, Uncle Doc, I got Queen. Queen's the best bitch out the litter. Mr. Shires give me an offer of three dollars for Queen. Glory Ned! Uncle Doc, I couldn't sell one of Spotty's pups even for a hundred dollars."

"Of course you couldn't, Sammy."

Sammy began stammering again. "See—well, see, Uncle Doc, I thought if I give Helen Queen—well, maybe Helen'd think 'bout Queen some and not 'bout her mother so much."

Going home, Dan Field was thinking about Sammy, Sammy the inscrutable, Sammy the nonchalant, but Sammy the Good Samaritan. Sammy who'd wheeled swill to the Mudtown children through bitter winter mornings, Sammy who'd championed Alexander, Sammy who'd painted the epitaph: "Cal, God's best

little lamb," and Sammy who had come bringing his frankin-
cense and myrrh to a little Jewish girl in her hour of need. *Thou
art my beloved son; in thee I am well pleased. . . .*

The office door opened and Pris entered.

Dan Field sprang to his feet. "Lady, you! Nothing the matter,
is there?"

Her eyes looked up into his. "Everything's the matter."

"What, my dear?"

"Dan, did you ever know that George was in love with a
Philadelphia girl named Larsen—Viola Larsen? He would have
married her if his father hadn't interfered."

Dan Field laughed. "My dear Pris, the Larsen episode happened
years ago. George has probably forgotten the lady ever lived."

Pris frowned. "Indeed he hasn't forgotten. He saw her the other
day in Philadelphia. But I don't mind. What I mind is the fact
they married me off to him. You know it's the truth, Dan. Ever
since I was born both families were resolved that George and I
would marry. It never dawned upon me that another man lived
who might love me, whom I might love. At least George knows
what it means to love and be loved, while I——"

"Pris," Dan Field interrupted, "why worry over something
which happened years ago? What if George did see the Larsen
woman? It is you he loves. You've led a good life together."

Again she frowned. "Dan, George has never really loved me. All
George has ever felt for me is affection. And affection is all I've
ever felt for him. You say we've led a good life together. Perhaps I thought it a good life because I never dreamed another
kind of life existed. I didn't know one could love someone so
much that nothing else mattered, not even your children."

She went to him and put her hands on his shoulders. Her
breath made the points of her breasts touch him, then leave, then
touch him again. Darling, darling, he was thinking, at last
you want me the way I want you. At last I might lift you in my
arms and carry you upstairs. I could put you on the big white
bed and loosen your clothes. I could run my hands over your
bare beautiful golden body. I could kiss your hair and your eyes
and your lips and your breasts and all the sweet flesh of you. But
no! It can't be, he started telling himself. It mustn't be, he kept
telling himself. If I take you our secret will be a secret no longer.

Your every glance, your every move would give us away. And you couldn't stand it. It would be a living death for you. Perhaps a time will come when a woman like you will dare face a love like this without becoming an outcast, when a woman like you will be able to divorce a man she does not love and marry another without becoming a pariah. But not today! Not today, darling! He heard her breath coming harder and felt the points of her breasts touch him harder, then leave him, then again touch him harder. Jesus! he swore to himself, I must keep my head. . . . I must keep my head. . . . Jesus! I must . . .

He stood away. "Sit down, Pris."

An instant she did not move, then she sank into a chair. He seated himself on the edge of the desk, his fingers fumbling with some sheets of paper. Those dear long thin white twitching fingers, she was thinking, which have lifted me out of the valley of the shadow of death.

"Dan, Dan dear, I——"

"You know, Pris," he interrupted, "your trouble is, the children are growing up. Every woman goes through this stage. Babies keep a mother busy. When they begin taking care of themselves somewhat, time lies idle on her hands. Now because your every minute isn't occupied you're concentrating upon George and making mountains out of molehills."

"No, Dan, no," she cried.

His voice still sounded calm. "What if George has never felt more than affection? You know, Pris, it's affection, not passion, which keeps a man by a woman's side through the years. The fire dies, almost always. . . ." He shuffled the papers between his fingers. "And truly, George's affection for you has been unusual. He and the Larsen woman had an affair years ago and he saw her a few days ago, you say. But he came back to you, didn't he? Good God, Pris, most men have dozens of women both before and after they're married!"

The shadows in her eyes deepened. "You, Dan, you've never had a girl."

Jesus! he swore to himself again. Jesus! Jesus! Better to end it all here and now so far as she was concerned.

He threw the papers on the desk. "You mean I have never had a girl here."

"Have you a girl some other place?"

He laughed. "A girl! My dear Pris, considering you're a married woman, you show very little understanding. I've half a dozen girls every time I go to New York."

She gasped, "You mean . . . you mean . . . ?"

"Of course. I'm not a monk."

She leaned toward him. "Dan, I don't care how many girls you've had."

Now what? he thought. Now what? What else is there to say? Suddenly he remembered the Boyds—and Sammy and Queen. Sammy the inscrutable, Sammy the nonchalant, Sammy the Good Samaritan, and Sammy who's just like George. Now he knew what else there was to say.

"Pris, have you heard that Vera Boyd hanged herself this afternoon?"

She gasped, "No. How horrible! But why, why would she do such a thing?"

"You must know they're Jews and have been socially ostracized. Eli said Vera could have stood anything, as long as she had him, except seeing Helen suffer. Until last fall Helen and Mollie Reynard and Bertha Richards were inseparable. Then Mollie and Bertha dropped Helen and the other children snubbed her. After having been a pariah herself Vera wasn't strong enough to bear Helen's suffering too."

Pris choked. "It doesn't seem possible such a thing could happen right here in Willowspring, Dan. Couldn't you do anything?"

He shrugged. "By the time I reached the Boyds' Vera was dead. I stopped at the manse coming home. When they first came here the Boyds attended the Presbyterian Church and Eli wants Vera to have a Christian burial."

"What did Mr. and Mrs. Culver say, Dan?"

"They were horrified, of course. Culver said he'd always meant to call upon the Boyds. For some reason he'd not gotten around to it but he and Mrs. Culver would go right down. Mrs. Culver would lay Vera out. They sent Laird after Ma Woodward."

Pris sighed. "It's the most terrible thing I ever heard. Didn't they have one friend?"

"Yes," Dan Field said, "they had one friend."

"Who?"

"Sammy."

"Sammy?" Pris echoed. "You don't mean my Sammy, Sammal?"

"I most certainly do mean your Sammy, Sammal."

Pris drew her brows together. "I don't understand. How could Sammy be their friend?"

"Sammy seemed to know how, Pris. When I left the Boyds' I found Sammy outside. He'd heard about Mrs. Boyd, he said, and wanted to know how Helen was. He'd brought one of the pups, Queen. He told me he'd had an offer of three dollars for Queen but a hundred dollars wouldn't buy one of Spotty's pups."

"What happened?" Pris asked.

"If a hundred dollars wouldn't buy one of Spotty's pups Sammy thought maybe if he gave Helen Queen maybe Helen would think about Queen some and not about her mother so much. Sammy went up on the porch and rang the bell. I stood and watched. Helen opened the door. Sammy said, 'Helen, I know you feels bad 'bout your mother. But I'm your friend and I want to give you Queen. For keeps.' Helen didn't say anything! She just took Queen and hugged the pup close. Then she looked at Sammy and smiled."

Pris shook her head. "It doesn't seem possible Sammy could do such a thing. He has always seemed absolutely indifferent, as if he didn't care about anyone nor want anyone to care about him. It's only lately that Rufe has acted indifferent. Until recently he brought me all his little joys and troubles. And Lillian isn't a great talker but she's been affectionate. Sammy, though . . . Why, Dan, since Sammy was a baby he never wanted a fuss made over him. He's not only seemed self-sufficient, he's seemed self-satisfied. I've always thought that Sammy is exactly like George."

"Sammy *is* exactly like George," Dan Field said.

Her eyes met his directly. "I know what you mean, Dan. Goodby."

He closed his eyes. He couldn't bear to see her go. He heard the door slam.

Going home, Pris told herself, Dan thinks no more of me than he does of Lillian, perhaps not half so much. And George must care. He must. . . . She held out a hand and the star sapphire gleamed. . . . I thought he had forgotten my birthday. . . .

George and Sammy, Rufe and Lillian . . . Imagine Sammy doing a thing like that! And Sammy is exactly like George.

Dan Field had no dinner guest this evening and the dessert happened to be rich pudding, consequently the candles did not flicker and dim an instant.

The meal over, however, Dan Field said, "Ackley, I want you to promise me one thing."

"Yes suh, I's willing to promise anything."

"No doubt." Dan Field smiled. "But I don't ever want to know how you make the candles flicker and dim."

Ackley looked positively hurt. "I wouldn't know what you all is talkin' 'bout, suh."

"Yes, you would, Mr. Ackley. And until I die I want to continue pretending that those candles flicker and dim an instant because the spirits of the South's dead truth blow a breath across their flames. Because if a man or a state or a nation is honest enough to acknowledge slavery, then it is possible to alleviate conditions. But if people hold others in bondage, either physically or morally or spiritually, and keep on insisting every soul is free —then there is no hope of redemption. Understand?"

Ackley blinked knowingly. "I understand, suh."

"What do you understand, Mr. Ackley?"

"I's a free man, suh."

Dan Field laughed. "You're about as free as Uncle Tom."

Ackley laughed. " 'Bout as free as Uncle Tom. Who am Uncle Tom, suh?"

Dan Field spoke soberly. "Uncle Tom, my good Ackley, is the black man's Jesus Christ."

"You don't say so, suh."

"I do say so. Uncle Tom gave his life so that black sinners might enter the kingdom of commerce."

"You don't say so, suh." Ackley changed the subject. "Mr. Doc, suh, have you all seen Little Flowah's mama lately?"

"Not recently, Ackley."

Ackley beamed. "Little Flowah's mama's going to produce some moh'."

Laughing inwardly, Dan Field asked, "How does Ferris like the idea this time?"

"Little Flowah's mama's husband am right well pleased this time, suh," Ackley informed.

Still laughing inwardly, Dan Field went to the office. He lighted a lamp and sat down at the desk. A great loneliness engulfed him. Always before had been the hope, the faint hope, the damn fool hope, yet a hope concerning Pris. Now all was over, finished! Still, here he could close his eyes and believe she was beside him again, her eyes shadowy, her lips saying she loved him, her breasts touching him. . . . He shivered. Ghosts! He opened his eyes. . . .

Lillian came through the door, her eyes wide, her cheeks flushed, her curls tumbling. She had never looked lovelier, nor more like her mother. Darling, he thought.

He said, "What are you doing here this time of night?"

She began to cry. "Uncle Doc, Uncle Doc . . ."

He took hold of her arms gently. "Whatever is the matter?"

"I'm—I'm dying, Uncle Doc."

"Nonsense! You're the rosiest-looking dying person I ever saw. Tell me the trouble."

Sobs wouldn't let the words come.

He shook her gently. "Stop crying and tell me what's happened."

She stifled the sobs. "Mama told me not to run and jump. . . . She told me . . . But after school today Prissy and I went to gather violets in the far fields. The fields were so green and the sun was warm and the air smelled so sweet I forgot about the violets. . . . I just ran and I ran and I jumped. . . . I never felt so good in my life. I kept thinking, I'm alive. I'm alive. Course I always knew I'm alive, 'cept I never knew I knew it before. Then—then a little while ago something terrible happened. And I am dying, Uncle Doc." She started sobbing again.

It came to Dan Field. She was almost twelve.

He pulled her onto his lap, held her close against his breast. "Miss Muffet, you're not dying. What happened to you happens to every healthy little girl."

She blinked back the tears. "Are you sure, Uncle Doc?"

"Certainly I'm sure. And it's the reason you were feeling so happy this afternoon and why the world looked more beautiful. And it's the reason you realized you're alive. Because before this afternoon you were a little girl but from now on you're going to be a woman, happy and alive."

She sighed deeply. "I guess if you say I'm going to be happy and alive I am, Uncle Doc. 'Cept I don't feel happy and alive this minute."

He stroked her curls. "I know you don't. I know. . . . What you'd better do, young lady, is run along home, tell your mother what's happened, and let her tuck you in your own little bed."

"Uncle Doc," she spoke anxiously, "don't you think Mama'll be mad 'cause I ran and jumped?"

"She won't be mad about anything, I promise you." He set her on her feet and arose himself. "I'll take you home, darling."

Suddenly she smiled and her eyes looked up into his. For the first time they didn't remind him of Pris. There was an archness about the glance Pris couldn't have achieved.

"You never called me darling before, Uncle Doc," she chirped.

Not aloud I haven't, he thought.

He said, "Don't you tell on me."

"I wouldn't," she assured seriously. "And I won't tell how sometimes you think you love me more'n anybody in the world. We'll have two secrets, *darling*."

"You mischief, you," he laughed. "Get along home before I spank you properly."

She laughed, too, and they went out of the office and down the street laughing.

Before the Albright gate she became sober again. "What shall I do, Uncle Doc?"

"Just go in and tell your mother. Everything will be all right, I promise."

"I guess everything will be all right if you say so, Uncle Doc. Only don't you come. I wouldn't want Mama to know I told you. I'll slip in the back door like I slipped out."

Dan Field was thinking, Someday this situation will be changed even as others.

He whispered, "Bless you, Miss Muffet."

She whispered, "Bless you, Mr. Spider."

She disappeared behind the house and Dan Field moved across the lawn. Hidden between two tree trunks, he looked through the sitting-room window. The family, except Lillian, were gathered under lamplight—Pris mending, Gramma Albright reading her Bible, Rufe staring straight ahead, Sammy examining a knife, George reading the *Ledger*, his broad back almost touching the pane.

What, Dan Field began speculating, what if I should walk into that room and tell George the truth? Tell him that Pris has never loved him, tell him that she loves me and has ever loved me, tell him that his life is a fool's paradise. After all, why should George's feelings matter? Certainly George has his good points, but what man hasn't?

Darling, I could take you to Vienna or Paris or Rome. . . . I could love you so much that nothing else would matter. And why not? Why not?

Lillian called, "Mama."

Pris answered, "Yes, dear."

"Mama, come here, please."

Pris put down her mending and left the room.

Miss Muffet, and Rufe the builder of a marble world, Dan Field thought, and Sammy the Good Samaritan . . . Pris's children but George's children . . . Suddenly he knew it wasn't only Pris he wanted. He wanted those children too. Life would not be life without them. And Bert—if it weren't for Bert his soul would be lost. . . . And poor little Prissy—she needed him.

His eyes went back to George, who was examining the contents of a box behind the *Ledger*. Dan Field could see what the box held: a string of pearls, to give Pris of course, perhaps tonight. . . . He remembered her eyes shining upon George the day he'd given her the star sapphire. . . . Pris and George would readjust their life, perhaps tonight. . . . Dan Field shivered and heard Eli Boyd's voice: "These spring evenings are chilly."

Jesus! he swore to himself, I'm becoming maudlin. I'm as wistful as a beggar brat outside a pastry-shop window. It's time I took myself to New York again. By God! I'll leave on the morning train and once there I'll get drunker than I've ever been and I'll find a woman whose hair is fair and whose eyes are gray and whose body is slim and I'll take her to bed and I'll close my eyes and for an instant out of all time I'll believe her flesh is the color of ripe wheat.

He was about to move when he saw a small shadow creeping through the darkness across the yard. Before the lighted window the figure stopped, raised a gun, and pointed it toward George's broad back. Dan Field sprang, grabbing the gun with one hand and thrusting the other over the figure's mouth. He dragged the culprit out of the yard, down the road.

Nearing the street lamp, he saw whom he held. "Ray!"

He pulled the boy to his place, pushed him through the office door onto a chair.

Sitting down, he examined the gun. "Whose musket is this, Ray?"

"Mr. Tatem's," Ray answered sullenly.

"How did you get hold of it?"

"He give me the loan."

"Did Red know you intended murder?"

"He didn't know nothing."

Dan Field rested the musket against the desk. "Why did you want to kill Captain George?"

Ray's eyes blazed. "'Cause I hates his God damn stinking guts."

"Why?"

Suddenly Ray's eyes stopped blazing and tears made puddles of the dirt on his cadaverous little face. "Let me go, Mr. Doc. Please let me go."

"I'll let you go very soon, Ray," Dan Field promised. "I'd like a talk first, though. Ray, I've been thinking a lot about you lately. I heard that in one year you've done four years' schoolwork. It's an almost unheard-of thing for a boy to be so smart."

Ray took a grimy fist, rubbed the tears and puddles, and wiped his nose across a ragged sleeve.

"What's more," Dan Field continued, "Bert says you want to be a mathematician, a man who knows everything about numbers. Bert also told me the tramp gentleman Mrs. Tatem ran off with gave you the idea. Do you still remember what the tramp gentleman said?"

Ray nodded, "I remembers all right."

"Would you care to tell me?"

"I don't mind. That thar tramp gentleman he says if'n yer knows nuff 'bout numbers yer kin find out anything in the world, like how fer it is round the world, or how many miles ter the stars, or whar the North Pole is at, or whar a ship still in the middle of the ocean is gonna land."

Dan Field nodded. "The tramp gentleman was perfectly right, Ray."

"I figgered he was, Mr. Doc. Know why?"

"Why, Ray?"

Ray's eyes gleamed now. "I figgered what's in this here world gits put here. And if'n things is here thar's gotta be a way fer ter find out all 'bout 'em. Even 'bout souls, Mr. Doc. The tramp gentleman says if'n yer knows nuff 'bout numbers yer could measure the depths of a soul easy as yer kin weigh the pounds of the body."

"How would you explain that, Ray?"

Ray smiled. "See, Mr. Doc, if'n yer weighs a body yer kin tell if'n it's fat or lean and if'n yer knows nuff 'bout numbers fer ter measure a soul yer could tell if'n it's good or bad."

Dan Field leaned forward and patted the boy's shoulder. "Ray, some of the smartest minds on earth today are thinking along those lines. Until this century people believed human beings and inorganic matter—that means anything not made of flesh, as the earth and trees and stars and stones—were made out of different material. Today men know everything is made of the same matter."

Ray gasped. "Do yer mean, Mr. Doc, yer and me and Captain George and dogs and stars and everythin's all made out'n the same stuff?"

"They are, Ray. What's more, some scientists are wondering if our souls may not be made of the same substance which, the way the tramp gentleman suggested, we'll be able to measure when we know enough about numbers."

"Them men's right, Mr. Doc. 'Cause souls they comes out'n heaven like 'lectric lights comes out'n heaven. And yer kin measure 'lectric lights, Mr. Doc."

"'Souls they comes out'n heaven like 'lectric lights comes out'n heaven,'" Dan Field repeated. "Ray, in the city of Baltimore, Maryland, stands a new school called Johns Hopkins. It has a physics laboratory, a workshop where men are trying to discover the truth about heaven and earth. How would you like to study at Johns Hopkins when you're older?"

"Me study thar?" Ray cried. "Yer means me, Mr. Doc?"

"Why couldn't a smart fellow like you attend Johns Hopkins one of these days? But, Ray"—Dan Field shook his head—"if I'd not been on the spot tonight you might have become a murderer. Anyhow, you'd have been a criminal, whether you killed Captain George or not. It would have been the end of all your chances to succeed. Through life you'd have been marked: He tried to kill a man."

Ray slumped, his expression miserable. "Mighty likely yer right, Mr. Doc."

"Why did you want to kill Captain George? Tell me."

Ray began talking quickly, the words rolling off his tongue. "I works hard and I works good. I shoveled snow and tended furnaces 'sides doing all the chores round home. But it takes me more'n four months fer ter earn the money. Twenty-four dollars and seventy-five cents is a hull heap of money fer ter git. Don't yer think, Mr. Doc?"

"I certainly do, Ray."

Ray nodded and the words continued rolling. "It is, Mr. Doc. I don't mind if'n Teacher she makes me sit off side 'cause I gits lice and stinks. Mam she washes fer folks and she says if'n she do wash us young'uns' duds we-uns jest gits 'em dirty agin. I was just ter plum wore out ter wash. . . . But see, Mr. Doc, this day I washes my duds and irons 'em good and I washes my head and my hands and face. Then I goes over town and I buys it."

"You bought what, Ray?" Dan Field asked.

Ray's eyes widened. "Why, the watch. . . . Oh, I fergits ter tell yer. It was a watch I was working fer ter git. Mr. Doc, it was beautiful. It was gold and it had little red stones—rubies, the lady says they was. The rubies wound round and round and makes a little clover on the gold and it was marked plain as yer nose, twenty-four dollars and seventy-five cents. I was mighty proud of that thar watch, Mr. Doc." He wiped away a tear.

"What happened to the watch, Ray?"

"I's telling yer, Mr. Doc. The lady she wraps a nice white paper round the box. I takes it 'long. When I git thar Captain George he was standing 'fore the gate. I guess I oughtn't ter have did it. 'Cept I didn't mean no wrong. I was mighty proud of that thar watch."

"What did you do, Ray?"

"I gives the watch ter Captain George and I says, 'Please would yer respectably give it ter her with my compliments?'"

"Give it to whom, Ray?"

"Why, ter her—Miss Lillian."

"Miss Lillian," Dan Field repeated. "Do you mean little Lillian?"

Ray nodded. "Yes sir, little Miss Lillian."

Miss Muffet, Dan Field thought. Miss Muffet . . . he worked more than four months to buy her a watch, while all the time his belly was so empty he was eating the Albright swill.

Ray was still talking, ". . . and I never did see her good till one night last summer. Yer had her out buggy riding, Mr. Doc, and when she gits out'n the buggy I was standing thar. She goes clost by, so clost I could of touched her, and I thinks, She's beautifuler'n any flower. Then the night 'fore Christmas I goes fer ter git yer ter born Noel. She opens the door and, Mr. Doc, she smiles at me."

She smiled at him, Miss Muffet smiled at him.

"Go on, Ray," Dan Field said.

"See, Mr. Doc, I wisht fer ter give her sumpin and I gits the watch. . . . But Captain George he opens the box and he sees the watch and he says, 'Yer want me ter give this ter Lillian?' " Ray began choking. "Captain George he throws the watch on the bricks and he stomps it ter pieces. He says, 'Yer filthy little swine, git out'n my sight or I'll break every bone in yer body.' "

Dan Field got to his feet and began pacing backward and forward. You poor little devil, he was thinking, oh, you poor little devil. You have no more chance of ever touching the hem of Miss Muffet's skirt than you have of catching a star between your grubby little fists. Catching a star . . . catching a star . . . catching a star. The words kept repeating themselves. Catching a star, and why not? *If'n yer knows nuff 'bout numbers yer could measure the depths of a soul easy as yer kin weigh the pounds of the body.* And what is a star and what is a soul? Dan Field asked himself. Someday men would know. Someday Ray Stoddard might know.

Suddenly the idea dawned. And why not? Dan Field asked himself. Why not? Money would take care of Lem and Myrtle; perhaps a small farm out in the country where Lem's green fingers might unearth some sort of salvation. Of course Ray's future would have to be planned methodically. But immediately

. . . He'd go away all right, Dan Field told himself, but not to New York.

He stopped still. He said, "These many a day I've been wanting to know what those fellows at Johns Hopkins are up to. How about the two of us going to Baltimore tomorrow, Ray, and finding out together?"

Ray raised his eyes wonderingly. "Yer mean yer wants me fer ter go to Johns Hopkins with yer?"

"I mean you, Ray."

Ray's brows met. "Would yer want the likes of me fer ter go?"

One of Dan Field's long white hands covered both Ray's grubby little fists tenderly, strongly. "Ray, I've only just discovered the fact myself but you are what I've been wanting to go places with me all my life."

Across Ray's dirty cadaverous little face a smile broke. "Then I's thinkin' I'd sure be mighty proud fer ter go, Mr. Doc."

Dan Field chuckled. "And I's thinkin' that one of these here days Miss Lillian Albright's gonna be mighty proud fer ter know yer, Professor Ray Stoddard."

Around ten o'clock Dan Field came downstairs and seated himself upon one of the chairs against which long ago crinoline rustled. But he did not pour himself a drink. He was thinking about the boy asleep in the big white bed, the bride's bed, the bed he'd sworn no one except Pris would ever occupy again. Dan Field smiled. Our right hand never knoweth what our left hand will do.

He had said to Ray, "Better stay all night. I'll have to get you ready for the trip."

He'd taken the boy upstairs, shaved his head over the basin, burned the hair, and soaked him in a steaming bath.

"Teacher will never make you sit off side again, Ray. Because never again will you have lice and stink."

Ray laughed. "I'll be mighty proud fer ter quit itching, Mr. Doc."

"Don't call me Mr. Doc any more, Ray. Just Dan. We're friends now."

"Yes sir, Dan."

"Don't say sir, son, just Dan."

"Yes, Dan."

When Ray was clean Dan Field rubbed him dry and covered his bones with one of his own undervests. Then he rubbed ointment on the scalp scabs where the lice had dug under the skin.

Presently he called, "Ackley."

Ackley looked through the bathroom doorway and his eyes popped. "What am going on, suh?"

"Ackley," Dan Field said, "Master Ray is going to stay all night with us."

"You means—you means, suh, Ray Stoddard's gonna——"

Dan Field interrupted. "That's what I mean, Ackley. Straighten this room and then fix him some supper. And listen, you black buzzard, if when you serve the food the candles flicker and dim I'll break every bone in your body! Understand?"

Ackley gulped, "I understands, suh."

"Then speak to Master Ray and smile."

Ackley smiled. "How-de-do, Mastah Ray."

Ray smiled, "How-de-do, Mr. Ackley."

"Don't say Mr. Ackley, Ray," Dan Field said, "just Ackley."

"How-de-do, Ackley."

Still smiling, Ackley's tone became dulcet. "Lil Mastah Ray, how'd you all like cream' chicken on toast, nice hot chocolate, and a lil bit of rice pudding?"

Ray gasped, "How'd I like it?" He looked up at Dan Field. "How'd I like it? Dan, yer knows I ain't hardly had a full belly oncet in my hull life."

You'll never have an empty belly again if I can help it, son, Dan Field thought, remembering. First thing tomorrow morning he'd tackle Lem about the farm, see Brown Walsh about his practice, then find some clothes, perhaps Sammy's, to cover Ray until the boy could be outfitted properly.

Ackley entered the room and handed him a book. "Mistah Fathah Callahan says to tell you all lots of folks round town's gonna be mighty interested in this book, suh. Need anything else tonight, suh?"

"Nothing more tonight, Ackley. Give my regards to Little Flower's mama and her husband. However, I'm leaving town on the morning train, so have my bag ready. And I want the rig hitched by six. Of course Master Ray is going along on the trip."

Ackley beamed. "Dat lil ol' Mastah Ray's one right sma't lil ol' boy. Good night, suh."

Dan Field's eyes dropped to the cover of the book Father Callahan had left.

The Fence
by
Timothy Albright

Dan Field opened the book and began to read:

The heavens hugged the earth, winding round about it blue plains and white billows as if to guard it from adversity. The heavens touched the earth, rugged mountains nosed against the clouds and sloped down to little hills and on to the lowlands. These hills are gentle hills under the ragged and crag-set mountains. One might lie on them all day and watch the clouds or sit and gaze with calm repose at the valley below. Above their reaches begins the creek, snuggling down through their grasses. Stream of moods—here it functions into a pool for fishes, now it scurries along in a narrow thread, there it slackens its pace to a mood of listless musing and murmurs across the village.

And the village—some giant Santa Claus might have built it just for fun. There were the shining big houses and the bright little cottages and the quaint little catchpenny stores. There were the flower gardens and the vegetable patches and the far fields where the violets grew in springtime. There was the courthouse with the town clock on top booming the hours and the half hours all day and all night. There were the bank and the livery stable, with the blacksmith shop behind clanging like a giant cymbal. There were the five tall-spired churches whose bells pealed on the Sunday air.

But around all the village was a fence. It was a very low fence; in fact it was so low that it could not be seen by human eye. Yet there was hardly a soul who'd been born in the village who had ever, whether from fear or indifference, stepped across the fence. . . .

Dan Field closed his eyes. Yes, he thought, there is a fence around the village and hardly a soul has ever stepped beyond. And too late for us now, Pris, my dear. Too late . . .

He opened his eyes. Or perhaps too early, Pris, my dear. But these children who are growing up, before the sun goes down on their day the four corners of the earth will meet and the skies will be no higher than their heads. And, Bert—Dan Field smiled—Bert, you will do those things I have left undone, your soul will be my soul marching on. And, Lillian—Dan Field smiled again—and, Lillian, you will be my heart. And, Ray . . .

Dan Field laughed out loud. "And, Ray, it's tomorrow. Who knows what you may become?"

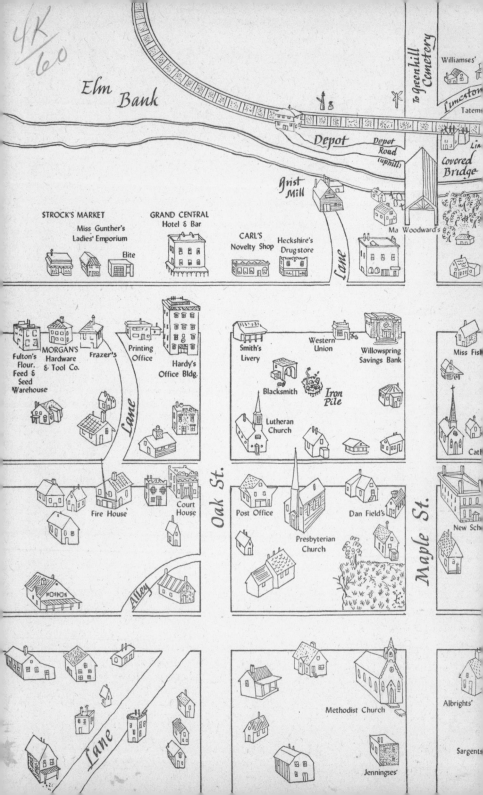

4K
60

Elm Bank

To Greenhill Cemetery

Williamses'

Limeston

Tatem

Depot

Depot
Road
(uphill)

Lim

Covered
Bridge

Grist
Mill

STROCK'S MARKET

Miss Gunther's
Ladies' Emporium

GRAND CENTRAL
Hotel & Bar

CARL'S
Novelty Shop

Heckshire's
Drug store

Ma Woodward's

Elite

Lane

Fulton's
Flour,
Feed &
Seed
Warehouse

MORGAN'S
Hardware
& Tool Co.

Frazer's

Printing
Office

Hardy's
Office Bldg.

Smith's
Livery

Western
Union

Willowspring
Savings Bank

Miss Fish

Blacksmith

Iron
Pile

Lutheran
Church

Cath

Lane

Fire House

Court
House

Post Office

Dan Field's

New Sch

Oak St.

Presbyterian
Church

Maple St.

Alley

Lane

Methodist Church

Albrights'

Jenningses'

Sargents